BY THE EDITORS OF CONSUMER GUIDE®

Favorite
HELPFUL HOUSEHOLD HINTS

GREAT POND PUBLISHING™

Louis Weber, C.E.O.
Publications International, Ltd.
7373 North Cicero Avenue
Lincolnwood, Illinois 60646

Manufactured in U.S.A.

10 9 8 7 6 5 4 3 2 1

Library of Congress Catalog Card Number: 86-60772

ISBN: 1-56173-865-4

Illustrators: Nan Brooks, Laura D'Argo, Jeff Mangiat, Mike Muir

Contents

CONTENTS

PART 2: HINTS FOR THE FAMILY

CONTENTS

PART 3: HINTS ABOUT FOOD

KITCHEN PLANNING AND ORGANIZATION

CONTENTS

CONTENTS

How to Use This Book

Taking care of a home and running a household smoothly is a major challenge, whether you're a single apartment dweller or the mainstay of a house full of children. And it's a challenge that presents a constant succession of responsibilities and chores, many of which you carry out almost without giving them a thought—unless it's to think, "I wish there were a faster, easier, better way to do this."

In fact, there often is a faster, easier, or better way to tackle the myriad small (and big) chores or problems that come your way day after day, and that's what this book is all about. FAVORITE HELPFUL HOUSEHOLD HINTS proves that a lot of people, you among them, apply a surprising amount of imagination even to the most run-of-the-mill matters. Tasks that you do so regularly that they're just part of a daily routine sometimes become sources of great ideas. When was the last time *you* hit on a great time- or money-saving idea that made you exclaim, "Now why didn't I think of that before?" And how many times have you learned of someone else's bright idea and been exasperated into saying, "Now, why didn't *I* think of that?"

Of course, no one person can have all the bright ideas, and that's why this book brings together over 4000 terrific hints for making your life run more smoothly and for making the way you handle everyday chores easier, speedier, more efficient, or more economical. It's a great resource for those days when nothing seems to go right, or those moments when a special problem has you beat. Every area of your household routine is covered, from cleaning just about everything around the home to indoor and outdoor decorating and repairs; from keeping the home safe for children to caring for your houseplants; common health concerns; from managing your money to finding extra storage space in odd corners you'd never thought of putting to use. There's also an extensive section on food purchasing, storage, preserving, and preparation, including scores of tips to save you time and money—like interesting ways to recycle leftovers.

THE FIRST SECTION of this book is "Hints for the Home," and it starts with a chapter on just about everything you need to know about whole-house care and cleaning. Learn how to keep your home looking its best from floors and furniture to the pictures and art objects that make the place especially your own. You'll find terrific tips on cleaning carpets and floors, furniture and upholstery, drapes and shades, the bathroom, and much more.

There are plenty of ingenious ideas here, and you'll be amazed by how much you can do with such ordinary household staples as club soda, vinegar, and cola (it's a great rust remover). You'll also learn how to get grubby fingerprints off the wallpaper (an ordinary pencil eraser may do the trick), and how to cope with impossible-to-get-at areas (use a cloth tied around the end of a yardstick to get behind the refrigerator). You'll learn how to make a do-it-yourself cleaner for glass windows. And did you ever think of using fabric softener to remove static "shock" from the carpet?

Some of the practical aspects of home ownership are covered in the next chapter, "Indoor Home Maintenance and Repairs." Here are hints designed to help you protect your investment in your home by keeping it in good shape, and save money by performing necessary repairs yourself. Here you'll find hints on maintaining and repairing flooring, stairs, windows, screens, and doors. Home electricity and plumbing are covered here, as are ways of keeping your home free from bugs and other pests. There's also a useful section on furniture care and refinishing.

"Home Furnishing and Decorating" comes next, letting you into all sorts of secrets to simplify home painting and decorating so that your do-it-yourself projects have that professional touch. You'll learn the most efficient shortcuts to a great paint job, and find out how to make wallpapering (even on the ceiling) easy. Even easy cleanup is covered here.

This chapter also lets you have fun with some really original thoughts—turn your bathroom into a picture gallery for all those odds and ends you don't have room for anywhere else; solve a bike-storage problem in a small apartment by hanging the bicycle on the wall as a highly unusual "sculpture." Learn how to make a small room look larger, and vice versa. Discover how many household items can, with a little imagination, be put to decorative use.

From here you move on to the exterior of your home. "Outdoor Home Maintenance and Repairs" helps you tackle outdoor painting jobs, roof repairs, and repair and maintenance of siding, gutters, and downspouts. You'll probably feel confident enough to tackle jobs you've previously left to the repair people. There are also some sound safety hints on using tools and ladders.

With your new-found confidence in your own skills, you can move on to "Hints for the Handyman or Woman," where you'll find space-and time-saving strategies for use in your workshop, hints for easy cleanup, and tips for woodworkers.

An important chapter on home safety follows. "Home Safety and Security" offers valuable information on how to identify and correct potential safety hazards in your home, how to guard against fire, and what to do (and not do) if a fire does occur. Learn how to protect your home (and yourself) from burglars and intruders, and how to safeguard your valuables. Here you'll also find excellent advice on making a home safe for children and teaching your children to be safety conscious. Good tips, too, on electrical and storm safety, and on safe handling of pesticides.

Both ecologically and economically, energy conservation is an important issue. Learn how you can help protect the environment and cut back on your utility bills from the chapter on "Saving Energy in the Home." This is where you get some solid advice on cutting heating and cooling costs and on energy-efficient use of water and electricity. There's even a special look at ways to save energy when you use your household appliances.

Now from the home to the garden, with an extensive chapter on "Gardening, Indoors and Outdoors." However large or small your yard—or even if you're working with a balcony or a window box—here's where you'll find professional tips on garden planning and planting, and caring for vegetables and flowers. There are also great tips on arranging and enjoying flowers, and keeping your houseplants healthy.

The first part of FAVORITE HELPFUL HOUSEHOLD HINTS closes with a look at your car. Are you getting the best mileage, and if not, why not? What simple steps can you take to keep your car looking good and running well? How can you be sure you're getting a good deal on a used car? Why is it a mistake to keep snow tires on your car longer than necessary? How can you extend the useful life of the tires on your car? When is the best time to rustproof? You'll find answers to all these questions and a lot more in this handy selection of hints for car owners. And you get some unusual safety tips—doesn't it make sense, for instance, to place strips of reflector tape on the insides of your car doors and the inside of the hood, so that if you have to leave the car on the roadway in a nighttime emergency other drivers will be alerted to the presence of a stationary vehicle?

You'll even find out how to get the car in and out of the garage without risking scratches from all the other stuff you keep in there. And if you have trouble positioning the car just right when you drive into the garage, your problems are over. Why *didn't* you ever think of painting guidelines on the floor? Or why didn't you ever think of suspending a tennis ball from the garage ceiling so that it will touch the windshield when you've driven the car just far enough in? You'll also find useful tips here for putting your garage to use as extra storage space.

"HINTS FOR THE FAMILY" is the title of the next section of FAVORITE HELPFUL HOUSEHOLD HINTS, and there really is something for everyone here. The logical starting place is "Getting Organized," which introduces you to all kinds of time- and temper-saving shortcuts to keeping the whole household running smoothly. Discover how to plan your activities to correspond to your personal energy level, how to color-code belongings so that other family members—not just you—can help keep their stuff under control and in the right places, and much more. You'll be amazed how much time and trouble you can save by employing these super-simple tips.

Then, because most people move at one time or another, there's a section on ways to make a move go as smoothly as possible—like planning a house sale ahead of time to get rid of unwanted objects, and packing a survival kit in case you get to your new home before the moving van arrives.

Next are all sorts of ways to make holidays the fun they should be, and to make gift shopping a pleasure instead of a chore. Along with innovative ideas for gifts, there are super ideas of recycling household throw-outs (paper towel tubes, brown paper bags, the newspaper comic strips) into attractive gift packaging. And if you never could figure out how to get the decorative bow on a gift package from home to party without crushing it, here's how: Just tape a plastic berry basket over the bow until you arrive at your destination.

"Money Management," which comes next, is an area where most people could use some helpful tips. What's the best way to handle monthly bills? Are you using your credit cards sensibly? Where do you go when you need a loan and want to make sure you don't get exploited? How much insurance do you need? Here, too, you'll find solid tips on buying or selling a home, renting (or renting to someone else), and landlord-tenant relationships.

Next comes a chapter of particular interest to parents. "Caring for Your Child" begins with sensible (and ingenious) ways to keep your baby or toddler not only well-nourished but also good-natured at mealtimes. Then there are important hints on children's health care, followed by great tips on making bathtime and bedtime go smoothly (for children *and* parents).

From the section on children's activities you'll learn that children don't always need expensive store-bought toys to have fun. Then you'll get a new look at how to stay sane during a children's party (let the kids finger-paint their own placemats, or frost the cake and decorate the cookies themselves). After that comes some practical advice on choosing and using baby equipment such as strollers and playpens—excellent tips especially for first-time parents.

Every cat or dog owner will find much of interest in the following chapter, "Caring for Your Pets." Find out how to give a pill to a protesting cat, how to bathe a dog without giving yourself a bath in the process, and how to keep your pet well-fed and well-groomed. There are good tips, too, on caring for birds, small mammals, and exotic pets.

The next chapter, "Clothes Care and Good Grooming," starts with laundry—an inescapable part of everyone's life and an area where "what do I do *now*?" problems occur all the time. Here are the answers to those cries for help—and often the answers are quite surprising. How do you get ballpoint pen marks off a shirt? Try sponging them with milk. Along with tips on how to tackle the toughest spots and stains, this chapter walks you through machine and hand washing; fabric care; handling special care items; and rinsing, drying, and ironing.

How to dress well without destroying your budget—now there's a dilemma that most people face at one time or another, and the section on choosing and caring for clothes gives you all kinds of valuable hints on how to look good without spending a fortune. Learn how to update last year's fashions with up-to-the-minute accessories, how to organize and store your clothes so that they last longer and look better; how to care for expensive furs and jewelry. And think how useful it would be to keep one foolproof, all-purpose outfit assembled and ready to go so that you'll never have any excuse for complaining, "But I've got nothing to *wear*." This chapter ends with some practical tips on children's clothes (color code boots so they won't get lost at school), and getting children *into* the clothes (a toddler trapped in a high chair can't bolt when it's time to get his coat on).

The next chapter, "Personal Care," is another great resource for hints on looking good without spending a lot of money on pricey commercial products. Learn how to make fine skin care products from such inexpensive ingredients as honey, oatmeal, lemons, eggs, or cucumbers. Find out how to keep your hair shiny and your hands beautifully groomed. And get some good advice on making the most of cosmetics and perfumes.

From looking good and dressing well to dressmaking is a logical step, and the next chapter proves that expert home dressmaking is within the reach of even the inexperienced sewer—especially the one who makes use of all these easy shortcuts to faster, more professional results. And for those who enjoy other types of needlecrafts there are original and helpful hints on knitting, crocheting, embroidery, needlepoint, and quilting.

THE THIRD PART of this compendium of wonderful household helpers shifts the emphasis to another major subject—food. Appropriately, the transition takes you straight to the kitchen. This chapter, "Kitchen Planning and Organization," deals effectively with making the most of your kitchen space (no one ever seems to have enough), using your appliances effectively, making the most of kitchen equipment and supplies, and speeding and easing kitchen cleanup, which is nobody's favorite activity.

Safe food handling is covered in the next section, along with a great selection of hints for preserving food at home—freezing, canning, and drying. Up-to-the-minute tips and techniques help you to top results, and you'll learn when you can substitute everyday kitchen utensils for expensive equipment.

The section on "Purchasing and Preparing Food" offers a wealth of fascinating information on how to select, handle, and prepare every type of food imaginable. There's something here for every taste and every occasion. Here are tips on sensible spending at the supermarket; selection of the best, most economical, and most nutritious foods; and dozens of really helpful (and often surprising) hints on foods from meat, fish, and poultry to breads and cakes to desserts and beverages. Picnics and barbecues get a lift from some good tips here, and there's a whole miscellany of useful odds and ends to round off this comprehensive food section.

"Diet and Nutrition" closes this food section, including hints for weight watchers and a whole section of suggestions for healthy lunchtime ideas to help you kick the junk food habit.

FAVORITE HELPFUL HOUSEHOLD HINTS has been organized to make it as easy as possible to find the information you're looking for as quickly as possible, but don't be too rigid about the way you use this book. Many subject areas "cross over" into each other. For instance, although there's a huge section on purchasing and preparing food, you'll find other terrific food hints in the home entertaining section. So be flexible. Browse through these pages and enjoy the ingenuity of the thousands of hints included here. One thing you can be sure of—anywhere you look you'll find the sort of terrific idea that makes you exclaim, "Now, why didn't *I* think of that?"

Part 1:

Hints for the Home

Whole-House Care and Cleaning

SUPPLIES AND
HOW TO USE THEM

You can eliminate tiny scratches on glass by polishing the affected areas with toothpaste.

A portable blow dryer can soften wax that has dripped onto wooden surfaces. Wipe away the wax with a paper towel, then rinse the area with a mixture of vinegar and water. Dry thoroughly.

The acid in vinegar makes it a good preventive wash for areas where mildew might form.

You can get stale odors out of sponges by washing them in the dishwasher, or by soaking them overnight in a bowl of bleach and rinsing them well the next morning.

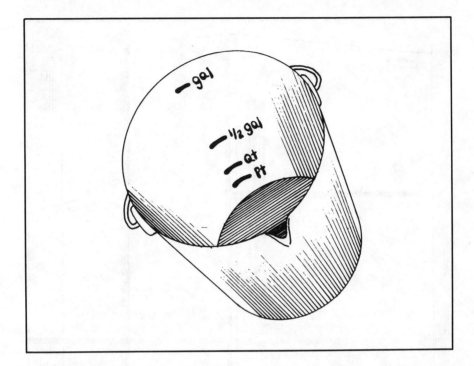

So that you don't have to guess when trying to mix correct solutions of cleaning compounds, use red fingernail polish to plainly mark pint, quart, and gallon levels inside a bucket.

Old toothbrushes can be put to good use as hair dye applicators, or as cleaning brushes for silverware, combs, and typewriter keys.

To clean your radiators, hang a damp cloth behind the radiator, then blow on the radiator with a hair dryer to force hidden dirt and dust onto the damp cloth.

Want to dust furniture quick as a flash? Dampen two old cotton gloves or socks with furniture polish, slip them over your hands, and then dust with both hands.

An automobile snow brush is perfect for cleaning under a refrigerator.

Dust and other debris often collect in hard-to-reach corners, such as behind large appliances, but you can reach easily into these corners with a yardstick. Make a yardstick "duster" by covering the end with a sock, secured with rubber bands, or by fastening a small sponge to the end of the yardstick with staples or rubber bands.

If you're tired of buying new dust mops because the old ones get dirty so quickly, cover your mop with an old nylon stocking. When the stocking gets soiled, simply discard it and replace it with another.

An empty soft drink carton is a good carryall for cleaning compounds as you work from room to room. When you're done, take the whole kit and put it away neatly below the sink.

When the suction tube on a spray bottle doesn't reach the liquid because most of the liquid has been used up, drop marbles or pebbles into the bottle until the level of the liquid rises enough to cover the end of the tube.

Instead of buying dust cloths chemically treated to "attract" dust, make your own from cheesecloth. Dip the cloth in a solution of two cups of water and a quarter cup of lemon oil and allow it to dry before using.

Paintbrushes make excellent dusters for small or hard-to-reach areas. Flick them along door jambs, around windows, and into corners where dust cloths won't fit.

To avoid snagging or harming delicate fabric when dusting ruffled or pleated lamp shades, use an old shaving brush or a baby's hairbrush. The bristles are soft and effective.

You can use a straightened wire hanger to unclog a jammed vacuum cleaner hose. Leave a small hook at the end of the hanger and maneuver it back and forth; then, see if the hose is free of debris by dropping a coin through it. If the coin rolls out the other end, you're ready to vacuum again. If it doesn't, you'll have to maneuver the hanger some more. Another way to unclog a vacuum cleaner hose is to push an ordinary garden hose through it.

Mend a torn reusable vacuum cleaner bag by pressing iron-on patches over the tears.

You can vacuum dust and lint from mops and brooms by holding them under the hose attachment.

To prevent a dust cloud from forming, empty a vacuum cleaner bag into a large plastic garbage bag; hold the mouth of the bag shut as you dump the dust inside it.

Although you use a chamois for cleaning chores, it requires gentle cleaning itself. Use natural soap, not detergent, rinse well, stretch to its original size, and dry away from direct heat.

Avoid crushing cobwebs on to the ceiling while cleaning; they will leave marks. Lift them off regularly with a mop or broom covered with a cloth, or with the brush attachment on your vacuum cleaner.

Run a coarse-toothed comb through brush bristles to help remove stubborn debris and soil.

To clean a dust mop without mess, slip a large paper bag over the head of the mop, secure the top, and shake so the dust falls into the bag.

Synthetic fabrics do not make good cleaning cloths. They are not absorbent, and they create static electricity.

It may not sound like fun, but you'll do yourself a favor over the long haul if you clean the attachment brushes and rollers on your vacuum cleaner regularly. Lint and thread buildup will hamper the appliance's performance over time.

An easy way to make an all-purpose soft soap is to shave two cups of hard bar soap into a large pot (two cups of powdered soap is a satisfactory alternative), add a gallon of water, and bring to a boil, stirring constantly to dissolve the soap. Simmer on low heat for ten minutes, then let the soap cool partially before pouring into clean containers. You now have a gallon of soft soap.

CARPETS AND UPHOLSTERY

Acid stains on a carpet or on upholstery should be immediately diluted and neutralized with baking soda and water, or with club soda. The same solutions will also keep vomit stains from setting.

If someone spills an alcoholic drink on carpet or upholstery, quickly dilute the spot with cold water so that the alcohol doesn't have time to attack the dyes. If red wine is the culprit, dilute it with white wine, then clean the spot with cold water and cover it with table salt. Wait ten minutes, then vacuum up the salt.

Use a paste of laundry starch and cold water to lift blood stains from carpet or upholstery. Allow the paste to dry, and then brush it away.

To remove chewing gum that is stuck on the carpet, press an ice cube against the gum. The gum will harden and can then be pulled off. Treat any last traces of gum with a spot remover.

Blot coffee stains quickly and dilute with plain water.

Use dry-cleaning fluid on tar spots, but apply it sparingly and blot regularly.

If there's candle wax on carpet or upholstery, put an ice cube in a plastic bag and hold it against the wax. When the wax becomes brittle, chip it away with a dull knife.

Here's another way to remove candle wax from carpet or upholstery: Place a blotter over the wax spot and press with a warm iron until the blotter absorbs the melted wax. Move the blotter frequently so that it doesn't get over-saturated.

You can occasionally remove crayon marks on carpet or upholstery by using the iron-and-blotter treatment that's effective with candle wax; you can also try dabbing at them using a cloth moistened with dry-cleaning fluid.

Dampen blood stains on carpet or upholstery with cold water. (Hot water *sets* the stains.) Then apply carpet or upholstery shampoo and follow this treatment by applying dry-cleaning fluid.

Absorb butter stains and other greasy household stains on carpet or upholstery with cornmeal, dried and ground corncobs, or dry-cleaning fluid.

To remove grease stains (except butter) on carpet or upholstery, scrape up as much spilled grease as possible and apply dry-cleaning fluid with a cloth. Or rub with paint thinner, cover with salt, and vacuum. Another alternative: Sprinkle with cornmeal, leave overnight, and vacuum.

Use hair spray to lift ballpoint ink stains from carpet or upholstery. Use dry-cleaning fluid, applied with a cloth, on other ink stains. Here's another way to cope with ink stains: Sprinkle them with salt. As ink is absorbed, brush the salt away and sprinkle again. Repeat as necessary.

Try to remove mildew from carpet or upholstery with white vinegar. If spots remain, rub with dry-cleaning fluid. Note: Eliminate moist conditions or the mildew will return.

Just as fabric softener takes static cling out of your laundry, it can remove static "shock" from your carpet. Spray your carpet lightly with a mix of five parts water and one part liquid softener and you won't have to worry about shocks when you touch metallic objects.

To raise depressions left in carpets by heavy furniture, try steaming them. Hold an iron close enough for steam to reach the carpet, but don't let the iron touch the fibers, especially if they're synthetic, because they could melt. Lift the fibers by scraping them with the edge of a coin or spoon.

Rugs will last longer if you occasionally rotate them to change areas of wear, or if you rearrange furniture to alter traffic patterns.

When a carpet thread is loose, snip it level with the pile. If you try to pull out the thread you risk unraveling part of the carpet.

To repair a large burned area in a carpet, cut out the damaged area and substitute a patch of identical size and shape. Secure the new piece with double-faced carpet tape or latex adhesive.

You needn't hide a carpet burn with furniture. If the burn isn't down to the backing, just snip off the charred part with fingernail scissors. However, if a carpet burn does extend to the backing, snip off the charred fibers and put white glue in the opening. Then, snip fibers from a scrap or an inconspicuous part of the carpet (perhaps in a closet). When the glue gets tacky, poke the fibers into place.

To prevent small area rugs from slipping out from under you, attach strips of double-faced carpet tape under the corners.

Has the pile on your shag rug flattened? You can raise it with a lightweight bamboo yard rake.

Should your spot-remover efforts alter the color of carpet or upholstery, try touching up small places with artists' acrylic paint. If that doesn't work, try a felt marker or a permanent ink marker of the appropriate color—and go slowly.

To remove wet latex paint spots on carpet or upholstery, dab with water. To remove wet oil-based paint spots, dab with turpentine, then absorb the turpentine with cornmeal. In either case, follow with an application of dry-cleaning fluid or shampoo.

If your pets have accidents on carpet or upholstery, blot the stains with water, then clean with club soda. A mix of equal parts of white vinegar and water is also effective.

Remove animal hair from furniture by wiping with a damp sponge. Dabbing with pieces of tape also works well.

You can remove soot stains by sprinkling generously with salt, allowing the salt to settle for several minutes, and vacuuming both salt and soot.

The best way to clean vinyl upholstery is with baking soda on a damp cloth, followed by a light washing with a dishwashing soap. Never use oil; it will only harden the upholstery.

If your carpet sweeper misses lint, string, and other small debris, just dampen the brushes.

Carpet odors can be eliminated by sprinkling baking soda on the carpet before vacuuming, or by doing the same thing with one cup of borax mixed with two cups of cornmeal. (Let the latter mixture stand for an hour before vacuuming.)

FLOORS AND FLOOR COVERINGS

You can remove heel marks from asphalt tile floors by rubbing gently with grade 000 steel wool dipped in liquid floor wax. Wipe with a damp cloth.

When cleaning an asphalt tile floor with water, use a well-wrung cloth or sponge; excess water can seep into the seams and loosen the adhesives that hold the flooring.

Use only solvent-based cleaners and polishes on cork tile floors. Water and water-based products are taboo on this type of flooring.

To avoid marking a cork floor, use an appliance dolly to move heavy furniture and appliances. Also, avoid the use of rubber compound floor protectors on furniture legs.

A mopped floor occasionally dries with a luster-dulling film; if you mop it again with water containing a cup or so of white vinegar the floor will glisten.

A pencil eraser or fine, dry steel wool is often effective in removing scuff marks left by shoe heels on resilient flooring.

Lift crayon marks from resilient flooring by rubbing them with toothpaste or silver polish on a damp rag.

Instead of using commercial preparations, you can "wax" a floor by washing it with warm water to which you have added two tablespoons of furniture polish and a half cup of vinegar.

Rather than wax floors on your hands and knees, stand and use a long-handled paint roller. A roller not only speeds up the waxing process, it makes it easy to reach under a radiator or built-in furniture.

To clean up raw egg dropped on a floor, sprinkle it with salt, let it sit for 15 to 20 minutes, and then sweep it up with a broom.

Instead of using a rag to apply paste wax to floors, get a better grip and protect your skin with a glove-type potholder or workman's glove slipped over your hand. Such gloves have the added advantage of being sturdy and easy to clean.

When washing highly waxed floors between waxings, use a solution of one cup of fabric softener in a half pail of water to prevent dulling the shine.

A few drops of vinegar in the water used to clean the kitchen floor will help remove particles of cooking grease that have settled from the air.

For a fast shine between floor waxings, put a piece of waxed paper under your mop and slide it around your floor.

After you've waxed a floor, wrap a bath towel around each foot and shuffle around the room to polish the floor in a flash.

When it's time for a new coat of wax on a linoleum or tile floor, remove the old wax by mopping with a solution of three parts of water to one part of rubbing alcohol.

WINDOWS AND WINDOW TREATMENTS

A liquid cleaner for glass can be made by mixing two cups of water and two tablespoons of liquid dishwashing detergent with two cups of isopropyl rubbing alcohol (70 percent). Stir until thoroughly mixed and then pour into a clean pump-spray bottle. The alcohol keeps the cleaner from freezing on the panes in cold weather.

Pure vinegar will remove stubborn hard-water sprinkler spots and streaks from a window.

Cloudy days are preferable to sunny days for window washing because direct sunlight dries cleaning solutions before you can polish the glass properly.

If you can wash one side of a window with horizontal strokes and the other side with vertical strokes, you'll be able to tell which side a streak is on.

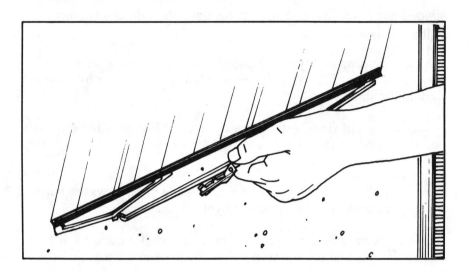

An old auto wiper blade makes a good squeegee for washing windows.

When washing windows, a soft toothbrush or a cotton swab is a useful tool for cleaning corners.

It is possible to clean upstairs window exteriors without using a ladder. Use a garden hose spray bottle attachment containing automatic dishwasher detergent; the spray leaves only a few spots.

To give an extra shine to window glass, polish it with well-washed cotton T-shirts or old diapers.

Polish windows to a sparkling shine with crumpled-up newspaper. The paper also leaves a film that's resistant to dirt.

Rubbing a clean blackboard eraser over a freshly washed (and dried) window gives it a diamond-bright shine.

To remove built up cooking grease or soot from window glass, use a solution of two cups of kerosene and one gallon of warm water. Rub it on with a soft rag and wipe the panes dry with a clean towel. Caution: Kerosene is flammable; don't pour it or use it near an open flame. The same cleaning solution (two cups of kerosene to one gallon of warm water) also protects window exteriors. Water drops will bead just as they do on a highly waxed car. Do not use this cleaner on any nonglass window.

To make an ammonia-based glass cleaner, mix two cups of water, one cup of isopropyl rubbing alcohol (70 percent), and one tablespoon of household ammonia. Pour into a clean pump-spray bottle.

Shades, Blinds, and Screens

Use wallpaper cleaner or an art gum eraser to lift spots from window shades.

If a nonwashable window shade needs cleaning, rub it with a rough flannel cloth dipped in flour.

A window shade that has too much tension can be removed from its bracket and unrolled by hand two or three revolutions to make it less tense after it is replaced.

A shade that won't lift properly needs more tension. Remove it, roll it up two or three revolutions, and reinstall it.

Use a silicone spray instead of oil on a window-shade mechanism. (Oil will soak through the wood roller and ruin your shade.)

The least expensive way to clean a nonwashable window shade thoroughly is to rub the surface with a rough, absorbent cloth dipped in cornmeal. The abrasiveness and absorption of the cloth and cornmeal pick up soil and grease. Terry cloth is good for this job, but an old sweatshirt turned inside out is even better. If you don't have cornmeal, dry kitchen flour can be substituted.

If you're interrupted while cleaning venetian blinds, clasp a clothespin to the last slat you cleaned so you'll know where you left off.

To prevent venetian blind tapes from shrinking when cleaned, rehang the blinds before the tapes dry.

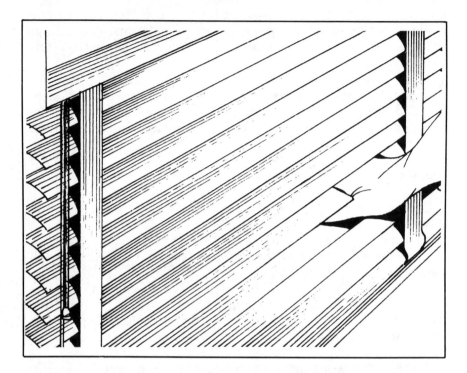

If you wear cotton gloves when washing venetian blinds you can use your fingers to rub the slats—this works better than any brush.

Another way to wash venetian blinds is to hang them from a clothesline and turn a hose on them. You can also wash them under the shower. Use mild soap and water.

To install a new venetian blind cord, tape or sew the end of the new one to the old one. Slowly pull out the old cord and you'll pull the new one into place at the same time.

Spray venetian blind pulleys with a silicone lubricant to keep them working smoothly.

An inexpensive but effective way to clean aluminum screens out-doors and keep them from pitting is with kerosene. Dip a rag in the kerosene and rub both sides of the mesh as well as the frames. Wipe off the excess. This is a good rust inhibitor for older screens, too.

Caution: Kerosene is flammable; don't pour it or use it near an open flame.

WALLS AND WALL COVERINGS

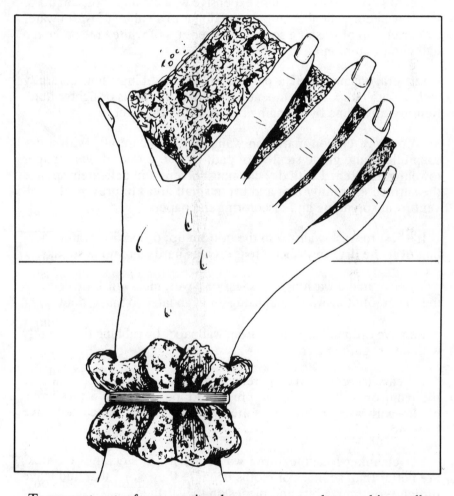

To prevent water from running down your arm when washing walls, fashion a bracelet from a sponge or washcloth held in place with a thick rubber band.

You can sponge washable wall coverings and some vinyls with a mild detergent. To find out how much elbow grease your paper can take, first work on a scrap.

Lift grease stains from washable wallpaper with a paste made of cornstarch and water. Alternatively, rub dry borax over stains.

There's no need to purchase expensive wall cleaner. You can make your own economical cleaner by mixing into a gallon of warm water a quarter cup of washing soda, a quarter cup of white vinegar, and a half cup of ammonia.

Lift crayon marks off a painted wall by rubbing them carefully with a cloth or sponge dampened with mineral spirits or lighter fluid. Remove any shine by sponging lightly with hot water.

To remove crayon marks on wallpaper, rub carefully with a dry soap-filled, fine grade steel-wool pad. Or use a wad of white paper toweling moistened with dry-cleaning solvent and delicately sponge the surface. Carefully blot and lift in small areas to prevent the solvent from spreading and discoloring the paper.

It's best to wash walls from the bottom up; otherwise, water trickling over the dry, unwashed areas creates hard-to-remove streaks.

You can make washing walls less of a wet, messy task by decreasing the amount of water and using an eggbeater to make thick suds.

Remove ordinary soil marks from wallpaper by rubbing them gently with an art gum eraser.

It's easy to remove transparent tape from a wall without marring the paint or wallpaper if you press the tape—through a protective cloth—with a warm iron to soften and loosen the tape's adhesive backing.

For cleaning rough-textured walls, old nylon stockings or socks are better than sponges or cloths because they won't tear and leave difficult-to-remove bits and pieces on the surface.

To remove grease stains from a grass-cloth wall or ceiling covering, apply an aerosol dry cleaner. Follow instructions carefully.

To remove a grease spot from nonwashable wallpaper, place a blotter over the spot and press it with a moderately hot iron. The blotter will soak up the grease. Repeat as required.

You can also use talcum powder to remove a grease spot on non-washable wallpaper. Dust on the talc with a powder puff, leave it for an hour and then brush it off. Repeat, if necessary.

Clean nonwashable wallpaper with rye bread. Make a fist-sized wad of bread and rub it across discolorations and dirt.

To remove white water marks from wood wall paneling, rub mayonnaise into them. Wipe off the mayonnaise 12 hours later. The marks will have vanished.

This inexpensive, make-it-yourself polish is excellent for restoring the beauty of wood paneling with an oiled finish. Pour equal parts of turpentine and boiled linseed oil into a jar, tighten the lid, and shake the liquid to blend it thoroughly. Pour a small amount of this mixture onto a soft cloth and rub up and down with the grain of the wood. The wood surface will appear oily, but within an hour the polish will be completely absorbed, leaving a lovely soft sheen on the wood.

Some cleaners can stain some types of brick. Test strong cleaning products on a small, inconspicuous area first, wait a week, and evaluate the results before doing the complete job.

If your spot-removal efforts change the color of brick, even out the color by rubbing another brick of the same color over the surface.

For best results, brick surfaces should be thoroughly saturated with clean water before and after cleaning.

Clean accumulated dirt and stains from a brick wall with a solution of hot water and an all-purpose cleaner. If the mortar between the bricks won't come clean, add chlorine bleach to the solution to help lighten the mortar.

When cleaning smoke stains from brick walls, wet the area below the smoke stain first so that any runoff won't set in the lower tier of bricks.

CLEANING THE BATHROOM

To make your own ceramic tile cleaner, put a quarter cup of baking soda, a half cup of white vinegar, and one cup of household ammonia in a bucket. Add one gallon of warm water, stirring until the baking soda dissolves. Wearing rubber gloves, apply the mixture with a scrub brush or sponge and then rinse. Mix a fresh batch for each cleaning.

To make your bathroom walls sparkle, rub the ceramic tile with car wax and buff after ten minutes.

To make your own heavy-duty grout cleaner, put three cups of baking soda in a medium-size bowl and add one cup of warm water. Mix the contents to a smooth paste and scrub into grout with a damp sponge or toothbrush, rinsing thoroughly afterwards. Mix a fresh batch for each cleaning.

A typewriter eraser from the stationery store is an excellent tool for cleaning the grout between bathroom tiles.

You can remove most mildew from the grout between tiles by rubbing it with a toothbrush or nailbrush dipped in laundry bleach. (Don't use abrasive powders or steel-wool pads or you'll scratch the tile.) Rinse with clear water after cleaning. If spots remain, you could camouflage stained grout with a white fingernail pencil or white liquid shoe polish. (If you get polish on the tiles, let it dry and then wipe it off with a rag.)

A ring around the tub can be rubbed away without cleaners with a nylon net ball or pad.

Cover a stubborn ring with a paste of cream of tartar and hydrogen peroxide. When the paste dries, wipe it off—along with the ring.

To enjoy your bath without worrying about leaving a tub ring, add a capful of mild liquid dishwashing detergent to the bath water.

To get rid of rust stains on a bathtub, try rubbing them with a paste of borax powder and lemon juice. If the stain persists, use a dry-cleaning solution.

To remove discoloration from a yellowed bathtub, rub the tub with a solution of salt and turpentine.

An old nylon stocking rolled into a ball becomes a nonscratch scrub pad for cleaning sink and tub.

Clean a rubber or vinyl bathtub mat by tossing it into the washer with bath towels. The terry cloth scrubs the mat, and everything comes out clean.

Shower enclosures are a chore to keep clean—but they can be less of a problem if you follow these suggestions: Keep mildew from taking hold by wiping shower walls with a towel after each shower, while you're still in the tub. When the walls need a thorough cleaning, run the shower water at its hottest temperature so the steam will loosen the dirt. Then, using a sponge mop, clean with a mixture of a half cup vinegar, one cup clear ammonia, and a quarter cup baking soda in one gallon of warm water. After cleaning, rinse with clear water. Note: Never use harsh abrasive powders or steel-wool pads.

Having trouble getting mineral deposits off a shower head? Remove the head, take it apart, and soak it in vinegar. Then brush deposits loose with an old toothbrush. Clean the holes by poking them with a wire, pin, toothpick, or ice pick.

Mix a half cup vinegar, one cup ammonia, and a quarter cup baking soda in a gallon of hot water to make a cleaning solution for porcelain, cultured marble, and fiberglass bathroom fixtures. Apply with a sponge and rinse well with clear water. Wear rubber gloves and work in a well-ventilated area when using this powerful solution.

The fastest way to clean chromium is with baking soda applied to the surface with a dry cloth. It will remove fingerprints, smudges, and even sticky residue with no further rinsing or wiping.

The least expensive way to clean up greasy film and smudges on chrome is to rub the surface with a dry cloth dipped in dry kitchen flour. The results are just as remarkable as with the dry baking soda technique given above.

Lemon oil will remove water spots on metal frames around shower doors and enclosures.

Glass shower doors will sparkle again if you clean them once a week with a sponge dipped in white vinegar.

Hand washing works better than machine washing for plastic shower curtains. You get fewer wrinkles.

If you wash the shower curtain in the bathtub you'll clean the curtain and the tub in one job.

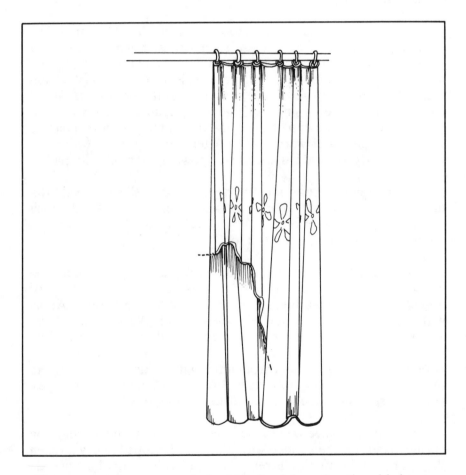

Keep a new shower curtain looking fresh by using the old shower curtain as a liner. Hang the new curtain on the same hooks, but in front of the old curtain. The old curtain will take the beating from water and soap scum while the new one stays clean.

To prevent machine-washed shower curtains from wrinkling, put them in the washing machine with a half cup of detergent and a half cup of baking soda, along with two large bath towels. Add a cup of vinegar to the rinse cycle, then hang the curtains up immediately after washing and let them air dry.

When you clean a plastic shower curtain, keep it soft and flexible by adding a few drops of mineral oil to the rinse water. Maintain the curtain's softness by wiping it occasionally with a solution of warm water and mineral oil.

Eliminate mildew by spraying newly washed shower curtains with a disinfectant.

Treat wooden towel racks with an occasional application of furniture polish to bring up the shine and give a protective coating.

To make your bathroom mirror sparkle, polish it with a cloth dipped in a borax-and-water solution or in denatured alcohol. Or polish with dry facial tissue, a lint-free cloth, paper toweling, or old nylon stockings.

Rubbing alcohol will wipe away hair-spray haze on a mirror.

You can defog a bathroom mirror quickly by spraying it with hot air from a hair dryer.

Mirrors in your bathroom won't steam up if you run an inch of cold water in the bathtub before adding hot water.

A quarter cup of sodium bisulfate (sodium acid sulfate) can be sprinkled into a wet toilet bowl for a single scrubbing and flushing. (Wear rubber gloves.) Let it stand for 15 minutes, and then scrub and flush as usual. Note: Never combine bleach with toilet-bowl cleaners; the mix can release toxic gases.

Rust stains under a toilet bowl rim sometimes yield to laundry bleach—but be sure to protect your hands with plastic or rubber gloves. (Note: Never combine bleach with toilet-bowl cleaners; the mix can release toxic gases.) Rub off truly stubborn stains with extra-fine steel wool, or with wet-dry sandpaper (available at hardware stores).

Cola that has gone flat can be spilled into the toilet bowl and left for an hour. The soft drink will clean the bowl.

Chemical toilet bowl cleaners should never be used to clean the bathtub or sink; the chemical will ruin the finish.

BOOKS AND RECORDS

Treat leather-bound books periodically with a light oil so that the leather won't dry out and crack.

If you arrange books at the front of shelves, air will be able to circulate and prevent mustiness.

Protect books from direct sunlight, which can fade the bindings and cause them to deteriorate.

To remove grease stains from books rub the affected areas with soft white bread crumbs.

Sprinkle damp book pages with talcum powder or cornstarch until the moisture is absorbed, then shake or brush the powder away.

To keep vinyl and imitation leather covered books looking good as new, wash them periodically with a mild detergent and then treat with a light coat of petroleum jelly or a vinyl dressing.

The fastest way to clean books is with the brush attachment on your vacuum cleaner. Tilt each book back one at a time on the shelf so you can remove the dust from the binding and book edges. Another rapid approach is to wipe books lightly with a clean, never-used paint brush—this is a very good way to handle books with the pages edged in gold leaf.

Badly soiled paper edges of a book can be easily cleaned with an art gum eraser. Hold the book firmly by the covers so it won't accidentally open and cause damage to the pages.

Remove dust accumulation from around the stylus or needle of your record player with an artist's brush dipped in isopropyl alcohol.

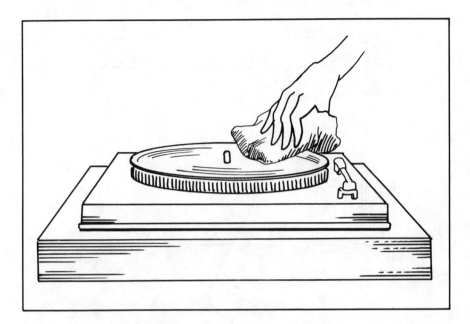

It is easy to clean lightly soiled records on the turntable. Gently hold a clean dust cloth on a record and allow the disc to turn at least three revolutions under the cloth. You'll be cleaning with the grooves, not across them, and so won't damage the record.

PICTURES AND ART OBJECTS

When cleaning picture glass, carefully dust the glass, and then polish it with tissues sold for cleaning eyeglasses. Avoid liquid cleaners because they could seep under the edge of the glass and spoil the photo or artwork. If you do use liquid cleaners, apply them to a cloth, *never* directly to the glass.

To make a tarnished gilt frame gleam again, wipe it with a rag dampened with turpentine.

To avoid damaging a picture or painting when polishing its wooden frame, spray the polish on a cloth, not on the frame, and then carefully apply to the frame.

To clean deeply carved picture frames, use a clean, dry, plastic squeeze bottle, pumping the bottle like a small bellows to blow dust from tiny crevices.

To wash fragile objects without breaking them, put them on a tray in the sink and spray them first with window cleaner or foam bathroom cleaner, and then with water. Let them air dry on a towel.

You can wash knickknacks more quickly than you can dust them. Swish them in water containing a touch of liquid detergent, rinse, and drain on a towel. If you want to make sure every crevice is dry, use a hair dryer.

Always keep ivory objects where light can reach them, because steady darkness causes ivory to yellow.

To clean a yellowing ivory object, cut a lemon in half, dip it in salt, and rub it over the ivory surface. When the surface is dry, wipe it with a damp cloth, then buff dry for a bright finish.

You can remove stubborn stains from ivory or plastic piano keys with a damp cloth dipped in baking soda, being careful not to let the soda fall between the keys. Wipe the keys off with another cloth, and buff them dry.

If the ivory keys of your piano look dull, brighten them by rubbing very fine sandpaper (400 or 600) along the length of each key *with the grain*. Then buff.

SILVER AND GOLD

To clean tarnished silver, place the items in a glass dish, add a piece of aluminum foil, and cover with a quart of hot water mixed with one tablespoon of baking soda. A reaction between the foil and the silver will remove any tarnish. Don't use this process on raised designs, however. You'll lose the dark accents of the sculpture.

If silver candlesticks accumulate wax drippings, place them in the freezer; when the wax freezes, you'll be able to peel it off.

An inexpensive way to clean gold is to mix one teaspoon of cigarette ash with enough water to form a paste. Rub the paste onto the surface of the gold with a soft cloth, rinse, and buff dry with a chamois. If no one in the house smokes, use baking soda instead of cigarette ash.

An easy way to clean silver is with ordinary baking soda. Make a paste from three parts soda to one part water. Using a soft cloth, rub the paste gently on the silver surface. Tarnish will disappear rapidly. After rinsing, buff the silver with a soft cloth to bring up the shine.

Make your own silver polish by mixing powdered white chalk with just enough ammonia to make a paste.

Silver polish that has hardened can be revived in no time: Add a very little warm water and mix until the polish is the consistency of cream.

SPECIAL SURFACES

You can strip cracked and peeling lacquer from coated brass objects with a solution of baking soda and boiling water (one cup soda to two gallons water). Let the article stand in the water until it cools, then peel off the lacquer. You can either have the piece relacquered or clean and polish it as for other brass.

A paste made of one tablespoon each of salt, flour, and vinegar is the most economical method for cleaning brass. Applied with a cloth, the paste is very effective in making tarnish disappear and the shine reappear.

Another quick and inexpensive way to clean brass is to dip a cut lemon in salt and rub it on the brass surface. Be sure to wash the brass in warm soapsuds afterward, and buff dry to bring up the shine.

To clean decorative copper objects, use a homemade paste of one tablespoon each of salt, vinegar, and flour. Rub over the surface and then wash the object in hot soapy water. Rinse and buff for a shiny finish.

Periodically coat unpainted iron surfaces with liquid wax and buff to preserve the highlights of the original finish and prevent rust.

Two tablespoons vinegar mixed with one tablespoon salt, or a cut lemon dipped in salt and rubbed over the surface, will clean copper effectively. Just remember to wash, rinse, and dry after this treatment.

Wine, fruit juice, or other acid foods cause permanent etching on marble. Wipe these substances off marble surfaces at once. Also, do not allow oily food substances to remain on marble; they will cause permanent stains.

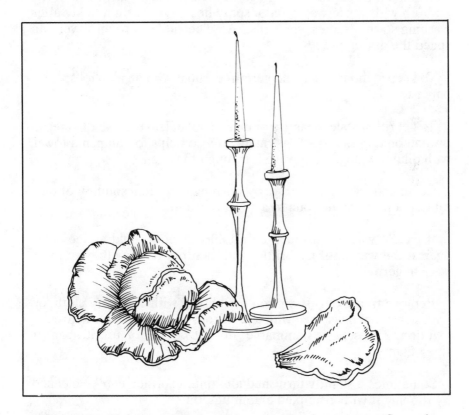

Here's an effective and unusual treatment for pewter. Save the outer leaves from a head of cabbage and use them to polish pewter. Rub the leaf over the surface and then buff with a soft cloth. You'll be amazed at the shine this simple technique gives.

Pewter objects will need less polishing if you use them regularly.

Wash pewter food containers and flatware immediately after use to prevent stains and pitting. Acid foods, salt, and salad dressing are particularly liable to cause harm.

CLEANING CHALLENGES

Lamp shades fixed to their frames with glue should be dry cleaned.

When lamp shades aren't glued to their frames, wash them in the bathtub with warm water and a spray hose. Dry them quickly after washing so the frames won't rust. An electric fan or hair dryer can speed the drying process.

To keep a phone clean and germfree, rub it with an alcohol-soaked paper towel.

To get rid of stale cigarette or cigar smoke, leave a dish of vinegar or ammonia in the room overnight. It also helps to dampen a towel with diluted vinegar and wave it through the room.

Clean and sweeten ashtrays by washing them in a solution of one tablespoon of baking soda to a quart of water.

If candle wax has dripped on a table or cloth, hold an ice cube against the wax until it's brittle, and then pry it off with a knife or your fingernail.

Remove traces of rust on iron by rubbing with an emery cloth, or with steel wool moistened with a few drops of turpentine or kerosene. Caution: Kerosene is flammable; do not pour it or use it near an open flame.

Sometimes a slightly tarnished aluminum surface can be cleaned by rubbing it with crumpled aluminum foil.

Some sturdy fabric flowers may be freshened when shaken in a paper bag with dry cut oats, cornmeal, or salt. More delicate blossoms should be treated according to the fabric from which they are made.

Black scuff marks on your luggage will rub off with lemon extract.

Clean colored leather luggage with mild soapsuds and a damp sponge or soft-nap cloth.

The best way to clean regular leather luggage is to use a soft, clean rag to rub in a few drops of baby shampoo, a small area at a time. Repeat until all surfaces are covered. Use the same cloth to buff the luggage to a natural sheen.

It is possible to clean a chandelier without taking it down; here's how. In a glass, mix a solution of one part denatured alcohol and three parts water. Cover the floor or table under the chandelier with newspaper or plastic and set up a ladder so that you can reach the pendants. Individually submerge the crystals in the glass for a few moments, swishing them back and forth a little, and then simply let them air dry.

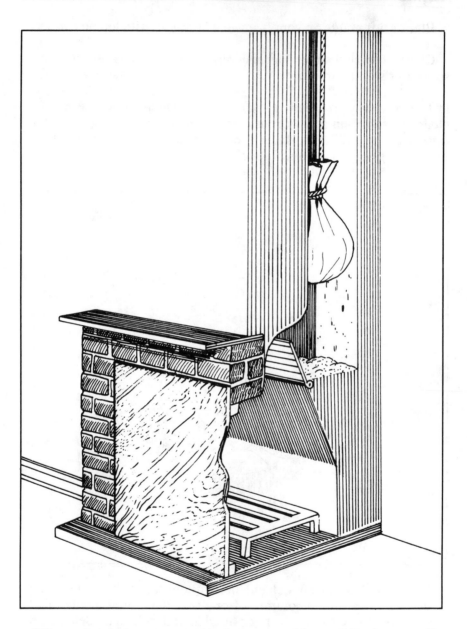

Why pay a chimney sweep to clean your chimney? Do it yourself this way. Open the damper and seal the hearth from the room with scrap lumber or a drop cloth secured with masking tape. If the flue is straight, fill a burlap bag with wadded paper and two bricks and then fasten it to a long rope. Go up to the roof and slide the bag up and down the chimney's interior five or six times to remove all soot. If the flue is curved, use two feet of tire chain or other heavy chain at the end of the rope, rather than a burlap bag. Slap the chain against the flue's sides as you raise and lower the rope five or six times. For the most efficient use of your fireplace, do this once a year.

To see if your chimney is free of soot after you've cleaned it, wait an hour or so for the dust to settle and then use a large hand mirror and a flashlight to examine the flue.

Fireplace smoke stains can be removed by washing them with a half cup of trisodium phosphate (TSP) mixed in one gallon of water. (Wear gloves to protect your hands.) You also can remove fireplace smoke stains by rubbing them with an art gum eraser, or by applying a paste of cream of tartar and water; when the paste dries brush it off along with the stains.

Fire-stained andirons can be cleaned by dipping fine (00) steel wool in cooking oil and rubbing gently. Apply a polish to bring up the shine.

If you can't get heating units clean with the vacuum cleaner and its attachments (dust brushes and crevice tool), use a solution of a half cup vinegar, one cup ammonia, and a quarter cup baking soda in a gallon of hot water. Wearing rubber gloves, apply this solution with a sponge or cloth, first placing newspapers under the heating unit to protect the floor.

Indoor Home Maintenance and Repairs

FURNITURE CARE AND CLEANING

Leftover tea makes a good cleaning agent for varnished furniture.

While waxing the furniture, also wax the insides of ashtrays. This makes them easier to clean.

Rub walnut or pecan meat over scratches in finished wood; the oil often hides them. Liquid shoe polish often covers scratches, too.

Wear cotton gloves to avoid leaving fingerprints while polishing furniture.

After polishing furniture, sprinkle on a little cornstarch and rub to a high gloss. Cornstarch absorbs oil and leaves a glistening fingerprint-free surface.

Paste furniture wax or oil furniture polish will camouflage tiny furniture scratches.

To treat scratches on natural wood or antique finishes, polish with a mixture of equal amounts of turpentine and boiled linseed oil. Apply with a clean, soft, damp cloth.

Any scratch made by a match can be removed by rubbing with a lemon wedge.

There are several ways to remove white spots, such as those left by wet drinking glasses. You can rub them with toothpaste on a damp cloth. (Try this on other surface stains, too.) Or rub them with paste furniture polish, any mild abrasive, or oil. Appropriate abrasives are ashes, salt, soda, or pumice: suitable oils are olive oil, petroleum jelly, cooking oil, or lemon-oil furniture polish.

You can tighten a loose furniture leg caster by wrapping a rubber band around its stem and reinserting it.

When wood fibers in a piece of furniture are merely bent, but not cut, straighten out any dents with an iron, set on medium, and a damp cloth. Place the damp cloth on a dent, hold the iron on it until the cloth begins to dry, redampen the cloth, and repeat the process as needed.

Tighten a cabinet or dresser knob by dipping its screw or screws in fingernail polish or shellac and reinserting the knob. When the polish or shellac hardens, the screws will be set and the knobs will be tight.

It's best to position a piano where the sun won't shine on it and where it's least likely to be exposed to changes in temperature or humidity.

You can unstick wooden drawers by rubbing contact surfaces with a bar of soap or a candle.

Paper stuck to a polished table can be lifted after saturating the paper with cooking oil.

A coat of wax prevents rusting on chrome kitchen chairs.

Decals will easily lift off painted furniture if you sponge them with vinegar.

To tighten wobbly wicker furniture, wash it outdoors with hot soapy water, rinse it with a hose, and let it air dry. The wood and cane will shrink and tighten.

Saggy wicker or cane seats can be similarly tightened by sponging them with hot water.

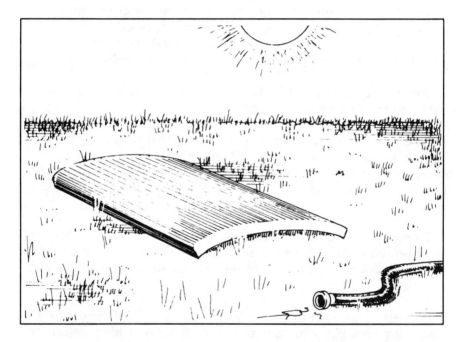

Sometimes a warped table leaf or other board can be straightened by exposure to wet grass and hot summer sun. For this treatment, water a grassy area thoroughly and set the board, concave side down, on the wet grass. As the dry side of the board absorbs moisture from the grass, the moist (convex) side is dried out by the sun and the board unwarps. This process takes no longer than a day.

Thread can serve as packing around a chair rung before it is reglued.

You can usually rub cigarette burns out of wooden furniture with very fine sandpaper or steel wool. Then, if necessary, color the area with shoe polish to match the rest of the surface.

If you need to pound apart sections of a chair that needs regluing, a soft mallet will provide enough power but will be much kinder to the wood than a hammer.

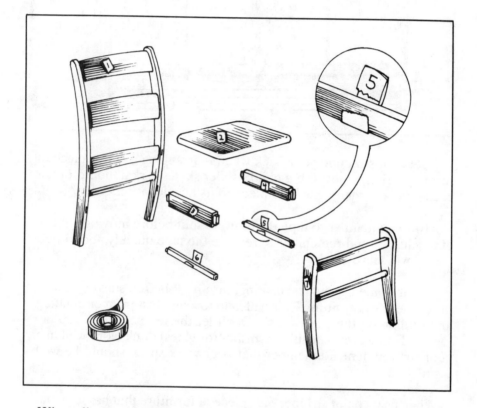

When disassembling a piece of furniture for repair, label or number the parts with pieces of masking tape so you'll know how to put them together again. Make a list describing which part of the piece of furniture each number represents. For example, number ten — top right-side rung (as you're facing the chair).

If a loose cane on a rattan chair is snagging your clothing or stockings, tame it with clear tape, or blunt it by dabbing on clear nail polish.

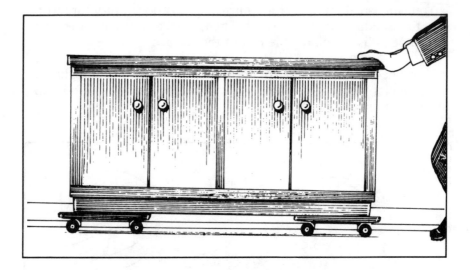

Instead of straining your back when rearranging a heavy piece of furniture, simply position a child's roller skate or skateboard under each end, and then wheel the piece to its new location.

Always remember to tape the drawers shut before moving a piece of furniture—and remember to remove the tape quickly, too, otherwise it will leave marks.

If your home has central heating, turn it off before starting to varnish a piece of furniture. This will help to keep dust from circulating and settling on the wet varnish. Don't let the temperature drop below 70°F, however, because varnishes (or glues) don't work well in a cool environment. Remember that your work space should be well ventilated.

When using paint stripper on a piece of furniture that has legs, put a tin can under each leg to catch drips. This protects the floor and lets you reuse the stripper that collects in the cans.

When gluing dowels, a dowel that's exactly the size of the hole it fits into can push much of the glue to the bottom of the hole and therefore not hold as well as it should. To avoid this, cut a few grooves in the dowel so the glue is distributed along its surface for a more secure bond.

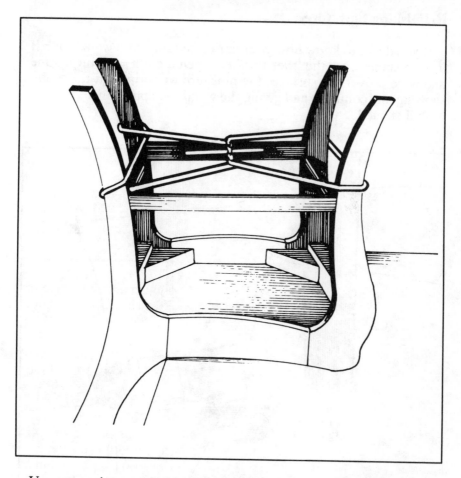

Use a tourniquet to hold a freshly glued chair rung firmly in place. Clamp the glued rung with a heavy cord wrapped around the chair legs. Use a dowel to twist the cord until the proper tension is reached, then prop the dowel to maintain pressure.

If a chair wobbles because one leg is shorter than the others, steady the chair by forming an appropriately shaped piece of wood putty to "extend" the short leg. When the putty dries, sand and stain it to match the leg and glue it in place.

When you're working with varnish, hold the container as still as possible so that bubbles don't form and spoil the smooth finish.

Refinishing Furniture

If you'd like to know how your unfinished furniture would look if it were stained, try the "wet test." Dampen a cloth with turpentine and wipe it over the surface; the moisture will bring out the grain, showing any contrasts and giving the wood the appearance it would have if stained.

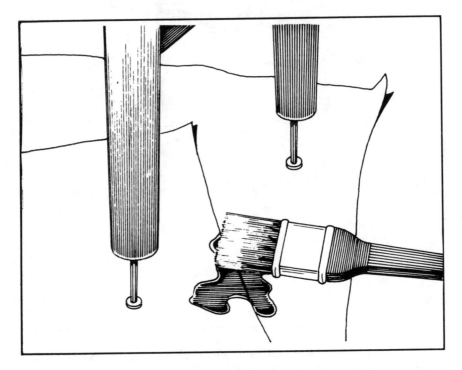

It's a practical idea to use newspaper to protect your floor or workbench when you're refinishing a piece of furniture, but the legs may stick to the paper. To avoid this, drive a nail part of the way into the bottom of each leg.

To sand a furniture spindle or rung without flattening it, hold a sandpaper strip behind the part, one end in each hand, and saw the ends back and forth to buff-sand the wood.

When refinishing, a flat rubber kitchen spatula can be a useful scraper for removing paint from curved or rounded surfaces, especially since it can be used even on delicate carvings. For greater versatility, buy both wide and narrow sizes.

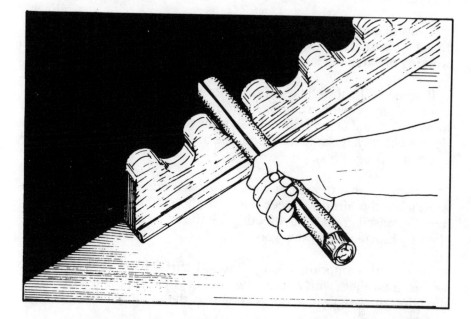

Sanding concave curves will be easier if you hold the sandpaper around a piece of dowel the same diameter as the curve or smaller. Or, slit a length of rubber garden hose and wrap the paper around it, with the ends held in the slit.

Many small items are useful for cleaning furniture crevices and cracks when you're refinishing. Enlist the aid of a nut pick, a plastic playing card, a plastic credit card, the broken end of an ice cream stick, the tine of an old fork, an orange stick, wooden toothpicks, or an old spoon.

If you need an unusually shaped smoothing tool for use on wet spackling compound and other wood fillers, try whittling an ice cream stick to the required contour.

To smooth wood evenly and thoroughly in the refinishing process, work with successively finer sandpaper grades. Between sandings, brush off or vacuum the sanding debris; then wipe the wood clean with a tack cloth.

A heavy string is useful when stripping the narrow turnings of a spindle furniture leg. Gently "saw" the string back and forth to remove the finish.

To avoid gouging wood when using a putty knife to strip furniture, round the putty knife's sharp corners with a fine-toothed file. If you're working on large flat surfaces, dull a paint scraper the same way.

If wood still shows ink stains, white water marks, splotches, or traces of any previous stain or filler after stripping, try wiping them away with liquid laundry bleach. To remove black water marks or to lighten chemically darkened wood, use oxalic acid (available in paint stores and drugstores).

Remember that treatment with any bleach raises the wood grain, even when the furniture piece has been thoroughly sanded. To prevent the raised grain from affecting the finish, resand to the level of the wood surface after the wood dries.

To obtain a smooth, evenly finished surface on open-grained woods, treat them with a filler after staining. First apply filler in the direction of the grain; then work across the grain to fill all pores completely.

If large knots in unfinished furniture are loose, remove them, apply carpenter's glue around their edges, and replace them flush with the surface. If small knots (pin knots) are loose, remove and discard them and plug the resulting holes with plastic wood or water putty.

For the most professional patching job, use shellac sticks to fill cracks and gouges since they leave the least conspicuous patch.

It will be easier to apply paint or varnish remover to a piece of furniture if all hardware has been removed. If you label the hardware along with a sketch of the furniture, it will also be easier to reassemble it correctly.

To help slow evaporation after applying a coat of paint remover—and give it more time to work—cover the surface with aluminum foil. Keep in mind, though, that paint remover stops working in any case after about 40 minutes.

You can make a template to patch damaged veneer this way: Lay a sheet of bond paper over the damaged area and rub a soft lead pencil gently over the paper. The edges of the damaged area will be precisely indicated on the paper so you can cut a pattern.

If hardware is spotted with paint or finish, drop it into a pan filled with paint remover. Let it soak while you work on the wood, then wipe it clean.

Small blisters on a veneered surface can sometimes be flattened with heat. Here's how: Lay a sheet of smooth cardboard over the blistered area and press firmly with a medium-hot iron, moving the iron slowly and evenly until the blisters soften and flatten. Leave the cardboard in place and weight the smoothed-out area for 24 hours.

For more durability, top an antiqued finish with a coat of semi-gloss or high-gloss varnish.

If you apply a protective shellac coating to cane chair seats they'll last longer and be easier to clean.

Wash-away paint and varnish removers should not be used on veneered or inlaid furniture pieces. The problem with wash-away removers is that water is the natural enemy of wood and certain glues. The water used to remove the chemicals must be removed from any wood furniture as soon as possible to avoid raising the wood grain or dissolving the glue.

Upholstering Furniture

When you reupholster furniture, put fabric scraps in an envelope and staple the envelope to the underside of the newly covered piece. That way you'll have scraps for patching.

When using ornamental tacks for upholstery, push extras into the frame in an inconspicuous spot so you have replacements if needed.

Before covering kitchen chair seats with plastic, warm the plastic with a heating pad so it will be more pliable and easier to handle.

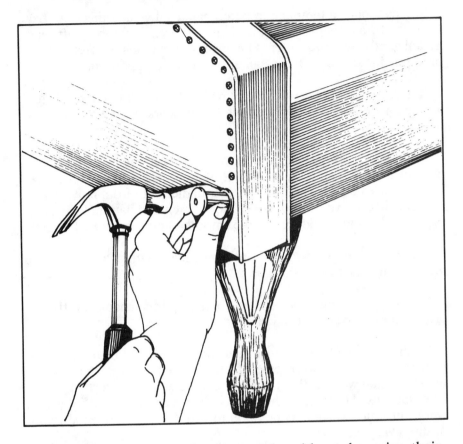

To hammer decorative furniture tacks without damaging their heads, place a wooden spool over each tack and pound on the spool.

When you're refinishing a piece of upholstered furniture and want to keep the upholstery, it's best to remove the fabric before you work on the finish—but only if you are sure you can put it back on again. If the piece is large, have a professional upholsterer remove and replace the fabric.

When examining a sample of upholstery fabric, fold the sample and rub the backs together to make sure that the backing is firmly bonded to the fabric.

You can test whether a fabric is likely to "pill" easily by rubbing it with a pencil eraser to see if bits of fabric appear.

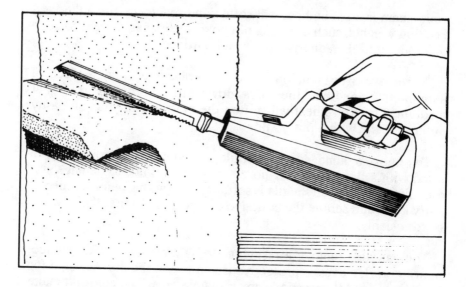

For speed and convenience, you can cut foam rubber upholstery padding with an electric carving knife.

FLOORS AND FLOOR COVERINGS

If you have a squeaky wood floor under tile or carpet, you may be able to eliminate the squeak without removing the floor covering. Try to reset loose boards by pounding a hammer on a block of scrap wood in the area over the squeaky boards. The pressure may force loose nails back into place.

You may be able to silence squeaky hardwood floors by using talcum powder as a dry lubricant. Sprinkle powder over the offending areas, and sweep it back and forth until it filters down between the cracks.

Try filling dents in a hardwood floor with clear nail polish or shellac. Because the floor's color will show through, the dents will not be apparent.

Sometimes you can flatten bulges or curled seams in a linoleum floor by placing aluminum foil over them and "ironing" them with your steam iron. (The heat will soften and reactivate the adhesive.) Position weights, such as stacks of books, over treated areas to keep them flat until the adhesive cools and hardens.

To remove a resilient floor tile for replacement, lay a piece of aluminum foil on it and then press down with an ordinary iron set at medium. The iron's heat will soften the mastic, and you can easily pry up the tile with a putty knife.

To remove a damaged resilient tile, soften it with a propane torch fitted with a flame-spreader nozzle. (Be careful not to damage surrounding tiles.) When the tile is soft, pry it up with a paint scraper or putty knife and scrape the adhesive off the floor so that the new tile bonds cleanly.

You can also remove a resilient tile by covering it with dry ice, wearing work gloves to protect your hands. Let the dry ice stand for ten minutes and then remove any remaining ice. The cold will make the tile brittle, so it will shatter easily. Chisel out the tile from the edges to the center.

Laying resilient floor tile will be easier if the room temperature is at least 70°F before you start, because tile is more pliable at higher temperatures. Put all boxes of tile in the room for at least 24 hours prior to positioning tiles on the floor. Try to keep the room temperature at the same level for about a week after laying the tiles, and then wait at least a week before washing the floor.

To prevent scratching the floor when moving heavy furniture across uncarpeted areas, slip scraps of old carpeting, face down, under all furniture legs.

After laying floor tiles, you can help them lie flat by going over them with a rolling pin.

If you want to replace a damaged area of resilient flooring, here's a way to make a perfect patch from scrap flooring: Place the scrap piece over the damaged area so that it overlaps sufficiently, and tape it to hold it in place. Then, cut through both layers at the same time to make a patch that is an exact duplicate. Replace the damaged area with the tightly fitting patch.

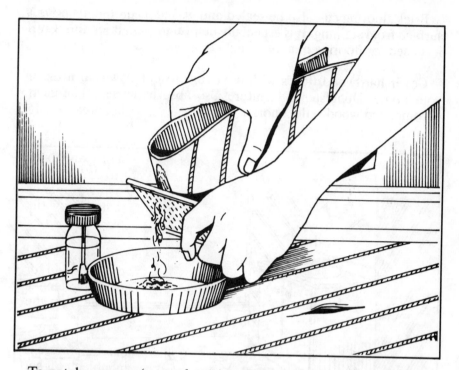

To patch a gouge (not a dent) in a resilient floor, take a scrap of the flooring and grate it with a food grater. Mix the resulting dust with clear nail polish and plug the hole.

Another way to camouflage a gouge or hole in a resilient floor is with crayon wax. Choose a crayon that matches the floor color, melt it, fill the gouge or hole, and then wax the floor.

Solvent-based cleaners and polishes preserve cork tile floors and should be used instead of water or water-based products.

So chairs won't scratch a hardwood floor, glue bunion pads to the bottoms of the chair legs.

Thumbtacks pressed into the bottom ends of wooden chair legs will allow them to slide more easily across a wood or tile floor.

If you're going to use flagstone or slate as indoor flooring, these porous materials should be sealed to keep them looking their best.

Brick flooring can also be sealed and waxed to protect its porous surface from staining. It is especially helpful to treat brick this way if it is used for flooring in a kitchen.

Cover hardwood floors with area rugs to cut down on noise in your home. Upholstered furniture also absorbs noise, while glass, chrome, and wood reflect noise.

To make a bathroom carpet fit perfectly, make a precise pattern with paper. Lay overlapped sheets of paper on the bathroom floor, tightly butted up against corners, walls, and obstacles. Tape the sheets together and cut. Turn the pattern over, face down, on the back of the carpet, trace with a pencil, and then cut.

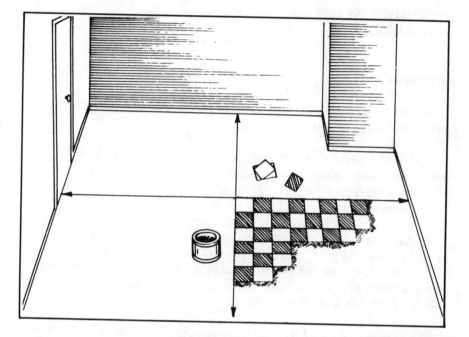

Install floor tiles from the center of a room outward, because the center of a room is where appearance and matching are most important.

Stairs

To stop squeaks at the front of a stair tread, drive pairs of spiral flooring nails, each pair angled in a V, across the tread and into the top of the riser below it.

Try eliminating squeaks in stairs by using packaged graphite powder or talcum powder in a squeeze bottle, applying the lubricant along the joints in the problem area.

If an application of graphite powder or talcum powder fails to eliminate a stair squeak, go under the stairs and drive wedges into the gaps between the moving components.

WINDOWS, SCREENS, AND DOORS

Windows

Spattered rain and dirt will easily wipe off windowsills that have a protective coat of wax.

Applying a reflective vinyl coating on the inside of your windows will both protect your furniture upholstery or drapery fabric from the fading effects of strong sunlight and help keep your home cooler in the summertime.

To free a window that's been painted shut, use a scraper, knife, or spatula to cut the paint seal between the sash and the window frame. Then, working from the outside, insert the blade of a pry bar under the sash and pry gently from the corners in. Lever the bar over a block of scrap wood.

When replacing a broken sash cord, consider using a sash chain, which lasts much longer.

Soften old putty for easy removal by heating it with a soldering iron, propane torch, or hand-held hair dryer. Or, if you prefer, soften it with linseed oil and then scrape it away.

To prevent a windowpane crack from spreading, score a small arc with a glass cutter just beyond the crack, curving around it. Usually the crack will travel only as far as the arc.

To remove cracked glass from a window without excessive splintering, crisscross the pane on both sides with several strips of masking tape, then rap it with a hammer. Most of the pane will be held together.

To make dried-out putty workable again, sprinkle it with a few drops of raw linseed oil and knead it until it is soft and pliable.

Before attempting to chisel dried and hardened putty from a wooden window frame, brush raw linseed oil over the putty's surface. Let it soak in to soften the putty.

If you try to open a window and it refuses to budge, tap a hammer on a block of wood at various places on the sash. (Don't hit the sash directly with the hammer, or you'll leave dents.) The tapping may jar the sash loose.

You can fill a pellet gun hole in a windowpane with clear nail polish or shellac. Dab at the hole; when the application dries, dab again—and reapply until the hole is filled. The pane will appear clear. A pellet gun hole in stained glass can be filled the same way.

When installing a new windowpane, speed up the process by rolling the glazing compound between the palms of your hands to form a long string the diameter of a pencil. Lay the "string" along the frame, over the glass, and smooth it in place with a putty knife.

When glazing windows, brush the frames where the putty will lie with boiled linseed oil to prevent the wood from drinking the oils from the putty.

If the putty knife sticks or pulls at the glazing compound when you're glazing a window, "grease" the knife by dipping the blade into linseed oil. Wipe off the excess.

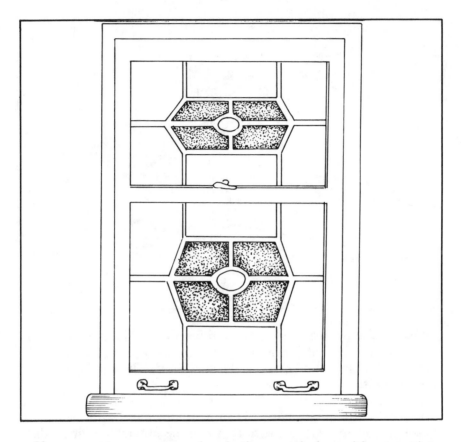

If you want to cover your clear bathroom window without putting up curtains, render the glass opaque by brushing on a mixture of four tablespoons of Epsom salts and a half pint of stale beer. Alternatives: Glue on stained-glass pieces, silver Mylar, or waxed paper. Double-duty alternative: Cover the panes with mirrored squares, which, as a side benefit, will make the bathroom seem larger.

When painting glazing compound, lap the paint slightly over the edge of the compound and onto the glass.

Draperies and Screens

Old keys make good drapery weights.

To keep drapery hem folds in position, insert wire solder or plastic-covered wire. Bend the wire into the desired shapes after hanging the draperies.

To prevent a curtain rod from snagging when sliding it through a curtain, slip a piece of aluminum foil or a thimble over its tip.

Do your draperies gap in the middle when you close them? They won't if you sew a small magnet into both center seams at the same height from the floor.

To make sure that curtain tie-backs are exactly opposite each other, use the bottom edge of the window shade as your guide when you install them.

Before washing a curtain, shake it outdoors to remove accumulated dust.

Heavy, lined curtains will absorb excess noise in a room. Placing heavy furniture against the wall facing noisy neighbors will also help cut down on sounds.

To keep aluminum screens from pitting, clean them outdoors (never indoors) with kerosene. Dip a rag in the kerosene and rub both sides of the mesh and the frames, then wipe off the excess. This is a particularly good rust inhibitor for older screens. (Since kerosene is highly flammable, it should always be stored in small amounts in a cool place. Never pour or use kerosene near an open flame.)

To repair a small tear in a wire window screen, push the wire strands back into place with an ice pick. If the hole doesn't close completely, brush clear nail polish or shellac sparingly across the remaining opening. Let the sealer dry, and reapply until the pinhole is transparently sealed. (Be careful not to let any sealer run down the screen; immediately blot any excess.)

If there's a clean cut or tear in a window screen, you can stitch it together. Use a long needle and a strong nylon thread or a fine wire. Zigzag stitch across the cut, being careful not to pull the thread or wire so tight that the patch puckers. After stretching, apply clear nail polish to keep the thread or wire from pulling loose.

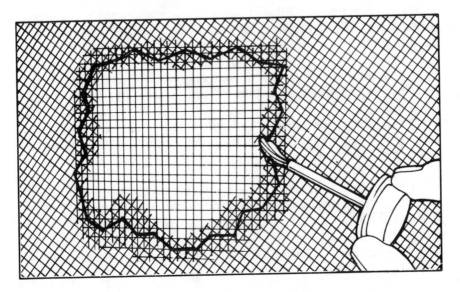

To close a large hole in a window screen, cut a patch from a scrap piece of screening of the same type as the damaged screen. Zigzag stitch the patch into place, and then apply clear nail polish to the stitching.

To repair fiberglass screening, lay a fiberglass patch over the hole or tear with a piece of foil over it and run a hot iron around the edges; the heat fuses the patch to the screen. The foil prevents the iron from touching the screen directly.

Lower rolled-up awnings after a storm to allow them to dry.

Clean awnings in the direction of the seam, not against it. As fabric awnings age, their seams weaken.

You can rejuvenate faded canvas awnings with a special paint available from awning dealers or paint stores.

Doors

If hinge screws on a door are loose because the screw holes have become enlarged, fill the holes with pieces of wood toothpick dipped in glue. When the glue dries, reinsert the screws. Or, wrap hinge screws with steel wool and reinsert.

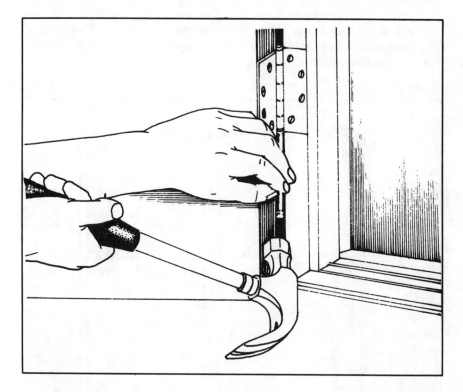

If you're trying to remove a door's hinge pin and the pin won't budge, press a nail against the hinge bottom and tap upward against the nail with a hammer.

If a door binds on the knob side when the door is closed, its hinges may be misaligned. If the top of the knob side binds, try putting a cardboard shim behind the bottom hinge. If the bottom corner binds, slip a cardboard shim behind the top hinge. To shim a door hinge, loosen the screws on the door frame side. Cut a shim from thin cardboard with slots to fit around the screws, slide it behind the hinge, and tighten the screws.

If a doorknob bangs against a wall, protect the wall by covering the knob with a slit-open powder puff.

For better control when lifting a door off its hinges, remove the bottom pin first. When replacing a door on its hinges, insert the top pin first.

If a door sticks at the sides, try to plane only on the hinge side. The latch side is beveled slightly and planing could damage the bevel. Plane from the center toward the ends.

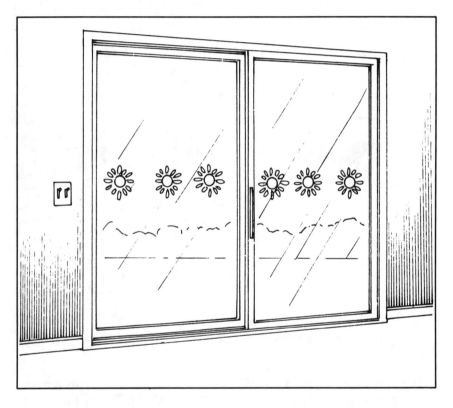

To prevent people from mistaking a closed sliding glass door for an open one, apply eye-level decals—at both adult and child levels if necessary—to alert people before they walk into the pane and possibly injure themselves. You can use the same trick to mark lightweight screens.

You needn't worry about oil dripping on the floor if you quiet a squeaky hinge by lubricating its pin with petroleum jelly rather than oil.

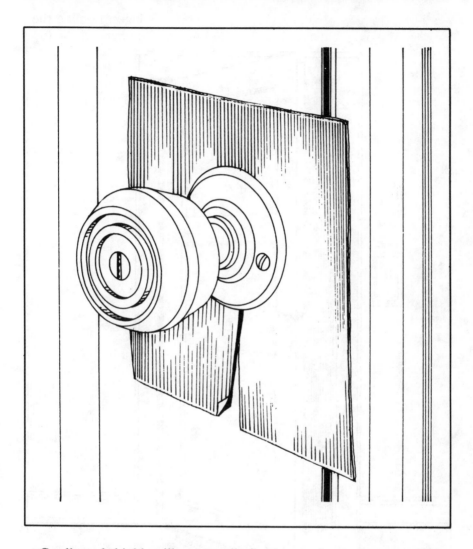

Cardboard shields will protect the finish on a door when you clean and polish door hardware. Fit the shields around the metal parts, holding them in place with masking tape.

If you have to remove some wood at a door's binding points, use a block plane on the top or bottom of the door and a jack plane to work on the side. Work from the ends to the center on the top or bottom edge, from the center out on the sides.

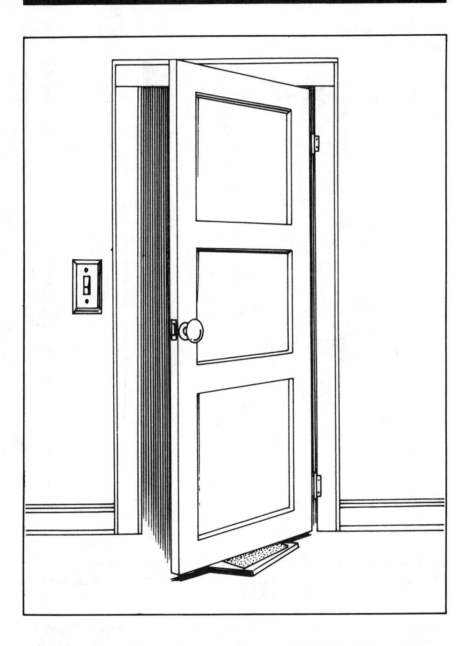

If you need to plane the bottom of a door because it scrapes the threshold or the floor, you can do so without removing the door. Place sandpaper on the threshold or floor, then move the door back and forth over this abrasive surface. Slide a newspaper or magazine under the sandpaper if it needs to be raised in order to make contact.

When you've fashioned a door to the exact size for hanging, bevel the latch edge backward just a bit to let it clear the jamb as it swings open and shut.

Before you replace a door that you have planed, seal the planed edges. If you don't, the raw wood will absorb moisture and the door will swell and stick again.

Graphite from a soft pencil can be used to lubricate a resistant door lock. Rub the key across the pencil point, and then slide it in and out of the lock several times.

If you want to replace an existing lock but you can't find a new one that will fit the existing holes, cover the old holes with a large decorative escutcheon plate.

To reduce noise in your home and cut energy costs at the same time, weather-strip all doors and windows.

HOME LIGHTING AND ELECTRICITY

Working With Electricity

Safety is an important consideration when you're working with electricity. To make sure that no one accidentally flips the circuit breaker back on while you're making electrical repairs, put a piece of tape—and a sign to let people know what you're doing—over the handle of the circuit breaker. The same applies to a fuse box.

Wait to work on a switched outlet or lighting fixture—even though you've flicked off the switch—until you have also deactivated the circuit. In many switching systems, parts of the circuit are still energized when the switch is off.

When working with electricity, insulate your pliers by slipping a length of small-diameter rubber hose on each handle. Wrap other metal parts with electrician's tape. Insulate the shank of a screwdriver by slipping a section of rubber or plastic tubing over it. Be sure to cut the tubing so that it extends from the handle down to the blade.

Replace a fuse with one of the same amperage as the one you took out. You risk causing an electrical fire if you use a fuse rated to carry more amps or if you try to bypass the fuse in any way.

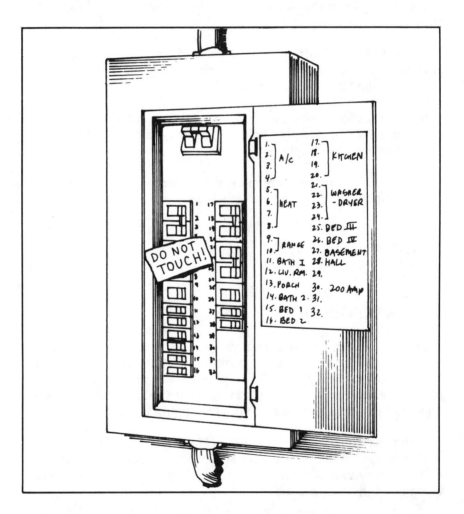

Save time ahead of time. Determine which circuits activate which outlets in your home; then diagram or print the information on a card attached to your circuit breaker or fuse box. When your electricity fails, you'll be able to solve the problem quickly.

For safety's sake, stand on a dry board when working with a fuse box or a circuit breaker box. Also use a wooden rather than an aluminum stepladder to minimize the risk of shock when working with electrical wiring.

Everyone in the family should know how to throw the master switch that cuts off all electrical current. Any time there's a chance of contact between water and electricity, avoid wading in water until the master switch has been shut off.

When maneuvering a section of electrical cable through a wall, play it safe and use roughly 20 percent more than a straight-line measurement indicates that you need. Often there are unexpected obstructions and the cable must be moved around. You can cut off any extra cable.

A blown fuse or a tripped circuit breaker is a sign of trouble. Locate and eliminate the problem before you replace a blown fuse or reset a tripped circuit breaker. Otherwise the problem will only recur.

Lighting Your Home

So that you won't be left in the dark if a bulb burns out in the basement, light the area with a two-socket fixture. If one bulb burns out, the other will still enable you to see.

If you're distracted by shadows that reduce visibility in your kitchen or workshop, replace incandescent fixtures with fluorescent lamps that provide even, shadow-free illumination.

If you're planning to replace a lamp socket, consider installing a three-way socket for greater lighting versatility. Wiring a three-way socket is as simple as wiring a standard on/off fixture.

Any change in a fluorescent lamp's normal performance, such as flickering or noticeable dimming, is a warning that the bulb should be replaced. Failure to replace the bulb can strain parts of the fixture; for example, repeated flashing wears out the starter and causes the starter's insulation to deteriorate.

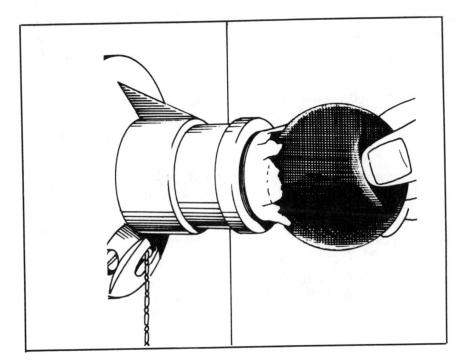

If it's difficult to remove a broken light bulb because there's little left to grasp, turn off the switch, jam a sponge-rubber ball against the jagged glass, and twist.

If your ironing board is set up in a poorly lit area you won't be able to see the wrinkles in your clothes. A directional light angled towards the ironing board and used to supplement your overhead lighting will allow you to see perfectly.

Good lighting is important in any area where you apply makeup or fix your hair. A light-colored counter helps reflect light up on to your face.

Luminous fixtures spaced about three feet apart on either side of a mirror and about 60 inches above floor level provide an ideal setting for personal grooming.

If you have a dark hall where it's necessary to use a light all day, choose a fluorescent fixture for maximum energy efficiency. You'll also need to change the bulb less often.

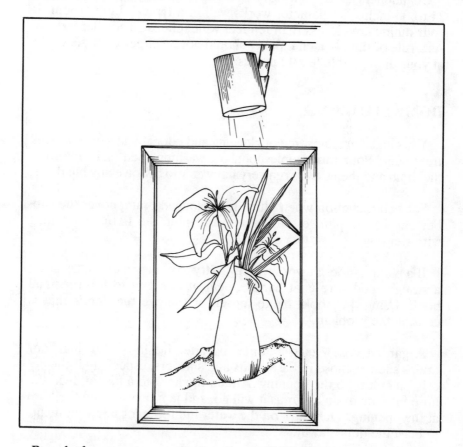

Proud of your art or antique collection? Highlight your treasures with accent lighting.

Shallow recessed fixtures spaced six to eight feet apart provide pleasant lighting in general living areas. Over a work surface, space fixtures about 18 inches apart for good illumination without shadows.

For maximum comfort and illumination, position lighting fixtures so that the bottom of the shade is at your eye level when you're sitting down.

Floor level lights directed upward toward your houseplants add drama and make interesting shadow patterns on walls and ceilings.

Chandeliers are dramatic and dress up a dining area. A chandelier 24 to 30 inches in diameter works well in a typical dining room. If your dining area is less than ten feet wide, choose a smaller fixture. As a rule of thumb, a chandelier should not be larger than the width of your dining table less 12 inches.

HOME PLUMBING

You can keep drains free of clogging and odors by this once-a-week treatment: Pour three tablespoons of washing soda (sal soda) into the drain and then slowly run very hot water to dissolve any build-ups.

For better suction when plunging a clogged drain, cover the rubber cap of the plunger with water and plug the fixture's opening with wet rags.

If a plunger doesn't work when you try to unclog a drain, try using a straightened wire coat hanger, bent at one end to form a small hook. Using the hook, try to loosen or remove the debris that is causing the problem.

A garden hose can sometimes be effective in unclogging floor drains such as those in basements and showers, especially if the debris isn't close to the opening. Attach the hose to a faucet, feed the hose into the drain as far as it will go, and jam rags around the hose at the opening. Then turn on the water full force for a few moments to blast the debris away.

If you hear a squealing noise when you turn the handle of a faucet, the metal threads of the stem are binding against the threads of the faucet. To fix this, remove the handle and stem and coat both sets of threads with petroleum jelly. The lubrication should stop the noise and make the handle easier to turn.

A moderately clogged drain can usually be unclogged if you pour down it a half cup of baking soda followed by a half cup of vinegar. Caution: The two ingredients interact with foaming and fumes, so replace the drain cover loosely. Flush after about three hours.

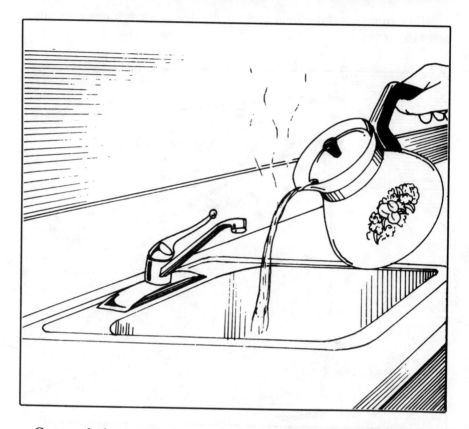

Greasy drains usually respond to this treatment: Pour in a half cup of salt and a half cup of baking soda, followed by a teakettle of boiling water. Allow to sit overnight if possible.

For a homemade, noncorrosive drain cleaner, mix one cup of baking soda, one cup of table salt, and a quarter cup of cream of tartar in a small bowl. Stir thoroughly and pour into a clean, covered jar. To use, pour a quarter cup of the mixture into the drain and immediately add one cup of boiling water. Wait ten seconds, then flush with cold water. Do this weekly to keep drains clog-free and odorless. (One blending of this mixture equals two and one quarter cups of cleaner.)

What can you do if too little water comes from the tank to flush the toilet bowl clean? Check the water level in the tank, and if it doesn't come to within one and one half inches of the top of the overflow tube, bend the float arm up slightly to allow more water to enter the tank.

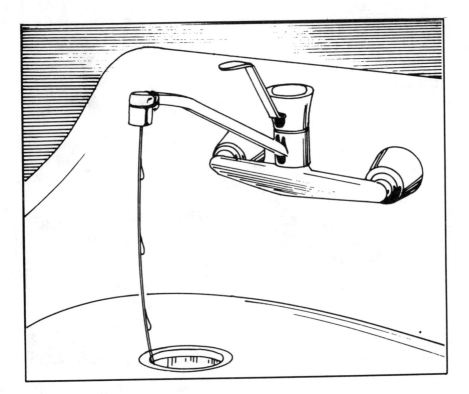

If a dripping faucet is getting on your nerves before the plumber arrives or before you have time to fix it yourself, tie a two-foot-long string around the nozzle, and drop the string's end into the drain. As the faucet drips, the drops will run silently down the string and away.

If there's very little water in a clogged toilet bowl, flushing will only cause the bowl to overflow. Instead, use a plunger to unclog the toilet; bring water from another source to cover the plunger cup for better suction.

To make a septic tank activator, combine in a large bowl two envelopes of active dry yeast with one pound of brown sugar; add four cups of warm water, stirring until the mixture blends completely. Set the mixture in a warm place for 10 to 20 minutes until it's foamy and its volume increases. Then flush it down the toilet.

If your water pipes bang and faucets leak, the water pressure in your home may be reaching or exceeding 70 to 80 pounds per square inch and you may need to install a pressure-reducing valve. You can measure the average water pressure in your house by attaching a pressure gauge to the cold-water faucet nearest the main shut-off valve.

If a water pipe is banging against a wall and causing noise, you can silence it by wedging the pipe off the wall with a wood block and clamping the pipe to the wedge with a pipe strap.

If you have a stretch of water pipe that often freezes, consider buying heat tape (sometimes called heat cable). The tape is wrapped around the pipe and an automatic thermostat starts the heat when the outside temperature drops to about 35°F.

When thawing a frozen pipe, start at the tap end and open the tap so that melting ice and steam can run off or dissipate harmlessly. If you start at the middle of a pipe, steam from melting ice may burst the pipe.

When you're using hot water faucets regularly, there's no danger of hydrogen gas building up in your water heater. But if you've been away for an extended period, this danger does exist. If you've been away for a while, open all hot water taps for a few minutes to prevent the danger of an explosion.

To clean copper pipe before sweat soldering, wrap a strip of emery cloth around the end of the pipe and move it back and forth as if you were buffing a shoe.

Most amateur plumbers are so proud of their first sweat-soldered joints that they immediately turn on the water—a big mistake. Allow the joint to cool naturally, because the sudden cooling effect of rushing water can weaken the joint and cause it to crack.

If a pipe springs a leak, consider replacing an entire section rather than just patching the leak. A pipe that is sufficiently corroded to leak in one place will often start leaking in other places.

Whenever you secure a pipe, be careful to anchor it so that it can expand and contract with temperature changes. If you place a bracket on a pipe, include a buffer fashioned from garden hose, radiator hose, foam rubber, rubber cut from old inner tubes, or kitchen sponges.

To avoid having the teeth of the wrench scar a chrome-plated plumbing fixture during installation, first wrap the fixture with a double coating of plastic electrical tape.

To keep the water shut-off valve in good working order, turn it off and then on again once every six months.

Make sure everyone in the family knows where in your home the main shut-off valve is located. Also make sure everyone knows how to use it. This could prevent flooding in an emergency.

PEST CONTROL

You can keep ants away from your home with a concoction of borax and flour. Mix one cup of flour and two cups of borax in a quart jar. Punch holes in the jar's lid and sprinkle its contents outdoors around the foundation of your home.

Bothered by ants and other tiny insects in your cupboards? Scrub the cupboards and then leave several bay leaves in each to discourage return visits.

Bat-proofing your property is a good idea if you've been infested once and want to eliminate future colonies. The strong odor a colony leaves behind attracts other bats even after the first group has been evicted.

If you see a bat in your house, try to knock it to the floor with a tennis racquet or broom. Once it's stunned, pick it up wearing gloves, or scoop it up with a piece of paper, and get rid of it. Never handle a bat with your bare hands because of the risk of rabies.

If bees are nesting in a wall but you don't know exactly where, tap the wall at night and decide where the buzzing is loudest. Because the temperature inside the nest is usually about 95°F, you may also be able to feel its heat through the wall. Double check by drilling a small hole in the suspect area. If the drill bit comes out with honey or paraffin on it, you've found the nest.

Some people are allergic to bee or wasp stings. If you know or suspect that you are one of them, never try to exterminate a nest yourself. Have someone else do it.

If there's a hornet, wasp, bee, or other flying insect in your house and you have no insect spray, kill it with hair spray.

If your home becomes infested with fleas, vacuum rugs thoroughly before spraying and throw out the dust bag at once.

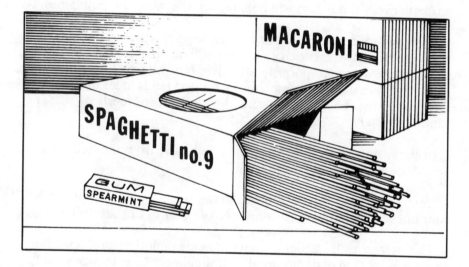

Mealworms, which are attracted to open packages of spaghetti, noodles, or macaroni, are repelled by spearmint chewing gum. You won't be bothered by the pests if you place a few sticks of wrapped gum in or near the packages. (Note: The gum must be wrapped so that it won't dry out and lose its scent.)

The scent of peppermint repels mice. To discourage these rodents, place sprigs of this herb where the rodents are likely to enter the house. You can achieve the same effect by soaking pieces of cardboard in oil of peppermint and leaving them in appropriate places.

Raw bacon or peanut butter makes good bait for a mousetrap; so does a cotton ball saturated with bacon grease. So that a mouse can't get the bait without springing the trap, make sure it will have to tug to remove the bait. If you're using peanut butter, dab some on the triggering device and let it harden before setting the trap. If bacon is your bait, tie it around the triggering device.

If you live in a multiunit building, any pest control measures you take individually will be ineffective in the long run simply because insects can travel from one apartment to another. To eliminate bugs completely, the entire building should be treated at one time.

Since mosquito larvae thrive in water, changing the water in the birdbath every three days will help reduce the mosquito population.

Because raccoons carry fleas, take immediate action if one sets up housekeeping in your attic or chimney. Chemical repellents such as oil of mustard are temporarily effective, but the smell may bother you as much as it does the raccoon. Your best bet is to let the animal leave, and then cover its entrance hole with wire mesh so that it cannot return.

In the spring, moving leftover firewood away from the house will help discourage insect infestations.

Centipedes prey on other bugs, so the presence of centipedes in your house may indicate the presence of other insects as well.

The presence of carpenter ants indicates another problem. Because they're fond of damp wood, you should check your pipes, roof, and windowsills for water leaks.

You can distinguish termite damage from other insect damage by examining any holes you find in wood. Termites eat only the soft part of wood, leaving the annual rings intact.

You can control roaches with a mixture of a half cup of borax and a quarter cup of flour. Sprinkle this powder along baseboards and door sills, or spoon it into clear jar caps positioned under sinks or under cabinets.

Remember that supermarkets and grocery stores almost always have roaches, so check bags and boxes when unpacking food at home.

To keep rodents out of your house, seal every opening they could squeeze through. Some need less than a quarter-inch space. Put poison in deep cracks or holes, and stuff these with steel wool or scouring pads pushed in with a screwdriver. Close the spaces with spackling compound mixed with steel wool fragments.

THE BASEMENT

You will have better daytime visibility in the basement if you paint window wells, basement walls, and basement ceilings white to reflect more outside light.

To guard against tracking dust or sawdust upstairs, carpet the basement steps. The nap of the carpet will brush dust or sawdust off the soles of your shoes.

If you have a moisture problem in your basement, you need to know whether the cause is seepage or condensation. To determine which of these causes applies, tape a hand mirror against a wall in the middle of a damp spot and leave it overnight. If the mirror is fogged the next morning, condensation is the cause of your moisture problem.

To get rid of condensation, either air the basement frequently or use the opposite approach—keep the basement doors closed and install storm windows in the basement to keep moisture out.

If basement moisture turns out to be seepage, you'll probably need professional help; in either case, however, it helps to wrap exposed cold-water pipes with nonsweat insulation and install a dehumidifier.

Home Furnishing and Decorating

GENERAL PAINTING TIPS

According to manufacturers' calculations, a gallon of paint will cover about 450 square feet. For estimating purposes figure 400 square feet of coverage per gallon of paint. Never try to "stretch" paint.

To determine the amount of paint required to cover a wall, multiply the height of the wall by its length, then divide by 400. By this reckoning, a gallon of paint will cover a 10- × 15-foot room with one coat. Two coats will take two gallons.

When painting a ceiling with a roller, it's not necessary to try to keep the roller strokes all the same length. The lines won't show when the paint dries.

If you use masking tape around windows while painting the wood-work, remove the masking tape immediately after painting. Otherwise it may pull off some of the paint.

If you want to paint a window frame and have no masking tape, use strips of newspaper dampened so that they will stick to the glass. Peel off the paper as you finish each frame.

To get paint drips off hardwood, ceramic tile, or resilient flooring, wrap a cloth around a putty knife and gently scrape up the paint. Then wash the areas with warm, soapy water. Don't use solvent if you can avoid it; it can damage the finish on the floor.

Decorative stencils can be expensive to buy. Make your own out of thin cardboard. Sketch a design, transfer it to tracing paper, and cut it out. Then lay this pattern on a piece of cardboard, trace around it, and cut it out.

If you're interrupted in the middle of a painting job, wrap a plastic sheet or aluminum foil around your brushes and rollers, just tight enough to keep the air out. The wrapping should be loose enough to avoid mashing the bristles on brushes or the pile on rollers. Leave brushes on a flat surface or hang them up.

Prevent drips when painting a drawer front by removing the drawer and painting it face up.

To avoid smearing when painting cabinets, paint the inside of the cabinets first. Then paint the tops, bottoms, and sides of doors before painting the door fronts. If you proceed in this sequence, you won't have to reach over already painted areas.

Protect doorknobs when painting a door by wrapping the knobs with aluminum foil or by slipping plastic sandwich bags over them.

When painting stairs, paint alternate steps so that you'll have a way out. When those dry, paint the others. Or, paint one side of each step at a time. Use the other side for foot traffic until the painted side dries, then reverse the process.

Where appearance isn't important, steps will be safer if you mix in a little sand when painting them (so that they'll be less slippery) and edge them with luminous paint (so that they'll be more visible).

If your wall-switch cover plate was painted over along with the wall and you now need to remove it, avoid flaking or chipping any paint by cutting carefully around the plate's edge with a single-edge razor blade. Remove the screws and lift off the plate.

Don't wipe your paintbrush against the lip of the paint can. The lip will soon fill up with paint that will run down the side and drip off. Use a coffee can to hold the paint instead.

Before painting a ceiling, turn off the light fixture, loosen it, and let it hang down. Then wrap it in a plastic bag for protection against paint splatters.

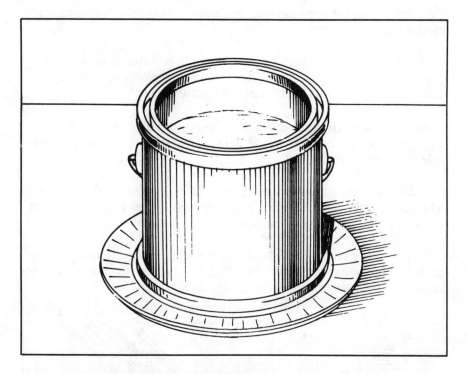

Glue paper plates to the bottoms of paint cans, to serve as drip catchers. The plates move along with the cans and are more convenient than newspapers.

If you don't want to—or can't—remove hardware when painting adjacent areas, coat the hardware with petroleum jelly before painting. You'll be able to wipe off any paint that gets on the metal by accident.

If the smell of fresh paint bothers you, you can eliminate it from a room in one day by leaving in the room a dish of ammonia or vinegar, or onion slices in a bowl of water.

To cut the smell when you're decorating with oil-based paint, stir a spoonful of vanilla extract into each can of paint.

If you want to be able to use a previous coat of exterior paint as a base for a new coat, the old paint should be no more than five years old. If you wait longer than that you'll have a major job of scraping, sanding, and spackling.

Wrinkling occurs when too much paint is applied or when the paint is too thick. You can correct wrinkling easily by sanding the surface and brushing on paint of a lighter consistency.

Artificial light darkens color, so your paint will look lighter in the daylight. If in doubt when at the paint store, take the container outside to examine the color.

Color can saturate your eyes. When mixing paint, look away at a white surface for several minutes to allow your eyes to adjust so that you can judge the color accurately.

To get the correct "feel" for spray painting and to determine the correct spray distance from the object to be painted, first experiment with a sheet of cardboard as the target area.

Make a paint holder from a coat hanger to keep your hands free when painting. Open the hanger and bend it in half; then bend it into an "S" to hook over the ladder and hold your paint can.

To avoid painting a window shut, gently slide the sash up and down as the paint hardens but before it forms a seal.

If you are working on a ladder in front of a closed door, lock the door so that no one can inadvertently swing the door open and send you sprawling.

Record how much paint is required to cover each room by writing the amount on the back of a light-switch plate. When you remove the switch plate before repainting, you'll be reminded of how much fresh paint you need.

Do tiny spots need a paint touch-up? If you use cotton swabs instead of a brush, you won't waste paint and you won't have to clean a brush.

Before using a new oil paintbrush, soak it for a day in a can of linseed oil. The brush will last longer and be easier to clean.

Cleanup and Storage

To avoid having to clean a paint roller pan, press a sheet of aluminum foil into it before use. When you're finished, simply wrap up the foil and dispose of it.

Why buy new paint thinner when you can reuse the old? Here's how: Pour paint thinner into an empty coffee can. After you've cleaned your brushes, cover the can tightly and let it stand for several days. When paint from the brushes settles to the bottom as sediment, drain off the "clean" thinner into another can and store for reuse.

To clean a paintbrush without making a mess of your hands, pour solvent into a strong, clear plastic bag, and insert the brush. Your hands will stay clean as you work the solvent into the bristles through the plastic.

To clean a paint roller after use, roll it as dry as possible, first on the newly painted surface and then on several sheets of newspaper. Then slide the roller from its support and clean it with water or a solvent, depending on the type of paint used.

Before capping leftover paint for storage, mark the label at the level of the remaining paint so you'll know without opening the can how much is left inside. Label the cans by rooms so there's no question which paint to reorder or use for touch-ups.

For easy cleanup of your paint tray, line the tray with a plastic bag before pouring in your paint. After the job's done, you can discard the bag without having to clean the roller tray.

If you store a partially used can of paint upside down, "skin" won't form on the surface of the paint. (Be sure lid is tight.)

If you must leave a paintbrush for a short time and don't want to clean it, wrap it in a plastic bag to keep it soft and pliable. Put it in the freezer to save it for a longer time.

Leftover paint that is lumpy or contains shreds of paint "skin" can be strained through window screening.

To keep a brush as soft as new, clean it and then dip it in a final rinse containing fabric softener.

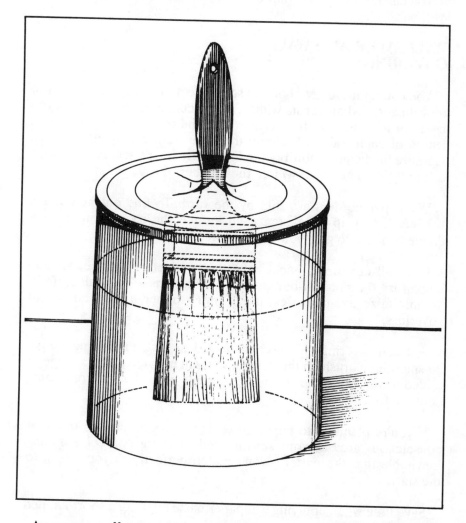

An empty coffee can with a plastic lid makes a perfect container for soaking brushes. Just make two slits in the center of the plastic lid to form an "X," push the brush handle up through the "X," and replace the lid. The lid seals the can so the solvent can't evaporate, and the brush is suspended without the bristles resting on the bottom.

White paint won't yellow if you stir in a drop of black paint.

A paste-type paint remover will remove paint spots from brick.

You can remove paint splatter from your hair by rubbing the spots with baby oil.

WALLPAPER AND WALL COVERINGS

You can figure to get about 30 square feet of coverage from a roll of wallpaper (whatever its width). To calculate how many rolls you need for a room, find the perimeter of the room by measuring the length of each wall and adding the measurements together. Then measure the height. Multiply the first figure by the second, and then divide by 30. The result will be the number of rolls you need.

Wallpaper borders are sold by the yard. To find out how much you need, add up the distance all around the room in feet, then divide by three to give you the yardage.

Foil wall coverings, because of their reflective surface, tend to emphasize the smallest bumps or imperfections in the wall surface. To minimize irregularities, use a lining paper under these wall coverings.

Foil wall coverings are easily damaged, so instead of using a regular smoothing brush on them, smooth them in place with a sponge or folded towel. Bond the seams in the same way—a seam roller may dent the foil.

If you're planning to paper all walls in a room, choose the least conspicuous area as your starting and finishing point. It's almost inevitable that the pattern won't match perfectly as you return to the start.

Save time when applying wallpaper paste by using a short-napped paint roller.

To make wallpaper hanging easier, a right-handed person should work from left to right and a left-handed person from right to left.

Tint wallpaper paste slightly with food coloring so that you can see exactly where you've applied it.

If there are stubborn grease spots on walls that you're going to paper, seal them with clear nail polish or shellac so that the grease won't soak through the new wallpaper.

However carefully you put up wallpaper, you may still find blisters. Fortunately, they are easy to fix. All you need do is slit the blister twice with a razor blade to form an "X", then peel back the tips of the slit, brush paste into the blister, and smooth the paper down.

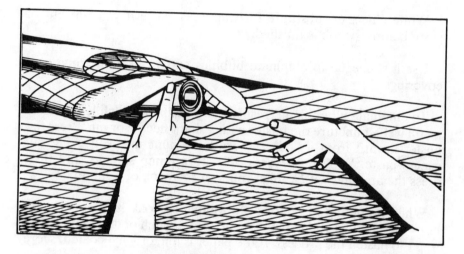

Wallpaper a ceiling with the strips positioned crosswise—they're shorter and more manageable. Accordion-fold each strip, pasted area against pasted area, and unfold it as you go along, supporting the paper with one hand and smoothing it onto the ceiling with the other.

When folding wallpaper accordion-style before hanging, the pasted side should not touch the patterned side at any point, and the paper should never be allowed to crease.

After wallpapering a room where there'll be a lot of moisture— such as a kitchen or bathroom—cover all seams with clear varnish to help guard against peeling.

When papering over wall anchors or places where you plan to reposition shelves or pictures, insert toothpicks in holes left by screws or picture hooks. As you cover these sections, force the toothpick points through the paper to mark reinstallation points for screws or hooks.

Save time when hanging the wallpaper itself by smoothing it with a clean, dry paint roller. If you attach the roller to a long handle, you can reach the ceiling or the tops of walls without climbing a ladder.

If you don't have a seam roller to use to tame a loose wallpaper seam, rub the seam with the back of a spoon.

White glue can substitute for wallpaper paste if you run out of paste before the job is finished.

Use a squeegee to eliminate bubbles and wrinkles in vinyl wall coverings.

To eliminate a bubble in freshly hung wallpaper—while the paste is still wet—puncture the blister with a sharp needle or pin. Press the blister inward from its edges toward the puncture, squeezing out excess paste. Wipe this excess off with a damp sponge, and then press the area flat with a seam roller or the back of a spoon.

When preparing to remove old wallpaper, soak it first with very hot water applied with a paint roller; add a touch of detergent to the water to hasten the process. If the paper is foil, or vinyl-coated, score its surface so water can penetrate.

When removing old wallpaper with a steamer, save the ceiling for last. As you work on the walls, steam rising from the applicator will loosen the ceiling paper. Much of it will start sagging from its own weight, and peeling it off will be easy.

Repairing Wallpaper

Save wallpaper for patching. Let it "weather" and fade at the same rate as the paper on the wall by taping a piece or two on a closet wall. If you do this, it will correspond in color density as well as pattern to the paper already on the wall.

If you don't have wallpaper scraps for patching, try touching up the design in worn areas. Carefully use felt-tip pens to restore rubbed or faded colors.

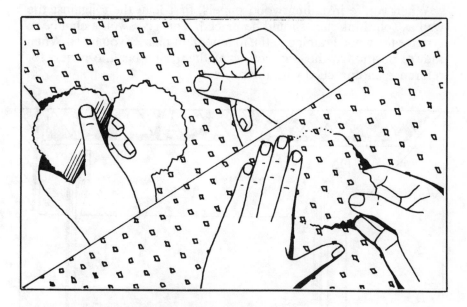

To repair a damaged wallpaper section, *tear*—don't cut—a patch from a piece that's been "weathered." Because less-defined torn edges blend imperceptibly with paper already on the wall, the patch will be virtually invisible. Note: Don't remove damaged wallpaper before placing a patch on it. Paste the patch directly over the damaged surface.

Other Wall Coverings

If you're stapling fabric to a wall and you want to mask the staples at the top and bottom, glue a band of fabric—or even a wide, contrasting ribbon—over these seams. You also can cover the staples with molding strips.

When paneling a room, let the panels acclimate to the room's humidity for 48 hours before positioning them. This helps prevent them from being installed too tightly or too loosely.

When applying wood paneling to a wall you can attach panels directly to the studs. However, panels attached this way tend to give a little and are not as soundproof as those installed over either a plywood or a gypsum board backing.

When you're installing wood panels, first lean them against the wall as you think they should be placed. This gives you a chance to arrange the wood graining in the manner that pleases you most. When they're positioned the way you want them, number the panels for reference and proceed with the project.

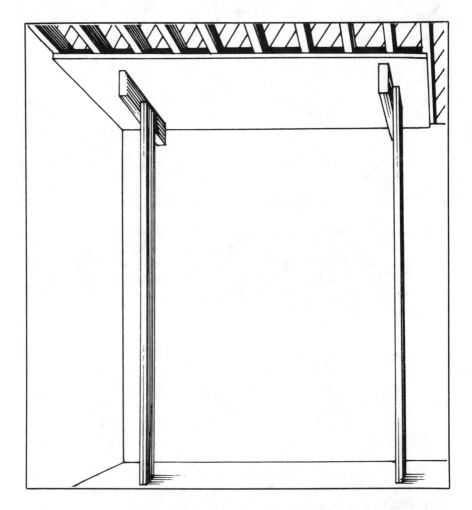

To save your arm muscles when installing ceiling wallboard, construct two "deadman" supports. These consist of 2 × 4s of the proper floor-to-ceiling length, including T-bars at their tops. They effortlessly support the panels while you do the final positioning and securing.

Instead of carrying large wallboard sheets into the house and possibly damaging them when navigating awkward corners, measure and cut them to fit before bringing them inside.

When using a handsaw or a table saw to cut a wood panel, cut the panel with the face up. When using a hand power saw, cut the panel with the face down.

Do you want to discourage nails from "popping" out of wallboard? Drive them in in pairs, spaced two inches apart. Each strengthens the holding power of the other. If you're driving nails into a stud where two wallboard edges butt up against each other, stagger the double nailing on each side of the interface.

To help absorb noise, install acoustical tiles on doors to playrooms. You could also reduce noise in your home by using such tile to line the rooms or closets that house central heating and air conditioning units.

Wall Repairs

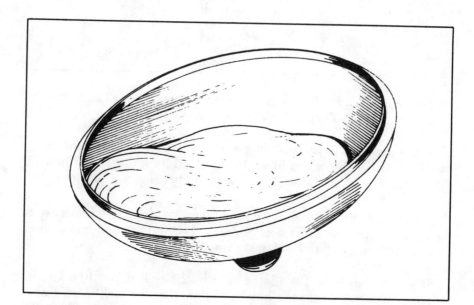

A saucepan lid makes a good container for joint compound, since the knob of the lid lets you hold the "bowl" easily during application. (When you've finished, make sure you rinse out the lid before any residue hardens.) Other easy-to-hold containers are a bathroom plunger or half of a hollow rubber ball.

To prevent a toggle bolt from slipping into a wall cavity before a hang-up is in place, insert a washer under the head of the bolt. (The hole needed for the bolt is normally larger than the head of the bolt.)

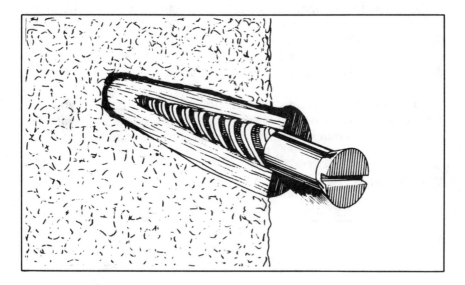

To hold a heavy bolt in a masonry wall, taper a dowel and drive it into a small hole. Then drive the bolt into the dowel.

If a screw hole in the wall has worn-down grooves, stuff the hole with a cotton ball soaked in white glue, and let it dry for 24 hours. You'll then be able to insert a screw securely using a screwdriver.

A beer can opener makes a good tool for cutting loose plaster out of a wall before patching a large crack. Use the pointed end of the opener to undercut and widen the opening.

It will be easier to fill a large hole in the wall if you first jam a piece of wallboard into the hole, and then mar the wallboard's surface so that it is rough. The spackle will adhere tightly to the wallboard piece and won't sink in and require further applications.

To patch a small hole in drywall you can use a tin can lid covered by a plaster patch. Thread a wire in and back out through two holes in the lid of the can and then slide the lid behind the wall through horizontal slits cut out from each side of the hole. Pull the lid flat on the inside, and hold it in place while you apply plaster.

Adding a tablespoon of white vinegar to the water when mixing patching plaster will keep the compound from drying too quickly, allowing you more time to work.

It's best to fill wide cracks in plaster from the inside out, pressing fresh plaster in with a putty knife or a trowel.

You'll be able to remove a damaged ceramic tile easily if you first drill a hole through its center and score an "X" across it with a glass cutter. Then chisel out the pieces.

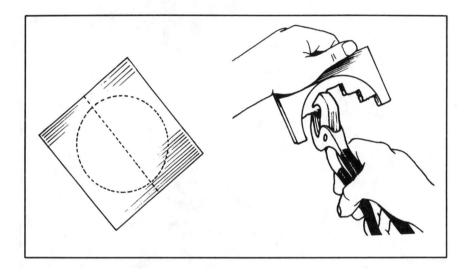

To fit a ceramic tile around the stem of a shower pipe, cut the tile in half and then cut semicircles out of each half with tile nippers.

When replacing an individual ceramic wall tile, it helps to tape it securely to surrounding tiles until its mastic dries.

PICTURES AND MIRRORS

Sometimes a picture that was positioned correctly won't hang straight. Wrap masking tape around the wire on both sides of the hook so that the wire can't slip. Or install parallel nails and hooks a short distance apart; two hooks are better than one for keeping pictures in their places.

Squares of double-faced tape affixed to the two lower back corners of the frame will keep a picture from moving. If you don't have double-faced tape, make two loops with masking tape, sticky side out. Apply to each of the lower back corners and press the picture against the wall.

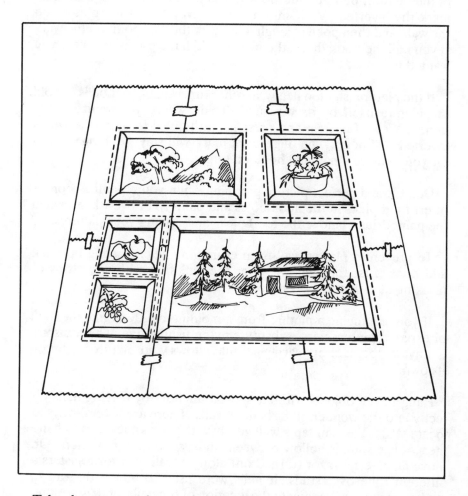

Take the guesswork out of arranging several pictures on the wall. Spread a large sheet of wrapping paper or several taped-together newspapers on the floor and experiment with frame positions. When you decide on a pleasing grouping, outline the frames on the paper, tape the paper to the wall, and drive hooks through the paper into the wall. Then remove the paper and hang the pictures.

Picture hanging can be frustrating if you simply try to "eyeball" the right spot to put the hook. Instead, place a picture exactly where you want it the first time with the following method. Cut a sheet of paper to the exact size of the frame. Position the pattern on the back of the picture, pull up taut the wire the picture will hang from, and mark the inverted "V" point on the pattern. Adjust the pattern on the wall, and then poke through it to mark the "V" point on the wall. If you nail the hook there, the picture will hang precisely where you wanted it.

If the picture isn't too heavy, another timesaving method is to hold the picture itself by its wire and decide where you want it positioned. Wet a fingertip and press it on the wall to mark the wire's inverted "V" point. The fingerprint mark will stay wet long enough for you to drive a nail and hook on target.

Don't lose a perfect picture grouping when you repaint a room—insert toothpicks in the hook holes and paint right over them; when the paint dries, remove the toothpicks and rehang your pictures.

To prevent a plaster wall from crumbling when driving in a nail and hook, first form an "X" over the nail spot with two strips of masking tape or transparent tape.

If you're hanging a picture from a molding but don't like the look of exposed picture wire, substitute nylon fishing line. The transparent nylon does a disappearing act that allows your picture to star on its own.

Hang heavy objects without special anchors by driving nails directly into the wooden studs behind walls. There are several ways to locate studs. You can tap a wall gently with your knuckles or a hammer. A wall sounds hollow between studs; solid on top of them. Or, move an electric razor (turned on) along a wall; a razor registers a different tone over studs. If nails were used to attach drywall to studs, a magnet will indicate the location of the nails, and, therefore, the studs.

When hanging a mirror with screws that go through mounting holes in the glass, don't tighten the screws all the way. Leave enough play to prevent the mirror from cracking if the wall shifts.

Hang mirrors to reflect *you* but not the sun; some mirror backings are adversely affected by direct sunlight.

Sometimes a picture that has been hanging for a while will leave darkish outlines on the wall because dust and dirt have collected against the frame. To prevent such build-up, allow better air circulation by holding pictures slightly away from the wall with thumb tacks pressed firmly into the backs of their frames. You can get the same result by fixing small tabs of self-sticking foam weather stripping to the picture backing.

HINTS ON DESIGN AND DECORATION

A room will appear larger if you paint an oversized piece of furniture the same color as the walls.

A small room can be made to look larger if you install mirrors on one wall to reflect the rest of the room.

If you want to make a large room seem smaller or cozier, choose a wallpaper with a large, bold pattern. However, don't choose a large pattern for a small room because it will make the available space seem crowded.

When selecting a wallpaper for a particular room, keep in mind the dominant colors already present in that room. One or more of those colors should be present in the wallpaper to tie the color scheme together.

To make a high ceiling seem lower, paper it with a bold pattern. To make a low ceiling seem higher, paper it with a small print or a texture.

A mural-pattern wallpaper makes a small room appear larger.

There's no need to invest in wallpaper to give your walls new life. A super graphic on the wall can make a room exciting. Or, if you have artistic ability (or just ambition), design and paint your own mural.

The texture of your furnishings can brighten or darken a room. Glossy surfaces like satin, glass, and tile reflect light and add brightness to a room; surfaces like brick, carpet, and burlap absorb light and make a room seem less bright.

In a low-ceilinged room, use vertical lines—high-backed chairs, straight draperies—to carry the eye upward and give an illusion of height. Horizontal lines—a long sofa or low bookcases—give a feeling of space and make high ceilings appear lower.

Small rooms will seem even smaller if filled with elaborate patterns or designs. Keep the furniture for a small room simple and the colors fairly restrained.

A darker color on the ceiling will make a high-ceilinged room seem more in proportion. So will low-placed, eye-catching objects such as a low coffee table, low-slung chairs, and floor plants.

In a long, narrow room, paint the end walls contrasting colors for a striking effect. Room dividers or furniture positioned in the middle of the room will give the effect of two rooms in one and lessen the feeling of length.

A favorite painting can be the inspiration for the color scheme of a room. Select one dominant color and several toning shades to create a pleasing combination.

You've fallen in love with an unusual wallpaper pattern but aren't sure whether you can actually live with it? Tape a sample to the wall of the room where you're thinking of using it and leave it there for a while. You may feel quite differently about it in a week or so.

If you are the wreck-it-yourself type of do-it-yourselfer, but can't afford professional help with your home decoration, consider swapping talents with a friend or neighbor. Perhaps you know someone who's artistic and would love to redesign or redecorate your room in return for your services as a babysitter, typist, or house cleaner.

If you use the same fabric on two different chairs, it will tie the decor of the room together.

To add color to matchstick blinds, weave rows of colored ribbon through them.

Matchstick blinds can disguise a wall of hobby or utility shelves for a clean, unified look. They also can be used to partition off a closet or dressing area where you would like a lighter look than a door provides.

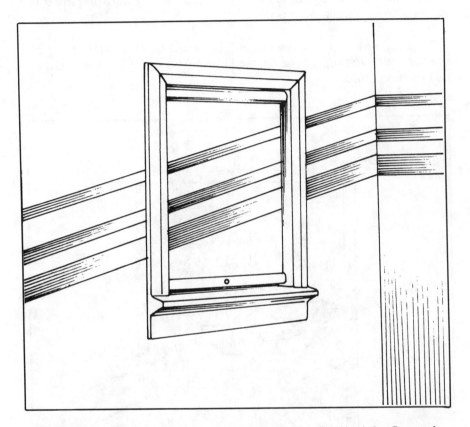

There is no need to invest in drapes if your budget is tight. Instead, brighten up inexpensive shades by decorating them with tape to complement the wall color or wallpaper, or by gluing fabric over them.

To give a room a soft glow, light objects in a room instead of the whole room. For example, spotlight a piece of art or a bookcase.

Decorative shades can make an attractive alternative to drapes—and may be a lot cheaper.

Hang shiny, metallic blinds vertically or horizontally to help re-flect summer sun. This works especially well in south and west win-dows where you can't construct awnings.

You can make a curtain panel from a bedsheet by knotting the top corners around a bamboo pole.

Your old removable-slat wooden blinds can be renovated. Spread the slats outdoors on newspaper and finish with high-gloss spray paint or brush-on enamel.

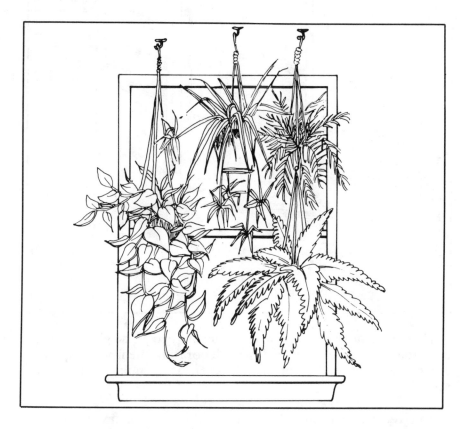

A screen of hanging plants can be a great substitute for curtains.

For an unusual window covering, attach wooden rings to a patch-work quilt and hang it from a wide, wooden rod. Don't do this, however, if the quilt is an antique that could fade or otherwise be damaged by exposure to sunlight.

If you have an Indian print bedspread that you don't use, hang it full-width across a window. Open it diagonally across half the window and secure it with a tieback.

Turn your bathroom into a miniature gallery with pictures you don't have space for elsewhere—so long as they aren't works that can be damaged by the humidity that collects in a bathroom.

If you don't want to buy furniture, you can rent it at surprisingly reasonable rates. Furniture for rent includes everything from sofas and carpets to lamps and works of art.

To make a quick floor covering for a beach house, stretch natural-colored painter's canvas from wall to wall, stapling it to the baseboards.

In a beach house, use roll-down window blinds to make a door for a doorless room.

Extra high-gloss vinyl flooring like that used on submarines and ships' decks makes fine flooring for lofts, darkrooms, and photo studios. You should be able to get it at an army surplus store.

Mexican serapes and Indian bedspreads make colorful, inexpensive tablecloths—great for picnics, too.

Fasten bright and colorful paper shopping bags to the wall for storage of art supplies and other lightweight items.

Keep your decorative baskets looking healthy by placing them away from dry heat.

A nonworking fireplace, primed and freshened with paint, makes a comfortable niche for a sewing machine table or an aquarium.

Display flowers in unusual vases—a crystal ice bucket, a fluted champagne glass, a bright coffee mug or jug. Flowers, in fact, look good in almost any container.

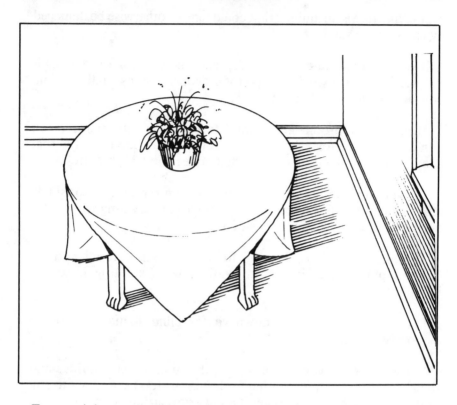

For a quick, easy, and inexpensive way to recover a chair, drape a twin-size sheet over the chair, and tie or pin the corners to fit. You can use the same trick to add interest to a small table.

You'll never have trouble tightening screws and bolts if you remember that, for most, right is tight and left is loose.

An easy way to give a room a facelift is to update hardware such as doorknobs, drawer pulls, and curtain rods.

Add a miniature hammock to a corner in a child's room to make a place for all his or her stuffed animals.

Replace a drab string cord or light-bulb chain with a piece of satin piping or silver cord. Thread a bright ceramic bead at the end of the cord for a finishing touch.

An adjustable curtain rod is a versatile support for a growing houseplant.

Even on fabrics treated to resist stains, blot up spills on upholstery immediately with a clean, dry cloth.

Look for levelers to compensate for uneven floors when buying tall pieces of furniture such as china cabinets and wall units.

If you must polish your nails on your polished wood desk or table, protect the surface with a towel or pad. Nail polish and remover are among the worst enemies of a wood finish. Medicines, perfumes, and alcoholic beverages are also among the chemical substances that can ruin a fine finish. Blot up such spills immediately.

Furniture upholstered in sturdy fabrics with a high content of durable fibers like nylon and olefin are good choices for a houseful of adventurous kids or playful pets—or adults who forget to take off their shoes before putting their feet up on the sofa.

Upholstered furniture should not be placed in constant direct sunlight or near heating outlets; these can cause fading or discoloration.

If someone in your family has allergies, check the materials used to fill upholstered furniture before you buy. Most states require furniture manufacturers to attach a label stating the materials used to pad the frame and fill the cushions—for instance, down, feathers, kapok, horsehair, or polyurethane. If you know one of the materials used is likely to be a problem for an allergy-prone family member, you can avoid that piece of furniture.

To brighten up the office, put pencils and pens in a flowerpot and use a music stand for a magazine rack.

To keep drying flowers dust-free, cover them with plastic bags punched with air holes. When the flowers have dried, spray them with hair spray. This will serve several purposes: The hair spray will give the flowers a clear matte finish, keep them from shedding, keep insects away, and protect them from moisture.

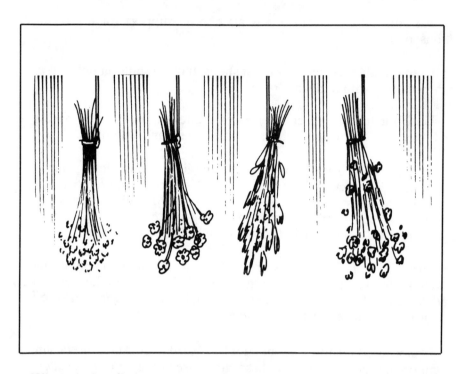

When drying flowers or vegetables, most have to be hung upside down in small bundles in a dark, dry place for a few weeks. Try hanging branches by strings of different lengths from coat hangers. This allows for good air circulation.

Some flowers and foliage can be placed in a vase without water and dried upright. Among them are pussy willows, wild grasses, and grains and flowers with large composite heads and sturdy stalks— for example, Queen Anne's lace and cockscomb.

A branch cut from any blossoming tree or bush makes an unusual centerpiece on a dining or coffee table.

Glue corn pads or pieces of felt to the rough bottoms of vases and art objects to keep them from scratching tables.

Use leftover dining room wallpaper to make matching place mats. Paste the paper onto sturdy cardboard, trim the edges neatly, and coat each mat with a plastic spray.

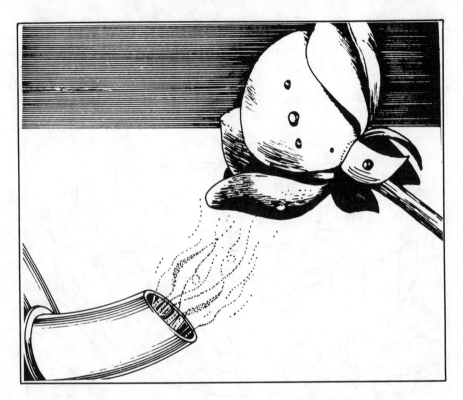

Perk up slightly wilted fabric flowers by holding them over steam from a teakettle or steam iron.

A handy deodorizer for wastebaskets: Place a sheet of fabric softener in the bottom of each.

An old dining table found at a flea market can make a great sofa-height coffee table. Just cut the legs to the height you need.

Change the look of an old formica table by laminating the surface with colorful fabric.

If you're serving messy finger food—fried chicken or ribs, for instance—provide finger bowls: Float lemon slices in small glass

115

dishes so that guests can rinse their fingers. Since finger bowls are an old-fashioned elegance and seldom seen these days, be ready to enlighten anyone who assumes that you're serving a rather odd sort of cold lemon soup.

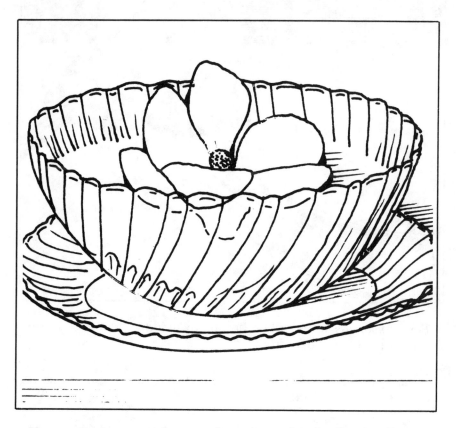

You can make unusual centerpieces in no time by floating flowers in clear glass dessert dishes. Fill the dishes half-way with water, cut the stems from the flowers, and place them in the dishes.

Dimestore bandannas make pretty, inexpensive pillow covers. Buy assorted colors for a striking effect. These bandannas also make wonderful table napkins—especially for a picnic or a barbecue.

Old, carved doorknobs, attached to each end of a dowel, make an attractive curtain rod. Paint or stain the knobs to match your furniture.

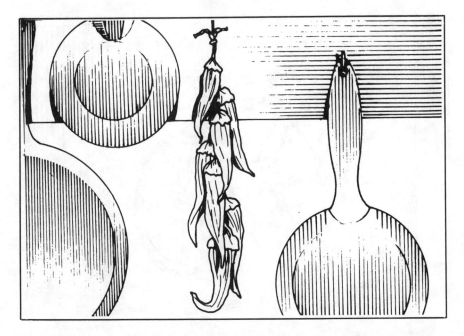

Hot peppers threaded on a long string make a beautiful kitchen decoration while drying. Garlic and onions also look attractive braided and hung on display.

You can make inexpensive bookcases out of flue tiles or conduit pipes. The cubbyholes are perfect for storing wine.

Solve a bicycle storage problem: A bicycle hanging on a wall becomes a piece of art as well as a means of transportation. A high-tech look for a teenager's room, perhaps?

You can make cheap floor rugs by stenciling canvas with nontoxic acrylic paints.

Make an extra closet into a book nook for quiet reading. Remove the door, and install a wall lamp, shelves, and a comfortable chair.

Place an unwrapped bar of soap in a drawer or linen closet to give lingerie and linens a pleasant scent.

An old kimono can be draped on a wall for an elegant splash of texture and color.

BEDS AND BEDDING

When storing linens, it's best to roll them around cardboard tubes rather than fold them.

When outfitting a guest room that's used infrequently, economize by choosing a cheaper mattress. It won't have to withstand daily use.

When shopping for a mattress, be sure that the clerk offering you advice is employed by the store and not by any particular bed manufacturer. A manufacturer's representative will have a vested interest in selling you his or her company's brand, which might be less suited to your needs than a product by another manufacturer.

Sometimes you can silence squeaky bed springs with a coat of spray wax. If bed squeaks are caused by springs touching the frame, pad the frame with pieces of sponge.

If bed slats sometimes slide out of place on the frame, keep them from moving so easily by slipping wide rubber bands over the slat ends.

If your innerspring mattress is showing uneven wear, turn it over and around, end to end, once a month.

When you purchase a new bedspread, consider buying a larger size than you need and then cutting the excess to make a matching headboard.

To give a guest room a clean and inviting scent, place an unwrapped bar of sweet-smelling soap under each bed pillow.

When buying an innerspring mattress, make sure it has thick, strong wire along its borders and a machine-stitched tape covering its outside edges.

Before purchasing a double mattress, lie down on it with your partner to be sure it gives both of you the desired support side by side and at your heads, shoulders, and hips. If one person rolls over, the mattress definitely shouldn't sway. If it does, try another mattress.

Make sure any mattress you buy is warranted against defects in workmanship and details for 10 to 15 years. Some guarantees aren't valid if the mattress isn't positioned on a frame that conforms to the manufacturer's specifications.

An adjustable ironing board placed beside a bed makes a perfect bed table for someone who's ill and confined to bed.

Bed manufacturers don't share a common system for rating mattress firmness. You'll have to judge each mattress by testing it, not by relying on a "soft," "medium," or "firm" tag.

Before washing a colored bedspread, dip a corner in a detergent solution to find out if the color bleeds. If it does, have the spread dry-cleaned.

The agitating movement of a washing machine may cause blanket fibers to mat. To avoid this, soak the blanket for ten minutes, then put it through a short wash cycle—preferably the cycle for "delicates" if your washer has one. Use fabric softener to increase fluffiness.

Here's an easy, inexpensive way to clean soiled mattresses or box springs: Use a solution of a quarter cup good quality dishwashing liquid and one cup warm water, whipped into a high foam with an eggbeater. Apply only the foam with a stiff-bristled brush, working on a small area at a time. When the entire surface is treated, go over it again with a damp sponge to remove any soap residue. Use an electric fan to speed drying.

Pillows stuffed with kapok (the silky covering of seeds from the ceiba tree) cannot be washed. Air them regularly to keep them fresh.

If you line dry a pillow that you have washed, be sure to change the hanging position hourly to dry the filling evenly and avoid bunching.

You can still wash a feather pillow even if the fabric is worn or the pillow heavily stuffed, but you'll need to wash the ticking and the feathers separately. Just secure the feathers in a large muslin bag, stitch the opening closed, and wash. Dry in the dryer with a pair of clean tennis shoes; this will help distribute the feathers.

If a sleeping bag can be machine-dried, throw in a clean, dry tennis shoe to prevent matting, and a clean, dry towel to absorb excess moisture.

Save a place on the closet shelf in each bedroom for the sheets and pillowcases you use in that room. That way you don't have to shuffle through the linen closet to find the right size or set.

Creams and lotions that are kind to your skin aren't kind to your pillowcases. Spread a hand towel over your pillow when you've treated yourself to an extra layer of moisturizer.

If you're good with an embroidery needle, monogram your children's bed linens. They may be more willing to make their own beds if their linens have the personal touch.

If one of your fitted sheets has seen better days, position a flat mattress pad in the center of it and stitch the pad in place. You now have an inexpensive fitted mattress pad.

STORAGE AND SAVING SPACE

If your home is built with studs and drywall, you can add cabinets between the studs, anywhere you need them—they won't take up any space at all. For example, put a liquor cabinet over your bar, or fashion a canned-goods pantry in your kitchen.

Pegboard is most often used on walls, but it can also be used as a room divider, or even to make the inside of a closet or cabinet door more functional. When installing pegboard, remember to provide space behind the panels for the hooks.

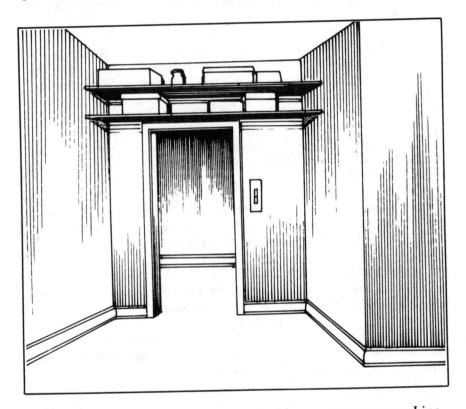

A hallway that's wide enough can double as a storage area. Line the hallway with shelves or shallow cabinets.

Use flat, roll-out bins for under-the-bed storage. They can hold bed linens, sewing supplies, and infrequently used items.

Nail coffee cans to the wall to make bins for clips, pins, or other small items.

To increase the capacity and efficiency of a drawer, outfit it with a lift-out tray. Fill the tray with items you frequently use, and use the space beneath the tray for articles you seldom need.

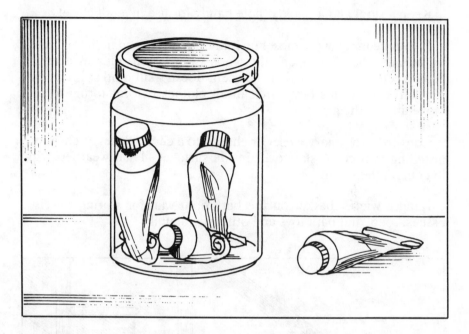

Glass baby food jars are ideal for storing nails and screws. Better yet, nail the caps to a wood base or wall plaque, and just screw the jars into place. And remember that partly used tubes of glue won't dry out if they're kept in a tightly closed jar.

Add more storage space in your bedroom by building a headboard storage unit. You can place books, lamps, or a radio on the lid of the unit and inside you can store extra linens and blankets.

For extra closet storage, see if your closets can accommodate a second shelf above the existing one. And if you install the main clothes-hanging rod high enough, you may be able to install another rod beneath it on which to hang shorter items such as slacks and shirts.

If you're in need of an extra closet for storing items like golf clubs, skis, and camping equipment, angle a decorative folding screen in a little-used corner.

Hooks, shelves, or hanging bins can transform the inside surfaces of closet doors into useful storage areas.

Keep a stool and a hooked pole handy for use in a tall closet.

If your cedar chest or closet no longer smells of cedar, lightly sand its surfaces. Sanding opens the wood's pores and releases a fresh cedar scent. Remember that the scent doesn't kill moths; it merely repels them. So, it's best to clean all clothes before storing to remove any moth eggs.

Convert an ordinary closet or chest into a cedar closet or chest by installing thin cedar slats over inside surfaces. Then weather-strip to contain the scent.

Hang a wicker basket on the bathroom wall for storing towels, tissues, soap, and bath toys and other incidentals.

Put the space under a stairway to work as a storage area. Construct a wheeled, wedge-shaped container that fits into the farthest area beneath the steps.

Another way to use a stairway as a storage area is to replace ordinary nailed-in-place steps with hinged steps. Use the space under the hinged steps to hold boots or sports equipment.

So that you won't misplace frequently used items, glue small magnets on the walls of the medicine cabinet to hold nail files, cuticle scissors, clippers, and other small metal objects.

Your medicine cabinet will stay neat and clean with "shelf paper" made of blotters that can absorb medicine or cosmetic spills.

Hang a basket near the front door and keep your keys in it, so you'll always know where they are. Use this basket also for bills and letters that need to be mailed. When you grab your keys, you'll remember to pick up the mail as well.

Install two rows of clothing and coat hooks on your closet doors —one down low for a child to use, another higher up for you to use.

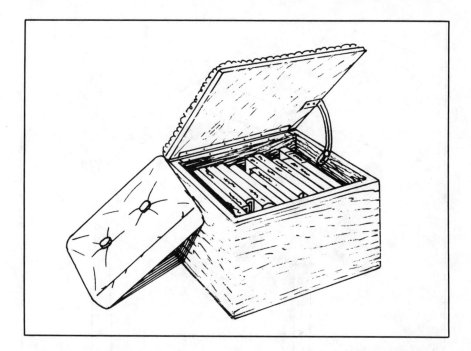

For a double-duty ottoman, build a plywood box with a hinged cover. Paint the outside or cover it with fabric, and then cover the top with scrap carpeting. Add a cushion for comfortable sitting, and store your magazines in style.

Extension cords won't get tangled when stored in a drawer if you wind them and secure them with rubber bands—or slip them into a toilet paper or paper towel tube.

Keep flashlight batteries fresh by storing them in a sealed plastic bag in the refrigerator.

When storing suitcases, put an unwrapped cake of soap inside each one to prevent musty odors from developing.

A metal garbage can is perfect for storing long-handled yard tools. Hooks can also be attached to the outside of the can for hanging up smaller tools. You can lift up the whole can and move it to whichever part of the yard you're working in.

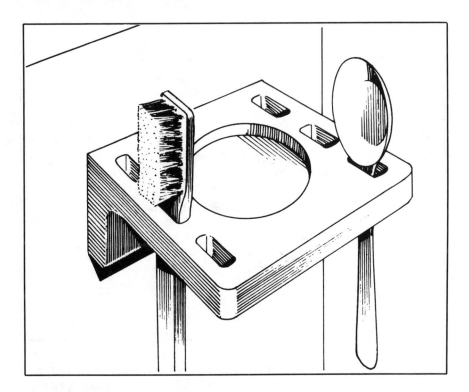

Use an extra slot in the toothbrush holder to keep a medicine spoon handy.

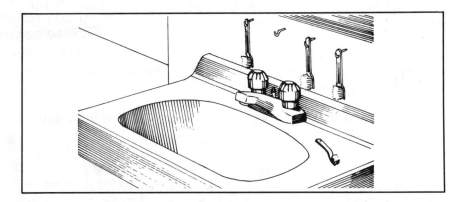

Keep toothbrushes handy but neatly out of the way on cup hooks attached to a wall or under a cabinet.

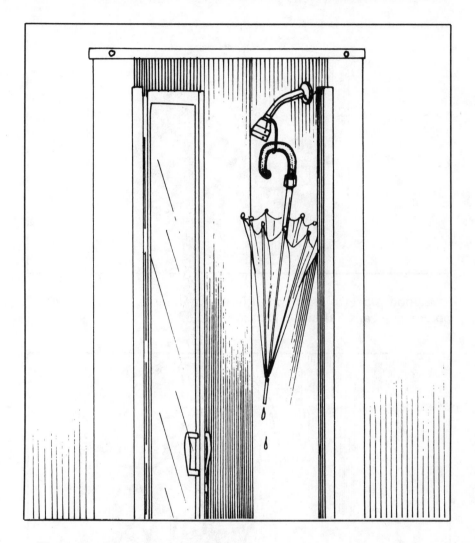

Keep your wet umbrella in the shower where it can drip away without making a mess. This is an especially useful strategy when you have company on a rainy day, and everyone has an umbrella.

You'll always know where your photo negatives are if you store them behind corresponding prints in your photo album.

Photographic film will stay fresh longer if stored in your refrigerator.

A good place to store small clothing items is in large, metal potato-chip cans—after the cans are washed.

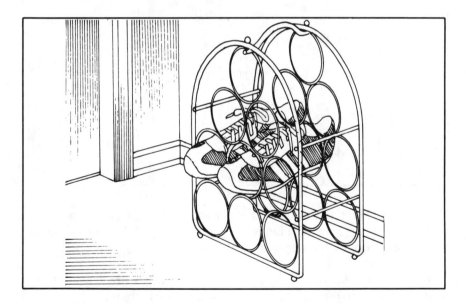

Put a wine rack next to the door and use it to store your sandy beach shoes and muddy running or gardening shoes.

Keep place mats flat and out of the way by hanging them on a clipboard hung from a hook inside a cabinet or pantry door.

To give yourself more storage space in a small bathroom, erect shelves in the "dead" wall space beside the vanity, over the toilet, or behind the door. Such shelves offer convenient storage without intruding on floor space.

If you're a total klutz with a hammer and nails and the thought of putting up shelves fills you with feelings of inadequacy, there are all kinds of ways to cheat. For instance, upend two narrow wastebaskets on your closet shelf and position another shelf across them. Or use sturdy boxes stacked on their sides to make compartmented shelf space—you can see at a glance what's stored in the boxes, and you can use the tops for little-used items.

To minimize breakages, store loose light bulbs in tumblers. A paper towel wrapped around the bulb before you put it in the tumbler provides added protection.

Make your shower curtain rod do double duty—attach extra curtain hooks to hold a back brush, a net bag for bath toys, each family member's washcloth, or a shower cap.

If you have troubles with bubbles and creases when applying adhesive-backed paper to shelves or drawers, try smoothing the paper with a blackboard eraser.

CHOOSING FURNITURE

It's risky to buy furniture off the back of a truck. The price—and the sample on view—may be attractive, and the cartons may even bear a good brand name, but by the time you find out that the boxed furniture is of inferior quality the truck and driver will be long gone.

Furniture items advertised for sale "as is" sometimes provide wonderful bargains, but you should be sure to identify the damage before the purchase. A minor scratch may be something you can live with (or fix yourself), but avoid structural damage unless you're willing to pay for repairs.

Good bargains are also available at "close out" sales, but be sure you won't want to match the piece later. A close out is a style the manufacturer is discontinuing and you will not be able to find replacements or additions once the consignment is gone.

The fabric on the arms of upholstered chairs and sofas will wear twice as long if the piece comes with matching arm caps.

Zippered sofa cushions should not be removed for cleaning or washing. Clean them according to the manufacturer's directions while they are on the pillow.

Vinyl-covered furniture may be a good choice for a family room or high-traffic area, but it's not invulnerable. Body oils and perspiration can harden vinyls, and tears are difficult to repair. Keep this in mind when making your choice.

Lightweight fabrics wear better when they are quilted; the quilting allows the fabric to "stretch" under stress.

The fabric used to upholster a piece of furniture can boost the price to a surprising degree. If you suspect that a piece you like owes its price to a lush fabric, ask if the piece is available with less pricey coverings.

Note that a fabric that has the design woven in is likely to be more serviceable than one that is printed only on one side.

If your household is particularly hard on furniture—or if you have cats—keep in mind that nubby fabrics are more likely to snag and pill than smooth ones.

There's more to upholstered furniture than meets the eye, so check the frame which supports it. Lift one end of the piece; it shouldn't wobble or creak. If it does, the construction may be inferior.

Push hard on the arms and back of an upholstered chair. You shouldn't be able to feel hard frame edges through the fabric. If you can, the chair is poorly padded and will wear out quickly.

Despite what you may have heard, you should not wash wood furniture with soap and water. Instead, use a solvent such as mineral spirits or naptha. (Avoid smoking or using electrical appliances during or immediately after cleaning with these substances, and dispose of the cloths used.)

Protect your wood table or desk by keeping a pad under your writing paper when using a ballpoint pen. It's easier than you think to lean on the pen hard enough for the point to mar the wood surface.

Moisten a duster with a spray polish before dusting furniture with a fine finish. A dry cloth can drive the dust into the finish and cause tiny scratches.

Before you go shopping for furniture, make a floor plan of your room. Use grid paper and a scale of one square on the grid to one square foot of floor space. Mark in doors, windows, heating outlets, electrical outlets, and other features that will influence where you can and cannot position a piece of furniture. That way you'll avoid buying a bookcase that blocks your most conveniently placed electrical outlets, or a sofa that has to sit on top of your floor heating duct. Take your floor plan and tape measure when you shop—a chair that looks quite small on the showroom floor may look a lot bigger when you get it into your living room or den.

If you move frequently, be wary of buying furniture with a specific location in mind. Look instead for items that are adaptable in style and color.

When buying furniture, comfort should be near the top of your list of criteria. You'll grow tired of even the most elegant chair if it's not comfortable to relax in.

It's a good idea to visit department stores that display furniture in room-style groupings. It's sometimes much easier to imagine how furniture will look in your own home if you see it in a home-like setting.

When selecting furniture, consider the traffic patterns of your home. That handsome coffee table that looks so good on the show-room floor will be a lot less attractive if it's going to block everyone's route to the kitchen or the stairs.

Fold a printed fabric and rub the printed sides together. If any of the print comes off, don't buy the fabric. It's an inferior product.

Tightly woven fabrics wear better than loosely woven ones. To check the weave, hold the fabric up to the light. Spots of light will show through a loose weave.

Vacuum your upholstered furniture weekly to remove dirt and grime that would otherwise get embedded in the fibers and cause the fabric to wear out faster.

Reverse loose cushions on your chairs and sofas once a week to ensure even wear and tear on the furniture.

Outdoor Home Maintenance and Repairs

OUTDOOR PAINTING JOBS

Spring is the ideal time to paint the exterior of a house. Do it as soon as the weather turns warm enough, but before the temperature gets too hot. In very hot weather paint dries too quickly and leaves marks where strokes were overlapped.

When painting the outside of your house, fold newspapers over the tops of doors and then close them. You won't paint the doors shut.

Don't use a flame to soften alligatored paint. The flame can shoot into a crack and ignite the sheathing.

Plant or prune shrubbery or trees so branches don't touch painted exterior surfaces. The undersides of leaves hold moisture long after a rain, and prolonged moisture causes paint to blister and peel.

When painting the exterior of your house, protect nearby shrubs from paint splatters by covering them with drop cloths or old sheets.

Paint will not bond on a surface wet from morning dew or on a prime coat not thoroughly dry. And without proper bonding, paint will peel. Be sure to wait for dew to dry before painting.

If using an oil-based paint on an area that has suffered mildew; add a mildew inhibitor to the paint. (This isn't necessary with water-based paints, which don't contain the oil that fungus feeds on.)

To prepare old wood for paint it's not necessary to remove the old paint. Simply seal all knots with thinned shellac and sand when dry. If the knot is loose, tighten it with wood caulking. After the caulking has dried, coat the spot with shellac, and then sand.

If paint is blistering on hollow porch posts or columns, trapped moisture could be the problem. Cure it by boring small ventilating holes at the top and bottom of each post or column.

Don't use a sander with a revolving disc to remove paint from wood siding. It will gouge the surface.

Use a wire brush to remove loose and peeling paint from curved metal surfaces. A scraper or putty knife will take such paint off flat surfaces. Use steel wool on rust spots, and a mirror to inspect the undersides.

Raw metal is coated with a protective, oily film that keeps paint from adhering properly, so it's best to paint galvanized metal after it has weathered for at least six months. If you prefer not to wait for the metal to weather, strip the film by washing the metal with pure white vinegar. Rinse the metal with water and allow to dry before painting.

The quickest way to paint a wire or chain link fence is with a sponge. Protect your hands with rubber gloves.

Use a roller to paint long, flat surfaces on a fence; the work will go much faster than if you use a brush.

TOOLS AND LADDERS

To keep your hands free while you're making repairs, make a holster for the nails and screws you'll need. Take a paper cup and make two vertical slits in it about an inch apart; the slits should be wide enough to let you slip your belt through them.

When working on a steeply sloped roof, keep your tools on a sheet of plastic foam. That way they won't slide off.

Need a place to hold your hammer when you're on the roof? Attach a shower curtain ring to your belt and slip the hammer through it.

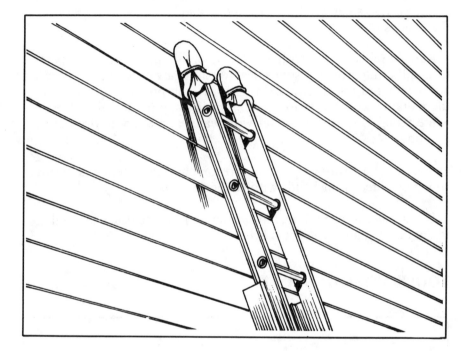

To avoid marring a paint job when leaning a ladder against clapboard siding, cover the top ends of the ladder with heavy woolen socks. The paint will remain unmarked.

When using an aluminum ladder, watch out for power lines: Aluminum *conducts* electricity.

If you're planning to work on a ladder extended to its full height, gain stability by lashing the bottom rung to two stakes driven into the ground under and to the sides of the ladder.

Before climbing up a ladder, test the bottom rung to make sure the ladder is solidly footed.

When positioning a ladder against a house or tree, it is safest to position it so that the distance from the base of the ladder to the house or tree is one quarter of the ladder's extended length. Otherwise the ladder may fall forward or tip backward.

The best way for a lone worker to raise a ladder is to pin its feet against the base of the house and push the ladder up from the other end, hand over hand, until it is upright.

Keep your hips within the ladder's rails. Extend the top two rungs higher than the place where you're working. The ladder should always extend up above the roof.

Make sure your ladder has firm support at the top. Placing it against a window sash or close to an edge means a slight shift could cause you to fall.

ROOF REPAIRS

If there's an unfinished attic or crawl space below a leaky roof, finding the leak shouldn't be too hard. Climb into this space and look around with a flashlight—it's easier to see a leak in the semidark, so don't turn on a light. When you find the leak, outline the wet area with chalk. If possible, push a piece of wire up through the leaky spot, so that it protrudes from the roof. This makes it easier to find the leak when you're working outside.

If possible, repair shingles on a sunny day. A wet roof is dangerously slippery.

You can repair split shingles temporarily even if you don't have any flashing. Put a piece of cardboard in a plastic bag and then slide the bag under the shingles.

You don't have to replace a cracked shingle if all the pieces are still in place. Pull out the obstructing nails and slide a piece of roofing felt or roll roofing under the shingle until it is behind the cracks. Drill holes for the new nails needed, then drive in the nails gently. Cover the nail heads with roof cement.

If black roofing drips tar down on shingles when you're patching, soak a rough rag or brush in kerosene and scrub the stains off right away.

New asphalt shingles can be put down over old asphalt, wood, and roll roofing if it's only one or two layers. If it's in three layers, the old roofing must be stripped off. Cedar shakes, slate shingles, or tiles, however, must be taken off.

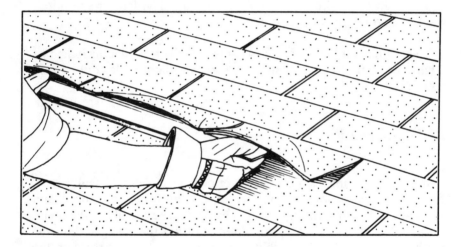

For emergency repair of a shingle, cut a patch to fit from a piece of sheet metal and slip it well under the shingle above the one you're repairing. Apply a coat of roof cement to the bottom of the patch, and tack in place. Cover the tack heads with cement. When you come back to do a more permanent repair later, pry up the patch.

If you want to replace a damaged shake and it doesn't come out easily, split it into several pieces with a hammer and chisel. Remove the pieces and extract the nails.

If the deck under old shingles is spaced sheathing, begin at the ridge so that debris does not fall through the spaces into the house.

To avoid having a new-looking, unweathered patch in repaired shingles or shakes, take replacements from an inconspicuous area of the house and use new shingles or shakes on that spot.

To make it easier to slide a new shingle up into place, round the back corners slightly with a sharp utility knife. Then lift the corners of the overlapping shingles and drive in a roofing nail at each corner.

Do not store asphalt shingles directly on the ground or on the roof overnight. Stack them on pieces of 2×4. When storing shingles, cover them with tarp rather than plastic, because moisture can condense under plastic. Stack shingles no higher than four feet.

GUTTERS AND DOWNSPOUTS

For best wear and protection, paint the outsides of gutters with oil-based exterior house paint, and coat the insides with asphalt roofing paint, which will make them resistant to rust.

Never rest a ladder on a gutter. It will bend the gutter out of shape, causing low spots where pools of water will collect when it rains.

When cleaning gutters, inspect each hanger for bent straps and popped nails as you work your way along the gutter. If the house has a fascia or board trim, check the gutter's alignment with it. The gutter should rest firmly against the fascia for maximum support.

Clean gutters by hand, then hose them down after you've removed the debris. This flushes out the remnants and gives you an opportunity to observe the flow of water and see low spots or improper pitch.

If you are replacing only a section or two of gutter, take a cross-sectional piece with you when buying a new one. You'll need an exact match of shape and metal.

Using a spray-on auto undercoating is a quick and easy way to repair your rain gutters. If you notice any gaps in the gutter, simply spray. If you have to patch a small hole, put a piece of screen wire over the hole and then spray on the undercoating.

Painting gutters is easy, but downspouts can be tricky. To protect the interior of the downspout against rust, drop a string with a weight on it down through the spout, and tie a sponge to the bottom end of the string. Use a sponge that must be compressed to fit inside the spout. Using plenty of paint, soak the sponge, and then pull on the string to squeeze the sponge up through the spout. The paint will spread evenly from bottom to top as the sponge goes up.

When installing a new gutter, get someone to help with lifting the gutter sections. Positioning long sections cannot be done by one person.

Check the nails or screws in the straps holding the downspout to your house. These can work themselves loose with use or age, or when a downspout has been used as a ladder support.

To keep downspouts clear, flush them frequently with a garden hose. If necessary, remove stubborn clogs with a plumber's snake.

SIDING MAINTENANCE AND REPAIRS

Cracked, warped, or loose siding should be repaired as soon as you notice it. Water works its way through such defects into the interior wall where rotting can take place undetected. If you don't have time for a thorough repair, seal splits with oil-based caulking compound and clamp them together by driving nails and clinching them over the boards. This is an effective short-term expedient.

Never caulk when the temperature falls below 50°F. For an emergency job in cold weather, use polybutane cord.

The best time to caulk is when painting the house. Apply primer to the seams first, then caulk. (Primer helps the caulking stick.) Allow the caulking to cure for a couple of days, then apply a finish coat. Be sure to use a compound that will take paint.

If you caulk in very hot weather and the caulking gets runny, place it in the refrigerator for an hour or two.

To remove white powdery surfaces on brick or concrete surfaces, go over them with a stiff brush. Wet the surface with a weak 5 percent solution of muriatic acid and water, leave the solution on for five minutes, then brush the wall and rinse immediately with clear water. Work a four-foot-square section at a time.

When mixing acid and water always add the acid to the water, *never* vice versa. Put on goggles, gloves, and an apron before mixing, and leave them on until after you rinse off.

To remove mildew from house siding, scrub the surface with a bleach and water solution (one cup of bleach to one gallon of warm water). Flush the area with clear water and allow it to dry thoroughly before painting.

OTHER OUTSIDE PROJECTS

Small cracks in blacktop can be patched with sand and liquid blacktop sealer. Pour sand along the crack to fill it part way. Then, pour the blacktop sealer into the crack over the sand, which will absorb the sealer quickly. If necessary, repeat until the surface is smooth.

Instead of using conventional stepping-stones, personalize your walk by having each family member put his or her handprint, name, and birth date in a square of wet cement. Mark other important dates in remaining squares.

When you're building a stone retaining wall, make sure you dig below the frost line for your footing, otherwise the wall could fall apart.

If you are erecting fence posts and don't have a carpenter's level, make sure they're vertical by visually aligning them with the edge of the nearest building.

Unless you're experienced, use a chain saw to cut only wood that is smaller than the length of the guide bar. If you bury the saw nose in wood, it is likely to kick back, making the saw difficult to control.

An apple corer from the kitchen makes a handy garden tool for removing thistles and dandelions from your lawn.

Fasten plastic sandwich bags over outdoor padlocks to prevent them from freezing during winter months.

Don't allow a carpet of autumn leaves to remain on your lawn over the winter. They'll form a mat and smother the grass beneath them.

Rake leaves on a dry day. On a wet day, the leaves will weigh twice as much.

Plant ivy or some other ground cover instead of grass in areas where it's difficult to maneuver the lawn mower. It looks good and, of course, you don't have to mow it.

Improve the looks of a carport with lattice work and hanging baskets. Close off the back of the carport with a trellis that will enclose the backyard seating area.

If you plan to install a skylight, position it on the northern slope of your roof. Because a skylight can really heat up a room on a sunny day, make sure the attic is well ventilated.

If you camouflage telephone poles or clotheslines with black paint, they seem to disappear.

When installing an antenna, position it where it cannot fall across a power line.

If water is seeping into your basement, inspect to see if water collects on the ground near the foundation of the house. Soil should slope away from a house, so if the ground is level or slopes in toward the foundation, you may be able to solve your seepage problem by regrading the soil so it slopes properly.

To keep water from collecting where a paved area meets the foundation of your home, undercut the joint, fill it with mortar, and then shape the mortar into a smooth curve with the back of a spoon.

Help prevent ice dams by installing insulation between the rafters in your attic. Use insulation with a vapor barrier and leave air space between the vapor barrier and roof boards under an underhang. The insulation should be six inches deep.

You can also prevent ice dams by providing ventilation for the attic through the soffit vent between lookout beams, which can be located by nail heads in the soffit.

The chimney in your home should be inspected each year just before the cold season to reduce the chance of fire and to increase efficiency.

You'll see more if you inspect the chimney from the top. On a bright day use a mirror to reflect sunlight down into the chimney. If you can't look down a chimney, inspect it with a strong flashlight and mirror from a fireplace or from the flue opening for a stove pipe.

If the chimney has crumbling mortar, be careful as you chip away cracked, loose mortar in preparation for tuck pointing or remortaring. A chimney in poor condition could topple at any time.

If you're shutting down your house for the winter, turn off the house water supply at the underground street valve.

Here's a fast way to clean the house water pipes of water when shutting down a house. After the water heater has been drained and everything else is empty, there may be water left in low spots in the horizontal mains. Just stick the end of a running air compressor hose into an opened outdoor hose faucet. The air pressure will shoot the water out wherever there is an opening. When only air comes out, you're done. This beats crawling under the house to drain pipes.

When shutting down your water system, open all the faucets and outdoor hose spigots to drain. Flush the toilet and sponge out remaining water from the tank. Drain or blow water out of fixture traps, including the toilet. After removing all the tap water from the sink and lavatory traps, fill the traps with a mixture of a little kerosene and a lot of denatured alcohol. Kerosene will keep the alcohol from evaporating. Caution: Kerosene is flammable; do not pour it or use it near an open flame.

Concrete Work

When you're pouring concrete steps, be sure to use solid objects as fillers; hollow objects buried in concrete—pieces of pipe, for example—have a tendency to float to the surface.

A smooth concrete surface is a hazard on outdoor steps. After the concrete has settled, but while it is still workable, run a stiff broom across the steps to roughen the surface.

If a hollow glass block in your garage wall breaks, clean the opening and soak some pieces of brick. Put the pieces into the opening and pack the hole solidly with concrete mix. You must use brick or the mix will fall out.

Make drilling in masonry easier by making a pilot hole with a masonry nail at the exact spot where you want to drill.

If you put sand on top of asphalt sealer it will prevent the sealer from sticking to your shoes.

You can prevent wooden forms from sticking to concrete by painting the parts that will be in contact with the cement with oil.

An old metal venetian blind slat can be used as a finishing trowel on small concrete jobs.

When setting a fence post in concrete, mound the concrete around the post so that water can't collect on top of it. Otherwise the concrete might form a shallow basin to retain water, causing even a post treated with a chemical preservative to decay eventually.

The Patio

Before constructing a curved patio, you can easily determine the precise contours you want by laying out a garden hose on the ground.

When laying a brick patio, start from a corner of the patio near the house and work outward toward the edges.

Laying a dry brick patio is quite simple. Dig out the area needed, edge the excavation with weather-resistant boards staked into place, and spread out a sand base two and one quarter inches deep. Spray the base gently with water, let it dry, and tamp it down until it's at a two-inch level. Position the bricks, fitting them tightly and making sure they're level. Pour sand on the bricks, sweep it into the crevices, sprinkle with water, and repeat as necessary to fill any gaps.

Nail kegs make good extra seats for deck or patio. Stain the kegs and make cushions for the seats.

When storing folding patio chairs, use old pillowcases as protective covers. Slip a case over each folded chair and pin closed. The fabric guards against scratches and dirt but doesn't trap moisture, as plastic bags might.

Keep weeds from growing in the cracks of your walks, patio, or driveway by dousing the cracks with salt or boiling salted water.

Waxing the ends and bottoms of the legs of wooden patio furniture helps protect against moisture that might be absorbed from standing rain water.

The metal edges of tubular patio chairs won't be able to cut through the rubber cups on the leg bottoms if metal washers are first inserted in the protective cups.

Drill holes in the seats of solid metal patio furniture to allow rain water to drain. If water is allowed to collect, the seats will rust prematurely.

Hints for the Handyman or Woman

GENERAL SHOP

To protect tools, it's best to store them so they aren't subjected to moisture. Keep a thin coating of oil on metal parts, wrap them in plastic wrap, or keep carpenter's chalk, which absorbs moisture, in the toolbox.

To sharpen scissors, use them to slice up several pieces of sandpaper.

A piece of garden hose, slit open, is a handy protective cover for the teeth of a handsaw between projects.

To guard the teeth of circular saw blades when not in use, store the blades in record album covers. You could even store them in an ordinary record rack in your workshop.

To clean small tools and protect them from rust, fill a bucket with sand soaked with motor oil and thrust the heads of small tools into it.

Store tools in a box containing oil-soaked sand if moisture is a problem.

You can clean tools without expensive cleaners. Pour a small amount of kerosene onto the metal part of a tool and rub vigorously with a soap-filled steel-wool pad. Then wad a piece of aluminum foil into a ball and rub on the surface. Wipe away the residue with newspaper, and coat the tool lightly with olive oil before storing. Caution: Kerosene is flammable; do not pour it or use it near an open flame.

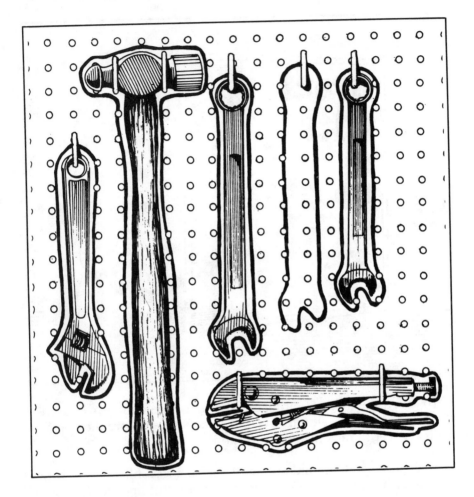

If you hang tools on pegboard walls, outline each tool with an artist's brush so you'll know at a glance where each tool goes. You'll also know when a tool hasn't been replaced.

If you want to remind yourself to unplug an electric drill when changing accessories, fasten the chuck key near the plug end of the cord.

Snow won't stick to your shovel if you give the shovel a coat of floor wax.

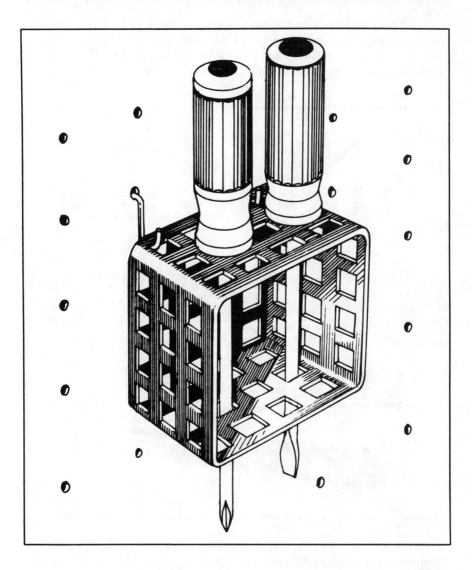

Keep screwdrivers handy—slide the blades through the mesh in plastic berry baskets nailed to the shop wall.

Paint all tool handles with an unusual, bright color, or wrap reflective tape around them; they'll be easy to identify if borrowed or left in the wrong place.

Don't take a chance of hitting a thumb or finger when hammering a small brad, tack, or nail. Slip the fastener between the teeth of a pocket comb; the comb holds the nail while you hold the comb. A bobby pin or a paper clip can be used the same way as a comb.

Here's a do-it-yourself rust-preventive coating for tools, outdoor furniture, and other metal objects: Combine a quarter cup of lanolin and one cup of petroleum jelly in a double boiler over low heat. Stir until the mixture melts and blends completely, and then remove from heat and pour into a clean jar, letting the mixture cool partially. Use the mixture while it's still warm, and don't wipe it off—just let it dry on the object. If there's any extra, cover it tightly, and rewarm it before you use it again.

To transform a hammer into a soft-headed mallet, cover the head with the sort of rubber tip used to prevent furniture legs from scratching the floor.

To retard moisture and rust, keep mothballs with your tools. If rust spots appear, rub them away with a typewriter eraser.

In your workshop, use a pocketed shoebag for such items as cans. The bag holds more and takes up less space than a shelf.

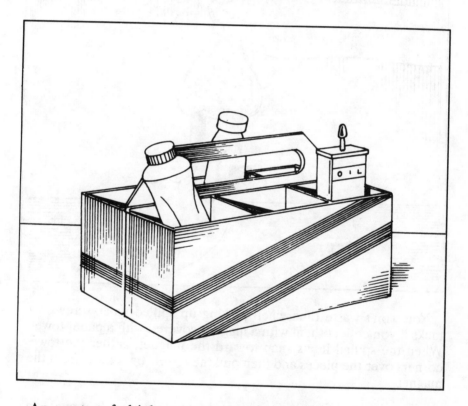

An empty soft-drink carton makes a convenient kit for holding and carrying lubricants.

Empy hand-cream jars are great storage containers for nails. The greasy film left on the side of the jar will prevent the nails from rusting.

If you need more workbench storage space, slide an old dresser under the bench and use the drawers for storage.

To keep the pores of your hands dirt- or grease-free, wipe on a thin coat of shaving cream before starting a messy task.

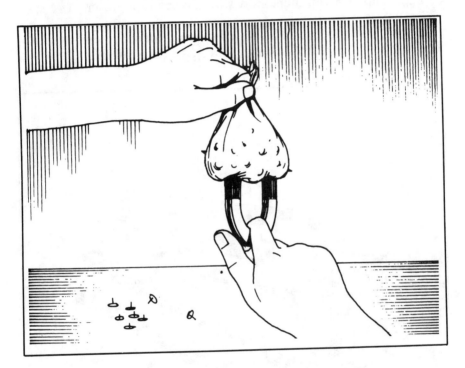

You won't waste time when picking up spilled nails, screws, or tacks if you collect them with a magnet covered with a paper towel. When the spilled items snap toward the magnet, gather the towel corners over the pieces and then pull the towel "bag" away from the magnet.

As an aid in measuring lumber or pipe, paint lines a foot apart on a concrete floor.

You can prevent a knot in nylon rope from working loose by holding it briefly over a small flame. The heat will melt and bond the fibers.

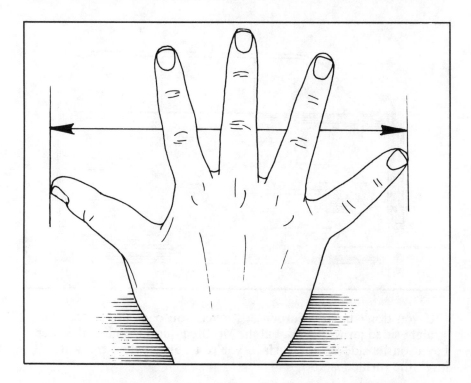

If you know the exact width of your hand with thumb and fingers spread, you can make rough measurements without using a ruler or tape measure.

Loosen a stubborn screw, bolt, or nut with a shot of penetrating oil. If you don't have oil, use hydrogen peroxide, white vinegar, kerosene, or household ammonia. Should these prove ineffective, heat the metal with an iron, rap it sharply with a hammer while it's still hot, and try again to loosen it. Caution: Kerosene is flammable; do not pour it or use it near an open flame.

You can work most rusted bolts loose by pouring a carbonated beverage on them.

If a bolt repeatedly loosens due to vibrations, coat the threads with fingernail polish and reinsert it. It won't loosen again. And if you need to remove it, you can break the seal with a little effort.

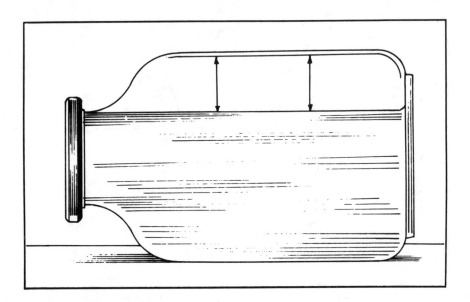

If you don't have a carpenter's level, you can substitute a tall, straight-sided jar with a lid. Fill the jar three-quarters full with water. Lay it on its side on the surface you're testing—when the water is level, the surface is, too,

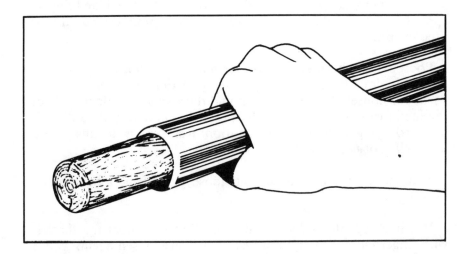

To prevent metal tubing from denting when sawing it, insert a round dowel that fits the tube's interior tightly.

For easy workshop measuring, fasten a yardstick to the edge of your workbench. Cut keyhole slots in the yardstick so you can remove it when you need it elsewhere.

If you're out of penetrating oil, you can substitute hydrogen peroxide or lemon juice.

An old nylon stocking makes an effective strainer if you're out of cheesecloth.

You can use a coping saw blade to remove a broken-off key from a lock. Slide the blade in beside the key, turn it toward the key so its teeth sink into the key's soft brass, and then pull the blade out along with the key fragment.

Dipping the ends of a rope in shellac will keep them from unraveling.

To hide a screw head, drill a counterbored hole, seat the screw, glue a piece of doweling into the counterbore, and sand it flush.

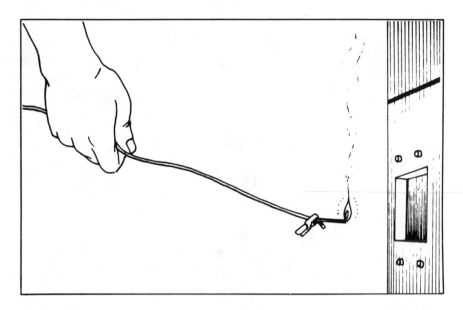

Avoid burning your fingers when lighting a pilot light with a short match. Simply clamp the match in an alligator clip at the end of a straightened coat hanger.

HINTS FOR WOODWORKERS

Plywood frequently splits when you begin sawing it. You can prevent this by applying a strip of masking tape at the point where you plan to start.

To prevent splintering or splitting when sawing, you can also pre-score the top layer on both sides, at the cutoff point, with a sharp chisel or pocket knife.

If you're buying plywood to use where only one side will be visible, you can save money by buying a piece that is less expensive because it's perfect on only one side.

Use expensive waterproof bond plywood only for outside use. Use less expensive water-resistant bond plywood when panels will be exposed to weather infrequently. And use relatively inexpensive dry bond plywood when panels will be used indoors.

You can saw a board into almost perfectly equal lengths without measuring it. Simply balance it on a single sawhorse. When the board stops wobbling, the center will be the point where the board touches the crossbar of the sawhorse.

To make any sawing task smoother and easier, lubricate a saw's blade frequently by running a bar of soap or a candle stub over its sides.

Saws cut more easily *across* the grain than with it. In ripping cuts there's a tendency for the blade to follow the grain, rather than a marked or scribed line, so watch carefully when making rip cuts or the cut might turn out wavy.

To prevent dimpling a wood surface when removing a nail with a hammer, protect the surface with a small block of wood or a shim; this, incidentally, will also increase your leverage.

To extract a nail without widening its hole or denting surrounding stock, use long-nose pliers and roll the pliers in your hand.

To prevent a saw from binding when ripping a long board, hold the initial cut open with a nail or wedge. Move the nail or wedge down the cut as you continue to saw.

Check that wood is perfectly smooth after sanding by covering your hand with a nylon stocking and rubbing it over the surface. You'll be able to detect any rough spots that remain.

Sandpaper clogs fast, and usually before it's worn out. You can clean clogged sandpaper and give it new life by vacuuming it or rubbing a fine-bristled brush back and forth across its grit.

Though a hacksaw is designed to cut metal, the thin blade is well suited for cutting small pieces of wood accurately.

When you drill through any kind of wood a certain amount of splintering will occur at the breakout point. (This is true regardless of the type of bit used, since wood has a composition that causes it to fracture rather than break.) You can prevent this breakout splintering by backing the stock with a piece of scrap.

Whenever there's danger of splitting a narrow section of wood with a screw, predrill a hole. Then the wood won't crack when you insert the screw.

Tack rags will last longer if they're stored in an airtight container to keep them from drying out. Airtight storage also prevents spontaneous combustion. (This safety tip applies equally well to other rags, coveralls, work gloves, and any other clothes that might absorb flammable oils and solvents.)

A plastic playing card or credit card can serve as a scraper for removing excess wood filler from a surface that you are repairing.

A salt shaker makes a good applicator for distributing pumice evenly on a wood surface.

When gluing two pieces of wood together, position the grain in he same direction. If the pieces are cross-grained and later swell due to moisture absorption, the joint will pull apart.

Home Safety and Security

PREVENTING ACCIDENTS
IN THE HOME

To avoid accidents, wipe up spilled water, grease, and other liquids from your kitchen, bathroom, and garage floors as soon as possible.

Secure throw rugs with nonskid pads and don't use them at the top or bottom of a flight of stairs.

If your throw rugs or runners do not have slip-resistant backing, use double-faced adhesive carpet tape on the backs of the rugs to keep them in place.

Rubber matting under rugs will also reduce the risk of the rug slipping and causing someone to fall. You can buy rubber matting that can be cut to size.

If your basement stairs are to be painted, add a little sand to the paint for a better grip, or install rubber or abrasive treads.

When handing a knife to someone else, always hold the point turned away from the other person.

If you staple burlap to the bottom step of a ladder, you'll have a scraper for your shoes. This way you won't have any slippery substances left on your shoes.

Don't put hot tea, coffee, or other hot liquids on a tablecloth that hangs way over the side of the table. Someone could trip on the cloth and spill the scalding liquid.

Keep the gas cooktop away from open windows where curtains could blow into the flames or where wind could extinguish the cooking flames.

Keep the handles of pots and frying pans turned inward on the kitchen range so that they cannot be knocked or tipped over by accident. This is especially important if there are young children in the household.

Guard your pet from drinking from pools of antifreeze which gather under cars—it's poisonous.

Keep a telephone close to your bed so you don't have to get out of bed or go to another room in order to call for help in an emergency.

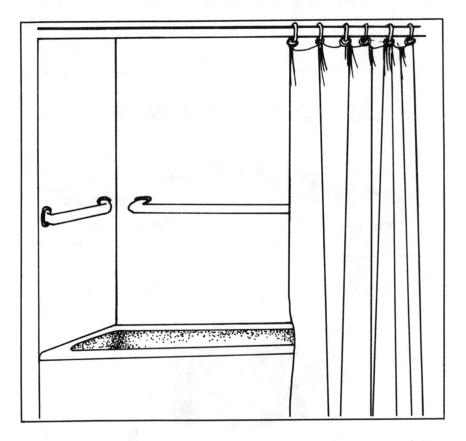

If an older person, or someone who is unsteady on his or her feet, lives in your home, install one (or preferably two) grab bars in bathtubs or showers.

One of your telephones should be accessible in the event of an accident which leaves a family member unable to stand to reach a wall telephone. This is especially important if there is an older person in your home.

When buying a step stool that you can use to reach high shelves or cupboards, choose one with a handrail to hold on to when standing on the top step. Always make sure the step stool is fully open and steady before climbing on it.

For an older person who is unsteady on his or her feet, a stool with nonskid tips can be used as a seat while showering or bathing.

Older people may risk burns from scalding water. If you set the hot water heater below 115°F you can avoid this risk. If your hot water heater does not have a thermostat, use a thermometer to check the water at the faucet.

Do you use your basement or garage as a general storage area? If so, there are probably many things you can trip over, including tools and sharp or pointed objects. If there's no light switch at the entrance to such a storage area, keep a flashlight handy. Or consider having switches installed.

Never remove the guards from your power tools. Tools used with the guards removed pose a serious risk of injury.

Handrails that don't run the full length of a staircase can be dangerous—someone may assume that the stairs end where the handrail ends and miss the last step. If necessary, consider extending or replacing the handrail.

If stair carpeting becomes loose, fix it at once. It's very easy to slip on loose carpeting.

If you're in the habit of placing items on the stairs to remind you to put them away next time you go upstairs or downstairs, try to work out a different reminder system for yourself. Someone may trip over items left on the stairs—especially in an emergency.

If the outside of your house is not very well lit, consider painting the edges of outside steps white so that they are easier to see in the dark.

When working in your darkroom, avoid using a fan when you're mixing chemicals. The fan may blow dry chemicals into the air.

Use disposable utensils such as plastic spoons and paper cups when mixing dry chemicals and dispose of the utensils safely after use.

FIRES AND OTHER EMERGENCIES

Preventing Fires

Distribute fire extinguishers in key areas such as the kitchen, bedrooms, workshop, and garage.

Walk your family through a fire drill so everyone knows what to do and where to go in case of fire. Make sure children know just where the family will reunite if they have to leave the house in case of fire.

Assign a special closet to combustible materials and dangerous tools that you don't want your children to touch. Put a good lock on the door and a heat detector inside to alert you to any fire danger.

Every room in the house should have at least two escape exits.

If you have school-age children, make sure that the school carries out regular fire drills and that the children know where to go and what to do in case of fire.

Don't overload electrical circuits with too many appliances.

Don't run extension cords under the rugs. The cords wear easily and may short out, causing a fire.

Nails or staples used to attach electrical cords to the walls or baseboards can damage the cords and thus cause fire or shock hazards. Tape cords to walls or floors instead of using nails or staples.

Replace frayed electrical cords before they burn or cause a fire.

Keep combustibles away from the furnace, which can give off flames or sparks at times.

To prevent grease fires, keep the stove clear of pot holders, paper napkins, and towels when frying food.

Keep baking soda on hand for extinguishing a kitchen fire in an emergency.

For basic protection at minimum expense, locate one smoke detector in the hallway near each separate sleeping area. (More complete protection calls for a detector on every level of a home.)

Don't mount a smoke detector in areas where the alarm can be triggered inappropriately such as by smoke from cooking, steam from the shower, or in the garage where combustion products from the car's engine can set it off.

Remember that smoke detectors are unreliable below 40°F.

Some fire departments supply stickers that can be placed in a window to alert firefighters to the presence of a child or an elderly or handicapped person. Inquire if such stickers are available in your locality.

If you live or work in a high-rise building, locate the fire exits on your floor. If an alarm sounds, remember that you should always use the fire stairs, not the elevator.

Learn to distinguish the sound of a fire alarm in your building from the sound of an elevator alarm bell. If you think someone's trapped in the elevator when, in fact, the building is starting to go up in flames, you could be in serious trouble.

An electrical outlet or switch that is unusually warm or hot to the touch may indicate a potentially dangerous wiring condition. In such a situation unplug cords, avoid using switches, and call an electrician to check the wiring.

Ceiling fixtures and recessed lights trap heat and overheating can lead to fire, so it's important not to use a bulb of too high wattage in such a fixture. If you don't know the correct wattage, use a bulb of 60 or fewer watts.

If you have a woodburning stove in your home, be sure it's installed according to local codes. Some insurance companies will not cover fire losses if the stove is not correctly installed.

Always extinguish the fire in a wood stove before leaving the house or before going to bed at night.

Unplug your hair dryer or any other small appliance used in the bathroom when you're not in the room. If a plugged-in appliance falls in the sink or tub it could cause a serious shock.

Don't let the cat sleep on top of your electric blanket while it's in use; the heat build-up can be dangerous.

An electric blanket should not be tucked in at the sides. It may overheat and start a fire.

Be sure to turn a heating pad off before you go to sleep. It can cause burns even at a relatively low setting.

To make a dry fire extinguisher, pour six pounds of fine sand into a large container and add two pounds of baking soda. Stir the mixture thoroughly. Keep the container in your shop, garage, or kitchen. This mixture can be sprinkled directly on small oil, grease, and petroleum product fires.

Fire Fighting Do's and Don'ts

Never use water on electric, oil, or grease fires. Water will only spatter the flames.

If you can't shut off the gas before fighting a gas fire, get out of the house immediately.

If you can't remove the fuel from a wood, paper, or fabric fire, cut off its air by smothering the fire with a coat or heavy woolen blanket. You might also cool the fire with water, a fire extinguisher, sand, or earth.

Even if a fire is confined to a frying pan or wastebasket, never spend more than 30 seconds fighting the fire. Small fires can grow with frightening speed.

Never re-enter a burning house for any reason. Leave fire fighting to the professionals as soon as they're on the scene.

Electrical and Storm Safety

Never place an electric appliance where it can fall in water.

Never touch an electric appliance while you are standing in water.

Don't place electric heaters near combustible materials.

As a safety precaution before leaving the house on vacation, unplug all electrical appliances except for those lights connected to automatic timers.

Animals are as curious and as susceptible to such dangers as electrical shock as children are. Block unused electrical outlets and keep electrical cords away from pets—puppies, in particular, are apt to chew on cords.

If you live in a storm-prone area, nail down roof shingles or use adequate adhesive to keep them from blowing off in a violent wind. For roofs with shingles that are not the seal-down type, apply a little dab of roofing cement under each tab.

Alert your local police department if you discover downed power lines. Set up barricades to keep others away from the area until help arrives.

A lightning protection system should offer an easy, direct path for the bolt to follow into the ground and thus prevent injury or damage while the bolt is traveling that path.

Grounding rods (at least two for a small house) should be placed at opposite corners of the house.

In a hurricane, don't go out unless you have to. However, if flooding threatens, seek high ground and follow the instructions of civil defense personnel.

Store a lantern, pick, shovel, crowbar, hammer, screwdriver, and pliers in your storm shelter. If the exit becomes blocked, you may have to dig your way out. Store canned food and bottled water, too.

The basement is not a good shelter during a tornado because it's too close to gas pipes, sewer pipes, drains, and cesspools. A better shelter would be underground, far from the house (in case the roof falls) and away from the gas and sewer system.

Keep an eye on large trees—even healthy ones—that could damage your house if felled in a storm. Cut them back if necessary.

A spare tire in the trunk of your car can be used as a life preserver in a flooding or drowning emergency. Make sure the tire is in good shape.

When a major storm is imminent, close shutters, board windows, or tape the inside of larger panes with an "X" along the full length of their diagonals. Even a light material like masking tape may give the glass the extra margin of strength it needs to resist cracking. Exception: When a tornado threatens, leave windows slightly ajar.

SAFE USE OF PESTICIDES

Never spray insecticides near a flame, furnace, lighted stove, or pilot light.

Keep insecticide sprays away from children, pets, dishes, foods, and cooking utensils.

When fumigating, use only the amount of pesticide required for the job.

Avoid contact with the pesticide and don't inhale its fumes.

Never flush insecticides down the toilet, sewer, or drains.

Never smoke while using pesticide, and wash your hands before handling a cigarette afterward.

As soon as you have used a space spray (bomb), leave the room. Close the room up tightly for at least half an hour, then ventilate.

Do not reuse insecticide containers. Rinse and dispose of them.

Never hang a chemically treated pest strip in a room where people will be present for any length of time, especially the sick, the elderly, or children.

HOME PROTECTION AND SECURITY

Plan to burgle yourself. In this game, you'll discover any weaknesses in your home protection system that may have previously escaped your notice.

Before turning your house key over to a professional housecleaner for several hours, make sure the person is honest and reputable as well as hard-working. Check all references thoroughly by telephone. If the housecleaner is from a firm, call your local Better Business Bureau to check on the firm's reputation. Make sure the firm insures its employees against accidents and theft.

Instead of keeping a spare key in a mailbox, under the doormat, or on a nail behind the garage, wrap the key in foil—or put it in a 35mm film can or a pipe tobacco can—and bury it where you can easily find it if you need it.

If your plans to be away from home have been publicized through a funeral, wedding, or similar newspaper notice, hire a house sitter. Burglars often read the newspapers to see who's planning to be away from home all day or for several days.

Lock up your home, even if you go out only for a short time. Many burglars just walk in through an unlocked door or window.

Your house should appear occupied at all times. Use timers to switch lights and radios on and off when you're not at home.

Ask your neighbors to use your garbage cans when you're on vacation, so your absence won't be so evident.

Safeguard your home by not leaving notes for workmen or family members on the door.

If you're going to be away from home for several days—or even for just one day—adjust your telephone ring to its lowest volume. To a prowler, an unanswered phone is a quick tip that your home is empty.

Let neighbors know of any suspicious-looking person or strange cars you notice lurking about.

To prevent burglars from stealing ladders stored outdoors, padlock them to something that cannot be moved.

To keep your tools from being stolen, paint the handles. Thieves avoid items that are easy to identify.

Trees located near windows, or shrubbery that might shield a burglar from view, ● be major flaws in your home protection plan.

Ask for credentials from any salesman who requests entry to your home—even security system salesmen. Many professional burglars use this cover to check out homes. If you want to buy an electronic alarm system, make your own contacts with reputable firms.

Dogs are among the best deterrents to burglars; even a small, noisy dog can be effective—burglars do not like to have attention drawn to their presence.

Be aware that trained guard dogs do not make good pets. Obedience training and attack training are entirely different, and only the former is appropriate for a house pet.

For the most effective alarm system, conceal all wiring. A burglar looks for places where he can disconnect the security system.

A door with too much space between the door and the frame is an invitation for the burglar to use a jimmy. Reinforce such a door by attaching a panel of three-quarter-inch plywood or a piece of sheet metal to it.

If there are door hinges on the outside of your house, take down the door and reset the hinges inside. Otherwise all a thief has to do to gain entry to your home is knock out the hinge pin.

You can burglar-proof your glass patio doors by setting a pipe or metal bar in the inside bottom track of the door slide. The pipe should be the same length as the track.

It's easy for a burglar to pry his way through rot, so replace rotted door frames with new, solid wood.

It's simple for a thief to break glass panels and then reach in and open a doorknob from the inside. A door with glass panels should be either fortified or replaced.

Locking Up Safely

Protect your windows with one or more good locks, an alarm system, burglar-resistant glass, or many small panes instead of one large area of glass.

When putting window locks on, have all the locks keyed alike and give each family member a key. Keep a key near the window where children can get it (but a burglar can't reach it) in case of fire.

After installing a window lock, drip some solder onto the screw heads. That will stop a burglar from unscrewing the lock after cutting a small hole in the window pane.

It can be a problem to lock an aluminum sliding window in a ventilating position. A locking sliding window bolt allows high security as it foils entry even if the glass is broken.

To help burglar-proof your home, install one-inch throw deadbolt locks on all exterior doors.

A spring-latch lock is easy prey for burglars who are "loiding" experts. Loiding is the method of slipping a plastic credit card against the latch tongue to depress it and unlock the door. A deadbolt defies any such attack. It is only vulnerable when there is enough space between the door and its frame to allow an intruder to use power tools or a hacksaw. But using tools takes time—to the burglar's disadvantage.

Change your lock cylinders from time to time, just in case someone has gotten hold of a set of your keys. If you lose your keys, change the cylinder immediately.

When you move into a new house, it's a good idea to change all the locks and tumblers.

In a rented house, install a double cylinder lock that requires a key to open it from the inside as well as from the outside. If a thief breaks through the panel and reaches in, he still has the lock to deal with instead of just a knob.

Protecting Your Valuables

A chiseled-out space in the top of a door makes a great "safe" for small valuables. Or you might devise a hiding place in a false ceiling.

Fireplace logs can be hollowed out to make hiding places, too. Other ideas include the underside of desktops, linings of drapes, underneath insulation in the attic, inside a lamp. Avoid the obvious places such as mattresses, drawers, inside figurines, behind pictures, and under carpets.

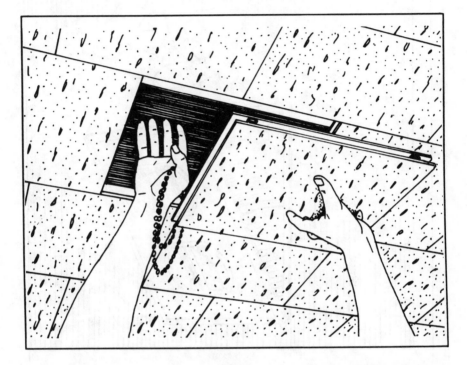

If you don't have a safe, or feel you don't need one, find good hiding places for your valuables in your home. An acoustical tile ceiling offers good hiding possibilities. Remove a tile and restore it afterward with magnetic fasteners or a similar device. However, be careful not to leave finger marks.

Hollow out the leg on a table or chair for hiding small objects. Drill from the bottom, then cap all the legs with rubber tips.

Many police departments offer a free "operation identification" program that includes home inspection, advice on protective measures, and use of an engraving tool to mark a code number that will identify your valuables in case of theft. Call your police department to find out if they offer such a service.

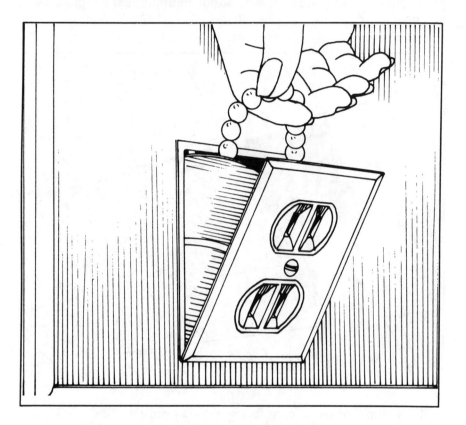

You can keep your jewelry safe by installing a wall-outlet safe. When the safe is closed, it looks just like an electrical outlet. When buying a wall safe, be sure it's fireproof as well as burglarproof.

Garage Security

If you frost or cover your garage windows, burglars won't be able to tell if your car is gone.

Keep your garage door closed and locked even when your car is not in the garage.

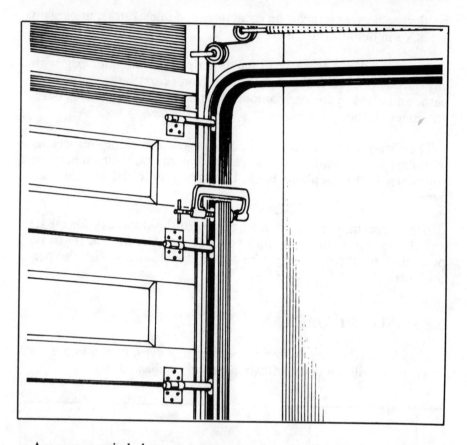

Are you worried about someone entering your house through your attached garage? If the garage door lifts on a track a C-clamp can provide extra security since the door cannot be opened if you tighten the C-clamp on the track next to the roller.

Another way to increase garage security is to install a peephole in the door separating the house from the garage. If you hear suspicious sounds, you can check without opening the door.

PERSONAL PROTECTION AND SECURITY

When shopping, watch for pickpockets in places like the check-out counter where you normally lay down your purse or parcel. Also be alert at store entrances, on escalators and in elevators, in bargain areas, or in demonstration areas.

When shopping, it's best to carry a zippered shoulder bag with any outside pockets facing toward you. Don't carry large amounts of cash, and divide your cash among the purse, your eyeglasses case, and inner clothes pockets.

There's no need to let people know that you live alone—especially if you are a woman. Do not list your full name on your mailbox or your entry in the telephone book. Use only your initial and your last name.

If a salesman or repair person comes to the door, ask for an ID and do not open the door until you have it. Ask for the ID to be pushed under the door. If you're still in doubt, check with the person's office.

KEEPING CHILDREN SAFE

Check all your child's toys to be sure any eyes, noses, knobs, or other parts will not come off when pulled or chewed.

In the bathtub, face your child toward the hot water faucet so he won't accidentally bump into the hot metal.

Don't hold a child on your lap while you drink or pass a hot beverage, or while you smoke.

A youngster at the creeping stage can grab lamp cords and pull lamps from tabletops. You can prevent this by wrapping all light cords tightly around table legs. Cover the wound cords with transparent tape if necessary.

Store all your poisonous materials on high shelves, out of the reach of children. And remember to label the containers.

Even though you keep all poisonous substances out of reach of children, tie a bell around all bottles and containers that hold poisonous materials to alert you to your child getting into something dangerous.

Some Poison Control Centers supply stickers to put on dangerous chemicals so that a child understands that they are harmful. Ask if these are available in your locality.

Never place pillows in an infant's crib, and keep the crib completely away from the cord of a venetian blind.

Never place a plastic bag or thin plastic covering within reach of an infant or small child, or near the child's bed.

Remove the plastic spray nozzle from old aerosol cans when you discard them. You reduce the risk of children finding the cans and spraying chemicals into their own or their playmates' eyes.

Keep home workshop tools disconnected, and lock switches and power supplies so a child can't turn them on.

If there are children in the house, block electrical outlets with plastic plugs.

If the knobs on your range are within your toddler's reach, consider removing them and storing them out of the child's reach when the stove is not in use.

A small child could choke on a large pill, so use liquid medication whenever possible. If a medication is not available in liquid form, mash the tablets and combine with juice or food (unless directed otherwise by your doctor).

If you use a medicine dropper to give your child liquid medicines by mouth, release the liquid slowly into a cheek; be careful not to point the dropper into the throat which might force medicine down the windpipe.

If there are children in the house, set the water heater below 115°F, which is scalding, so that children won't harm themselves if they run hot water.

You'll have a better grip on a soapy baby if you wear a soft cotton glove on one hand.

To prevent a curious toddler from opening kitchen cabinets and drawers, slide a yardstick through the handles of adjacent drawers and cabinets.

If your small child can't remember which is the hot water tap and which is the cold, make it easier by marking the hot tap with red tape.

Line the tub or sink with a towel or diaper before bathing a baby. The child won't slip around so much and will feel more secure.

To prevent a child from accidentally locking himself in the bathroom, make sure the door has no fastening—like an inside bolt—that cannot be opened from the outside. Or remove the lock altogether and instruct everyone in the family to knock when the door's closed.

Similarly, make sure that your child cannot accidentally get locked in a closet or other confined space. Check all knobs and locks in the house and remove any that suggest possible hazards.

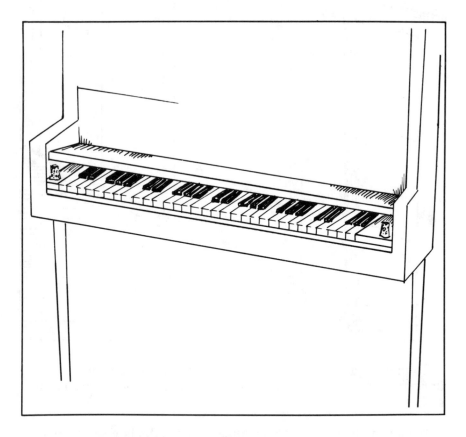

If you have a piano in your home, a toddler could accidentally drop the lid over the keys on his or her fingers. Guard against this by fastening an upright cork at each end of the keyboard.

A child's fingerprints are a sure means of identification and many organizations recommend that parents have children fingerprinted. Some police stations offer this service—they make one set of prints that parents keep. Ask if this service is available in your locality. Do-it-yourself fingerprinting kits are also available.

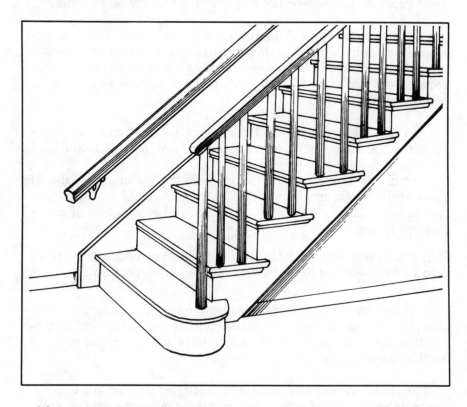

Make it easy for small children to go up and down your stairs. Add a temporary handrail at child-height on the wall opposite the permanent handrail.

Kids love T-shirts, tote bags, buttons and other items with their names on. Such easy identification, however, makes it easier for a stranger to greet a child by name, thus appearing to be a friend. Teach your young child that someone who knows his or her name can still be a stranger to whom "stranger danger" rules apply. To be on the safe side, avoid having your child wear identity-revealing items of clothing.

Although it's not wise to have a child wear clothing that reveals his or her name to strangers, a young child can carry an ID in an inconspicuous place when you take him or her to a zoo, circus, or fair. Attach a stick-on label listing the child's name or phone number inside the child's purse or tote bag, or inside a pocket. Then if a child gets lost, you will be notified over the loudspeaker system.

When you take older children to a large, crowded place, such as a zoo or a ballpark, decide on a prearranged place where you will meet if you get separated accidentally. Agree to go directly to that location at a prearranged time, or if you have failed to meet up after a certain length of time.

For your child's safety when bicycling, make sure he or she carries identification including his or her name, address, and phone number.

A child with a medical condition, diabetes, for instance, should carry at all times identification that includes the child's medical condition, doctor's phone number, and details of medication or emergency treatment.

If you fasten bells out of a child's reach on exterior doors, you'll know when your toddler is headed outdoors unsupervised.

A toddler may find it difficult to walk on a hard surface with his first pair of hard-soled shoes. You can make it easier for him by glueing thin strips of foam rubber to the shoes' soles. Or, put strips of masking tape on the bottoms of his shoes.

If an adult sits next to a restrained toddler while traveling in a car, the child will be happier and the trip will be more pleasant.

The following houseplants are poisonous if swallowed or chewed and should be kept out of the reach of children: Poinsettia, mistletoe, rhubarb, laurel, rhododendron, azalea, cherry boughs, and daphne berries.

Your school-age children should never reveal to callers that they are home alone. Teach them to tell phone callers that you can't come to the phone right now, but if they'll give a number you will call them back. Work out a strategy with your children—and remember that it need not require the child to tell a deliberate lie. Even if you are an adult, there is no need to let strange callers know if you are alone in your house or apartment.

Your children have reached the age where they're too grown-up to go to an after-school babysitter? Make sure they understand that if they come home and find a door or window open or any signs that the home has been disturbed or entered, they should *never* enter. Be sure they know to go straight to the nearest phone and call first the police, then you.

Children old enough to answer the door should be able to see who's there, just as you do. Install a second peephole low enough for youngsters to use.

Saving Energy in the Home

CUTTING HEATING COSTS

To check the efficiency of the heating system in a home you're thinking of buying, change the thermostat setting—raise it if it's cold outside and lower it if it's warm—and then see how fast the room heats up or cools down. It should take no more than half an hour for the home to reach the desired temperature.

Periodically cleaning the squirrel-cage-type blower in a forced-air heating system will improve its efficiency and lower the system's operating cost. A vacuum cleaner hose attachment and a stiff brush are effective cleaning tools for this purpose.

Installing a window greenhouse in one or more of your house's south-facing windows is an unusual (and effective) way to gain extra heat for your home in winter, to reduce the loss of heat to the outdoors in the evening, and, of course, to provide an encouraging environment for plants. Such greenhouses can fill even east or west windows if you install reflectors to catch more of the sun's rays.

Your heating system will operate at peak efficiency only if it's clean, so regular maintenance means savings on fuel bills.

For each degree you set your thermostat above 70°F, you can expect a 3 percent rise in energy costs. For most people, a 65°F daytime setting and a 55°F nighttime setting is acceptable.

Exercise caution in setting low indoor thermostat temperatures. Older people may require temperatures above 65°F to protect them from hypothermia, a possibly fatal drop in body temperature. People with circulatory problems or those taking certain types of drugs may also be vulnerable. In such instances, ask your doctor about recommended winter and summer thermostat settings.

Reduce the thermostat setting before you go to bed at night; cutting back for several hours will measurably decrease fuel consumption.

To avoid having a thermostat turn the heat on or off when it's not necessary, make sure it doesn't misinterpret the true warmth of your home. This can happen if the thermostat is positioned in a drafty area, placed on a cold outside wall or near a fireplace, or installed too near a heat-producing appliance such as a TV set or a lamp.

Take advantage of the fact that a large group of people generates heat—reduce the thermostat setting when you're entertaining a crowd.

It takes less energy to run a thermostatically controlled electric blanket than it does to maintain daytime thermostat settings throughout the sleeping hours.

Next time a banging radiator is driving you crazy, make a quick check with a level. The radiator should slope down on one side, toward the pipes and the boiler. If it doesn't, you can stop the banging by propping up the outside legs.

Turn the thermostat to its lowest setting if you won't be at home for a few days. You can turn off the heating system completely if there's no danger of pipes freezing while you're away.

A portable hair dryer can be helpful in checking where doors or windows need additional weather stripping. Move the air stream along the interface between a door and its frame or a sash and its frame. Have someone on the other side of the door or window follow the dryer's movements with his or her hands. Where heat is felt leaking through, you need a patch job.

Walk around the house with a candle on a cold windy day to see where cold may be entering around doors and windows.

To maintain your home's temperature, latch the windows—instead of merely closing them—for a tighter seal.

During winter months, cooking foods slowly in the oven at low temperatures will provide extra heat to help warm the house.

Hot bath water will help keep your bathroom warm in cold weather months if you leave it to cool before draining the tub. The water will also add humidity to contribute to the comfort of your home.

When caulking several joints, start with the smallest joint and recut the tube's nozzle as necessary for successively larger joints.

Loose-fitting windows can lose heat up to five times faster than windows that fit properly. To check a window for air leaks, feel around the edges for air movement on a windy day. Or light a candle or match and move it around the edges; if the flame flickers, heat is being lost and weather stripping is needed. Weather stripping is also needed if ice or condensation builds up on a storm window; this is a clue that air is seeping around the interior window.

A room will stay warmer in cold weather if curtains fit tightly against the window's frame so that warm room air doesn't move across the cold window surface. A fixed valance at the top and sides of the curtains will help, and so will weighting or fastening the curtains at the bottom.

If you plan to install new shades or blinds to help keep your home warm, consider mounting them outside the frames. If they're installed inside window frames air can leak along the edges, but outside mountings help reduce the flow of cold air.

A simple strategy like keeping your windows sparkling clean in winter can help warm your home. Spotless window glass lets in more sunlight than grimy panes.

It's best to remove window screens before winter arrives because fine-mesh screen can reduce by up to 20 percent the amount of warming sunlight entering your home.

Because a great deal of heat is conducted through large, overhead garage doors, a significant amount of heat can escape from a home that has an attached garage but no insulation between the house and the garage. An insulated and weather-stripped garage door, therefore, can save you money, even if the garage is unheated.

If your garage is incorporated into your house and has living space above it, insulate the garage ceiling to reduce the flow of cold air into the living areas.

Acoustic tiles or foam panels on an upstairs ceiling will add insulation; consider this as an alternative to repainting.

A build-up of frost or moisture on the inside of storm windows indicates that damp air is leaking into the space between the two windows. To correct this problem, weather-strip the cracks.

Save on heating costs and stay comfortable in cold weather by dressing to retain body heat. Layer your clothing: wear lightweight basic garments, such as a shirt or blouse or short-sleeved sweater, covered by heavier garments, such as a sweater vest, and topped with a warm jacket or sweater jacket. If you become too warm you can adjust your own body thermostat by taking off a layer.

Many types of weatherstripping must be installed with nails. You can use any type of hammer, but a magnetic tack hammer works best for driving small brads in cramped areas.

To speed the installation of weatherstripping, try stapling instead of nailing it.

Keeping your home well caulked is one of the best ways to save energy. When you caulk, make sure joints are thoroughly dry—you can dry deep crevices with a cloth stretched over the blade of a putty knife, or with a blast of hot air from a hair dryer.

Radiator reflectors—insulation boards with aluminum or another shiny material on one side—reflect the available heat back into the room. Make your own by covering one side of cut-to-size insulation board with aluminum foil (shiny side out) or some other shiny material, and fastening the board to the wall behind the radiator. Be sure that the reflector doesn't touch the radiator—if it does it will send heat into the wall behind it instead of into the room.

Make a low-cost draft guard to lay across the bottom of your door. Sew together the sides and one end of a four- to five-inch strip of fabric (recycle an old sheet or skirt), and fill it with sand. Sew the open end. The draft guard should be a few inches longer than the bottom of the door.

Make a simple draft detector by clipping a piece of tissue or lightweight plastic to a coat hanger, and hang it in front of a suspected leak. The movement of the paper will indicate the location of the leak.

Woodburning Stoves

When installing a woodburning stove, select a brand made of steel or cast iron for safety. Be sure that the stove carries a label indicating that it's been tested for reliability.

When purchasing a used stove, carefully check the condition of the hinges, grates, and draft louvers, and the sturdiness of the legs. Reject any stove with cracks.

A stove should be installed only over a fireproof material such as brick or stone, or an asbestos plate covered with metal made especially for the purpose.

Have the elbows, joints, flue, and chimney of a stovepipe thoroughly cleaned once a year.

Keep easily flammable materials such as newspapers and magazines, wooden furniture, and firewood logs at a safe distance from your stove.

Before operating a newly installed stove, read the instruction manual for safety tips, or contact your local fire department for safety specifications on the stovepipe and flue.

Never use lighter fluid or other flammable liquids to start a fire. Place kindling wood and crumpled pieces of newspaper under your logs to help fan the flames.

The only material suitable for burning in a wood stove is dry, seasoned firewood.

Fireplaces

Empty cardboard milk cartons make wonderful kindling for fires. So do candle stubs.

When burning fireplace logs, sprinkle salt on them periodically. You can reduce soot by two thirds by doing this.

To make newspaper logs, coat a three-foot dowel, or a section of broomstick, with paste wax. When the wax dries, buff it to a smooth finish. Place a newspaper on a large flat surface; hold the dowel firmly at each end, and roll sheets of paper onto the dowel as tightly as you can. (Tightly rolled logs burn much longer than loosely rolled ones.) Continue to roll paper onto the dowel until the roll is three to three-and-a-half inches in diameter. Carefully holding the paper in place, fasten the log firmly at each end and in the center with thin wire. Slide the dowel out of the roll, and repeat to make as many logs as needed. Two to three thick newspaper sections make one log.

Add a curved-tube convection heater to your fireplace to draw more heat from the fire into the room, instead of letting it escape up the flue.

A curved-tube heater that has a blower unit can double the amount of heat thrown into a room from your fireplace. Be sure to select one that's big enough to fill the opening.

When you're not using the fireplace, be sure you're not losing heated air through the chimney; remember to keep the damper in the fireplace closed except when a fire is burning.

A fireplace draws air from the house to keep the fire going, so if your furnace is operating and warming up the air while the fireplace is going, the net effect is that you're paying to heat air that is going right up the chimney. The best way to correct this problem is to install an outside air vent directly in front of the fireplace. The fireplace will then operate on outside air instead of on your heated air. It's also a good idea to close the doors to the room where the fireplace is being used.

CUTTING COOLING COSTS

Solar reflective films applied over your windows in warm-weather months will reduce the amount of light and, therefore, of heat that enters your home.

Since cold air falls, you'll get better air circulation from a room air conditioner if you aim its vents upward.

If you have a forced air heating system but use window air conditioning units, be sure to close the heating system vents so cold air doesn't escape through the ducts and fall to the basement.

To keep air conditioning to a minimum, be sure you're not over-heating your home needlessly. Draw your draperies against direct sunlight, and switch off lighting fixtures when you're not in the room. If you have the facilities, consider barbecuing outdoors so that you can keep the kitchen cool.

If you install your air conditioner thermostat away from heat-producing appliances and direct sunlight, it won't "think" the room is warmer than it really is and work overtime. Also, place any outdoor portions of your unit or a central unit where they'll receive the least direct sunlight.

Using a patio cover will reduce the load your air conditioning unit bears in the summertime. The cover shields the concrete from sunlight that would otherwise reflect and radiate into your home. Conversely, removing the cover in winter months lets you take advantage of the heat generated by reflected sunlight.

Keep furnishings away from air conditioning vents so that the cold air can circulate freely.

Save on energy costs by turning off your air conditioning unit when you leave home. If you're gone every day, install a timer control to keep the unit off until shortly before you return in the evening. (You can manually override the timer when you're at home.)

Awnings and canopies can keep your home cooler in the summertime.

Odors emitted by a central air conditioner usually indicate condensate drain fungus. You can eliminate the smell by pouring laundry bleach into the condensate pan to kill the fungus.

Ceiling Fans

With an old-fashioned ceiling fan, avoid using a light dimmer switch as a variable speed control. A light dimmer switch can't handle the electrical load involved. Use only a speed control and lighting fixture outlet designed for your specific brand of fan.

Don't install an old-fashioned ceiling fan too close to curtains; the blades could rip them away from the window.

Never install an old-fashioned ceiling fan on a ceiling that's less than eight feet high, since the blades twirl about a foot lower. If the ceiling is too low, the blades are close enough to head level to be dangerous.

ENERGY-EFFICIENT USE OF APPLIANCES

Laundry Appliances

About 95 percent of the energy used by a washing machine goes into heating the water. A machine with a cold rinse cycle will save some of that energy and cost you less to operate.

You'll use less electricity when running your washing machine if you select the shortest cycle and the coldest water temperature appropriate for the type of fabric being washed.

Using the correct amount of detergent in your washing machine actually saves energy. Too much detergent causes oversudsing, which can put strain on the machine.

Because some fabrics require less drying time than others, try to run loads of similar fabrics in your clothes dryer.

Save energy by drying clothes in consecutive loads; the dryer retains heat from one load to the next.

The Refrigerator and Freezer

Position a refrigerator where there's plenty of air circulation. A refrigerator uses more energy when located near a stove or a heating vent.

To lengthen the life of your refrigerator and increase the unit's efficiency, periodically vacuum the dust that collects on the coils at the back of the refrigerator.

Make sure your refrigerator is standing on the level; if it isn't, it may be working harder than necessary.

Your refrigerator or freezer has to work extra hard to maintain the correct cold level if it is heavily frosted. Defrost when the frost is no more than a quarter-inch thick.

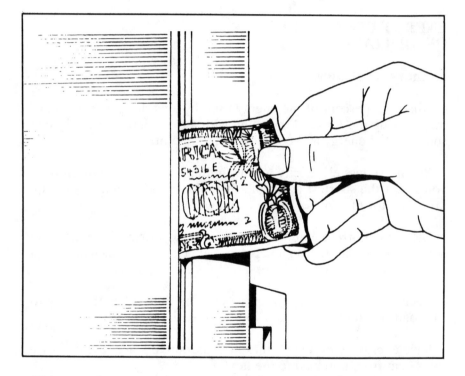

If you notice water standing in the bottom of your refrigerator, there may be an air leak around the door. To test the gasket, close the door on a dollar bill. If the bill pulls out easily, the gasket needs replacing.

A good way to keep your freezer from expending too much energy is to put it at the lowest setting that keeps ice cream firm. If your ice cream is rock-hard, the setting is unnecessarily high.

Going away for the weekend? Turn the cold control on the refrigerator down to the lowest point short of defrost before you go.

Your freezer should be kept as full as possible for most energy-efficient operation. If you don't have enough food packages to fill the freezer space, use extra bags of ice.

Don't put uncovered liquids in the refrigerator. They will add to the humidity and make the compressor work harder. Always cover liquids for refrigerator storage.

Take large items for defrosting from the freezer and let them defrost in the refrigerator overnight. They will help cool the refrigerator as they defrost, thus cutting down on the refrigerator's energy use.

Don't defeat your refrigerator by putting hot, just-cooked food into it. Allow foods to cool to room temperature before storing them in the refrigerator or freezer. (But don't let cooked foods stand too long before refrigerating.)

To conserve refrigerator and/or freezer energy by minimizing loss of cold air, plan ahead and put in or take out as many items as possible each time you open the unit.

The Range

Whenever practical, use small cooking appliances, such as an electric frying pan or toaster oven, instead of your range. These small units are energy-efficient and throw less heat into your kitchen.

To conserve energy when using the stovetop units on an electric range, turn off burners a short time before cooking is complete. With electric burners, the cooking process often continues for as long as five minutes after the burner is turned off.

You'll use less energy when cooking if you cook with as little water as possible; small amounts heat more quickly.

Another energy-saving tip: Put a lid on the pan you're using because water boils faster when covered.

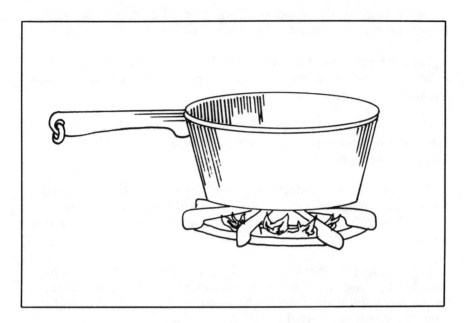

Sensible use of pots and pans can save energy when you use your range. Fit the pot or pan to the burner; a small pot or pan on a large element wastes heat, and a large pot on a small element is inefficient.

To save on heat costs, don't turn on an element or burner until the pot or pan is on the stove. If you're going to simmer, turn down the heat as soon as the liquid reaches the boiling stage. Adjust the setting to just keep the contents boiling; a higher setting wastes energy.

Copper and stainless steel cookware usually require lower heat settings than aluminum cookware.

It's important to keep pan bottoms clean because a layer of soot decreases heating efficiency on any type of stove. Shiny pans are particularly efficient on an electric range.

Since a great deal of heat escapes each time you open the oven to examine what's cooking, you can conserve energy by minimizing the number of times you peek at the food inside. (During the summer, heat that escapes when you open the oven also puts extra strain on your air conditioner.)

To save energy when using your oven, don't preheat it unless required. If you must preheat, put the food in as soon as the oven reaches the desired temperature.

Cook as many items as possible at one time to save energy. If you have a double oven, use the smaller one whenever possible.

Try cooking food items in the oven-usable paperboard containers in which they're packaged. You'll save from 10 to 20 percent of the oven energy normally required. The containers withstand temperatures up to 400°F. Don't, however, try to reuse them.

A self-cleaning oven will use less energy if you start the cleaning cycle right after cooking, when the oven will already be on its way to the high temperature needed for cleaning.

Dirty reflectors under the heating elements on your electric range are both unsightly and wasteful of energy. Reduce fuel costs by keeping the reflectors clean.

Other Appliances

You'll waste energy by running a partial load in the dishwasher. Wait until you have a full load. Turn off the drying cycle and allow the dishes to air dry for further energy savings.

Locating your dishwasher near your water heater is one way to reduce heat loss, because shorter water lines lose less heat than longer ones.

Color television sets use almost twice as much electricity as black-and-white sets. If you have both, it will cost less to watch a black-and-white movie on a black-and-white set.

If you want a mini-TV that's truly portable, make sure it operates on both AC or DC current. However, if you don't plan to use it outdoors, consider getting a larger set, with a larger screen, that operates on household current only. Though still portable, it'll cost less than a true mini.

Before you buy any TV set, study the picture it produces under lighting conditions similar to those of the room in which you'll watch at home. If you're not satisfied with the picture, look at other sets.

ENERGY-EFFICIENT HOME LIGHTING

To save energy, convert incandescent fixtures to fluorescent wherever practical. Fluorescent tubes illuminate more efficiently than incandescent bulbs.

To make sure that bulbs in remote places (attic, basement, garage, or closets, for example), aren't left burning, install automatic switches that shut off the lights in a room when the door is closed.

Another way to monitor lights in remote areas of the house is to install a switch with a red pilot indicator. When the red light glows, you'll know lights in the basement, garage, etc. have inadvertently been left on. These remote switches are available from hardware stores.

Three-way bulbs, like dimmers, let you adjust lighting intensity to your needs and can save electrical energy. If a fixture won't take a three-way bulb, reduce the size (wattage) if you need the bulb only for general light.

If you install bright security lights, consider controlling them with a photoelectric cell or timer that turns the lights on at dusk and off at dawn; this means you can avoid burning the lights unnecessarily.

It is important that light fixtures be kept clean, because a dusty or dirty light fixture will absorb light, decreasing the amount of illumination reaching areas where it's needed. A dirty fixture may therefore prompt family members to turn on additional lights that shouldn't be necessary.

White or light-colored lamp shades capitalize on the light produced by lamp bulbs. With such shades, a lower-wattage bulb can produce the same amount of light as a higher-wattage bulb screened with a dark-colored shade.

Getting rid of a decorative outdoor gas lamp can save you money in energy costs. However, if you need outdoor light for visibility or security, consider converting a gas lamp to electricity. This will reduce energy consumption considerably, especially if the lamp is turned on only when necessary.

To save energy, use one large bulb rather than several smaller ones. It requires six 25-watt bulbs to produce the light of a single 100-watt bulb.

If you turn a three-way bulb to the lowest level while watching television you'll both save energy and reduce glare in the room.

Fifty-watt reflector floodlights are recommended for directional lamps such as pole or spot lamps. They require half the wattage of standard 100-watt bulbs, yet provide nearly the same amount of illumination.

The smallest diameter recommended for a lamp shade is 16 inches. Anything smaller will waste electricity by not diffusing enough light to be functional.

In high-intensity portable lamps, you can substitute 25-watt reflector bulbs for the 40-watt bulbs normally used; you'll get approximately the same illumination while consuming less energy.

ENERGY-EFFICIENT WATER USE

Increase the efficiency of your water heater by spreading the family's baths, dishwashing, and laundry throughout the day. Also consider showering rather than tub bathing because a short shower consumes four to eight gallons of hot water, while a bath uses 20 gallons or more.

Another way to make your water heater still more efficient is to use cold rather than hot water for washing clothes. Many fabrics and detergents are designed for cold-water washing.

If your water heater is warm to the touch, it is not well insulated and is wasting energy. Wrap insulation around the tank to solve the problem.

A moderate temperature setting further increases a water heater's efficiency. (It is also safer for children and elderly or infirm people to keep the temperature setting below the scalding point of water.)

If you have a swimming pool, economize on your water bills by filling your swimming pool with rain water. Attach an elbow connection to the gutter spout on your house and run a pipe from the elbow connection to your pool.

To prevent water from cooling as it travels to your plumbing fixtures, wrap hot water pipes with insulating material.

Sediment buildup can slow your water heater's recovery rate. If you notice a marked drop in recovery time, drain the sediment from the tank.

To prevent sediment from building up in your water heater, drain the heater periodically. Perform this maintenance step early in the morning, before anyone has used hot water and disturbed the water in the tank.

If you have an electric water heater, check with the power company about obtaining an off-peak meter. An off-peak meter allows your heater to operate at times when the company has power to spare, and you may be able to buy electricity at a lower rate.

You can further conserve energy by turning off your water heater if you plan to be away for a few days.

Hot water can cool very quickly as it makes the long trip from the basement to a second-floor bathroom. Consider locating a water heater centrally, perhaps in a small closet in the kitchen. It's also important to have the water heater in a place as warm as is practical. The warmer the environment, the less the water has to be heated.

Gardening, Indoors and Outdoors

CARING FOR INDOOR PLANTS

If you love indoor plants but don't want to invest a lot of time and effort in taking care of them, select large, mature, well-established plants. They usually need less attention than young plants that are just getting started.

To cut down on the time you spend on your indoor garden, choose plants that have more or less the same water, light, and temperature requirements. Pot them in the same mix in containers of the same type and size. Then all you will have to do is give them all the same amount of light and water.

If children or pets keep knocking your plants over, try double-potting. Put the plant and its original pot inside another, larger pot with rocks or gravel between the two. This will add both size and weight and should stabilize the plant.

Cats are territorial animals, so don't position a plant in the cat's favorite place in the sun. Also, if your dog likes to people-watch through the window, leave that spot free.

Here's a novel but effective way to grow parsley indoors: Slice sponges in half and sprinkle them with parsley seeds. Arrange the sponges on dishes in a sunny location, keep them moist, and watch your parsley grow.

To speed up seed germination, place seed trays on top of your refrigerator, where the 72° to 75°F heat emitted will promote steady growth.

Repot plants only when needed. Spring is the best time because it favors new growth.

If you have plants that need to be brought in and potted for the winter, line the pots with plastic. Leave some excess plastic over the edge of the pot, and punch a couple of holes in the bottom for drainage. In spring, when it's time for transplanting, lift the soil and the plant out of the pot by the plastic.

All plants need adequate light if they are to grow properly. Here's a way to test how much light your plants will get in a given location: Place a sheet of paper where you want to put a plant, and hold your hand a foot above the paper. If your hand casts a sharp, well-defined shadow, you have bright light. If the shadow is fuzzy but recognizable, you have filtered light. If all you get is a blur on the paper, your light condition is shady and you will have to choose your plants carefully or consider supplementing the available light.

Sharp white stones laid over the top of the soil in the pots will discourage the cat from sitting on your plants. So will chicken wire or hardware cloth fitted over the top of the pot and around the plant.

Cats like to nibble on houseplants, but may be deterred if offered a plant of their own, such as a box planted with grass. Sod is preferable to grass planted from seed. The cat will probably use the box for other purposes before the seed gets a chance to sprout.

To a certain extent, plants move toward light by themselves (this turning toward the light is called phototropism). You can keep a plant standing straight by turning the pot a quarter of the way around every once in a while.

If your houseplants seem to be suffering from lack of light, wash the windows. Dirty windows can cut down on light transmittal by as much as 40 percent.

Humidity for plants can be increased in several ways. Group the plants closer together. Put a layer of pebbles or perlite in a metal or plastic pan, place the pots on the pebbles, and keep the water in the pan just below the bottoms of the pots. Or increase the amount of moisture in the air by using misters or foggers.

Water that has been sitting for some time is best for watering plants. It will have reached room temperature (some plants dislike cold water) and a lot of the chlorine will have evaporated.

Plants don't like softened water. If you have an ion exchange water softener, get your plant water from the tap before it goes into the softener.

Sand or perlite added to your plant mix will improve drainage. Or enlarge the hole in the bottom of the pot or use more crocking (broken clay pots).

Self-watering pots and plant waterers that work by means of wicks, gravity, or capillary action should be used only with plants that prefer to be evenly moist or wet. Some of these devices do a beautiful job on water-loving plants, but they are not satisfactory for plants that like to dry out between waterings.

A dried-out houseplant can be revived by sinking the pot in tepid water until the air bubbles come out. Next time, remember to water *before* the soil shrinks away from the edge of the pot—that means the root ball has dried out.

There's nothing you can do to save an over-watered plant that has rotted. However, you can clip still-healthy leaves or stems and root them to start new plants.

Increase light reflection by using aluminum foil or sharp white rocks on top of the soil in the pots.

Mist plants early in the day so that the moisture will evaporate by afternoon. This lessens the chance of water collecting on the leaves and spreading disease, or getting trapped in the center of the plant and causing rot.

If you keep houseplants near a window, protect them in very cold weather by covering the window with a thin sheet of plastic.

Do something special for your plants. Feed them dried blood (high in potassium), ground up eggshells (which contain calcium and some nitrogen), or a diced banana skin (high in potassium). Work these substances into the soil.

Cigar and cigarette ash is as bad for plants as smoking is for people. So don't let guests stub out their cigarettes in your plant pots.

Houseplants that like to be evenly moist will survive your absence for a couple of weeks if you water them well and put them on a tray of wet gravel inside a large, clear-plastic dry cleaning bag (a terrarium tent).

Before going away on a trip, put water in the bathtub and set your large plants on top of bricks; the bricks should be placed on end with the tops just out of the water. Cover the plants and tub with a sheet of clear plastic, and set your bathroom light on a timer to give 12 hours of light a day.

As an alternative, when you go on vacation, set all your houseplants on old towels folded in a few inches of water in the bathtub. The plants will absorb the water as they need it.

Succulents (such as cacti) will survive your absence if you water them well and move them out of direct light before you leave.

Unflavored gelatin dissolved in water is a good, nitrogen-rich plant food. Use one envelope of gelatin to a quart of liquid, and water the plants with this mixture (freshly made) once a month.

You can make a potting soil that is suitable for most houseplants by mixing together four cups of black soil or potting soil; four cups of leaf mold, peat moss, or spaghnum moss; four cups of coarse sand; two to four cups of activated charcoal; and one tablespoon of steamed bone meal. This mix should be "cooked" in the oven at 200°F for 30 minutes before use. (It will smell awful, but your plants will love it.)

To make your own potting soil for plants with very fine roots, decrease the black soil and sand in the previous recipe to three cups each, and increase the peat or spaghnum moss to six cups.

To make your own potting soil for cacti, decrease the black soil and leaf mold or moss to two cups each, and increase the sand to six cups.

When reusing old pots, free them of pests or disease by this method: Wash them in hot water and then soak overnight in a solution of one part chlorine bleach to eight parts water. Rinse well next day.

Give newly potted plants a little less light for the first few days.

Tin tops from cans can be used to provide drainage in plant pots. Bend them slightly so that they cover the hole with the concave side down, leaving plenty of room for excess water to drain out.

If you have to transport your plants from one location to another, here's a sure way to prevent the soil from spilling. Crumple dry newspaper into balls and pack it around the base of the plant on top of the soil. Lay strips of masking tape over the top of the balls of paper and stick them onto the sides of the pot. This creates a "tape net" to keep the paper and soil in place.

Cool the water in which you've cooked spaghetti or potatoes and use it to water your plants. The starch is good for them.

After you boil eggs, use the cooled water on your houseplants. It is packed with growth-stimulating minerals.

Water from an aquarium is perfect for fertilizing houseplants, as is water in which fish has been frozen.

You can "water" a terrarium simply by patting the inside of the glass with a wet paper towel.

An ordinary basting syringe is also useful for watering a terrarium.

If you're not sure whether a houseplant needs watering or not, poke your index finger an inch into the topsoil. If the soil there is moist, don't water. If it's dry, do.

Plants originating in deserts and dry areas like to be drenched and then permitted to dry out. Do this by soaking the plant in its pot in a bucket or sink filled with tepid water until no more air bubbles emerge. Remove the pot from the water and let it dry out before drenching again.

Put a gloss on the leaves of your houseplants by swabbing them with a soft cloth dipped in glycerin. Unlike other gloss-producing substances, glycerin won't collect dust.

One of the quickest ways to clean the leaves of a houseplant is with a feather duster.

Container gardening lets you garden even if you don't have a garden—and gives you extra space if you do. Items that can be recycled into planting containers include tin cans, old washtubs, plastic bottles, old tires, sewer pipes, plastic bags, wire screens, the kids' outgrown little red wagon, and all sorts of other household discards.

Use an egg carton for a seedling nursery. Place half an eggshell in each compartment, then fill with loam and your plant seed. When the seedlings are ready to be transplanted, plant the shell and the plant. The eggshell will decompose and enrich the soil. Egg cartons only work, however, for small-rooted seedlings; fast-growing young plants like tomatoes need more space.

You can unwittingly bring bugs into a house by taking houseplants outside for extra sun and then returning them to their places indoors. If you take plants outdoors, keep them isolated from other houseplants for three or four weeks after you bring them back into the house. If you detect bugs on the plants, wipe the stems and leaves with a mild soap-and-water solution.

If you pinch new shoots at the growing points, you'll encourage branching, which produces more growth for flowering.

If you suspect that one of your houseplants has a pest problem, attach a pest strip, then cover the plant for a few days with a plastic bag. By the time you remove the bag, the plant should have perked up.

In order not to dislodge newly planted seeds, place the containers in a shallow dish of water so that moisture can be absorbed from underneath.

Water bulb houseplants from the bottom also. Fill a pie pan with water and let the plants sit in it for a while.

Use a mister to water delicate seedlings.

Any container used as a plant pot must have drainage holes. If you're recycling a container such as a yogurt cup or margarine tub, make holes in the bottom and stand the pot on a saucer.

Use pieces of Styrofoam for a lightweight drainage layer in the bottom of a hanging planter.

Slip shower caps over the bottoms of hanging planters to catch the overflow when watering. The caps can be removed after an hour or so.

Handle prickly cactus plants with ice tongs to protect your fingers.

If your dish garden contains any cactus, place a newspaper strip around the cactus to protect your fingers while transplanting.

If you favor high-tech decor, use plastic wastebaskets instead of expensive planters for your indoor greenery. Wastebaskets are usually available in whatever colors are currently favored by the interior design business, and they're so cheap that you won't mind switching if fashions—or your tastes—change.

Place a spider plant in a room where someone smokes frequently, because your friendly spider plant does more for you than add a touch of green to your home—it also helps clean your air. Within 24 hours your spider plants will clear your air of carbon monoxide from tobacco smoking or unvented kerosene heaters. The spider plant also helps remove the vapors of formaldehyde, a suspected carcinogen released by many building products and home furnishings. Researchers have found that 8 to 15 spider plants (the typical hanging basket or six-inch pot size) will purify the air in an average-size insulated apartment or home.

Other plants which lower pollution levels in your home are the Chinese evergreen, which looks somewhat like a philodendron, the peace lily, and plants of the peperomia family. However, these don't do quite such a good job of air cleaning as the spider plant.

Treat an ailing houseplant by dribbling a tablespoon of castor oil on the soil in the pot; then water thoroughly.

A plant will live longer if you don't let it go to seed. Cut blossoms off when they begin to fade.

If you think that worms in the soil of your potted plants may be eating away at the roots, place a slice of raw potato on the surface soil in each pot. The worms will crawl out to get at the potatoes, and you can capture and destroy them.

If you have the space, you can grow vegetables indoors in artificial light. Lettuce does especially well when grown under fluorescent plant lights. Plant your lettuce garden in the basement, the attic, or anywhere the temperature stays between 65°F and 70°F during the day and drops about ten degrees at night.

Old sponges cut into squares are great for covering drainage holes in flowerpots.

You can make hanging mini-planters from egg-shaped panty hose containers. Puncture holes in the sides and insert string for hanging.

Use a knitting needle to test whether or not your houseplants need water. If the needle inserted into the soil comes out dry, water the plant.

During cold-weather months, a room filled with houseplants will benefit from the moisture provided by a portable vaporizer.

A freestanding stepladder makes a good display stand for plants.

If you have opened bottles of club soda left after a party, feed the contents to your houseplants or outdoor plants. Flat soda is beneficial to green, growing things.

Water ferns periodically with tea, or mix wet tea leaves into the potting soil.

Most plants benefit from pinching, but palms are an exception. It's fatal to pinch back palms.

Cracked walnut shells, marbles, stones, or fruit pits can be used to provide drainage at the bottom of a houseplant pot.

When you water a houseplant, water it slowly and thoroughly until the water runs out of the bottom of the pot. If you have the plant in a saucer, empty the saucer after the plant finishes draining.

Chlorine in water can give houseplants brown tips. To avoid this, let tap water stand for a full day to let the chlorine evaporate; then water your plants.

Plant a garlic clove beside a houseplant to keep all types of pests away.

It's hard work rotating a big, heavy planter so that the plant gets sun all around, but you can simplify the task by sitting the pot on a lazy Susan.

YOUR OUTDOOR GARDEN

Try to position your tall-growing plants on the north and northeast side of your garden so that they won't overshadow other plants.

When you're planting a vegetable garden in the city or on a small lot, try to avoid setting your plants in the shade of buildings and large trees. Besides blocking sun from your garden bed, trees will also compete for the available soil nutrients and moisture—remember that a tree's root system can reach beyond the span of its branches.

When cultivating the soil in your garden, remember that good soil is slightly lumpy. If you work it until it's too fine, it will pack hard when it rains or blow away in a strong wind.

To find out what kind of soil you have in your yard, try this do-it-yourself texture test: Take a small handful of moist garden soil and hold some of it between your thumb and the first knuckle of your forefinger. Gradually squeeze the soil out with your thumb to form a ribbon. If you can form a ribbon that stays together for more than one inch, you have a heavy clay soil. If a ribbon forms but holds together for about three quarters of an inch to one inch, you have a silty clay loam. If the ribbon breaks into shorter pieces, the soil is silty. If a ribbon doesn't form at all, the soil is sandy.

Start a compost pile in fall with dried leaves from the yard. Keep vegetable and fruit peelings, eggshells, tea and coffee grounds, etc. in a plastic bag and empty them onto the pile when the bag is full. All add valuable organic matter to your garden soil. Kick more leaves over the scraps.

Never start a compost pile when there is the danger of attracting rats, and never put meat scraps or bones in the compost pile.

When planning your garden, remember that vegetables grown for their fruits—tomatoes, peppers, eggplants, for example—need a minimum of six to eight hours of direct light a day. If they don't get enough light they may produce a leafy green plant but little or no fruit. Crops that are grown for their leaves and roots will produce satisfactory crops in light shade.

Work the soil well before planting root crops. If they have to negotiate lumps, stones, or other obstructions, vegetables such as carrots and parsnips will grow forked or distorted instead of straight.

Save garden space by companion planting—for instance, plant fast-growing lettuce between your tomato seedlings. By the time the tomatoes need the space the lettuce will have been harvested.

Extend your gardening season with a cold frame that uses solar heat to warm your plants.

Keep seed packets in the refrigerator or some other cool place till you're ready to plant the seeds. The refrigerator is also the best place to store leftover seeds. Put them in a glass jar with a bit of silica gel and screw the cap on the jar tightly.

Buy a watering can that's short enough to fit under both the kitchen tap and the outside faucet so that you can fill it easily without a lot of twisting and maneuvering.

Water gently, because a sharp jet of water can wash away the soil and expose the roots. A sock tied over the nozzle of the hose effectively breaks the force of the water.

In a small garden, save space by growing cucumbers upright on a fence or trellis.

Plastic jugs (milk jugs, for instance) with the bottoms removed make good insulators to protect young transplants from cold night temperatures. Two-pound coffee cans with both ends removed also work well.

Don't know what sort of fertilizer to feed your plants? Remember that phosphorus encourages root growth and fruit production; nitrogen is necessary for leafy growth; and potassium promotes root growth and disease resistance. A complete, well-balanced fertilizer contains these ingredients in fairly equal proportions. Apply fertilizer at the rate of about one pound per 100 square feet, or ten pounds per 1000 square feet.

To make sure you plant your seeds in straight rows, make a simple planting guide from two stakes with a string stretched between them. Or use the handle of your rake to make a trench in which to plant the seeds.

If you're short on garden space, try growing corn in an old washtub.

Seeds won't germinate if they're planted too deeply. Follow this guide: Small seeds should be planted one-quarter to one-half inch deep; medium seeds a half to one inch deep; and large seeds one to one and a half inches deep. Very tiny seeds can just be pressed into the soil.

Lots of beginning gardeners hate to thin plants because of the "waste." But unless plants are thinned you'll get a poor crop because individual seedlings will be fighting each other for space, moisture, and soil nutrients. Always thin as directed on the seed packet.

Never transplant seedlings directly from indoors into the garden. They must be hardened off by being exposed gradually to outdoor conditions: Put the containers outside during the day and bring them in again at night for a couple of weeks before setting the seedlings out in their permanent location in the garden.

You can grow many small vegetable varieties successfully in hanging baskets. Cherry tomatoes look delightful in a hanging basket.

Plant sweet-scented flowers—stocks or lavender, for example—under your windows; they will perfume the house.

Never use grass clippings from a lawn that has been recently treated with a herbicide as mulch or compost on your garden.

If the weather becomes very hot before your transplanted seedlings have had time to become accustomed to garden conditions, provide shelter by propping a board so that it will shade the young plants.

If you garden in containers or raised beds, remember that your plants will dry out faster than those in a regular garden bed and will need more frequent watering.

Each year, keep a notebook in which you record your garden's progress. Note dates of plantings and fertilizings, which plants did well or not so well, harvest dates, and problems with weeds, bugs, or lack of rain. You'll have a useful gardening guide to refer to next season.

When you're watering your plants, try to avoid getting water on the leaves, which can spread disease.

Peas don't like hot weather; harvest them before the summer heat gets too intense.

When buying tomato plants for the garden, look for plants that are short, stocky, and bright green in color. Be sure not to plant your tomatoes until the soil is warm and the danger of frost has passed.

If your tomato seedlings are too "leggy" plant them deeper and on a slant, so that the plants don't get top heavy.

To protect your corn crop from birds, tie paper bags over the ears.

Grow rosemary and bay in clay pots buried just beneath the surface of the soil in your garden. This makes it easier to move them indoors when the weather gets cold; they're temperature-sensitive and may not survive winter conditions outdoors.

Certain herbs spread so fast outdoors that they'll take over the garden unless you control them. For example, wild marjoram, tarragon, and mint are perennials that flare out in all directions from season to season. You can restrict them with a sunken section of stovepipe that confines their roots; a large coffee can with both ends removed works well, too.

Herbs can be frozen, dried, or stored in oil or vinegar. Cut them just before they flower, when their oils are most abundant. The best time to cut herbs for storage is at mid morning on a sunny day.

For a garden that's relatively pest-free in the spring, scrupulously clean out all old vines, stalks, stems, and rotten fruit in the fall.

A plastic paint pan makes a perfect planter when decoratively wrapped with aluminum foil.

Chives are resistant to both pests and viruses. Extend some of this immunity to the rest of your plants by feeding them chive tea. Chop the leaves finely and cover with boiling water (a half cup of chive leaves to a pint of water). Infuse the tea for 15 minutes and cool. Spray the mixture on your garden.

To make a garden for strawberries, attach an old gutter spout to a fence and fill it with soil.

Plant horseradish near your potatoes; it helps keep potato beetles away.

Plant onions next to beets and carrots to keep bugs away.

Basil planted near your tomatoes helps discourage worms and flies.

Before resorting to pesticides, remember that a strong jet of water from a garden hose will dislodge aphids, mealy bugs, cabbage worms, spider mites, and young scale.

Grapes don't continue to ripen after they've been picked; unripe grapes can be left on the vine until the first light frost.

Plant tulip bulbs late in the fall, after you've planted other bulbs, Plant all bulbs with the pointed end up.

Dig up gladiolus corms in the autumn, dry them in the sun for seven days, then store them during the winter in a dark, dry, cool place.

Unless the outdoor temperature is extremely cold, you can plant roses as late as November.

A two-foot-long branch about as thick as your little finger can be cut from a willow tree and planted in moist soil to start a new tree.

Replace the bottom of a wooden box with chicken wire to make a colander for garden vegetables. Before you bring them inside the house, place your vegetables into the box and spray them with the garden hose to wash off dirt and bugs.

To prevent the rain from splattering soil from a window-box onto your windows, top the soil with a layer of gravel.

The trunk of a hollowed-out tree makes a great planter. Line the trunk with plastic and fill it with rocks (for drainage) and soil.

Flowers that spread are good choices for a tree-stump planter—they'll spread out attractively over the wood.

A very small garden can be organized to give you both flowers and vegetables. Try planting beans with sweet peas, tomatoes behind the marigolds, and peppers among the petunias.

Because thyme, marjoram, and parsley don't grow higher than a few inches, plant them where they won't be overshadowed by other plants. Low-growing herbs make a delightful edging for a flower bed or a path.

Coriander, tarragon, and dill grow to a height of two feet or more, so plant them against a wall or toward the back of a flower bed that backs onto a fence or wall.

Make a homemade pesticide by mixing one tablespoon of biodegradable detergent to a pint of water and using it to spray both sides of the plant leaves. After an hour, spray or hose down with clear water.

Rhubarb, which contains poisonous oxalic acid, is effective against aphids and red spider mites. Pour two pints of boiling water over a pound of chopped rhubarb leaves and let it set overnight. Next day strain and add a tablespoon of detergent to the liquid. Spray on vegetable crops, but not within a week of harvesting. Keep your kids and pets away, too.

During the early stages of infestation by larger insects, you can often hand-pick the bugs and their eggs from the leaves or brush them into a jar coated with detergent.

If tiny worms infest the soil where your ferns are growing, you can get rid of them by pushing matches in the soil, sulphur ends down.

Discourage flies from swarming around garbage cans by washing the cans thoroughly, letting them dry in the sun, and then sprinkling dry soap into them.

To control flies and gnats, make sure garbage cans have tight-fitting lids, and attach impregnated resin strips to the can lids.

Pestered by slugs and snails in your garden? It will help if you get rid of their hiding places. Put scratchy sand or cinders around each plant, or arrange cool shady spots they can crawl under so you can collect them in the morning. A saucer of flat beer set into a depression in the soil will also attract slugs—they'll fall in and drown.

Dogs and cats can be repelled by a mix of two cups of isopropyl rubbing alcohol (70 percent) and one teaspoon of lemon grass oil. Brush or spray the liquid on areas you want dogs and cats to avoid.

If you want your garden vegetables to ripen faster outdoors, place aluminum foil beneath them to reflect the sunlight.

To encourage ivy or myrtle to root, pin vines to the ground with hairpins.

The best time to water gardens and lawns is early in the morning. Early morning watering lets the sun dry the leaves quickly, preventing the spread of spore and fungus diseases that thrive in moist conditions.

Always soak the soil thoroughly when watering. A light sprinkling can do more harm than no water at all because it stimulates roots to come to the surface, where they're killed when the sun bakes down on them. Never water from above, because many diseases are encouraged by wet leaves. Direct water at the soil gently to avoid washing the soil away and exposing the roots.

Select a watering can made of lightweight material. Remember that you'll have to lift and carry it when it's filled with water.

Dogs, raccoons, or opossums will leave your trash cans alone if you sprinkle ammonia around each can. Soak your garbage bags with full strength ammonia for double protection.

If you don't like getting your fingernails dirty when gardening but find it difficult to work in gardening gloves, dig your nails into a bar of soap, or coat the undersides with nail whitening pencil. Your hands will wash clean easily.

Crushed eggshells scattered on your garden will boost plant growth.

When rinsing dirty vegetables just pulled from the earth, collect the dirty water to pour back on your garden. It is rich in nutrients that can help the other plants grow.

You'll avoid getting pricked when you're pruning thorny tree branches and bushes if you use a big pliers to grab the branches.

It's best to finish pruning by August so any new growth can harden before winter. When you prune, always cut flush, leaving no stubs to decay.

Harvest radishes when they're one inch in diameter; larger radishes are tough.

Old car tires make firm anchors for outdoor garbage cans.

A sturdy wooden coat hanger is great for storing a garden hose. Wrap the hose around the hanger and hang it in the garage.

Fix a small leak in a plastic hose by touching it very lightly with the tip of a hot ice pick. The plastic will melt and seal the hole.

Here's help for haphazard gardeners. Paint the handles of your small garden tools a bright color—anything but green—so that you can find them more easily where you left them while you went in to answer the phone.

If your gardening gloves don't protect your hands adequately when you're pruning prickly bushes, wear oven mitts instead.

The plastic foam meat trays you buy your steaks and chops on make useful kneelers for working in the garden.

If you find that two hands are one hand too few when trying to transfer raked leaves to a leaf bag, clip the bag to a fence with clothespins. Then you only need to hold it open with one hand, leaving the other hand free for scooping up the leaves.

Another way to fill lawn and leaf bags without hassle: Fit the bag into a garbage can and dump in several armfuls of leaves. Remove the bag, and the contents will form a base so that the bag sits solidly on the ground while you fill it to the top. (If you fill the bag to the top while it's still in the garbage can, you'll have a hard time getting it out again.)

ARRANGING AND ENJOYING FLOWERS

When you're cutting flowers from your garden, carry a bucket of water in which to place the blooms as soon as they're cut.

The best time to cut flowers is early in the morning when they're full of moisture from the previous night.

If you want to give short-stemmed flowers more length, slide them into soft-drink straws before putting them in a vase.

If you refrigerate a vase of flowers each night, the flowers will last longer.

If you want flower buds to open faster, put the stems in a container of warm water.

When you receive a box of cut flowers from a florist, recut the stems to encourage maximum water intake.

Cut flowers from the florist are expensive. Fill out a small bouquet with interesting foliage. Foliage is generally more long-lasting than flowers, and with luck and good care some foliage can be kept attractive for months. Fresh cut flowers can be added to the foliage arrangement as the old ones die off.

To encourage carnations to last longer, add a little boric acid to the water in the vase.

Cut flowers last longer if you cut their stems at an angle. To avoid mashing, use a very sharp knife or pair of scissors. Also, always cut the stems under water so air bubbles won't form.

If a flower vase is leaking and you can't figure out why, turn it upside down over a light; the light will shine through any holes or cracks.

Long-stemmed flowers will stand erect in a wide-mouthed vase if you make a lattice across the top of the vase with transparent tape.

Hair rollers tied together and stood on end at the bottom of a vase will help hold flowers securely in place.

Flowers loosely arranged in a vase will last longer than tightly packed ones.

An easy way to make a slightly cracked vase serviceable again is to use a sturdy plastic bag as a liner. The weight of the water will keep the bag in place.

You can fix a small hole in a flower vase by dripping melted candle wax over it from the inside of the container and allowing the wax to harden. As an alternative, drip epoxy glue on a hole or crack and let it harden.

Car Care and Maintenance

CLEANING THE CAR

A box of baking soda is a useful addition to your car-cleaning supplies. A half inch of baking soda in the car ashtrays helps eliminate stale tobacco smells. It also makes it easier to extinguish cigarettes.

A baking soda solution will remove salt deposits from the paintwork on your car. Extra dirty spots will come clean and shiny if you apply baking soda with a damp sponge. Rinse well with water.

Rub baking soda into fresh stains on car upholstery. When completely dry, brush or vacuum off.

A baking soda paste (three parts baking soda to one part water) is good for removing corrosion build-up from your car's battery terminals. The paste is slightly alkaline, which means it actually neutralizes corrosion. (Always be careful when working around a battery; it contains a strong acid.)

A light coat of petroleum jelly on battery posts and cable attachments retards corrosion.

Bird droppings, insects, and tar marks may be easier to remove from your car if you hold a cloth saturated with cooking oil on the area until the material will lift off.

When polishing your car, use a soft-bristled brush to remove dried polish around trimwork. The brush works better than a cloth.

Tar remover is useful for removing gummy substances that have stuck to the lower sides of the car body.

When waxing your car, be sure to get wax into all the crevices in the car body. Wax will prevent water from getting under trim pieces and areas that are subject to rusting. Use a soft-bristled brush.

If you've applied wax to your car too thickly or let it set too long after drying, the residue will be difficult to remove. If this happens, apply a light dusting of cornstarch. The cornstarch will absorb the dried residue without removing the wax finish, and you'll be able to wipe it away.

You know you've done a good wax job on your car when water beads on the surface. Areas that have not been waxed will become unevenly wet and will stay that way until evaporation takes place.

If you want your tires to shine like new again, clean them off and apply a coat of clear self-polishing floor wax.

Keeping tires clean can be a problem, because various restrictions on the use of phosphates in commercial cleaners have resulted in some products that do not do a very good job. (Trisodium phosphate, for example, will remove any stain from a whitewall tire.) If phosphates are banned in your area, substitute an abrasive household cleanser. Apply it with a damp cloth and use a scrub brush to work it into discolored areas of the whitewall. Rinse with clean water.

Do not put too much faith in paints that claim to renew the appearance of whitewall tires. These are only stopgap measures. These coatings have a glossy white look when first applied, but they soon yellow and fade.

Keep your car mats looking new and make them easier to clean by coating them with a liquid wax shoe polish.

Wash your car on a cloudy day (or park in the shade). Avoid using hot water and soaps or harsh detergents, which can bleach the paint and cause streaks that are impossible to remove. Use a mild liquid dishwashing detergent for best results.

On a hot day, park your car in the shade to polish it. Heat from the car's surface will interfere with the cleaning action of the polish. If you have to stop work before you've finished polishing the car, don't stop in the middle of a panel; you'll leave a visible line.

A musty odor in a trunk will disappear if you leave a coffee can containing cat litter in the trunk overnight.

Keep an extra kitchen mop in the garage to use when washing the car. The mop will clean a wide area on the top, hood, and trunk of your car, and you won't have to reach or scrub as much.

After cleaning large areas of chrome, protect them with a coat of durable clear acrylic. You can buy it in spray cans in auto supply stores.

Cleaning your car's engine is a messy job, and not easy, but it is rewarding. Once you've done it, however, you may find that your car won't start. If this happens, the spark plugs may be wet. Wipe them off with a clean cloth. If the car still won't start, check for excess moisture at the ignition coil and distributor. Wipe these components dry with a clean rag.

When cleaning engine parts, use only cleaners designed for the job; never use gasoline or lacquer thinner which give off toxic fumes. Both gasoline and lacquer thinner have such low flash points that no spark is needed to cause them to burst into flame.

Remove all smoking materials before cleaning the exterior of a car battery. Batteries can be highly explosive.

Do your wiper blades streak or smear the windshield of your car? It may be because the blades are hardened or cracked and should be replaced, but the problem may just be a dirty windshield or dirt on the blades themselves. Before changing the blades, see if washing them and the windshield with soap and water will do the trick.

Chattering windshield wipers may be caused by an improper wiper arm tip adjustment. Turn on the wipers; when they are at mid-stroke, shut off the ignition. Remove the blades and check to see if the arm tip is parallel to the windshield glass. If not, use locking-jaw pliers to bend the arm parallel to the glass. If this does not correct the problem, replace the wiper arm.

CAR MAINTENANCE AND REPAIRS

If you do not have a workbench, set up a makeshift work area near your car with a picnic table or a sturdy plywood panel supported on two trash cans. If you work outdoors, be sure there's an outlet where you can plug in a trouble lamp if your chores continue after dark. Also, have a sturdy plastic sheet or some other waterproof cover at hand to protect your tools if it rains suddenly.

Keep a good flashlight in your auto repair toolbox. It is often easier, quicker, and more effective to use a flashlight to spot an area than a standard trouble light.

You can save a lot of time and trouble by including a selection of popular-size nuts, bolts, washers, and lock washers, plus sheet metal screws, plastic and electrical tape, penetrating oil, sealers, and other commonly used materials in your "shop" inventory.

Assuming you are buying tools for the car you now own, you will probably be investing in standard rather than metric sizes. However, with metric fasteners becoming more common, consider phasing metric sizes into your collection. More new cars are requiring metric tools.

If you're making your first venture into do-it-yourself car maintenance, look for sales of complete sets of tools. You can buy a basic set that includes most common sockets, open-end wrenches, hex keys (for hex head bolts) and other miscellaneous necessities for about $50. This way you can save about 30 to 40 percent as compared to buying individual pieces.

If you are tuning your car and a fastener is difficult to remove, apply a little penetrating oil and allow it time to work. When you remove parts, arrange them in the order of removal and place them in a tray or other container so they won't get lost. This also eases reassembly.

When checking the gap on a spark plug, use a round-wire gap gauge. A flat gauge can give you an inaccurate reading.

Tires and Tire Pressure

A good investment is an accurate tire pressure gauge, which can be purchased for a few dollars. Do not rely on the accuracy of a gauge mounted on a hose at the service station. Such gauges are often mistreated and are frequently inaccurate.

To extend the life of your tires, make sure you rotate them periodically.

Radial tires normally bulge slightly when properly inflated, whereas belted-bias tires do not. If your car is equipped with radial tires, it is best to use a tire pressure gauge to check pressure rather than trying to check it visually.

Never deflate tires because they indicate an overinflated condition when hot. When they cool, they will return to their normal inflation pressure.

You can identify probable inflation problems by visually checking your belted-bias tires. An underinflated tire wears more rapidly on the outer edges of the tread because the too-soft body of the tire tends to flex more at the center, with most of the weight of the car being supported by the sidewalls. An overinflated tire will show the greatest wear at the center of the tread pattern. The tire is distended at the center where the greatest concentration of weight is placed.

Always check tires when they are cool. Tires properly inflated at one temperature may become overinflated or underinflated as the temperature changes.

If you have your car tires rotated, you can choose whether to have the spare tire included in the rotation. Spacesaver spare tires, however, should not be included in the rotation; they are designed only for emergency use.

Repair of a puncture on a tubeless tire should be performed with the tire dismounted from the rim. Any on-the-wheel repair should be considered only an emergency measure and should be corrected properly as soon as possible. If the tire casing is not patched on the inside, air—under pressure—can make its way inside the plies, causing ply or belt separation. Eventually, this can ruin your tire.

If you car is carrying a heavy load or pulling a trailer, add two to four pounds more pressure than normal when you check the tires.

Painting and Body Work

Rubbing alcohol on a clean rag works well for cleaning a sanded metal surface before priming.

When applying primer to an area of metal before painting, do not attempt to cover the area completely with a heavy coat of primer. Best results are obtained by applying several fine, misty coats. The same applies to the first coat of paint used over the primer; after the first coat, you should still be able to see plenty of the primer through the paint. Subsequent fine, misty coats will complete the job.

When applying primer from a spray can, hold the nozzle at least 12 inches away from the object being sprayed. If it's closer, you're likely to get runs. If you do find that the primer runs, allow it to dry thoroughly, then sand the run with #400 sandpaper, wipe the area clean, and apply another coat of primer.

After touching up the paintwork on your car, allow the paint to dry for at least two days. Then apply a little rubbing compound with a clean, soft cloth to rub the paint out. This will result in a more professional-looking job. Rubbing compound applied according to the directions on the product adds luster to the paint and helps it blend in with the older paint.

If the nozzle on a spray can is clogged with paint, pull the nozzle off the can and soak it in paint thinner or another petroleum-based solvent to clear the passage. When the nozzle is clean again, replace it on the can.

A shallow scratch on your car can be removed with rubbing compound on a soft, slightly damp rag. Using the tip of one finger, gently rub the compound back and forth—never in a circular motion—along the scratch until the scratch vanishes. Remember that rubbing compound is an abrasive that can remove paint and primer, so stop as soon as the scratch disappears.

To make it easier to apply primer or paint to a chipped spot on paintwork, cut a small hole about twice the size of the chipped area in a piece of thin cardboard and hold the cardboard with the hole a few inches away from the chipped area; then spray.

An ordinary wax crayon can cover scratches on your car's finish. Match the color of the crayon to your car and rub it over the scratches. Buff the area with a cloth.

Weather-strip cement can be used to resecure glued molding that has come loose from your car. Apply a thin line of weather-strip cement along the middle of the back of the molding and press into position—make sure you position the molding correctly the first time, because the cement dries quickly.

Those decals and stickers some cities and communities require you to display on your car windshield can be a real problem to remove once they've expired. Make the task easier by using a sharp, single-edged razor blade held in a pair of pliers to reach awkward corners.

How to get that bumper sticker off your chrome bumper? Soak the sticker with a petroleum-based solvent and use a plastic ice scraper to scrape the softened sticker from the chrome.

Rustproofing

Rustproofing compound can make rubber brittle; avoid getting it on rubber seals, tubes, and gaskets.

If you get rustproofing compound on paint, rubber parts, or yourself, remove it with kerosene or a mineral solvent. Caution: Kerosene is flammable; do not pour it or use it near an open flame.

For best results from a professional or do-it-yourself rustproofing job, it should be done before your car has been driven for three months or 3000 miles. Only during this approximate period can you expect to prevent rust from getting started.

Rustproofing is less advisable after your car has been exposed to a season of road or marine salt. Because rustproofing compound can seal in moisture, rust that has already started and has not been removed will continue its development.

In checking your car for signs of rust, inspect closely any bubbles or blisters in the paint. If they are soft to the touch, the metal beneath is probably being eaten away by rust. Any rust should be treated quickly.

CAR SAFETY AND CONVENIENCE

Always keep an emergency box in your car. You should have a blanket, flares, small shovel, cat litter or sand, a sterno stove, dry soup mix, water in a plastic bottle, and a flashlight.

Keep plastic gloves and rubber bands in the glove compartment of your car to protect your hands if you have to tinker under the hood. Slip the gloves over your hands and sleeves and hold in place with the rubber bands.

Keep an old window shade in your trunk. If you have to change a tire, unroll the shade on the ground to protect your clothes from the dirty roadway.

If your car door locks are frozen, hold a flame under the key for a few seconds and insert the key into the lock. The heat from the key should loosen the locks.

If you don't have an ice scraper at hand, use a credit card.

An old nylon stocking kept in the trunk of the car comes in handy when you have a flat tire. Rub the stocking around the tire; the hose will snag on the nail or tack that caused the flat.

If you find yourself on the side of the road with a rusted jack and no oil can, take the dipstick from your engine and let a little of the oil drip onto the jack.

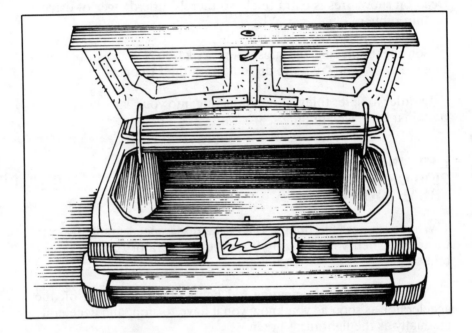

If you have to pull over to the side of the road or highway, reflector tape strips placed on the inside face of your car doors will alert motorists approaching from behind you in the dark. Also, tape placed on the inside of the hood will alert oncoming cars to the presence of a stationary vehicle.

Keep a blackboard eraser in the glove compartment for cleaning off steamy windows.

When jump-starting a dead battery, line up the two cars so they're facing each other, but be careful not to let them touch. Touching can lead to electrical shorts and dangerous sparks.

Back your car into the garage in cold weather; if you need to use jumper cables, the car will be in the correct position.

When purchasing a set of jumper cables, be sure they're equipped with a good electrical conductor, such as copper. Copper carries electrical current much better than aluminum and most other metals.

Don't spend a fortune on new snow tires. Buy recapped ones. The tread on snow tires is extra thick, so there's little danger of driving on thin rubber.

Consider replacing the mushroom locks on your car door with tapered ones. They're more difficult for a thief to open.

In order to deter thieves from breaking into your car, always try to park in a busy, well-lit area.

GETTING TOP PERFORMANCE FROM YOUR CAR

Whenever possible, increase and decrease speed gradually; you waste gas when you suddenly floor the accelerator or slam on the brakes.

Conserve gas by anticipating red lights. Take your foot off the accelerator as soon as you know you'll have to stop, and accelerate gradually as the light turns green.

You can also cut gas consumption if you shift into neutral when you stop for a traffic light. This takes the load of the transmission off the engine. Shifting into neutral is particularly important when you're using the air conditioner, because the engine idles more easily in neutral and handles the drag of the air conditioner with less strain.

Learn to "trick" your automatic transmission in order to save gas. Here's how: As you accelerate to over 30 miles per hour, ease off the accelerator a bit, which will allow the automatic transmission to shift into high gear earlier than it would otherwise. Once it's shifted, continue accelerating, if need be, to reach your desired speed.

When coasting down a hill or toward a stoplight, keep the engine running (it's needed for control of the car), but take advantage of gravity and ease up on the accelerator as you start down a hill.

If you get in the habit of releasing your parking brake before you turn on the ignition, you won't damage your car by accidentally driving with the parking brake on. Don't rely on a dashboard "parking brake on" light.

Check to see if the battery fluid is frozen before you try to boost a run down battery. If it is frozen, jumper cables can damage the battery and possibly cause an explosion.

Save money by avoiding so-called "super" spark plugs. They cost too much to be economical, even in the long run. It's best to stick to plugs recommended by the car maker and change them every two years, or more often, as the owner's manual directs. Economize by buying them at department stores rather than car dealerships, and learn to install them yourself.

You can extend the useful life of your car significantly by changing the oil and oil filter even more frequently than the manufacturer recommends.

You can help avoid sudden engine breakdown by replacing fan belts or alternator belts before three years are up.

You'll save money with a rental car if you fill it with gas before returning it. Many car rental companies charge more for the gas if they fill up the car from their own pumps.

You'll waste time and gasoline by letting your car warm up excessively. After 30 seconds of idling, even in the coldest weather, your car should be ready to roll.

It's best to keep the fuel level above the "empty" zone because once it falls below that level you risk dredging up the sediment that collects at the bottom of the gas tank. This can lead to inefficient engine operation because of a clogged fuel filter and gas line. By leaving it to the last minute to fill up you also, of course, run the risk of running out of gas altogether.

Filling your tank only when it's three-quarters empty will save you weight—six pounds for each gallon you leave out—and allow you more miles per gallon. It also prevents condensation, which can freeze and block gas lines in cold weather. If you always top off your tank, you'll be driving with more weight than necessary.

You'll save on fuel consumption if you remove old spark plugs on schedule. If one plug out of eight is misfiring, you're losing an eighth of the engine's output. Even if the engine misfires on one cylinder for only a short period—for example, at start-up when cold—you're running raw gasoline out of the exhaust pipe.

You'll save on gas if you get yourself ready to drive before starting the engine. Adjust the mirrors and the seat and put on your glasses and seat belt—*then* switch on the ignition.

Parking in a garage protects your car from wear and tear—and against theft—and also saves on both heating and cooling costs. In summer, the shade cools the car's interior, so you don't have to turn on the air conditioner immediately. In winter, the engine stays warmer in a garage than it does outside, which means it starts more quickly and requires less time to warm up.

Keeping snow tires on during warm-weather months may reduce fuel efficiency, because the tread pattern and weight of snow tires make the engine work harder. Snow tires also wear faster than standard tires in warm weather, since the rubber compound used for them isn't particularly suited to high temperatures. So, switch to standard tires as soon as you're confident that spring has arrived.

Radio stations in most big cities broadcast rush-hour traffic reports. You'll save time and energy if you check these reports when you leave your house or work and then alter your route if there's a tie-up on your usual route.

If you drive to the same destination each day, experiment with alternative routes because the quickest distance between two points isn't always the straightest line. Time yourself, consider how many stoplights or traffic jams you must wait for along each route, and measure the distance with your odometer. One route may take you a few blocks out of your way but allow you to bypass a bottleneck, save time, or save gas.

Because a heavy car uses more gasoline than a light car, you'll save if you clear your trunk of unnecessary ballast—tire chains and snow tires; sandbags; golf clubs; bowling balls, etc.

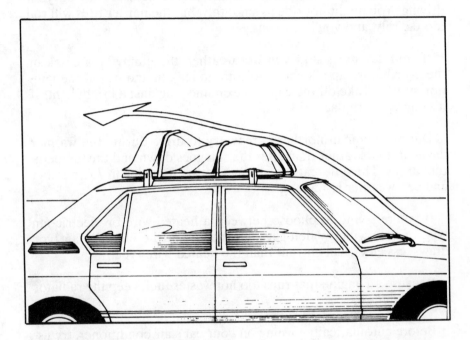

A roof rack loaded with suitcases or boxes can decrease highway mileage significantly, but you can minimize the loss if you take advantage of aerodynamics and arrange items so that the load is lower at the front than at the back.

For better mileage, use radial tires. They provide up to 6 percent better fuel economy than bias tires, and they roll more smoothly and last longer, too. On balance, the longer life makes up for the higher initial cost. A good set of radials will nearly duplicate the traction capability of most snow tires, yet they'll be more economical in use.

Check your air filter regularly and replace it if it's clogged. If a clogged air filter keeps air from reaching the carburetor, the engine will be harder to start and will use more gas.

At least once a week, check your tires to see if they are under- or overinflated. Also check tire tread for excessive wear.

You can save gas by riding on harder tires. Usually two pressures are given for tire inflation: One for an unloaded car; the other, as much as six pounds higher, for a loaded car or one that's to be driven long distances at high speed. Use the higher pressure for all your driving. You might not ride as smoothly, but the harder tires will roll more easily, and you'll save gas.

If your car starts slowly in wet weather, there may be a crack in the distributor cap allowing moisture to leak in and out of the ignition system. Take off the cap and examine it against a bright light. If it's damaged, replace it.

During winter in northern areas, try to drive during the warmer daylight hours rather than after the sun goes down and the temperature drops. The difference in mileage between driving in 75° weather and 25° weather is 1.5 mpg.

If you're trying to choose between a heated-wire or electric-fan type of rear window defogger, consider that the electric-fan type draws less electrical current than the heated-wire type.

Because an engine that runs too hot wastes fuel, keep the radiator completely full.

Before automatically turning on your car's air conditioner, try using the air vents. Many newer cars have a ventilation system that can keep air inside the car fresh and cool even in hot weather.

BUYING A NEW OR USED CAR

Check out the used car dealer before you check out the used car.

When buying a used car, make sure you check the exhaust. Put the car in neutral and press firmly on the gas pedal. If you see white or bluish smoke, it means the engine is worn, so don't buy the car.

Never buy a used car at night. Used car dealerships usually have strings of incandescent light bulbs strung up all over their lots because the lights give "sparkle" to the cars. As you walk around the cars, the reflections may distract you from any defects the cars may have.

If there are new rugs or floor mats on the floor of the used car you're looking at, check underneath to see if they're covering rusted out areas of the flooring.

Deciding what you want from a car will help you determine what size and model to purchase. If you're looking for economy, buy the smallest car that meets your major driving needs. If you plan to drive the car for the remainder of its useful life, buy a mechanically uncomplicated car.

The fenders, doors, and other body parts of new and used cars are often aligned through the use of shims. At the factory, these shims are painted the same color as the car. However, body repairmen often use shiny, new, cadmium-plated shims, which should alert you to the fact that a used car has been in a collision.

When choosing carpeting for a car or van, consider opting for 100 percent nylon. Polyester carpeting looks beautiful when new but deteriorates faster than nylon.

When inspecting a van you're thinking of buying, examine the paneling. Some builders use inexpensive pressboard paneling with a thin, imprinted wood-grain veneer. Better shops, however, use real wood panels or wood panels covered by heavy vinyl with a wood-grain pattern. Vinyl paneling stands up well to wear and resists scratches even better than real wood panels.

Select tires for a van on the basis of your driving needs rather than on style. Pay attention to the load range of the tire and the tread pattern, because there are tires for highway driving, and tires for off-road work. Keep in mind that larger tires with aggressive tread designs tend to be rough-riding and noisy for general use.

The odometer of a used car has probably been turned back if two or more digits don't align with the other numbers.

If a used car dealer has nothing to hide, he won't mind if you drive a car to your mechanic and let him look it over.

Since car troubles seem to multiply after three years, look for a used car less than three years old.

THE GARAGE

If you never are quite sure when to stop when you pull into your garage, suspend a ball on a string from the garage ceiling to act as a parking guide. Hang the ball so that it almost touches the windshield at eye level when you are seated at the steering wheel. When you drive in, stop just before the ball touches the windshield.

Luminous stripes painted on the rear garage wall can help you center your car when parking.

A "padded" garage can help you avoid scratching your car when pulling in and out. Attach sections of inner tube to both sides of the entranceway, if that is your problem area, or anywhere else that there's a danger of scratching the car.

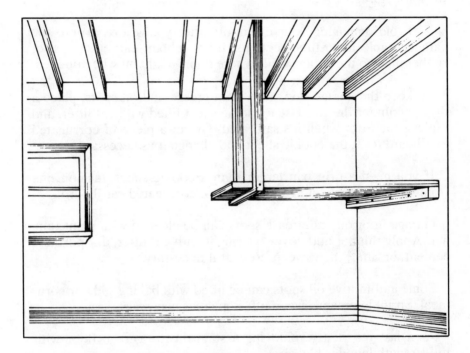

Save floor space in your garage by storing storm windows or screens overhead in a simple storage rack attached to existing ceiling joists.

To soften the blow in case you accidentally collide with the garage's rear wall when parking, cushion the wall with an old tire hung at bumper height.

Maximize garage floor space by painting white lines on the floor to outline parking areas for bicycles, the lawn mower, and other large objects. Then they'll be out of the way when you want to park the car.

If you need to maximize garage floor space, try hanging items such as rakes and shovels on the walls. Gain more room by filling the top half of the garage's rear wall with shelves or cabinets in which to stash small tools, automotive supplies, and garden accessories. Position these cabinets high enough to allow the hood of your car to fit underneath. Overhead, lay a platform across the ceiling joists so that you can put the space between the ceiling and roof to work for storage, too.

To avoid damaging your car doors after you've driven into the garage, staple inner-tube sections, foam rubber, carpet scraps, or rubber mats to the garage walls where doors might hit when opened.

To keep the garage floor free from grease and oil spots, place a drip pan under the car. Use a cookie sheet filled with cat litter, and replace the litter when it's saturated. Or cut a piece of corrugated cardboard to fit the cookie sheet and change it as necessary.

If you need a drip pan larger than a cookie sheet, fashion one from aluminum foil stapled to a piece of corrugated cardboard.

Garage floor oil and grease spots can be cleaned with paint thinner. Apply thinner and cover overnight with cat litter, dry portland cement, or sand; then sweep. Repeat if necessary.

Some automotive oil spots can be lifted with baking soda or cornmeal. Sprinkle on and sweep off. Repeat as necessary.

As a last resort, try removing a stain on the garage floor with full-strength laundry bleach.

If all cleaning attempts fail, you can camouflage garage floor drippings with paint. Apply a black stripe the width of the space between the car's tires. The stripe doubles as a parking guide.

If your wooden garage door is hard to open, it could be because it is not completely painted or sealed and so has swollen. (An unpainted door can bind at the edges and seem heavy.) To remedy this, let the door dry out thoroughly over several dry days, and then seal it by painting all surfaces, including edges.

Part 2:

Hints for the Family

Getting Organized

RUNNING A HOUSEHOLD SMOOTHLY

Decide on the time of day when your energy level is highest and do your least favorite chore then. You'll find you can get through it much more easily. Wind down the day with one of your favorite things, no matter how simple.

If you have trouble getting started in the morning, get organized the night before. Lay out your clothes, measure the coffee, and set the breakfast table before you go to bed.

Pin the menus for the week on a bulletin board—with the recipe titles and cookbook page references—for everyone in the family to see. The first one home can start the meal.

To save time and energy at the grocery store, make out your shopping list in the same order as the food is stocked in the store aisles.

Keep a large empty drawer, storage box, or laundry basket handy for instant cleanup when an unexpected guest is on the way.

Designate one area of your home, even if it's only one drawer somewhere, for filing business papers, bills, letters, and clippings.

When lining garbage cans with plastic trash bags, nest several bags into a can at the same time. Then remove the bags, one by one, as they fill.

Take a check from your checkbook and put it in your wallet so that you'll always have an extra when you find yourself down to your last check—or if you've forgotten your checkbook. Be sure to record the amount of this extra check in your checkbook when you use it.

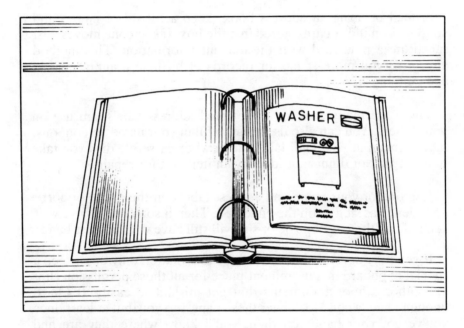

The instruction booklets that come with appliances won't be so easily misplaced if you keep them handy in a notebook. Paste the back cover of each booklet against one of the notebook's three-hole-punched sheets, and you'll know just where to find the information when you need it. The same goes for household documents, mortgage agreements, insurance policies, and so on.

Add shelves above your washer and dryer to hold colored plastic baskets—one color for each family member. When you take clean clothes out of the dryer, sort each person's clothes into the appropriate basket. Family members can then pick up their baskets and fold and put away their own clothes.

Assign a color to each family member and color code items throughout the house. Schoolbags, umbrellas, ponchos, coat hooks, storage boxes, and lunch boxes can all be color coded this way.

Color code your address book. Use different colored pens to write in friends, relatives, business acquaintances, club members, school personnel, and service people like that wonderful handyman someone told you about. You can use the same color system when marking up your wall calendar.

Instead of using an address book, keep a record of names and addresses on index cards stored in a file box. If someone moves, just substitute a new card with the current information. This method also gives you more space for records of birthdays, anniversaries, and clothing sizes.

There are many uses for the printed address labels you use on your letters. You can also use them to fill in your name on coupons; label items that you lend; label the bowl or casserole dish you take to a pot luck or dinner; or identify an item left for repair.

Use one of your name and address labels on the inside of correspondence as well as on the envelope. Then if someone you've written to loses the envelope he or she will still have your address handy.

If you have several children (or, for that matter, only one), keep a special clipboard in a prominent place for all those permission slips and other school documents that get mislaid so easily. It's hard enough to get a child to deliver these papers to you, but at least once you've got your hands on them you'll know where they are and when they have to be processed.

Another way of keeping track of the kids' communications from school: Keep a horizontal file in the kitchen, assign a tray to each child, and make a rule that after-school snacks are in order only *after* the day's papers are deposited in the right file.

Keep a small notice board near your phone for the names and phone numbers of your children's friends. That way, you'll know who to call when you come home to a note that says "gone to Tom's, back later" thirty minutes before your youngster is due at the orthodontist's office. Make it a wipe-off notice board if your children are at the age when they change best friends more often than they change their shoes.

No one in your house ever wants to read the magazines you subscribe to until the day *after* you've donated them to the dentist's office? Follow office procedure by stapling a photocopied routing slip to each magazine as it comes into the house. Leave a space for family members to mark articles or pictures they want to clip when everyone's through with the publication. That way, if anyone misses the final installment of a serial or a special-interest article at least it won't be your fault.

Large detergent boxes cut on the diagonal are perfect for filing special issues of magazines that you want to save.

A seam ripper is perfect for clipping recipes, coupons, and so on from newspapers and magazines. Keep one (with the safety cap on) near your favorite reading chair.

Felt-tipped pens will last longer if you store them with the writing end down, so that the ink keeps flowing into the tip.

If you carry pencils in your purse or briefcase, keep them in a plastic toothbrush holder. You'll find them more easily and the points will be less likely to snap off. This is a good tip for the children's school bag pencils, too.

If you have young children and use babysitters, paste one of your own name and address labels near (or on) the telephone. Then the babysitter who knows you as "the lady across the road" but doesn't remember the street number of your house will have the full address right there if it's necessary to make an emergency call.

If the wrapping paper on a package you are mailing won't stay in place while you tape it, slip a couple of rubber bands around it. It will be much easier to apply the tape accurately and tightly.

A toothpick dipped in rubbing alcohol makes short work of cleaning the crevices around the buttons or dial of a telephone.

Rubbing alcohol on a lint-free cloth does a good job on grubby typewriter keys.

To make slide and photo showings more enjoyable, label the film as soon as it's developed with place, date, and any other information needed for identification.

Organize your records by category with the help of stick-on colored dots. All your classical records can be coded with one color, rock music with another, musicals with another, and so on.

Make an efficient cleaning apron from a compartmented shoe bag by attaching strings and filling the pockets with rags, polishes, brushes, and other lightweight supplies.

At the end of the tennis season, coat the strings of the family's rackets with petroleum jelly before storing. It will keep the strings supple.

Petroleum jelly is a good alternative to chalk or candle wax for lubricating drawers that won't open smoothly.

Keep appliance cords and extension cords tangle free by storing them in the tubes from paper towel rolls.

Help your children learn to make their beds by marking the centers of sheets, blankets, and spreads with an appliqued design or colored thread. Even a young child will see that when the little line of teddy bears is in the middle of the bed, the sheet is on straight.

Keep extra clothespins in the coat closet and have your family use them to clip together gloves, boots, and sneakers so that you waste less time rummaging through piles of partner-less items. If your child takes a clothespin to school in his or her tote bag, it can be used to clip boots or gym shoes together for easy retrieval at the end of the day.

The nonskid cutouts you use in the tub are just as effective on a slippery high chair seat. Your baby will feel safer and more secure.

Snap-shut shower curtain hooks can effectively keep curious toddlers out of your cupboards. Lock two hooks together across the handles of each cupboard.

Those compartmented hanging closet organizers for shoes can be put to all sorts of uses. They're ideal for storing sweaters, underwear, socks, needlework supplies, and many other space-hungry household items. And you can see at a glance just what's in there.

Computers and VCRs

Try not to position your computer in a carpeted room. Static from the carpet may damage the computer circuits or even wipe out data on your disks. If you must keep the computer in a carpeted room, buy an antistatic mat or use an antistatic spray to reduce build-up on the carpet.

Occasionally wipe your computer keyboard with a clean, lint-free wiper. You can use an antistatic cleaning fluid if necessary, but spray it on the cloth, not on the keyboard.

Air must circulate freely around the computer and peripherals to avoid building up heat. Never block the slots that allow cooling air to circulate. If you add a number of circuit boards, you may need a fan. Check with the dealer to see if you need to use a fan with your computer.

Cigarette smoke, humidity, and dust can harm your computer. Try to keep the appliance clear of such conditions. Cover the keyboard, printer, and peripherals when not in use.

Be sure to use correctly wired three-wire electrical outlets for your computer system. The three-wire plug grounds the equipment, avoids electrical "noise" from the motor of your refrigerator, and minimizes interference with TVs and radios.

When you buy a computer, check your homeowner's insurance policy to find out if you're covered if your computer is stolen or damaged.

It's a temptation to buy economy-priced tapes for use with your videocassette recorder, but it may end up being a costly mistake. The use of poor quality tapes is one of the major causes of VCR problems. Stick to premium quality tapes by reputable manufacturers.

For best results, replace your VCR tapes after every hundred or so re-recordings.

PACKING AND MOVING HOUSE

Packing Your Belongings

Save space by not packing the unbreakable contents of tightly loaded drawers. Simply tape the drawers in place with strips of wide masking tape. To minimize tape marks, remove the tape as soon as the furniture arrives at your new home.

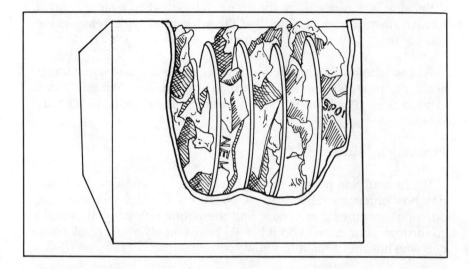

Plates are less likely to break if they are packed standing on edge. To minimize breakage of glass items, place the heavier ones on the bottom and the more delicate ones on top. Excelsior or pieces of crumpled newspaper make good packing material. If you have several days to pack before moving, dampen the excelsior so it will shape itself to the china and glassware.

Get carpets and slipcovers cleaned before you move. They'll come back wrapped and ready to go.

Small linens such as towels, washcloths, and pillowcases can also serve as packing material for dishes and glassware—and they don't waste space.

If you pack books so their spines are alternated, they will take up less space. (It may be cheaper to ship books via the United States mail, since the post office offers an inexpensive, fourth-class book rate.)

To prevent odors from developing in the refrigerator or freezer during the move, put several charcoal briquettes inside the unit to absorb the odors. Or fill the refrigerator or freezer with wadded-up newspapers. The paper will absorb any moisture and help prevent odors.

Because furniture casters sometimes fall out when a piece is lifted, remove them ahead of time. Tie them together with heavy twine, and tag them so you know which piece of furniture they fit.

As you tape up each packed box, place a piece of kite string underneath the tape, leaving about an inch sticking out. When it's time to unpack, just pull on the string, which will slit right through the tape.

Planning a Move

When notifying people about your move, be sure to include utilities, post office, social security, publications to which you subscribe, doctors, insurance companies, and the phone company. If you also go through your address book, you'll be less likely to overlook someone who'll want or need to know you're moving.

To save time and eliminate confusion when the movers arrive, draw a floor plan of your new home ahead of time. Sketch in and number your furnishings the way you want them arranged. Tag furniture pieces to correspond to the floor plan so the movers know where to put each piece.

Moving will go more smoothly if you make a master checklist of everything that must be done in connection with the move. So that you don't fall behind, schedule a deadline for each task.

If you're going to move a considerable distance, get your youngsters into the act. Encourage them to look up facts on your new location at the library, and let them help you plot the most convenient route on a map. If you're moving only a short distance, let them examine the new house and neighborhood before the move.

When leaving your previous home, empty the children's rooms last, and restructure their rooms first when you've arrived at your new home. This helps them adjust psychologically.

Having a Moving Sale

If you hold a house or garage sale to dispose of unwanted items before moving, you'll not only make money, you'll save money by not having to pay for transporting unwanted possessions.

Your sale will be more organized if you categorize odds and ends in bins. For example, have one bin for kitchen gadgets, another for books, and another for records.

To keep pairs of shoes together, tie them with yarn or string.

To get the best prices at your moving sale, clean and shine the objects you're selling—and display them creatively.

To display the clothes you're selling, rig up a clothesline. You can also throw an old sheet over part of the clothesline for a makeshift dressing room.

Make sure you have plenty of newspapers, old boxes, and grocery bags for packing up the items purchased.

Moving Into Your New Home

If you have access to the new home a day or so before the van arrives, you could set off a bug bomb or spray. (Even if you don't see bugs, there may be some.) This way, you won't worry about your family, your pets, foods, or furnishings during the spraying.

If you're going to arrive before the movers, consider bringing a book, radio, or portable television with you to while away the wait.

Take a survival package along with the family so you can camp in your new home until the moving van arrives. Include instant coffee, cups, spoons, soap and towels, a can and bottle opener, some light bulbs, a flashlight, toilet paper, cleansing powder, and a first aid kit. Also be sure that daily medications travel with you.

If you drive to your new location and arrive late, spend the first night at a motel rather than trying to "settle in" when everyone's tired. Everything will seem much more manageable in the morning.

HOLIDAYS AND
GIFT GIVING

You can fireproof a Christmas tree by spraying it with a half gallon of lukewarm water to which you've added one cup of alum, four ounces of boric acid, and two tablespoons of borax, thoroughly mixing all ingredients. If there's any solution left, pour it into the water in the tree stand.

Gingerbread men are not just for eating. They make attractive ornaments on the Christmas tree or strung across a room. Before you bake them, punch holes in the head with a straw so that you will be able to thread yarn through them for hanging.

Make your fresh tree last longer by cutting the trunk by one inch on the diagonal and standing it in a water base; replenish the water daily.

If you're going to plant a "living Christmas tree" on your property, do it long before the ground hardens. Dig a hole big enough to accommodate the burlap-covered roots of the tree, then cover the surface of surrounding ground with a thick layer of mulch. The tree should be well established by the first snowfall, and it will look spectacular when it is decorated with lights.

To keep small children or pets from toppling the Christmas tree, place the tree in a playpen "fence."

Divided egg cartons make safe storage containers for small Christmas ornaments.

When it's time to put away the Christmas ornaments, buy an extra box of hooks and pack them away too. Next year you'll have extra hooks for the new ornaments.

Postage stamps stuck together? Put them in the freezer for a while. They'll usually come apart with no damage to the glue.

If you're sentimental about greeting cards you've received and want to preserve them, coat them lightly with hair spray to prevent the colors from fading.

Instead of commercial cards, send personalized season's greetings on notepaper trimmed in red or green. Decorate the envelope with seals or stickers.

A pair of candlesticks with candles makes an attractive gift, but how do you make sure the candles don't get broken in transit? Wrap them in tissue and put them in a paper towel tube before wrapping the whole gift.

Display your Christmas cards by stringing them up against a staircase banister or pasting them around a large wall mirror as a decorative border.

Make up next year's holiday card list from the return addresses on the envelopes of this year's cards.

Get into the holiday mood by making festive barrettes. Glue decorative strands of ribbon to the top side of the barrette. At the ends of the ribbons tie small pinecones, feathers, or jingle bells.

If you're the sole guardian of the keys to the family car, the trunk of the car is a great hiding place to stash gifts until Christmas morning.

Fill an old mason jar with pretty pebbles and seashells collected at the beach, tie on a ribbon, and give as a decorative doorstop.

Use recycled lace and pretty fabrics to make beautiful Christmas stockings.

Keep a few "general interest" items in stock to avoid embarrassment when you've forgotten to buy a gift. Holiday cookies, preserves, or other food gifts are acceptable to most people—and you can use them yourself if you don't give them away.

So that one person doesn't do all the work, invite family and friends over to help cook the holiday meal.

Shopping Strategies

Team shopping with a friend who has similar needs and interests can save time and money. You'll give each other helpful advice on making the right purchases.

To keep track of children when you're shopping in crowded holiday stores, dress the kids in bright colors; a brightly colored hat is especially visible. Have small children carry identification in a pocket or on a sweater under their jackets. (A visible name tag makes it too easy for a stranger to greet the child by name.) Or hire a sitter to take care of the kids while you shop alone.

If hiring a sitter while you go shopping for gifts will dent your budget, perhaps you can do a deal with a friend who has children the same age as yours: If she (or he) sits for your children while you go shopping alone, you can return the favor in kind.

If you're taking a child shopping for his or her own gifts for family or friends, limit the outing to the child's shopping only—don't try to combine it with yours. Help the child make a list of possible gifts and how much he or she budgets for each one. Make the occasion special by finishing up with a movie or some other treat. If you have several children, make the occasion even more special for each one by taking them separately.

So that your children have a chance to buy Christmas presents without your finding out what they're choosing for you, have a neighbor or a friend take them shopping. You can return the favor with your neighbor's children.

Before the Christmas season begins, start a file of gift ideas clipped from mail order catalogs and newspaper ads to spur your thinking once you begin to shop.

Consolidate your gift shopping by buying as many as possible of your gifts in one department of one store.

Don't start on your shopping trip without an organized list of who you're buying for along with their special interests, their color preferences, and their sizes.

Holiday shopping won't seem a hassle if you can schedule your shopping excursions at off hours: Right after the stores open, in mid-afternoon (2:30-4:30 P.M.), or late enough in the evening to avoid the after-work crowd. Try to avoid the crowds on weekends and lunch hours.

To lighten your luggage at holiday time, have the store mail your gifts directly to the recipients.

If you're short on time and patience, ask your favorite department store if they have a shopping service. You tell them what you want in any given price range, and they'll shop, gift wrap, and deliver for you. Sometimes this service is free; other stores charge a service fee.

If you procrastinate and need a few last-minute gifts, investigate smaller stores that specialize in hardware, health food, lingerie, etc., for some suitable items.

If you can face the stores *after* the holiday, you'll find Christmas cards, ornaments, gift items, wrapping paper and ribbons, etc., on sale at greatly reduced prices. Stock up for next year—you'll save money now and time and energy when the Christmas shopping season rolls around again.

Encourage neighborliness by planning a caroling party; make it an annual event.

For a festive holiday get-together, have a Christmas cookie exchange. Invite neighbors and friends and ask them to bring some of their favorite cookies.

Save assorted cartons and boxes throughout the year, and have the children assemble them into a holiday castle. Spray-paint with gold or silver, and sprinkle with red and green glitter.

Special Occasions

A hurricane lamp filled with colored glass ornaments makes a lovely centerpiece for your holiday table.

Wrap a baby gift in a receiving blanket or diaper.

Think big when buying baby shower gifts. Babies are often ready for the six-month size within a couple of months of birth. Also, every mother needs baby shampoo, soap, washcloths, crib sheets, soft towels, disposable diapers, baby sleepwear. And what about something nice for the mother-to-be, too?

Natural dyes can be used to color Easter eggs. You'll have green eggs if you boil them with grass; red if they're boiled with beets; and yellow if onion skins are in the pot.

It's easy to make a heart-shaped cake to serve on Valentine's Day. Just bake a round cake and a square one. Face the square one toward you, point forward like a playing card diamond. Slice the round cake in half and position the two halves against the diamond's uppermost sides. Frost and serve.

Don't throw out the pumpkin seeds when you're through carving a Halloween pumpkin. Salt the seeds and dry them in the oven for a tasty and nutritious snack.

For a practical but pretty shower present, buy a laundry basket and attach kitchen gadgets and towels with colored ribbons.

Gifts and Gift Wrapping

When you make a gift of stationery, include some stamps. This is an especially thoughtful touch if the recipient is someone who can't get around much—a person in a hospital or nursing home, maybe.

When bringing fresh flowers to a friend, put the stems into a balloon with a little water in it; secure with rubber bands. The flowers stay fresh and are easy to carry.

For a friend who hates housework, give a gift certificate for one day's professional cleaning service.

On Mother's Day, use an oven mitt as the wrapping for a small gift, especially if the practical mitt hides something exotic—like a piece of jewelry or a bottle of perfume.

Young children don't classify clothes as legitimate birthday or holiday gifts, but you can keep their faces from falling on the big morning by hiding an inexpensive "real" gift inside the clothing.

A straw basket filled with special soaps, a nailbrush, and good facecloths makes a wonderful house gift.

Make a loaf of bread and wrap it up along with a jar of homemade preserves as a delicious and practical gift.

Need an unusual gift for a friend? Paint a pillow with nontoxic acrylic paints and personalize it with your friend's name, dates or place names important to that person, or a special design or message.

Instead of buying a box of note cards as a gift, make up a package of the lovely art reproduction postcards you can buy at museums.

If you're mailing cookies, minimize breakage by packing them in fluffy, unflavored popcorn. The recipient can eat both the cookies and the packing.

If it's not too used-looking, smooth out wrapping paper from gifts you've received and use it again. And don't forget that you can iron paper that's not too flimsy.

For friends who enjoy the beach or have the luxury of their own swimming pool, a set of plush bath towels is a welcome gift.

If you have any artistic talent, put an original ink drawing on the cover and on several inside pages of a notebook, and give it to a friend to use as a diary or personal record-keeper.

A promissory note of a certain number of hours of babysitting is a great gift for parents.

Enlarge the cultural horizons of a friend: Give records of music from Latin America, Italy, Germany, or some other country.

Organize your gift-wrapping chores by storing wrapping paper rolls in a narrow wastebasket, along with scissors, tags, transparent tape, and marking pens of assorted colors.

If you're not sure how much to cut from a large roll of wrapping paper for a particular package, first wrap a string around the package, cut it so there's a slight overlap, and use it as a measuring guide.

To wrap an oversize Christmas gift, why not use a paper Christmas tablecloth? It is easier to handle than several sheets of ordinary wrapping paper.

Pack gifts in practical baskets or decorative tins or containers. Your gift will be doubly useful, and you won't have to buy wrapping paper and ribbon.

Don't throw out the tubes from paper towel rolls. The tubes make versatile containers for all kinds of odd-shaped small gifts, from strings of beads to rolled up scarves or handkerchiefs. Roll the tube in gift wrap and tie at both ends with ribbons.

Odd-shaped cartons and boxes that you've saved over the year also give you useful resources for odd-shaped gifts that are difficult to pack.

Dress up and decorate wooden clothespins to resemble storybook characters, and use them as Christmas tree ornaments or gift-package decorations.

Old maps and pieces of sheet music make fine wrapping paper.

To press wrinkled ribbon flat, pull it through a hot curling iron.

Instead of tying a package with ribbon, glue on dried leaves and flowers to decorate. Or simply paint a ribbon on your gift-wrapped box.

Make small squares of wrapping paper double as gift tags. Fold a piece in half, punch a hole in the corner, and write your message inside.

You'll always have last-minute gifts on hand if you remember to buy doubles of things you need yourself. Such items as jellies and preserves, correspondence notes, and toiletries make suitable gifts. You can also take advantage of sale items and specials that look like suitable standby gifts. Store these potential gift items in a particular spot. This is also a great way to stock up on holiday stocking stuffers for the children.

Fill a small basket with spices as a gift for someone who loves to cook.

Have a writer on your gift list? He or she will appreciate a supply of legal-size lined yellow pads in a monogrammed leather case, or even without the case.

Have a child paste a small, current picture of himself to a piece of cardboard and draw a decorative design or border around it. Then frame the whole thing as a perfect gift for a relative or friend— especially someone who lives far away and doesn't get to see the child very often.

Newspaper and brown paper bags make strong and surprisingly attractive wrappings for packages.

Wrap gifts in color comic strips or bright magazine covers and artwork.

Blow up a balloon, paint the recipient's name on it, and tie it to your gift.

To protect a gift bow on a package from being crushed in transit, keep a plastic berry box taped over it until you arrive at your destination.

A gift for a teen can be wrapped in a colorful bandanna.

Paint the recipient's name and the year on a shiny Christmas bauble and tie it to your gift. Your friend can hang the bauble on his or her tree as an annual reminder of you.

If a paint or wallpaper store will give you old wallpaper sample books, you can use the sample pages as gift-wrapping paper—elegance at no cost at all.

Dress up a plainly wrapped package by spelling out the recipient's name or a greeting from letters cut from newspaper or magazine headlines.

Check out the accessories in a fabric goods store for unusual trims to decorate your package.

HOME ENTERTAINING

Preparing for a Party

Keep a record of the parties and get-togethers you've given, along with guest lists and menus and what aspects of the event were—or weren't—a success. It will make useful reading next time you plan to entertain.

If you plan a menu of limited courses, everything can be set out buffet style. That way you'll be able to enjoy the meal along with your guests, instead of running back and forth to serve.

So you won't forget anything that needs to be done for your party, do your planning on paper—including a time schedule.

Co-oping a party is a great way to entertain, especially if your schedule leaves little time for elaborate preparations. Arrange for everyone to bring something, and you provide the ambiance and the wine.

If you're planning on a house full of guests for a holiday party, don't forget to rent or borrow an extra coat rack so that you won't have to pile coats on a bed.

If possible, do most of your party cooking in advance so you won't be stuck in the kitchen away from your guests.

For crisp summer napkins, use men's white linen handkerchiefs.

Bagels fresh from the bakery make unusual napkin rings.

Make your buffet convenient for you and your guests by wrapping place settings of silverware in napkins and placing them in a basket.

Preparing for a party is much easier if all your entertainment equipment is stored together in one place.

For easy party serving and cleanup, use one big platter to hold the entire main course. Arrange all the food in an attractive manner and serve.

A good substitute for a regular bar can be made by setting out an attractive tray of drinks, glasses, and accessories on a convenient table or counter.

For a special occasion party, send balloon invitations. Inflate the balloons with a balloon pump, and write the invitation on them with a felt-tip marker. Then deflate the balloons, put them in envelopes, and mail to your guests.

If you're serving separate courses, keep a tray handy between courses and at the end of the meal for clearing the table. It will save you a lot of trips between table and kitchen. ·

Remember to keep nonalcoholic drinks—juices, soda, etc.—on hand for guests who don't drink alcohol.

Invite your friends to a make-a-pizza party and see how creative you all can be.

An easy and pleasurable way to entertain is to invite friends to your home for a relaxing Sunday brunch.

If you've invited more guests than your dining table will accommodate, but still want to offer a sit-down dinner, extend the table by topping it with a large piece of plywood. Cover the table first with table pads or foam rubber both to protect the surface and to keep the plywood from slipping.

A quilted mattress pad, cut to size, makes a perfectly satisfactory cover to protect your tabletop.

Party Food Made Easy

You can prepare vegetables for a party one or two days ahead of time. Cut up the vegetables, wrap them in damp paper towels, put them in plastic bags, and refrigerate.

If you don't feel confident about timing several courses, serve a casserole in an attractive dish.

Don't try out a new recipe on guests. Prepare it first for family members or close friends. You'll be sure of the taste and the length of time it takes to prepare.

For an easy party menu, set out different types of salad vegetables and a lot of toppings and let guests create their own salads. Make sure some of the ingredients are interesting or unusual enough to add a festive feel to the meal. Add some bread and wine to make the meal complete.

Large green peppers make ideal cups for dips. Slice off the tops of the peppers, scoop out the seeds, and fill the centers with your favorite dip. A loaf of bread sliced in half horizontally, with each half hollowed out, makes a container for a heavier dip or spread—a thin mixture would seep into the crust and then all over the table.

A creative way of serving vegetables for dips is to line a wicker basket with lettuce and then fill the basket with carrots, mushrooms, cauliflower, celery, and other vegetables.

A hollowed-out half melon makes a perfect container for cut fruit.

An ice bucket can be used as a serving dish, because its insulation keeps foods appropriately hot or cold.

Don't despair if you don't have as many dessert dishes as you have guests; you can serve most desserts just as easily in wine glasses.

Lay a damp napkin on a serving tray so that tumblers and dishes won't slide off.

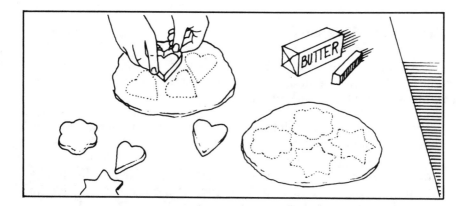

You can make individual butter servings look different if you put pancake-size dollops of softened butter on a cookie sheet, set the sheet in the refrigerator till the butter hardens, and then cut the butter into various shapes with your cookie cutters.

Party Drinks

If you're making any kind of fruit juice punch, freeze some of the juice in a large bowl or container, and use it instead of ice cubes. The punch won't be watered down.

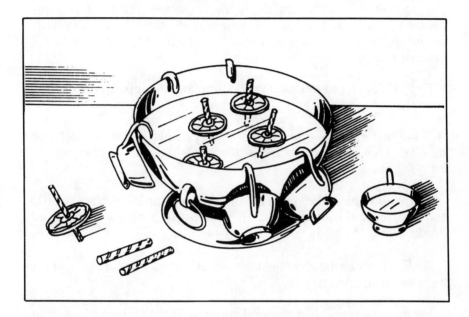

A pretty party garnish for punch is peppermint sticks pushed through the centers of lemon or orange slices.

When you're storing wine for any length of time, keep it in a dark place.

When you buy ice for a party, keep it from melting by placing the bag of ice on dry ice.

If you have leftover tea or coffee from a party, freeze them in ice cube trays. Use the cubes to chill iced tea or coffee without diluting the flavor.

An empty wine bottle may be attractive enough to save, but you won't want it if there's a cork stuck inside. If you can't fish out the cork, pour ammonia in the bottle and put it where there's plenty of air circulation. The ammonia will make the cork disintegrate in less than a week.

Before pouring beer, make sure the glass or mug is really clean. The slightest trace of soap, lint, or grease will cause bubbles to cling to the side. Next, tilt the glass or mug and start pouring beer down the side, then quickly straighten the container and pour into the center to minimize the foam. If you *prefer* a thick head, simply increase the pouring distance between the beer bottle or can and the glass or mug.

Dry drinks served before a meal stimulate the appetite more than sweet drinks.

Wine that must be opened with a corkscrew should be stored on its side. This keeps moisture in the cork and makes opening the bottle easier.

If you don't have the space in your refrigerator to keep soft drinks and beer cold during a party, fill your bathtub with ice and store drinks there.

Since wine can be damaged by vibrations, store it away from a staircase or machinery.

Ice for a party will last longer if you first freeze an inch of water in the bottom of the ice bucket.

Entertaining Ideas

If you want to give your entire house a refreshing scent—perhaps before a party—sprinkle cinnamon on a sheet of aluminum foil, put it in a hot oven, and leave the oven door open.

You can also make your house smell good by placing a solid room deodorizer beside an air-return vent of a forced-air heating system. The air will recirculate and carry the fresh smell to every room.

You can make a room smell pleasant by dabbing perfume on the cool bulb of a lamp. As the bulb heats, the scent will permeate the air.

Lighting a group of birthday candles with a short match can result in burned fingertips. A better idea is to use a lighted strand of uncooked spaghetti. The same trick works for lighting a candle in a long, deep container.

If a candle is too large for a candleholder, shave off some of the excess wax and then hold the candle bottom over a lighted match for a few seconds. When the wax softens, squeeze the candle into the holder. But make sure that the candle is not so much too big for the candleholder that it will make it top heavy and liable to fall.

To make candles burn slowly and evenly, with virtually no dripping, put them in your refrigerator for several hours before your guests arrive.

When a large decorative candle burns down in the middle and becomes hard to light, don't discard it. Instead, drop a small votive candle into the cavity to make the candle as good as new again.

You can snuff out a candle flame with kitchen scissors.

Handtowels for your guests can be rolled up and put in a pretty basket in the bathroom.

Because not everyone operates on the same morning schedule, let house guests know where to find everything they need to make their own breakfasts.

Guests sometimes feel more comfortable if they don't feel that you're doing all the work. One way to let them share is to write down some simple chores on slips of paper in a basket, and let your guests choose one at random. Some chores the guests can help with are emptying the trash, locking windows, cleaning up after breakfast.

If you're having guests, supply the guest room with books and magazines, an extra robe, and a tray to keep all personal things in one place.

A thoughtful way to thank your host and hostess for time spent as their house guest is to send pictures of your time together pasted into a scrapbook.

Money Management

SENSIBLE SPENDING

It pays to use "cents off" coupons when buying food. Little by little, the savings add up over time. Look for such coupons in your daily newspaper as well as in shopper "throwaways" and mailers.

Save on supermarket costs by preparing shopping lists for a full week of planned menus. Always plan menus so you can make good use of store specials and leftovers.

You'll come out ahead if you avoid buying nonfood items offered for sale in supermarkets. Shop for such items at discount outlets that specialize in nonfood products, where you'll usually find these products priced lower.

Trade your extra food discount coupons with neighbors and friends, or form a club in that neighborhood that meets at intervals to exchange coupons.

Take a calculator with you to the store. It makes it much easier to figure out price comparisons and make sure you're getting the best deal.

It's convenient to buy sandwich fixings ready sliced, but it costs less to buy meats and cheeses in chunks and slice them yourself.

When you budget, be sure to set both short-range and long-range goals. Goals might include a new car next year, a university education for a child ten years down the road, and retirement for yourself in 25 years. Setting goals gives you the incentive to control your spending.

A simple way to budget if there's more than one worker in your household is to use one of your paychecks each month to meet a big expense, such as an installment payment or the rent, and to use all other paychecks to cover the monthly expenses.

When budgeting, you needn't trace every expenditure down to the last penny. This wastes too much time (and often causes family arguments). Instead, overlook the inevitable small items that you can't seem to track down. Most people have a few dollars' worth of such unaccountable expenses every month. Attempting to pinpoint them entails useless bookkeeping.

Are you financially constricted because several large household payments fall due within a short time? Consider arranging a more convenient payment time for some of them. For example, if taxes *and* an insurance premium are due the same month, contact the insurance company to see about rescheduling your premium due date.

One simple way to keep expenses down is to pay credit card bills before additional service charges become due. You can also make budgeting easier on yourself if you establish when your regular bills come due each month, including credit card accounts, and work out the most convenient order in which to pay them over the course of the month. If you get organized in this way you can avoid service charges wherever possible, and you can avoid being hit with a whole bunch of bills that have to be paid at the same time.

Rule of thumb: The maximum amount of credit and installment debt payable monthly should never exceed 25 percent of your monthly gross salary before deductions.

So that too many family expenditures don't occur simultaneously, stagger the medical and dental checkups of family members.

You'll get much more for your shopping dollar if you don't automatically associate brand names and high prices with high-quality merchandise. Some of the best bargains (still high quality) are lower priced or generic.

Shopping by mail can save time, energy, and gasoline, but what happens when something you've ordered for a special occasion arrives too late? Just send it back, unopened, marked "refused." Provided the package is unopened, you will not have to pay the return postage.

You are under no obligation to return items that are sent to you in the mail provided you did not order them. If something is sent to you *without* your authorization, consider it a gift.

Don't accept a C.O.D. delivery for a neighbor unless you're sure the goods have actually been ordered. If you can't check, or your neighbor has not asked you to accept the package in his or her absence, send the package back.

Don't allow yourself to become financially strapped by letting a door-to-door salesperson fast-talk you into signing a sales contract. If you *do* sign, and if the item costs $25 or more, federal law lets you cancel the contract within three business days and receive a full refund within ten days.

November is a good time to buy men's and women's overcoats at reduced prices; that's when merchants offer bargains to hype pre-Christmas business.

Money-wise shoppers take advantage of storewide clearance sales after Christmas, Easter, and July 4th. You'll find bargains galore in linens, clothes, and scores of other items.

The best time to buy back-to-school clothing for youngsters is at the *end* of September.

You can curtail hospital expenses if you try to avoid being admitted on a Friday. Friday admissions result in longer stays than admissions on another day. For the shortest length of stay try to have yourself (or any family member) admitted on a Tuesday.

When you purchase furniture it makes good financial sense to buy the best quality you can afford. Cheap furniture wears out or goes out of style quickly—necessitating the purchase of more cheap furniture. High-quality furniture generally remains in style longer and stays in good condition for many years.

The best time to buy furniture is in June.

Cut down on your magazine subscription bills by trading magazines with your neighbors and friends.

To conserve money, pay cash for things you'll soon use up, such as food items and cleaning supplies. Use credit only for things you'll continue to use after you've finished paying for them, or for emergencies such as medical bills.

When shopping for durable items, save on gasoline and wear and tear on your car by using mail order catalogs.

Another advantage of shopping by catalog is that each item is described in elaborate detail. You can pick and choose at leisure the product that best suits your needs.

Avoid wasting money on a service contract when you buy an expensive appliance. The contract price will typically be low for the first year when you can reasonably expect that nothing in the appliance is likely to go wrong. However, for each succeeding year, when things are more likely to go wrong, the contract may cost you more than it's worth paying.

When a repair estimate is more than 15 percent of an appliance's replacement cost, seriously consider buying a new appliance.

If you really don't need a second car, make do with only one car and rearrange your schedules and appointments accordingly. You'll save a considerable amount of money each year.

Consider leasing a car rather than buying one. Not only will you tie up less capital, but you won't be burdened by insurance and maintenance costs.

Planning to take a package tour of several European countries? If you go in October, odds are you'll pay significantly less than you would in June, July, or August. Wherever you go, in fact, off-season rates are likely to be cheaper.

To save money on vacations, try home-swapping for a stated period of time. For example, if you live on the Canadian border and would like to spend a week or two in Tampa, Florida, try to locate someone in Tampa who would like to spend a week or two on the Canadian border. Thousands of people do this each year.

Don't be afraid to ask for a hotel room price when you make a reservation. Hotels generally have three room categories: Economy, standard, and luxury. An economy room may provide all the comfort and amenities that you need.

Never enter a financial negotiation without options. Having options places you in a better bargaining position.

Whenever you create competition for something you possess, the item rises in value. Obviously, when buying a product or service, the more people who want your money, the further your money will go.

If you have something difficult to negotiate—a concrete item that can be stated numerically, such as price, interest rate, or salary—cope with it at the *end* of a negotiation. By this time the other side has already made a hefty expenditure of energy and a substantial time investment.

Take a pocket calculator with you when shopping for an expensive item. Ask to be permitted to "work out the numbers" in front of the salesperson who wants to serve you. Then frown thoughtfully while tapping the calculator's keys. This procedure is almost guaranteed to restore an atmosphere of reasonable give-and-take in a bargaining situation.

BANKING AND CREDIT

Put your money in a bank where interest is compounded semiannually or quarterly rather than yearly. Your money will work harder for you.

If possible, never withdraw funds from a savings account before the stated interest payment date. If you do withdraw prematurely, you'll lose all the interest due for that particular interest period.

In case you're hit by unforeseen big expenses—such as unexpected home repairs or a sudden illness in your family—have an emergency fund in your savings account equal to at least two months' income.

Even after you've paid off a loan, continue paying out the same amount to your own savings account every month. You are used to making the payment, so you won't miss the amount so much.

If you find it difficult to save money, force yourself to do so by purchasing United States savings bonds under a payroll savings plan where you're employed, or by means of a bond-a-month plan at your local bank. You can build sizable savings over the years by authorizing small, regular deductions from your paychecks. There may be shrewder ways to invest, but there are no better ways to save. When you've built up a nest egg, divide it among several sound investments.

When you receive a check, deposit it at once. Many banks won't honor checks that are two or three months old.

A good way to save money is to put aside, at the end of each day, every bit of change you have in your pockets or in your purse or wallet including single dollar bills. Faithfully deposit this amount in a bank or a savings association once a week.

Because you always want your money to be working for you, don't keep more than is necessary in a no-interest checking account, unless maintaining a minimum balance qualifies you for free checking or other benefits.

To remain on good terms with your bank, remember that endorsing a check and depositing it doesn't mean you have that cash to draw on immediately. When making the deposit ask the teller how long the check will take to clear; then you'll know when you'll be able to write your own checks against it.

It doesn't pay to postdate a check, because a bank may refuse to accept it or may hold it until its date is reached. The bank's caution is understandable: If the check is charged to your account before you expected it to be, it might cause other checks that you've written to bounce.

Managing Your Credit

It's smart to obtain maximum lines of credit well in advance of need. If a credit card grantor opens your account with several hundred dollars' worth of credit, request an increase after six months, even though you may not actually need it. Continue to pump up your credit availability until you achieve the maximum line. That way, it's there when and if you do need it.

Planning to move out of the area covered by your local credit bureau? You may have trouble reestablishing credit quickly. For fast action on new credit applications, have in your possession several copies of your credit file from the bureau covering the area where you used to live.

Maintain your credit standing if you're temporarily unable to make a payment on a debt. See your creditor and discuss rearranging the payment schedule with him. Most creditors are understanding about this. They're *not* understanding if you try to avoid them.

In order to avoid being irritated by a collection notice that you know is due to a creditor's error (a not uncommon occurrence), pay the item in question if it's less than $25. Immediately forward your statement, with a complete explanation of the error, to the creditor. Your account should reflect a correction within 30 days.

A good way to keep out of credit binds is to pay off a series of payments completely before committing yourself to a new series of payments for something else.

Try not to put down less than a one-third cash payment when purchasing a car, or to let the financing extend past 36 months. With less than one-third down, a car's depreciation is likely to reduce its market value faster than you can shrink the balance of the loan.

Puzzled as to where you stand with your credit accounts? You needn't be. Simply put aside a special place for storing all credit slips. Periodically review the slips to see how much you owe, and determine whether or not you can afford to buy more on credit at that particular time.

Whatever you do, don't sign a credit contract that contains a "balloon" clause. A balloon clause stipulates a final payment that's much larger than any of the installments that precede it. If you discover such a clause too late, you may lose property after having paid a hefty part of its price, or be forced to refinance at disadvantageous terms.

Thinking about taking out a second mortgage to finance a vacation, to buy an automobile, or to consolidate bills? Although your home could be used as security for such a loan, it's probably best to take out a personal installment loan instead. Second mortgages should not be used for casual expenditures.

Offer the best security you can when taking out a loan. When you secure a loan with top-notch collateral, you usually get it at a cheaper rate than on your signature only.

Always make sure that all collateralized loan balances are less than the collateral's value. For instance, auto loans that entail a lien on the car should be reduced more rapidly than the decline in the car's resale value.

It's foolhardy to use emergency funds as collateral for a loan. If you default in payment and the funds are seized, you'll have painted yourself into a corner should any catastrophe occur.

Keep away from any loan that permits repossession of the property purchased without providing cancellation of the full amount of the indebtedness at the time of repossession.

To save on interest charges when borrowing money, make the largest down payment possible and repay the balance in the shortest time possible. (It's always expensive to make a small down payment and to extend the life of a loan excessively.)

Having trouble making monthly loan payments? Consider slicing the remaining payments in half by extending them over a longer time period.

Taking out a loan to finance a vacation? For the sake of personal psychology as well as your budget, make certain you can pay it up within one year. If you can't, you may grudgingly be paying off this year's vacation when next year's vacation time rolls around.

It doesn't pay to borrow money from small loan companies, because their interest rates are often significantly higher than those of banks or established savings and loan associations.

Avoid commercial debt poolers. They will charge you as much as 35 percent of your debts for lumping them together and collecting one regular periodic payment from you.

BUYING INSURANCE

Shop around when buying a health insurance policy. Compare the loss ratios of different companies. A loss ratio is the percentage of premiums that a company pays back to its policyholders in benefits. A high loss ratio means a good value for you. A company which returns 60 percent of its premiums to policyholders is a better value than one returning only 30 percent.

Rule of thumb for how much life insurance you need: The equivalent of four to five years' earnings.

Avoid having too many different life insurance policies. Consolidate your program into a few policies rather than buying half a dozen different policies. Your premium will be considerably lower.

If you're carrying more whole life insurance than you need, you can switch to a universal life policy for a better return on your money.

It's best to have an insurance agent who's roughly your own age. If his or her insurance needs are probably quite similar to your own, the agent may have a better understanding of your requirements.

Unless you're totally satisfied with the transaction, you're under no obligation to purchase an insurance policy. Keep in mind that the inflated price sometimes quoted by one insurer over another is purportedly due to so-called "service." Never accept this as a valid reason for an extreme cost difference between two policies that are otherwise roughly identical. Make certain the price you pay is truly competitive.

You may be able to save money by paying insurance premiums annually, rather than quarterly or twice a year.

You should be prepared to prove any insurance claims. One of the best ways is to take some photos of the insured property—inexpensive photos of every wall in every room—and store them somewhere outside the home for safekeeping. If a claim has to be made, these pictures will show exactly what the property looked like before it was damaged.

Maintain only the auto insurance coverage you need. You may wish to dispense with collision and comprehensive coverage on older cars if you can afford to pick up any possible losses yourself. You should, however, have liability insurance on every car you own.

Buy substantial deductibles on auto insurance, if you want to save money on your comprehensive and collision coverage. Doing so enables you to reduce your premium anywhere from 45 to 56 percent.

Are you 65 years of age or older? Take advantage of the fact that in many states auto insurance rates are substantially lower for people in this age bracket.

BUYING, SELLING, OR RENTING A HOME

Buying a Home

Generally it pays to buy rather than rent a retirement home. Buying gives you equity and a significant tax advantage over renting.

Your object in a home investment should be to improve your financial position. When inflation gallops ahead and everything else costs more, your home investment will go up in value because it can't be duplicated or replaced for less. In fact, many home investors acquire a substantial nest egg without any real knowledge of real estate.

If you expect that your income may fluctuate or be interrupted in any way, or that you may even stop earning at all, don't invest in a home.

Before buying a home, determine what zoning regulations cover the site on which it stands. For example, if you plan to expand the house in the future, will you be able to do so? Sometimes a house in its existing form uses up the maximum space allowed by the local zoning ordinance.

It really doesn't make sense to purchase an expensive house in a neighborhood that heavily features less expensive houses. If you want an expensive house, you'll get more for your money in a neighborhood where all houses are in the high price range.

If you want to hire an architect but the job fee seems too high, consider buying the architect's advice on an hourly basis.

When you're looking at homes, it's best not to take small children with you. They're too much of a distraction. What's more, the owners of the homes you inspect (as well as the realtor) can offer you a better look at the premises, and provide more helpful information, without the children around.

Study classified ads in newspapers to gauge the going prices for houses in any given area, and to measure the price levels in one area against the price levels in another. This enables you to narrow your choices among the sections of town you might be interested in. If advertised prices in a given section are consistently higher or lower than what you'd like to pay, rule out that particular area.

Corner lots were once considered desirable, but they aren't today. In addition to having the equivalent of two front lawns to maintain, corner lots pose a safety hazard for small children because of increased traffic at intersections.

When examining houses, don't be overly impressed by cosmetic touches or window views. Concentrate on important issues: Sound construction, convenient arrangement of rooms, adequate space, and so on.

If you stubbornly hold out for a lower price when the asking price for a house actually is reasonable, you may lose the house altogether.

It's almost always more advantageous for a home investor to seek the longest mortgage term available. A term of 30 years or more to repay is better than a term of 20 or 25 years.

If there's a mortgage outstanding on a house you plan to buy, consider assuming the mortgage from the seller. An existing mortgage probably carries a lower interest rate than the general going rate. Remember, though, that you'll need the consent of the lender before you can assume the seller's mortgage.

If you can manage to pay relatively large monthly payments, the odds are that you'll be able to get a larger mortgage loan, pay if off faster, and pay reduced finance charges.

Would you like to begin home ownership with lower monthly payments than a conventional mortgage allows? See if you can get a graduated payment mortgage (GPM) through an FHA-insured program or through a federally chartered savings and loan association. The total cost of your graduated payment mortgage will be higher over the life of a 25- or 30-year mortgage, but if your income is modest, you'll be able to purchase a home sooner.

Refinancing is a way for a homeowner to realize a return on real estate without selling it. Some homeowners, especially those who live in areas where property values have steadily increased for many years, routinely refinance each time the equity in their homes rises sufficiently so that the ratio of the loan to the equity dips below 60 percent. They hike the loan back to 75 percent of the value of a new mortgage and use the money they derive from doing so for other financial ventures.

When purchasing urban property, be sure to obtain title insurance. A title insurance policy doesn't insure against every conceivable loss that might occur, but it does insure against defects that might normally appear in the records.

An open-end mortgage enables you, the borrower—after paying off part of the loan—to reborrow up to the amount of your original mortgage. This is a financially sound way to pay for home modernization, repairs, remodeling, or expansion.

The ideal insurance policy should protect the homeowner against all of the hazards itemized in the basic HO-1 (homeowner's) policy, plus $100,000 or more of personal liability, plus any perils that frequently occur in the area, such as snow damage or floods. The policy should provide living expenses in case the home is damaged by fire or other disaster, and it should cover the full replacement cost of personal property that might be stolen or damaged. It makes sense to interview three separate agents before deciding on a policy.

As the value of your home increases, make sure your insurance company provides an "inflation rider" in its policy. An inflation rider automatically increases coverage as the value of your home increases.

Home Improvements

When improving a home for resale, make only improvements that will boost the sale price. As a rule of thumb, don't invest money in improvements unless you'll get back two dollars for every dollar you've put in.

Owners who keep their property for less than three years after making an improvement seldom recover their entire remodeling costs, so plan well ahead when you consider major improvements.

As a rule, a new or modernized kitchen, an additional bathroom, a finished family room, or an extra bedroom will return only 50 to

75 percent of its cost if the home is sold within a year or two. The idea is to make improvements that—in addition to making the home a more pleasant place in which to live—will pay for themselves as the value of the home appreciates overall over several years.

What options are open to the homeowner contemplating an improvement but reluctant to pay the prevailing labor rate? Try talking to the maintenance engineer in a nearby apartment building. These people often have plumbing and carpentry skills, and they may be happy to obtain part-time work.

An advertisement in the classified section of the newspaper can also help you locate someone with good repair skills who will charge reasonable rates.

Selling a Home

Unless you are experienced in real estate matters, it's best to use a broker when you sell your house—and this is required by law in many areas. There's an incredible maze of unexpected paperwork that accompanies the transaction.

A realtor can cull out people who are just "window-shopping" for a house, and aren't really serious about buying. When you advertise a house yourself, you may attract crowds of window-shoppers who will waste your time.

Trying to appraise your own home objectively is almost impossible. For instance, portions of your home that you regard as assets may be seen as liabilities by potential buyers. Let your realtor guide you.

Remember that a realtor doesn't necessarily want the selling price of a home to be as high as possible. A broker's primary concern is to close the sale. This entails seeing to it that the buyer and the seller agree on a mutually acceptable figure. A broker makes no deal and earns no money unless he or she can mediate a compromise between the seller's asking price (normally too high) and the buyer's offering price (normally too low).

The best times to sell a home are early spring, late summer, or early fall. The urge to buy and to move are strongest in the spring. However, late summer and early fall are also big moving times because families want to get resettled before the start of a new school year.

Nine times out of ten, selling a home is easier if you use a realtor. But you may be able to sell your home on your own without much effort in a strong sellers' market. If a lot of people are moving into your community but few homes are being built to accommodate the newcomers, you should be able to sell without too much difficulty.

When you're having an open house to show your home to prospective buyers, be sure to clean the house from top to bottom. Trim your bushes and mow your lawn; put on the air conditioner if it's a hot day; open all curtains and draperies; and have plenty of cookies, tea, and coffee available.

When you have prospects in to examine your house, try to keep the premises as quiet as possible. Switch off the TV set, put your pets in the backyard, and request that your children play quietly (if they're younger) or turn off the stereo (if they're older). This will ensure that distractions in your home won't prevent visitors from forming a valid opinion of the structure itself.

Don't fall victim to the "one more fool" theory, which emphasizes that, regardless of the price, eventually someone will come along who'll pay even more than the present bidder.

Ten percent above market value is probably too high a price to ask for an owner-sold home. Just slightly above market value is more realistic.

When negotiating any real estate transaction, don't parade your enthusiasm. Always behave as though you're under no pressure whatsoever and have all the time in the world.

When buying or selling real estate, don't make any concessions without getting equal—or larger—concessions from the other side.

Reluctance on the part of a property seller to answer all questions within a reasonable time is a strong indication that the property isn't as good a buy as the owner would have you believe.

Real estate closings can be disasters unless you're appropriately prepared. Appropriate preparation means that all documents must be submitted to all involved parties in advance, so that there's time to spot errors, raise and resolve objections, and make corrections.

There's no such thing as a standard real estate contract. There are certain printed forms that sellers insist upon. Legally, however, contracting parties are free to phrase their agreements in any manner they please—as long as the agreements are valid in the eyes of the law.

Renting a Home

A smart way to live rent-free and beat inflation in the process can be to purchase a duplex, a triplex, or a quadruplex. Live in one of the units yourself and defray—or completely pay for—its cost by renting the other units.

Don't put your money into property that you plan to rent to others if you can't cope calmly and rationally with frozen pipes, overflowing toilets, malfunctioning heating and cooling systems, and nonpaying or irresponsible tenants.

When searching for properties to rent to other people avoid those that are overequipped (and therefore overpriced) for their location. Select properties with no more features, equipment, or amenities than your prospective renters are likely to want. Remember, it's easier to add amenities and raise rent than to remove amenities and lower rent.

If you're looking for rental properties, concentrate your efforts in the lower to middle range of the local price structure. Why? Because higher-cost single-unit houses frequently return less in rent—in proportion to the outlays they require—than lower-priced houses.

Purchasing a house to rent to others can give you a substantial annual yield for each dollar you invest. The right house, with the right financing, can return 20 to 40 percent or more to you each year via tax shelter, rental income, and capital appreciation.

Don't expect the impossible. A rental property will rarely—if ever—be at its optimum level of general maintenance and repair at all times.

Don't invest in an apartment building if its vacancy rate is eight percent or higher.

If you're renting out a building, an effective way to depreciate it is to put the building itself on one depreciation schedule—let's say 25 years—but put its major components, such as central air conditioning, on shorter, more realistic schedules.

Many "pyramid" builders (those who use property to buy other property) don't hold on indefinitely to every property they acquire. Instead, they purchase speculative properties, rehabilitate them, push the rents upward, and sell them (roll them over) to other investors at a profit.

If you own a rented home, the rental income you receive can offset the monthly mortgage payments. In fact, a home with an older mortgage at a low interest rate can often bring in rental income that's substantially higher than the mortgage payments.

To maximize the rental potential of a second or vacation home, make sure it has the potential for four-season occupancy. If the structure will be snowbound two-thirds of the year, consider something more versatile.

Insist that prospective tenants for rental property have gross monthly incomes of no less than three and one half times the rent you're charging. If their monthly income is only three times the rent you're charging, regard that as a warning and back off.

When renting property to others, painstakingly spell out all operating rules in your leases. These rules should include the maximum number of occupants allowed in a given unit.

Never offer to rent property without first obtaining a detailed written application. Otherwise, you may be making yourself vulnerable to a professional deadbeat, or setting yourself up for a housing discrimination suit.

Rental tenants will stay with you longer and will take better care of your property—possibly even improve it—if they feel you're giving them a fair deal. However, do not hesitate to take action against tenants who take advantage of you.

PLANNING FOR RETIREMENT

Check your Social Security account every two years to make sure you're being credited for the proper amount of contributions. Contact the Social Security office nearest you to obtain a statement of your payment record.

Even if you plan to work past retirement age, apply for Social Security three months before the month in which you reach full retirement age. That way you should be admitted to Medicare Part A (hospital insurance) and Part B (medical insurance) without losing any months of coverage.

If you're buying a retirement home, consider relocating close to public transportation. You might then be able to avoid the expenses of running a car.

Don't rely on Medicare to cover all your hospital costs. As comprehensive as it is, Medicare pays for only 40 percent of the average beneficiary's total health care expenses. It's up to you to plug the gaps with a supplemental health insurance policy.

Be wary of "work-at-home" schemes that focus on retired people as their market. Only a tiny fraction of the population has ever made money addressing envelopes at home, or selling "much needed items" to their neighbors. These schemes are frequently scams.

If you're going to buy a retirement home, make sure to choose one that's not too big for your needs.

Caring for
Your Child

FEEDING BABIES
AND TODDLERS

To prevent an active baby from tipping over his high chair at mealtimes, latch the chair to a wall with a childproof hook and eye.

If a child tries to slide out from under the tray of the high chair, make the chair less slippery by fastening a rubber sink mat to the seat.

Attach a towel bar to the back or side of a high chair and use it to hang a washcloth and bib.

A rubber suction soap holder keeps a baby's plate or bowl from slipping on the tray of the high chair.

To warm an eight-ounce bottle of formula in a microwave oven, use high power for 15 to 30 seconds for room temperature formula and 30 to 60 seconds for formula that's cold from the refrigerator. Test the milk on the inside of your wrist before feeding the baby.

If you're nursing but need to give supplemental bottles occasionally, consider using powdered formula. That way you can mix the amount you need instead of opening a can for just one bottle.

Spread a large plastic garbage bag under a high chair to catch spills.

Plastic or metal high chairs can go right into the shower for fast cleanup. If you run the hot water, even caked-on foods will wipe off easily.

You can regulate the flow of liquids from a baby bottle by loosening the bottle collar slightly if the flow is too slow or tightening if the flow is too fast.

If you mark the ounces on the baby bottle with nail polish, you'll be able to read them even in a dimly lit room at night.

If the holes in a baby bottle nipple are too small, you can enlarge them by lodging toothpicks in the holes, then boiling the nipple for about five minutes and allowing it to cool. If the holes are too large, reboil the nipple.

Baby bottles won't tip over in the refrigerator if you stand them in a soft drink carton.

You can keep nipples from deteriorating as quickly by occasionally brushing them with a salt solution.

Bottle nipples stored in a cool, dry place will last longer.

A baby can be weaned gradually from a bottle by letting him drink directly from the familiar container, but with the nipple removed or replaced by a soda straw.

You can clean bottle nipples in the microwave oven by boiling them in water in a glass jar. If you add a teaspoonful of vinegar to the water, mineral deposits won't collect on the jar.

If you use disposable plastic bottles to feed your baby, you need not sterilize them; they are sterile when you first take them out of the package. Bottle nipples, however, should be sterilized before each use.

Breast milk for your baby can be refrigerated if it is to be used the same day. Otherwise, freeze it. It can be frozen for up to two weeks.

If air bubbles do not form when your baby is drinking from a bottle, loosen the cap. If you tilt the bottle so that the nipple is filled with liquid, there will be less chance of the baby swallowing air.

Mixing your baby's cereal with a vitamin C source, such as a fortified fruit juice, helps the infant's body use the iron in the cereal.

Even young babies like their food to look interesting. Give your baby foods with different colors.

At bedtime, it's better to give a restless baby a pacifier than to give a bottle of milk or juice—the sugar in the liquid could stay in the infant's mouth long enough to harm developing tooth surfaces.

When your baby is ready to start feeding himself, choose a spoon with a rounded bowl and a short, straight handle, and a fairly deep dish with straight sides. The most practical time to let a baby practice self-feeding is when you're planning to bathe him afterward anyway—because you'll almost certainly need to.

Store packaged baby cereals in a cool, dry place away from other grain products that may attract bugs. They should also be kept away from strongly flavored vegetables, which give off odors that the cereal could absorb.

How many times have you seen a bored, hungry baby cause an uproar in a restaurant, probably giving her parents indigestion and drawing hostile looks from other diners? To avoid having the situation occur when you take your baby to a restaurant, take along this survival kit: Small plastic suction dish; lidded cup; disposable bib; safety belt or harness; small toys; baby food mill.

If you're taking a young child somewhere where you figure food will be a necessary distraction, take along a bagel threaded on a loop of ribbon. The child can hold onto the bagel or the ribbon, so there's double insurance against the bagel getting dropped or lost, and a bagel doesn't make loud crunches at quiet moments.

If you have a dishwasher, set your water temperature at 180°F to sterilize baby utensils along with family dishes.

If you put glass marbles in a sterilizer, they will attract water minerals and help keep baby bottles clear of deposits.

Your baby is less likely to suffer the pain of trapped gas if fed in as nearly upright a position as possible. The bubble at the bottom of the baby's stomach can then rise and be burped easily.

You'll be more comfortable when nursing if you sit in a cushioned rocker armchair; or on a sofa that has low arms.

While feeding a baby, leave a heating pad in the crib so that it will be comfortably warm when you put the baby down for a nap.

If you take a baby on a long trip, regular formula or milk in baby bottles may spoil. Instead, put only the measured amount of powdered formula or milk in the bottles. When you're ready to feed the baby, just add water to a bottle and shake it.

An ice-cube tray can be used to freeze blocks of baby food for individual servings.

For baby food that's free from lumps, put enough food in the blender to cover the blades one inch.

If you can't unscrew the lid of a baby food jar, punch a small hole in the lid to break the vacuum seal. The lid should twist right off.

Here's a practical idea: When your baby is learning to drink from a cup, let her do it in the bathtub where spills don't matter.

Help your toddler handle cereals and soups by serving them in a mug or bowl with a handle that he can hang on to.

If your kids are picky eaters, try them on miniature meat loaves made in muffin tins.

For a picky toddler, put small quantities of different foods into compartments of a muffin tin and lunch becomes a game. Do the same for a child who is sick in bed.

When a child is first trying to drink from a cup or glass, make the utensil easier to grip by putting several wide or strips of tape around it.

An egg poacher is a useful utensil for warming baby foods. It even has compartments for different foods so they don't all get squished up together.

You can make sloppy joes more manageable for your children if you start with unsliced hamburger buns. Cut a quarter-inch-thick layer off the top of each bun to make a lid and scoop out just enough bread to leave a bowl with sturdy walls. Fill the hole with sloppy joe mix and then press the lid firmly back in place.

An ice cream cone makes a novel, edible container for tuna, egg salad, cottage cheese, or yogurt.

BATHTIME AND BEDTIME

You'll have a better grip on a soapy baby if you wear a soft cotton glove on one hand.

You'll stay dry even if the baby splashes if you clip a towel around you like a bib. As a bonus, the towel will be at hand when the bath is over.

Line the tub or sink with a towel or diaper before bathing a baby. The child won't slip around so much and will feel more secure.

When bathing a baby, use soap sparingly to avoid depleting the baby's protective skin oils.

When you do use soap on your baby, you'll find that a pump dispenser designed for liquid soap will be easier to handle than a cake of regular soap. The dispenser lets you keep one hand on the baby while quickly dispensing just the amount of soap you need with the other hand.

When selecting a baby tub, twist it to make sure that it stays solidly in shape. A sturdy tub makes transporting water easier.

You won't get powder on the baby's face if you put the powder into your hand and then apply it to the baby.

If your infant doesn't like to be bathed, he or she may feel more secure sharing a bath with you.

To keep soap or shampoo out of an infant's eyes, gently rub petroleum jelly on his or her eyelids and eyebrows. The jelly will make the shampoo run sideways rather than downward.

A tip for bathing a small child in a large tub: Set a clean plastic clothes basket in the tub; fill the tub with water and set the child into the basket.

Decorative nonslip tape or cutouts in your tub or shower give your toddler a better footing.

Many toddlers insist on washing themselves but find bars of soap too slippery to deal with. Solution: Stuff a sock with small chunks of soap and fasten the open end. The child will be able to work up a lather and the sock won't slide around. Or let the child use liquid soap.

To avoid scarring when bathing a child who has chicken pox, gently pat the child dry so that blisters or scabs are not disturbed.

The sound of running water simulates intrauterine sounds, so you might be able to lull a restless baby to sleep with a tape recording of water filling the tub.

If you try to keep a baby's surroundings totally quiet during naps the baby will get to the point where he or she can't sleep through any noise at all. It's much better to maintain a normal, reasonable noise level so that the child learns to sleep just about anywhere.

A small inflatable plastic pool makes an ideal bed or playpen for an infant when you're traveling. Inflate the pool and line it with a sheet or blanket. There are no hard edges and the baby can't roll out either.

A baby who hasn't yet learned to turn over is safer lying on his or her stomach to sleep. That way, a baby who vomits is less likely to choke.

Avoid the use of foam rubber pillows for a child with hay fever. Although these pillows are considered nonallergenic, they may breed molds as they age.

A padded laundry basket or a padded dresser drawer makes a good bed for a visiting infant.

A large bed sheet provides an infant with a clean play area on a motel floor or on a grassy area outdoors.

YOUR CHILD'S
HEALTH CARE

Syrup of ipecac, which is given to induce vomiting in cases of swallowed poison, should be in every medicine cabinet. If you keep on hand two small bottles, each containing a single dose of two or three teaspoonfuls, it will be ready for immediate use and you won't have to waste time measuring in an emergency.

Keep an antihistamine, in tablet or liquid form, in your medicine cabinet. Correctly administered, it will reduce the itching and swelling of insect bites and minimize the itching of chicken pox, poison ivy, and other rashes.

If you disguise medication in a small quantity of juice, ice cream, or applesauce, be sure the child takes the whole amount. What's left on the spoon will not aid the child.

When your child is over five or six, help him learn to swallow a pill by placing it on the back of his tongue before giving him something to drink. Start with relatively unimportant medication—like a children's pain reliever for a headache—so that he'll be prepared when it comes to taking important medication.

Children hate to have adhesive tape removed from their skin, but the tape will come off painlessly if your first rub the tape with a wad of cotton soaked with baby oil.

If a child has a toothache, apply an ice pack to the jaw. A warm compress may just make the pain worse.

You don't have to wreck your child's jeans when he has his leg in a cast. Open the inside seam and insert a long zipper. When the cast comes off, you can easily remove the zipper and stitch up the seam.

A cast on an arm or leg can cause skin chafing and irritation. This can be eased by rubbing the edges of the cast with petroleum jelly. Baby powder on the edge of the cast also helps relieve irritation.

A soft terry washcloth is much kinder to a tender nose than tissues when a child has a cold.

If growing pains are frequent and severe, sturdier shoes may alleviate the problem.

A warm application to the neck is an old remedy that works to relieve hoarseness.

A cut near the joint of your child's fingers can be immobilized by splinting the fingers until the cut has healed.

A bedboard under the mattress (a piece of plywood will do) helps relieve discomfort when a child has back pain.

Good liquids to give a dehydrated child are fruit juices, weak tea with sugar, ginger ale, colas or other carbonated drinks, or gelatin desserts (which can be given in liquid or jelled form).

You may be able to control diaper rash simply by changing the brand of soap you use or your method of washing the diapers.

When a child balks at swallowing a vitamin or a pill, bury it in applesauce or some other palatable soft food.

Do not use a kitchen spoon to administer medication. Use a specially marked measuring spoon for medication; you can buy one at any pharmacy.

A child who's sick in bed needs company, but you still have to get on with chores, right? Solve the problem by cleaning out his closet or toy box while you chat to him.

Clear liquids are best for a child who is dehydrated, but if you want to give skimmed or whole milk, dilute it by half with water. This will reduce the salt content.

Your daughter has just had her ears pierced and you fear that an infection is developing? Soak the earlobes in a warm Epsom salts solution (a quarter cup of Epsom salts to a pint of water).

Warm water soaks or warm salt water rinses (one-half teaspoon of table salt in half a glass of warm water) help clear up gum boils.

If your child repeatedly develops ingrown toenails, shoes that are too small or too pointed could be the cause.

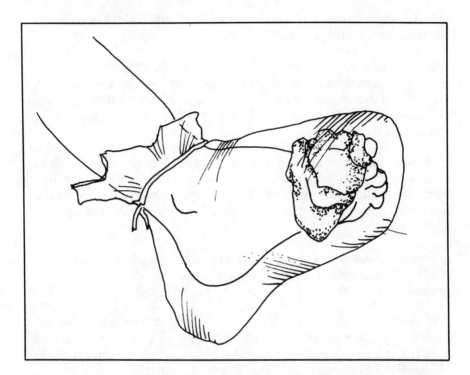

If an embedded toenail cannot be removed because the area is too tender, try prolonged soaking in a strong Epsom salts solution (one cup to one quart of water). Cover the lower foot and toe with a bandage or cloth, soak thoroughly in the solution, and encase the dripping foot in a plastic bag. In this manner the nail can be soaked for hours with little effort.

A paste of moistened meat tenderizer applied to the bites of stinging insects may give immediate relief.

If your baby has heat rash on her face, rest her face on an absorbent pad in the crib to minimize dampness.

Sponging your child with diluted rubbing alcohol helps relieve heat rash. So does cornstarch applied lightly with a powder puff.

Help correct a tendency towards pigeon toes by teaching your child to sit cross-legged when he sits on the floor rather than on his haunches with his toes directed outward.

Cut fingers or toes will heal better if kept immobile. Try splinting the fingers or bandaging toes together.

Instead of throwing out old white socks your children have outgrown, recycle them as bandages for skinned elbows and knees. A sock with a toe cut off slips over an elbow, the heel portion covering the joint. The cuffs of the socks make effective bandages for an injured knee.

If your child has a knee injury that requires him to avoid activities such as stair climbing, bicycling, running, and jumping, have him wear an elastic knee support. The support may not be medically necessary, but it will remind him to take it easy until the knee is strong again.

If your adolescent is prone to athlete's foot, have him or her avoid plastic- or rubber-soled shoes and use cotton socks for absorption, preferably white to avoid contact dermatitis from dyes.

If your child develops perleche—cracks at the edges of the mouth—have her brush her teeth with table salt or bicarbonate of soda instead of toothpaste. After the condition clears up, try using different toothpastes, or ask your dentist for advice.

Don't try to test a child for fever by feeling his or her head. The only accurate way of registering a child's temperature is with a thermometer. The most reliable reading is obtained with a rectal thermometer, although it takes a little longer than an oral thermometer to register the temperature.

You can sufficiently restrain a baby while you take his or her temperature rectally by placing the child face down on a solid surface and putting the heel of your hand firmly on the lower back.

An uncooperative toddler can be firmly clasped between your thighs, and bent forward over one leg in a position to expose the target, when you need to obtain a rectal temperature reading.

You can use any lubricating ointment to grease a thermometer for rectal use, but the best is a water-soluble gel because it readily washes off in cold water.

Blisters caused by friction or burns should never be broken, but covered with gauze and bandages. If a blister is already opened, clean it with soap and water and bandage the area.

BABYSITTERS

Before you leave a new babysitter with your infant, take the sitter on a tour of your home, especially the kitchen and the baby's room. Make sure the sitter knows where to find everything he or she may need, including clean diapers and a change of clothes for the child.

If your baby is at the shy stage, have a new sitter come in ahead of time to play with the baby, feed him, or get him ready for bed while you're around.

When you leave your child with a sitter, write down any special instructions and be sure the sitter has a note with the address and phone number of the place where you can be reached. If you will be inaccessible by telephone, arrange to call the sitter at a certain time.

Be sure your babysitter understands your rules about having a companion over or making phone calls while he or she is in charge of the child. No sitter should bring a friend or anyone else to your home without your knowledge and permission.

CHILDREN'S ACTIVITIES

Toys and Games

Any door or wall can be made into a blackboard with chalkboard paint from the paint store.

A large household sponge can double as a washable blackboard eraser.

Make an indoor sandbox from an old plastic dishpan. Spread newspaper and plastic bags underneath to catch spills.

Plain oilcloth tacked to the wall of a child's room or the family den makes an easy-to-clean area for the little ones to practice their graffiti. The oilcloth is easy to replace, and encourages the children's large-scale artistic talent without wrecking the wall.

A plastic wastebasket of a suitable size can make an impromptu bucket-type seat for a child. Cut away part of the front and sides, making sure that all edges are smooth, and put a pillow in the bottom. You can tape the edges where you made the cuts for extra safety.

Enlarge the play space in your child's room by moving the dresser into the closet. You should still have plenty of space for hanging clothes above a low dresser, and having all his or her clothes in one area may encourage the child to keep the room neat (if you're lucky).

Those stackable kitchen bins that you find in the hardware store make excellent storage for small toys, coloring books, art supplies, and all those odds and ends it's so hard to find a home for. The bins come in bright colors so you can easily coordinate them with the color scheme of the room.

Snap-on plastic shower curtain hooks can hold toys and rattles on a baby's crib.

An old tractor or truck tire makes a great outdoor sandbox. Just be sure there are no sharp metal edges.

Cover the edges of swing seats with slit sections of garden hose to soften the blow if a seat swings into a child.

You can extend the life of cardboard games, paper dolls, and jigsaw puzzles by spraying them with shellac.

Stuffed toys that are not washable can be cleaned with dry cornstarch. Rub it in, let stand, and then brush it off.

If a youngster complains that his sled doesn't zip down a hill fast enough, spray the bottoms of the runners with vegetable oil.

Keep old greeting cards in a box and bring them out on days when the kids are complaining that "there's nothing to *do*." Let them cut up the cards to make collages or art projects. This way they can recycle used cards into new ones to send next year.

Cutting down the legs of an old, adult-size table makes a play table just the right height for children.

Carry a powder puff and a box of cornstarch to the beach for dusting sand from your child when it's time to leave.

Gather beach toys in a mesh vegetable bag to rinse them of sand easily.

Save money by making your own fingerpaints for your youngsters. Mix a quarter cup of cornstarch with two cups of cold water and boil the mixture until it thickens. Pour it into containers and add food colorings.

Another method for making fingerpaint or decorative play plaster: Mix two cups of soap flakes and two cups of liquid laundry starch in a large bowl. Blend with a wire whisk or an electric beater set at high speed until the mixture has the consistency of whipped cream. For color, add four to six drops of food coloring and beat the mixture again. Mix a fresh batch for each play period.

An easy recipe for play dough: Combine two cups of flour and one cup of salt with just enough water to make the mixture rubbery and soft. Keep it tightly sealed when not in use to keep it from drying out.

Wrap crayons with masking tape so that they'll be less likely to snap in half when your child uses them.

Kids can make a lot of mess with paint. Make their artistic endeavors easier on yourself by inserting the paint container into an opening cut in a sponge. The sponge will hold the container steady and soak up any drips.

A flip-top bandage container makes a strong storage container for crayons.

Proud of your child's early attempts at artwork? Preserve the freshness of the colors by coating each creation with hair spray.

If your little girl wants to dress up like a lady, let her make her own necklaces. Dip dry macaroni in a variety of liquid food colors, drain it, and let it dry. Then have the child string the bright pieces with a blunt needle and thread.

Add glitter to the soap flakes you use as decorative "snowy" covering for children's holiday art projects.

If there are a number of young children in your neighborhood, you can set up a baby-sitting co-op. Parents share the child care and the kids make new friends.

Preschoolers can have a lot of fun decorating orange juice cans as pencil holder gifts. String, noodles, wrapping paper, cutouts, etc. are all suitable decorative materials.

Liquid starch is a good substitute for glue. So is clear nail polish.

Can't get your kids to settle down to write a letter to a grandparent or relative? Have them send a drawing instead. If possible, use an envelope large enough to hold the work unfolded, and slip in a piece of cardboard to keep it flat. Have the child do a small design on the envelope, too (if she's not out of patience by then), and you've got a letter that's almost as good as a gift.

To improvise a hobby horse, stuff a sock, insert a broomstick all the way into the heel and tie the sock on tightly. Decorate it with a face and mane.

You don't know what to do with all those crayoned pictures that your child brings home, but you haven't the heart to throw them away? Keep them and let the child use them as wrapping paper for gifts for friends and classmates.

A specially good piece of artwork that your child has done makes a fine gift for a grandparent or godparent. You'll be surprised how sophisticated young art can look when smartly matted and framed. (Remind the child to sign and date the piece.)

Fill your little ones' Christmas stockings with dime store items—crayons, bags of gold stars, felt-tip markers, colored chalk, etc.—which will keep them occupied all winter long.

Mount greeting cards, magazine cutouts, etc. on cardboard. Then cut them out in irregular patterns for do-it-yourself puzzles.

To make stilt walkers, remove the lids from two tin cans. Punch two holes in the bottom of each can near the edges. Thread strong string through the holes and tie a knot to secure. The child can slip his elbows through the looped string. Really small children can start with tuna cans.

The back of a child's bedroom door is a perfect place for a cork bulletin board.

Children can make place mats by arranging leaves on burlap and covering them with clear plastic wrap, secured on the wrong side with tape.

If you lack space for storing a toy train, devise a simple pulley and rope system to raise the train board to the ceiling of a child's room. If you paint the underside the color of the ceiling, the board can hang camouflaged.

You can make a child's ball that won't break either heads or windows from an old sock stuffed with panty hose.

Save the plastic caps from empty toothpaste tubes, and fill them with clay. Kids can use them as miniature flower pots to decorate their dollhouses.

Reinforce the spines of children's school textbooks with strips of colored insulation tape.

When rubber gloves spring a leak, cut off the fingers to make finger puppets.

You can turn a closet with a three-panel door into a puppet theater. Remove the middle panel and hang a rod with a curtain from the inside of the closet. Replace the doorknob with a latchless wire pull so your child can't get locked inside.

You can use screw-on earrings as miniature clamps for model building.

Traveling by car with children can be enjoyable if you plan ahead. Take along a plastic shopping bag filled with paper and pens, crayons and coloring books, books, and a favorite game.

Kids can make easy hand puppets out of old socks.

Make a flute from a paper tube by punching it with holes an inch apart and covering one end with waxed paper.

Cut a hole in the cover of a shoebox and stretch five rubber bands across it lengthwise to make a splendid banjo.

Take a trip to the woods with your children. Collect seeds and pods of all kinds for decorating the house and gift packages during the holidays.

A piece of tissue paper placed between the pages of a child's coloring book will prevent colors from smearing.

While traveling, kids can color and play games on a lap tray; a cookie sheet makes a good tray.

A sheet of flexible, transparent plastic is perfect for children to write and draw on. If they use washable pens the plastic will wipe clean.

If your children enjoy exploring neighborhood streams and ponds, make sure the glass jars they use to hold their "catch" are shatterproof: Just wrap tape around the jars so that if the jar is dropped the tape will cushion the glass.

You can make a good "fishing net" for your young explorers by attaching a kitchen strainer to a broom handle.

If you're taking a bevy of little ones to a movie or museum, take along a tote bag for mittens, scarves, hats and all the other paraphernalia they collect. You may have to carry the bag, but at least you won't spend half an hour trying to round up everyone's belongings.

Even before a child can read, he or she can learn to put clothes in the right places if you cut out magazine pictures of socks, shirts, pajamas, etc. and paste them on the front of the child's dresser drawers.

Almost any strong cardboard box, covered with bright paper, makes a useful extra toy box. Use leftover wallpaper from papering the child's room for an attractive coordinated look.

If you've papered your child's room with a paper featuring storybook figures, cut out some of the figures to make decals for other pieces of furniture. This way you give the room a designer look without paying designer fees, and you can even use the figures as teaching tools—socks go in the drawer with the orange tabby on, pajamas in the one that has the grey kitten, and so on.

Figures cut from wallpaper also provide a cheerful border or pattern to brighten up a cheap white shade over a child's window. Or, have the child use crayons or markers to draw his or her own design on the shade—rainbows, balloons, a big sun shining down on flowers in a garden.

If your children strew toys all over the house (and where are the children who don't), try this time and temper saver: Keep one of those mesh kitchen carts on wheels in an inconspicuous corner for instant cleanup before dinner or when guests are due. Then the kids can pile all their belongings into the cart and wheel it all out of sight. A cart with several shelves is the best bet.

Don't pack the plastic sled away at the end of the snow season. Use it in summer to trek beach gear and toys across the sand—much easier than carrying an armload of buckets, beach balls, and sopping wet towels.

Beach toys tend to look much like one another. Avoid summertime arguments by putting each child's initials on his or her toys with indelible marker or nail polish.

When the kids are out playing, put a clock facing out into the yard on a windowsill. They won't keep coming in to ask you what time it is, and they won't be able to excuse lateness on the grounds that "we thought it was *much* earlier than that."

Children's Parties

At a birthday party, cover the party table with shelf paper and let each guest decorate his or her own place with nontoxic felt-tip markers. The kids can decorate white paper plates and cups the same way. It will keep the kids busy and save you money—plain paper utensils are much cheaper than the party kind.

Create an autograph tablecloth at your child's next birthday party. Have the guests sign their names, then embroider over each signature or outline the names in permanent dye. Use the cloth at future birthday celebrations, adding new names each year.

Have an undecorated frosted birthday cake ready, as well as a big dish of sugar cookies. Let the birthday child decorate the cake from jars of instant frosting while the rest of the kids decorate cookies with frosting, jelly beans, candy hearts, gumdrops, chocolate pieces, etc.

Sometimes birthday candles drip wax into the frosting and discolor it. You can prevent this by securing each candle with a marshmallow—an easier method than trying to get the candles to stand straight in those tiny decorative holders.

Cut circles of bread with a cookie cutter, and set out spreads and make-a-face decorations: Raisins, colored candies, pretzels, carrot and green pepper sticks, etc. Let the children design their own open-face sandwiches.

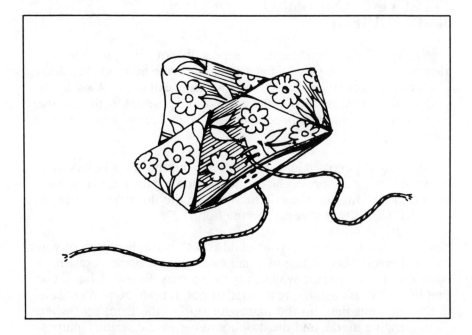

Keep old wallpaper books or wrapping paper and have each child at a birthday party make his or her own hat. Provide scissors, yarn for the ties, newspaper for making streamers, and a stapler.

Instead of using one of your good tablecloths for a child's party, spread a large, colorful bath towel on the table. It looks festive, absorbs spills easily, and washes quickly. A bright sheet works well, too.

If your child has a summer birthday and you have a garden, have an outdoor picnic or barbecue party—a great way to keep the birthday cake off your furniture. Do keep the insect repellent handy, though.

Start a holiday tradition by having each child select a special ornament for the Christmas tree each year. Store these in a box for each child, adding new ornaments every year. Once the children have grown, they'll have accumulated a whole set of ornaments to take to their own homes, and each one will bring back good memories.

SELECTING AND USING
BABY EQUIPMENT

When you're expecting a baby, especially your first, it's a temptation to go out and buy every baby product on the market—but don't. Buy an item only when you're sure your baby will use it. Also, before making the purchase, divide the price of the product by the number of months your baby will be using it. Then decide whether it's a necessity or a luxury.

One safe and economical alternative to purchasing a bedroom set for your toddler as soon as he or she gets too big for a crib is to pack the crib away and put the crib mattress on the floor. Your little one can't fall far if the mattress is on the floor.

Make a habit of having your child travel in the backseat of your car, and bring along a bag of small toys, games, books, crayons or other distractions to help while away the journey. Research has shown that in a car crash a child, restrained or not, is up to 50 percent safer in the backseat than on the passenger side in the front seat where glass, bending metal, and the dashboard can cause serious injuries.

Anything that keeps a child happy during a car trip is okay, right? Wrong. Toys that fasten onto the front of children's car restraints—plastic steering wheels, for instance—are potentially dangerous in a crash. Instead, take along harmless toys to keep the child busy during the trip—soft toys, dolls. paper and pencil games, puzzles for an older child, and so on.

If you will be walking a lot on cracked and bumpy sidewalks, look for shock absorbers on the stroller you buy; your baby will have a less jarring ride.

For maximum safety, the seat belt on a stroller should actually make contact with even the smallest baby's waist. Check before you buy.

To prevent a curious child from getting his or her fingers crushed, give your youngster a toy to play with while you collapse and fold the stroller. Then the child won't try to help you and risk getting hurt.

When looking at playpens, press on the floorboard to test a playpen's strength. Select a floor that holds steady without bending to your pressure—remember that your baby will jump around in a playpen enough to cause a thin floor to crack.

It's a wise precaution to fasten down the floor padding of a playpen. Sew two fabric strips on each side of the pad; the strips should be long enough to be tied across the underside of the playpen in order to hold the pad securely in place.

An automatic baby swing can sometimes be useful because the repetitive tick-tock often lulls a fussy baby into contentedness. If you have a choice, choose a swing with the longest running time. Otherwise you'll find that the baby has barely dozed off before the swing stops moving and the cessation of the comforting rhythm wakes her up.

Swings take up a lot of floor space. Before you buy one, check how easily it can be stored and whether you actually have room for it.

When your tot is ready to try a potty chair, he may be more amenable to using one he's chosen himself. So take him with you to buy it—but only after you've narrowed the choices to two models, either of which you can live with. A small child can't usually deal with multiple-choice decisions.

Caring for Your Pets

GENERAL CAT AND DOG CARE

Use your own comfort level as a guide to how weather is likely to affect your pet: If it's too cold or hot for you to be outdoors, your pet shouldn't be out either.

Don't leave your pet in a car in hot weather, even if the windows are open. Heat builds up very quickly in a car and can cause collapse or even death.

On a hot day, be vigilant about an animal's water supply. Fill your pet's bowl with cold tap water and freshen it often.

To avoid colds, keep your pet inside for several hours after a bath.

Whenever you give a command to your dog or cat, first establish eye contact. Eye contact tells the animal that you mean business.

Never give a young child a kitten or puppy (or any small animal) as a pet. The child may not understand that rough handling can cause the animal serious injury.

Never give a pet to any child without getting a parental okay.

When disciplining an animal, never call his name and then administer a punishment. Calling his name should be reserved for good things.

Never discipline a pet after the event. An animal cannot connect your present displeasure with a past misdemeanor.

It's not necessary to buy an expensive pillow for a dog or cat's sleeping basket. Two or three old towels will do just as well.

Carpet scraps make a perfect lining for a pet's bed or basket.

A wooden barrel, turned on its side and appointed with a pallet filled with wood shavings, makes a cozy doghouse. You'll need to provide a covering or "door" for the front of the barrel in cooler weather.

If you want to keep pets off the furniture, tuck mothballs in under the cushions.

Spraying a pet in the face with water from a plant mister will also discourage unwanted behavior.

Animals like sameness in their home surroundings. If you make extensive changes in your home or apartment, don't worry if your cat or dog loses his appetite for a few days. When the animal gets used to the new surroundings, his desire for food and water will return. The same thing may happen if you move to a different house, have houseguests, or have a new baby in the house.

Feeding Pets

Don't be misled into buying high-priced packaged food for dogs because it looks appetizingly red, like hamburger. A dog can't discern the difference between red and gray or brown. It's what's in the food that counts, not what it looks like.

In general, "dry" dog food is more nutritious than "wet" dog food. This also applies to cat food. Any time you get a new pet, however, check with your veterinarian for dietary recommendations.

A teaspoon or so of oil mixed into your pet's food every day will make his coat glossy, and stop dry-skin scratching. If the oil gives the animal diarrhea, however, withdraw the oil from the diet. If dry skin continues to be a problem, consult a veterinarian.

Never offer your dog or cat pork chop bones, chicken bones, or fish bones. These can splinter into sharp pieces and catch in your pet's throat. Make sure, too, not to leave these bones in the garbage where an enterprising pet can get at them.

Don't feed your dog immediately before or after exercising the animal.

If you must give your dog a bone, give only marrow or knuckle bones that have first been boiled to remove fat and grease that might cause diarrhea. Take the bone away as soon as it starts to splinter.

If moist pet food is not eaten within two hours, refrigerate it. Dry food and biscuits are the only foods that can be left out for any length of time.

Never offer your pet any food that's spoiled or moldy. Food that's unsafe for humans is also unsafe for pets.

If your pet has a water dish outside and always knocks it over, substitute an angel food cake pan for the dish. Put a sturdy stake through the pan's center hole and into the ground, and even a frisky dog won't be able to knock it over.

If you have both a cat and a dog, and the dog steals the cat's food, put the cat's food on platforms out of the dog's reach or behind a barrier the dog can't squeeze his nose through.

Do not feed dog food to a cat, or vice versa. The two animals have entirely different dietary needs.

If you have more than one cat, give each one its own food bowl. Separate the bowls by at least a foot at feeding time.

If you're going to change your pet's diet, do it gradually. A too-sudden change may be a shock to the animal's system. Cats and dogs—just like their wild ancestors—don't usually object to a monotonous diet.

Pet store owners are not necessarily reliable sources of information on animal nutrition or care. If you have questions about your pet's diet or health, see a veterinarian.

To prevent your dog from straining with impacted feces, add a teaspoon of cooking oil to each plateful of food.

Traveling With Your Pet

If you want to take your cat on a car trip, first take him for short rides; increase the time each trip so he gets used to the car.

If your pet is traveling in a carrier, put some of his favorite toys inside to make him feel more secure. Or line the traveling container with an old sweater of yours—the familiar smell will comfort the animal.

Before traveling with a pet, let the animal get used to the pet carrier. Leave the carrier out where the animal can smell it, explore it, and sleep in it.

Don't feed your pet for six hours before a car trip. If he has a tendency to car sickness, try to avoid giving even water for two hours before you leave home.

When you travel with your pet in a car, bring along a plastic freezer container of frozen water. As you travel, the water will thaw, and your pet will have a fresh drink ready.

If possible, carry water from home for your pet. The different mineral content of water in a new location could give him diarrhea.

When traveling with a dog, make sure he's on a leash before you get out of the car at your destination. Otherwise he may get over-excited and jump out of the car—and, possibly, get hit by another vehicle.

If you're traveling with a cat, keep the carrier firmly closed and don't release the cat until you get indoors. If the cat panics and jumps out of the car in a strange place you'll have little chance of finding him again.

GROOMING AND PEST CONTROL

When you bathe a dog or cat, make certain the water temperature is roughly 100°F. Warmer or cooler water will cause your pet distress and may make him difficult to handle.

When your dog or cat starts to shed hair, usually after the cold-weather months, massage his coat with your hands, then stroke the animal from head to tail with your palms. Get rid of loose hair this way and you'll have less all over the house.

Fleas spend more time off your dog or cat than on. If you see evidence of fleas, vacuum weekly (especially in dark corners and crevices) and then throw out the vacuum bag. Spray commercial insecticide around the house periodically for a few months.

If your dog smells bad but there's no time to give him a bath, rub baking soda into his coat and brush it off.

Check carefully for fleas when brushing or combing your pet, especially around the ears, face, and tail.

When you bathe a dog or cat wash the head, ears, and neck first. If you don't, any fleas that are on the animal will take refuge there while you clean the rest of his body. Be careful not to get shampoo in the eyes.

An important reason to keep your cat or dog free of fleas is that children have been known to get tapeworms from swallowing infected fleas. Fleas sometimes carry tapeworm eggs in their stomachs.

Always air out a flea collar for several days before putting it on your dog or cat, otherwise the chemicals may irritate his skin. Keep the collar away from both people and pets while it airs.

Avoid applying excessive amounts of flea powder to the coat of a dog or cat, and brush off all excess within 30 minutes of application. If your pet tries to lick off the flea powder he may get sick, so watch him while you're waiting to brush off the powder.

To eliminate fleas, try not to let your cat hunt; wild animals are often flea-infested and the fleas carry tapeworms. Empty the cat's litter pans frequently, and wash them periodically with a disinfectant.

A handful of naphthalene flakes in the vacuum cleaner bag will kill fleas vacuumed out of the carpet. Be sure to throw out the vacuum bag afterward.

A little brewer's yeast added to their food makes some animals less attractive to fleas.

Never use a flea collar at the same time as flea powder or flea sprays. This constitutes a harmful overdose.

Mixing onion or garlic salt with your pet's food may repel fleas. Also try mixing cedar shavings with your pet's bedding.

Groom short-haired dogs once or twice a week with a grooming comb. Long-haired coats need bristle or wire brushes and pet combs with rounded teeth.

Comb out a long-haired dog before a bath. Then you won't have to untangle wet hair.

Burrs will be easier to comb from your dog's coat if you first crush them with a pair of pliers.

If a skunk sprays your dog, it will help to wash the dog with tomato juice, then with shampoo and water. (Do this in a well-ventilated area.)

When washing your dog in the bathtub, prevent clogged drains by placing a piece of nylon netting over the drain to collect hairs.

If washing your dog normally leaves you soaked with suds, make yourself a coverall apron by cutting holes for your head and arms in a plastic trash bag.

If you scatter fresh pine needles under your dog's sleeping pad, fleas will keep their distance. If he sleeps in a doghouse, wash it out periodically with salt water; salt also repels fleas.

Your pet's ears should be cleaned once a month. Clean only that part of the ear canal that you can see, using a cotton swab soaked in mineral oil or alcohol. Wax protects the ear canal, so a small amount is beneficial.

Don't worry if your dog or cat drinks from the toilet (and most do). Water in a flushed toilet bowl won't harm your pet in any way.

But don't let a pet drink from a toilet that has a cleaner or freshener in the tank or bowl—the chemicals are toxic. Keep the seat down any time there are chemicals in the bowl.

If he handles the noise, vacuum your dog's coat when he starts shedding in spring.

Ticks can be pulled out with a tweezer. If you try to burn them out with a match, you could burn your pet.

Keep your cat or dog away from dieffenbachia; it's poisonous. And at Christmas, watch out for mistletoe berries and poinsettia; they're both poisonous too.

Worming medications are dangerous if used· incorrectly. Never worm your cat or dog with any medication not prescribed by your vet.

Don't worry if your cat or dog eats grass; many animals actually graze.

CARING FOR
YOUR DOG

If you want a dog that will live for a long time, pick one of the smaller breeds. Generally, the larger the dog, the shorter the life span.

If a young puppy has "garlic breath," don't worry. This is normal and shows the presence of "good" bacteria in his mouth. The odor will disappear in a few months.

Don't be alarmed if your dog twitches or jerks spasmodically when asleep. He isn't having convulsions; he's just dreaming.

It's not that difficult to give a dog a pill. Grasp his muzzle in one hand, then gently press the dog's lips over the upper teeth with your thumb on one side and your fingers on the other. Firm pressure will force the dog to open his mouth so that with your free hand you can place the pill as far back in the mouth as possible. Hold the dog's mouth closed and rub his throat to stimulate swallowing.

If your dog won't take a pill readily, try disguising it in a piece of cream cheese, which most dogs will eat without complaint.

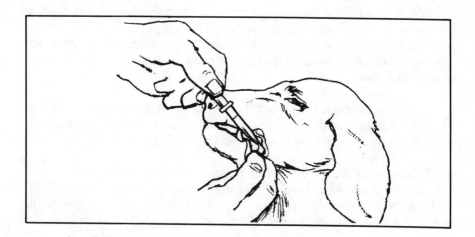

If you have to give a dog liquid medication and you know he's going to put up a fight, have him stand on a towel or bath mat in the tub. You'll have him in a confined space so he'll be easier to control, and any medication that gets spilled will go in the tub and not on your carpet. Pull out the dog's lower lip at the corner to make a pouch, and use a dropper or a syringe to place the medication in the pouch, a little at a time. Rub his throat to stimulate swallowing.

Don't feed a dog milk under the mistaken impression that it's good for his teeth. It will probably give him diarrhea.

If a dog shows the signs of shock after being injured or involved in an accident, keep him warm and don't change his position too suddenly. Sudden movement can cause shock to move to the irreversible stage. Shock is an emergency condition; an animal in shock needs to be kept warm with blankets and hot water bottles and transported promptly to the veterinarian.

If you need an outdoor stool sample from your dog, try not to include any soil in the sample. Dirt can contain harmless soil worms that may hamper the diagnosis.

Before buying a puppy try to check out his parents. The parents should be friendly and outgoing. If they're vicious or shy, the puppy will probably be the same.

When walking a puppy, keep him away from the droppings of other dogs. A disease known as parvovirus kills 75 percent of the young dogs under five months of age who contract it. (Older dogs are more or less immune.) Most puppies contract it through contact with infected feces.

Remove the leash from your dog when in the car. A leash can get caught in door handles or other projections and cause injury to your pet. But put the leash on before you let the dog out of the car.

When you start training your puppy—the best time to start is at the age of seven weeks—don't let the family get in on the act. Only one person should do the training, and it should be someone with patience who will also be spending a lot of time with the animal.

In training a dog, use one-word commands because they're clear and easy to understand. Don't expect a dog to understand complicated language structure.

In hot weather, it's best to exercise your dog early in the morning and late at night. Midday heat could be dangerous.

If the pads of your dog's feet become dry or cracked, rub a little petroleum jelly into them.

If your dog has just been clipped, make sure you don't walk him in strong sun; he could get sunburned.

It's important to wash off your dog's feet in the winter, because he will probably pick up salt and chemicals from the street and these substances can injure his feet, especially if the pads are cracked.

If you have to leave your dog alone at home, leave your radio on. The accustomed sounds will reassure your pet and make him feel less abandoned. The sound of the radio also deters would-be house-breakers by making it seem that someone's home.

To wipe away the rheum that gathers at the corners of your dog's eyes, use a dab of cotton dipped in a boric acid solution.

CARING FOR
YOUR CAT

Cats keep themselves clean by licking their fur, and sometimes the hairs collect in the stomach and form hairballs. The easiest way to treat hairballs is to give the cat a preparation that will coat the stomach and combine with the hair so that it can be passed in the stool. White petroleum jelly is an excellent coating agent. Put a teaspoonful or two on the cat's mouth and paws and let him lick it off.

Cats love to play with yarn or string, but such games can be fatal. If your cat has swallowed yarn or string, give white petroleum jelly to ease the passage of the material through the system.

Ear mites are a common problem with cats. If you notice black, brown, or gray waxy material in the ear instead of the usual clean pink surface, the cat may have mites. When giving medicine prescribed for mites, add some to the cat's tail too. Since a cat often sleeps with his tail curved around the body, the mites can infest the tail, thus reinfecting the cat's ears.

If you have more than one cat and one gets ear mites, chances are the others will too. Have them all checked by the veterinarian.

When petting your cat, always stroke in the direction in which the fur lies. Being stroked the wrong way irritates rather than soothes your pet.

Discourage your cat from leaping onto your stove, particularly if it's a smooth-top electric stove. Cats are heat-seekers by nature, and could burn themselves severely by getting too near to one of the active elements.

It is not unkind to keep your cat indoors, particularly if he has the companionship of another cat. Cats that are allowed to roam can get into fights with other cats, be attacked by dogs, or get hit by cars.

If your cat spends time outdoors, make sure he wears a collar with an ID tag carrying your pet's name and your phone number. A cat collar should have an elastic insert so that if the collar gets caught on a branch or fence the cat can slip his head right out of the collar and avoid choking.

If you do let your cat roam free, attach a bell to his collar as a warning to birds. Make sure his tags are on, too.

Animals' appetites lessen in warm weather. If you have a kitten, give him small amounts of food frequently on hot days. Don't let him fast too long.

If you give your cat vegetable oil for constipation, never put the oil directly into your pet's mouth. It may trickle into the breathing tubes and lungs. Instead, mix the oil with food.

Don't let a cat eat a dead rat or dead mouse. Not only does the rodent have internal parasites that will be transmitted to the cat, but it may have been poisoned, and the poison that killed the rodent could kill the cat.

Don't put off having your cat neutered because you think the animal will get fat afterward. Neutering doesn't make a cat fat; obesity is caused by too much food and too little exercise.

If you have to give a cat medication, place him on a bath mat or small rug that he can dig his claws into. Better yet, put the cat on the floor and squat down with your pet between your knees.

If a cat is too sick to clean himself, keep him brushed and rubbed down. Wipe runny eyes often.

Cats are prone to diabetes. If your cat is diabetic, have your vet show you how to give the required insulin injections. If you do this faithfully, diabetes will not shorten your cat's life.

When a cat gives birth to kittens, don't handle the newborns and keep children and strangers at a distance. Interference may upset the mother, and she may reject the kittens.

If a cat's membranous eyelids half-cover his eyes, it's a sign of illness—generally intestinal. Consult the veterinarian immediately.

Constant discharge from your cat's eye can be a symptom of either local infection or systemic disease. This is another case for the veterinarian.

If a kitten dies suddenly with no outward sign of illness, he probably had feline distemper. Your other cats should be vaccinated immediately.

Prefer home-raised kittens to those found in all but the most reputable pet stores.

Cats, like people, can have dental problems. A little dry food in the cat's diet helps prevent tartar buildup, but doesn't replace an annual dental checkup by the vet.

To give a cat a pill, hold the animal firmly on your lap or between your knees. Grasp the head on either side of the jaw so that the cat has to open his mouth. Place the pill as far back in the throat as possible. Close the cat's mouth and rub his throat gently to stimulate swallowing.

If your cat has a fever, don't give aspirin without a veterinarian's recommendation. Your cat will have trouble detoxifying and excreting it.

Cats are private creatures. If your cat has to stay overnight in a cage at the veterinarian's, take along a brown grocery bag with the edges turned back and ask the veterinarian to place the bag on its side in the cage. Your cat will have a place to retreat from the unfamiliar sounds and smells of the veterinarian's premises.

Raw liver is a natural laxative for a constipated cat. Give small servings no more than twice weekly. Adding a little milk to cat food might also work.

If your cat has diarrhea, cooked liver might help. Persistent diarrhea calls for veterinary attention.

If your cat will cooperate, clean his teeth once a week with a child's toothbrush or a cotton ball dipped in warm water.

Groom your cat regularly to help keep him free of hairballs. Brush short-haired cats daily. Long-haired cats should be combed first to get loose hair out, then brushed. Groom more frequently in hot weather when cats are shedding old fur.

If you encounter matted or tangled fur when combing a long-haired cat, use your fingers, not the comb, to separate the tangles.

When brushing short-haired cats, be sure to brush between the shoulders where the cat can't reach to groom himself.

If a cat appears malnourished even though well fed, has frequent loose stools, a lackluster coat, and a bloated stomach, you should suspect worms. Consult a veterinarian.

If you have two cats, one may suddenly react with hostility when the other returns from a trip to the vet. The stay-at-home cat is reacting to the strange smells his companion has brought back from the veterinarian's and will soon become friendly again.

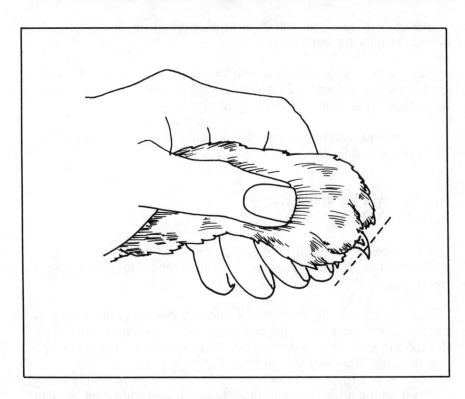

Your cat's claws will be easier to trim if you press the paw to expose the nails. Use special clippers from the pet supply store (never use human nail clippers on a cat). Cut the nail well clear of the quick—the pink line you can see running through the nail. The illustration shows how to cut a cat's nails.

When you clip your cat's nails, don't forget the dewclaws, which are equivalent to the nails on the human thumb.

Cats normally don't need bathing, but if your cat does need a bath, get a friend to assist. If you don't have help, place a small washable rug or Turkish towel over the side of the basin or tub for the cat to cling to. A cat gets panicky on a slippery surface where he can't get a foothold. Hold the cat with one hand and lather quickly with the other.

A double kitchen sink is best for giving cats baths—one side for soaping, the other for rinsing. Two plastic dishpans are also good.

Before bathing a cat, put a drop of mineral oil in each eye to prevent irritation from the soap.

After bathing your cat, rinse him with water and add a little vinegar for the second rinse. Blot the fur with a towel, then let the cat finish the drying process by licking the fur.

It's better to towel-dry a cat after a bath than to use a hair dryer. The noise of a hair dryer can terrify a cat.

BIRDS, SMALL MAMMALS, AND EXOTIC PETS

When holding a pet bird, be very gentle. Bird bones are so fragile that even the slightest pressure on the wrong spot can cause a fracture.

You won't be doing a pet bird a favor by putting it outside in its cage to enjoy fresh air. Wild birds will flutter around, attracted by the food in the cage, and your pet bird may pick up some of the parasites and diseases they carry.

Never let a pet bird loose in the kitchen. It may land on a hot pan or burner. And don't let a bird loose in a room where an electric fan is operating. Many birds fly into whirling fans and damage or destroy themselves.

If a pet bird breathes through its open mouth, you know it's sick. Buy a bird antibiotic at the pet store, pulverize it, and add it to your bird's drinking water. If this doesn't help, get it to the vet.

When you buy a parakeet, buy a young one. Older birds are less likely to become attached to their owner.

If a parakeet's beak becomes soft, add a few drops of cod-liver oil to its diet.

If you have a pet canary, protect it from drafts and from direct sunlight. Either can be fatal.

Don't buy a canary between July and October, which is the canary's molting season. A sudden environmental change during that period may send it into shock.

If you're buying a parrot, buy one born and raised in this country rather than one that's been imported. Domestic birds are likely to be healthier.

If you have a parrot, be ready for a lifetime relationship—it may live longer than you do. Never sell it to someone else because it will probably die of heartbreak if you do. Parrots become extremely attached to their owners.

If you want a parrot whose imitative speech most closely resembles that of a human, purchase the rather drab-looking African Grey.

Not every bird of the same species relishes the same type of food. For example, some parrots love spinach leaves and apple slices. Others prefer eggs, cheese, or tiny chunks of meat. Experiment to discover your pet's food preferences.

If you want a truly affectionate budgerigar, pick a male. They're friendlier than females.

It's easier for a girl or woman to train a budgerigar to speak because higher-pitched female voices are more like the budgie's than male voices.

Should a budgerigar regurgitate, don't worry about it. It's normal for healthy adult birds to do it periodically, since this is the way they feed their young. The habit is programmed into them.

Should your budgerigar escape from its cage and be difficult to catch, wait until dark. It can't see in the dusk as well as you can, and will make no attempt to avoid you.

If you have a pet reptile, such as a lizard or snake, and need to clean its terrarium home, have a duplicate (empty) terrarium handy in which you can place your pet while touching up its quarters. Otherwise it may escape.

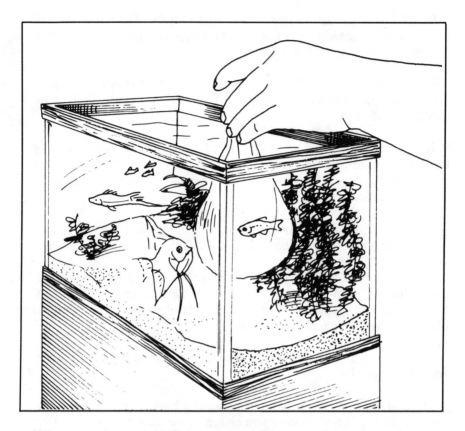

When you buy a goldfish at a pet shop and bring it home in a small plastic bag partially filled with water, float the bag in your home aquarium for 30 minutes before releasing the fish. This helps the fish adjust to the tank's water temperature.

Handle a pet salamander or newt with wet hands. The rough texture of dry skin may injure it.

If you have an adult land tortoise as a pet, you needn't confine it in an enclosure. Give it the run of your house or apartment. It will discover cozy places to sleep in and warm places to sun itself. Feed it slices of ripe fruit and pieces of leafy vegetables, and provide it with a nontippable pan of water to drink from.

If you keep aquatic turtles in a smartly appointed tank, feed them in another tank that you can empty with a minimum of fuss—they're very messy eaters.

Be careful about moving a small animal's cage from one location to another. An animal has a strong sense of territory, and may be seriously upset by relocation.

Avoid sudden gestures when handling small mammals. They're easily frightened and may bite you in fear.

If you have a pet rabbit (and no cat or dog), don't be afraid to let it loose in the house. It can be trained to use a litter pan filled with paper shreds. Keep an eye on it, however, to be sure it doesn't nibble on the furniture legs.

Don't be surprised if a pet rabbit eats some of its own droppings. The droppings contain B vitamins necessary for the rabbit's health.

If you have rabbits, don't keep two males together in the same cage or hutch. They'll probably fight like gladiators.

Never lift a rabbit by its ears. Doing so may damage the musculature around the head and make the ears floppy.

When picking up a pet mouse, lift it by the root of its tail, not the tip. The skin at the tip of the tail is likely to slide right off.

If you have pet mice, make sure they have a piece of unpainted hardwood to gnaw on. If they don't gnaw on something hard their front teeth will grow so long that they'll have difficulty eating.

It's best not to expose a hamster to direct sunlight for a prolonged period. If you do, it may die of heatstroke. Hamsters are nocturnal animals and prefer subdued light.

Never try to raise wild animals as pets. They can't usually be tamed, their behavior is unpredictable, and it's cruel to keep a wild animal in captivity unless you have all the resources and facilities—and knowledge—necessary for its care.

Never touch a wild animal that approaches you, even if it seems tame. The local animal control unit should deal with any out-of-the-ordinary animal visitors.

Monkeys don't make good pets. They tend to be destructive, ill-tempered, and apt to bite. Also, a solitary monkey is always unhappy. Simians crave the company of their own kind.

If you do have an exotic pet and it gets sick or acts strangely, call the nearest zoo or nature center. Their trained personnel can tell you what to do.

When approaching any injured animal, speak in a calm, soothing tone. Don't shout or cry out, which will only upset the animal more.

If an animal has been injured, always restrain him physically before you try to determine the extent of the injuries. If possible, have someone else hold the animal while you make the examination.

In the case of a suspected back injury, try not to move the animal more than absolutely necessary. Slide a board or plank under the animal and use strips of cloth to strap the animal to this improvised stretcher. Then take the animal to the veterinarian as quickly as possible.

If your pet appears to have broken a limb you can fashion a temporary splint out of a newspaper or magazine wrapped around the limb. Tie the limb to the splint firmly (but not so tightly as to cut off the circulation), and take the animal to the veterinarian.

In case of small heat burns to your pet, apply cold water or an ice pack to the affected area immediately. Never put grease or butter on a burn—it can make it worse.

Clothes Care and Good Grooming

LAUNDRY: USING THE WASHER AND DRYER

Always sort your laundry by color. Make three piles: One for white or predominantly white articles; one for light colors and pastels; and one for bright and dark-colored items. The third pile may have to be separated into colorfast and noncolorfast items.

If you have a large load, further sort it into lightly soiled, moderately soiled, and heavily soiled items. Then you may be able to do the lightly soiled items on the gentle cycle, which is easier on the clothes than the heavy-duty cycle needed for very dirty items.

Synthetics, blends, and permanent press fabrics should be washed separately from natural-fiber fabrics without special finishes.

To prevent tangling in the machine, tie and buckle all sashes and belts before laundering.

When preparing the wash, turn all pockets inside out to get rid of debris, and turn down the cuffs at the bottom of sleeves and pants and brush away soil.

It may seem like a chore, but you'll save time in the long run by mending seams, tears, and holes before laundering the garment. The damage could get worse during laundering and you'll have more work to do. Remember the proverb: "A stitch in time saves nine...."

Before washing a garment, check the label to see if the item has been pretreated for shrinkage. "Sanforized" clothing shrinks less than 2 percent after washing, but a "preshrunk" item may shrink as much as 5 percent. That much shrinkage can really affect the look and fit of a garment, so adjust washing and drying temperatures accordingly.

Load an automatic washer to capacity, if possible, to save time and energy. However, to keep wrinkling to a minimum, loads of permanent-press or synthetic-fiber knits should not be so large that items can't move freely in the washer.

To minimize wrinkling and shrinkage when washing delicate and permanent-press items, always use at least a medium water level setting for both the wash and rinse cycles, no matter how small the load.

Clean your washing machine periodically to get rid of accumulated soap scum and hard-water minerals. Run the machine through a warm water cycle to which you've added a gallon of distilled vinegar.

For the best circulation when using an automatic washer, mix small and large items in each load.

To dispense overabundant soapsuds in your washer, sprinkle table salt into the water.

You can get rid of grease and grime on shirt collars and cuffs by rubbing in a thick coating of chalk; allow this to sit overnight and launder as usual.

When laundering greasy work clothes, add a cup of kerosene to the soapy water for a cleaner wash. Or pour a bottle of cola into the wash water—cola loosens grease stains. Caution: Kerosene is flammable; don't pour it or use it near an open flame.

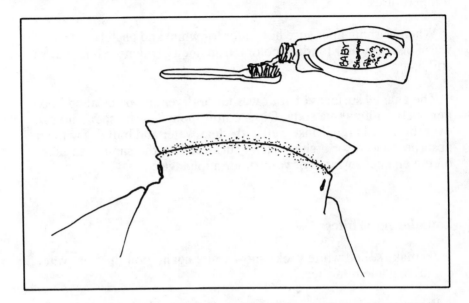

To remove dirty rings from shirt collars, apply a little baby shampoo to the area and scrub with an old toothbrush before laundering.

You can prevent fabric colors from bleeding by adding two or three teaspoons of salt to the wash and rinse cycles.

To boost the effectiveness of detergent for heavily soiled or greasy wash loads, add one cup of ammonia to the wash water.

If a lot of lint is being deposited on your wash, you may be using too little detergent. Increase the amount of detergent to help hold lint in suspension so it can be flushed down the drain.

Prevent snags in polyester garments by turning them inside out before laundering.

Flame retardant items should not be washed with soap or with nonphosphate detergents containing sodium carbonate. Either will cover up the flame retardant properties.

A general rule to follow in cleaning synthetic fabrics: Wash the clothes in warm water, rinse in cold water, and tumble dry at low temperatures.

When washing linen, use hot water for white and pastel colors and warm or cool water for dark colors. Iron linen garments while they're still damp.

The enamel surfaces of your washer or dryer can be cleaned inexpensively with baking soda. Dip a damp sponge in the soda and rub over the soiled area. Rinse well with clear water and buff dry with an absorbent cloth for a shiny clean surface. Use the same treatment on the enamel surfaces of your other appliances.

Laundering Whites

To make soiled white socks snow white again, boil them in water containing a lemon slice.

White socks will come cleaner if soaked in baking soda and water to help loosen dirt before washing.

Never launder white nylon with colored fabrics; a color transference may take place.

Enjoy truly white handkerchiefs again. Add a touch of cream of tartar to the wash water.

To prevent nylon from yellowing, presoak in a baking powder and water solution.

White synthetic items should be washed only with other white fabrics.

Laundering Darks

If you wash dark clothes separately you won't have light-colored lint to cope with.

Dark clothes and corduroy won't show lint after washing if you turn the garments inside out before washing.

Black lingerie and other black clothing tends to look brownish after several washings. To restore the pure black color, add bluing, coffee, or strong tea to the rinse water.

Wash, dry, and iron jeans inside out if you want them to retain their color instead of looking faded.

Bleach

When you use laundry bleach it should be poured into the wash water or otherwise diluted. Bleach should never be poured directly onto fabrics.

When bleaching, always bleach the whole item and not just a single stain.

Use the hottest water possible when using a bleach; this improves its performance.

To bleach delicate fabrics such as silk safely, use one part 3 percent hydrogen peroxide mixed in eight parts of water.

When washing synthetics that contain spandex (foundation garments or swimwear, for example) use only an oxygen or sodium perborate bleach.

Whiten diapers with less bleach by adding one-third cup baking soda to the beginning of the wash cycle.

Avoid using chlorine bleach on resin-finished rayon; it may cause the fabric to discolor.

If you find an unexpected rip or tear in a garment and want to know if it has been caused by bleach, inspect the edges around the area. If the fabric has been damaged by bleach, the edges will be weak and will tear easily. Yellowish discoloration is also an indication of bleach damage.

Fabric Softener

Fabric softener should not be used in combination with another laundry product, such as a water conditioner, in the rinse cycle. Stains may result.

You can remove stains caused by fabric softeners by rubbing the area with a liquid detergent or prewash spot and stain remover, and then rewashing the article.

Adding fabric softener to the final rinse water will reduce clinging when you wear your knit garments.

Too much fabric softener reduces the absorbency of diapers, so do not use it for each washing.

You can reduce static electricity effectively on acrylic fabrics if you add fabric softener only every third or fourth time they are washed.

When laundering baby clothes, it's best to use fabric softener sparingly because some babies are sensitive to softener build-up.

Cotton towels and washcloths will lose their absorbency if you use too much fabric softener on them; use it only occasionally.

If a laundered garment feels greasy or slick, you may have used too much fabric softener. Leave the softener out of the next few washes to see if the condition improves.

If you use a sheet-type fabric softener, you can use it in the washing machine's rinse cycle for loads that you plan to air dry rather than machine dry.

The Rinse Cycle

There will be no soap residue on machine-washed clothing if you add a cup of white vinegar to the final rinse water. For hand washing, add a proportionately smaller amount of vinegar to the rinse water.

A few drops of vinegar added to the rinse water will reduce static electricity in synthetic fabrics or curtains.

Bath salts added to the final rinse water will give underwear a nice fresh fragrance.

If you want to eliminate suds from a sink so that you can run the rinse water simply sprinkle salt on the suds.

To remove detergent and alkaline residue from diapers, add one cup white vinegar or a half cup borax to the final rinse water.

A handful of baking soda in the next-to-last rinse will keep diapers soft and fresh smelling.

Machine and Line Drying

Instead of running your clothes dryer in winter, hang your laundry in the basement to humidify the house and cut your energy costs.

Don't overload your dryer. Overloading causes wrinkles, wastes energy, and prolongs drying time.

Polyester knits should be removed promptly from the clothes dryer to prevent wrinkling and shrinking.

Line dry white and light-colored items in the sun to bleach them snowy white. Line dry bright-colored items in the shade.

When using a wire coat hanger to drip-dry clothes, cover the hanger with a towel or aluminum foil to avoid getting rust spots on the clothes.

When machine drying, shake out each article before placing it in the dryer; this speeds up drying time and reduces wrinkling.

Smooth clothes as you hang them on a clothesline, running your fingers down seams and along collar fronts and cuff edges. This eliminates a lot of ironing later.

Always wipe a clothesline clean with a damp cloth before hanging clothes.

Attach items to a clothesline by their sturdiest edges.

Silk should be dried out of the sun; sunlight weakens the fabric.

Wash plastic clothespins in mild soap and warm water in the sink, or in a mesh bag in the automatic clothes washer. Wash wooden clothespins in hot water and dishwashing detergent.

A permanently pleated skirt will keep its freshly pressed look after washing if you gather the pleats together tightly and carefully slip a nylon stocking down over the skirt before hanging it up to dry.

Machine washable slipcovers will fit smoothly after laundering if they're put back on the furniture while still slightly damp. As they dry completely, they'll shrink into place.

Be sure that cotton garments are completely dry before storing. If you put them away damp you could be inviting mildew damage.

LAUNDERING BY HAND

Silk can be hand washed in cool water with a mild soap. Air dry silk garments away from direct heat or sunlight.

When hand washing silk, use a shampoo containing protein. The protein in the shampoo feeds the protein in the silk.

Woolen garments should be washed in lukewarm water to prevent shrinking. Lay them flat to dry so that they won't lose their shape.

To prevent stretching, knit garments should be washed by hand and laid flat to dry. Place the wet garments on heavy towels, and replace the towels twice a day until the clothing is dry. Never put knit garments in direct sunlight—they will fade.

If you trace around a wool sweater on a large piece of paper before hand washing, you'll have a pattern to use when reshaping the sweater for drying. Cut out and discard the paper "sweater" and use the outside frame as your guide.

A half tablespoon ammonia added to a dishwashing detergent solution for hand washing a soiled sweater helps remove the soil without harsh rubbing.

If you love wool but can't wear it because it makes your skin itch, see if adding two tablespoons glycerin to two-and-a-half to three gallons of lukewarm rinse water softens the sweater and makes it easier to wear.

The alkaline content of soap can damage wool fibers. Use an appropriate nonsoap detergent, and make sure it is thoroughly dissolved in the wash water.

When hand washing a sweater, it's best to reach under it to lift it; if you pull it out of the water, it might stretch.

Give extra softness to hand-washed sweaters by adding a capful of cream hair rinse to the rinse water.

When washing by hand, use towels to blot excess moisture from sweaters, stockings, panties, and bras. Hang to dry only if the weight of the water won't stretch these items out of shape. Otherwise dry them on a towel-covered flat surface.

Add a few pinches of table salt to the water when hand washing a garment with both light and dark colors; this prevents the darker colors from running.

SPECIAL CARE ITEMS

Clean felt fabrics by wiping them with a dry sponge. If a more thorough treatment is necessary, hold the material over the steam from a teakettle and then brush lightly with a dry sponge or lint-free cloth to smooth the surface.

Place panty hose, knee-highs, and other small items in a mesh bag before washing in a machine; they will be less likely to get tangled or damaged.

To machine wash fragile garments, put them in a pillowcase and close it with a plastic-bag tie. Wash the bundle on a gentle cycle.

Unless the label states otherwise, you can wash your suede-look-alike skirts and shirts. If you add a couple of towels to the washing machine at the same time you'll find your mock suede items come out of the machine with a softer, smoother surface.

Turn a turtleneck sweater wrong side out before you put it in the laundry hamper. When it's washed, any makeup or skin oils that have come off on the neck area will be exposed to the suds and will come clean faster.

To prevent fraying, wash a foam rubber pillow in its case. Then air dry the pillow. Do *not* put it in the dryer.

Glycerin will keep plastic items such as shower curtains and baby pants soft and pliable; add several ounces to the rinse water.

Plastic or rubber rainwear should be air dried, not put in a clothes dryer.

Some down-filled garments can be machine washed using cold water and a mild detergent. Rinse well until the water shows no more suds, then machine dry at very low heat. Add a large bath towel or sneaker to the dryer to help rotate the garment.

When storing heirloom linens or baby clothing, preserve them in "mint" condition by washing and rinsing them, then rinsing again in a vinegar and water solution. Avoid starching or ironing and, if possible, dry them in the sun. Finally, wrap each item separately in tissue paper, placing extra paper between folds.

A little liquid detergent may be all you need to remove grass stains from washable fabric shoes. Or try a prewash spot and stain remover.

Hand wash quilts filled with cotton batting; machine washing is too harsh and will cause the batting to bunch.

Launder a patchwork quilt using the method recommended for the most delicate fabric in the quilt.

Lift a fresh grease spot from a nonwashable fabric shoe by sprinkling the spot with cornstarch; allow the cornstarch to soak up the grease for a few minutes and then brush it away.

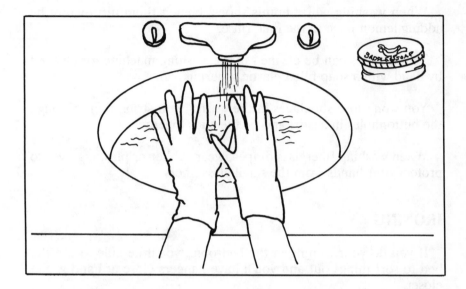

Hand wash leather gloves in saddle soap while they're on your hands, but don't rub them. Rinse them well and remove them. If they're hard to remove after washing, run a stream of water into them.

Before drying leather gloves you've just hand washed, blow into them to help reshape the fingers. When the gloves are almost dry, put them on once more, flexing the fingers to soften the leather. Then take off the gloves again, and dry them flat.

Once leather gloves have been dry cleaned, they should not be washed.

Hand wash rayon fabrics in warm water and let them drip-dry. Iron the garment on the wrong side while it's still damp.

If you spray new tennis shoes with starch before wearing them, dirt can't become embedded in the canvas and the shoes will always be easy to clean.

Nylon fabrics can be machine washed and dried at low temperatures. Add a fabric softener to the final rinse water to reduce static cling.

When washing white tennis shoes, bleach them ultra-white by adding lemon juice to the final rinse.

Tennis shoes can be cleaned in the washing machine, or cleaned by hand with a soap-filled plastic scouring pad.

You won't lose shoelaces in the wash if you string them through the buttonholes in a shirt and tie the ends together.

When washing fiberglass drapes, wear rubber or plastic gloves to protect your hands from the small glass fibers.

IRONING

If you do your ironing in the bedroom, you'll be able to use the bed to sort things out and you'll have hangers close at hand in the closet.

Always arrange your ironing paraphernalia according to whether you're right- or left-handed. If you're right-handed, pile up the clothes to be ironed on your left, and position the clothes rack to your right. If you're left-handed, reverse these directions.

A piece of lightweight muslin or batiste makes a perfect, inexpensive pressing cloth.

When ironing, keep thread, needle, and extra buttons handy for making necessary repairs before an item is pressed and stored in the closet.

When ironing, progress from articles or garments needing the lowest temperature to those requiring the highest temperature. And start with small areas, such as cuffs, before progressing to larger areas.

To make your ironing board cover fit perfectly, place it on the board while it's still damp from the washer, and let it dry in place.

To avoid scorching the fabric you're ironing, put it between two sheets of aluminum foil. The iron will glide smoothly over the foil and its heat won't scorch the fabric.

To prevent wrinkles, keep moving freshly ironed surfaces away from you.

Starch pillowcases lightly to make the fabric more resistant to stains from face and hair creams and oils.

To prevent collars, cuffs, and hems from puckering, iron them on the wrong side first.

Iron collars and cuffs from the ends toward the center for best results.

Iron double-thickness fabric on the inside first, then on the outside.

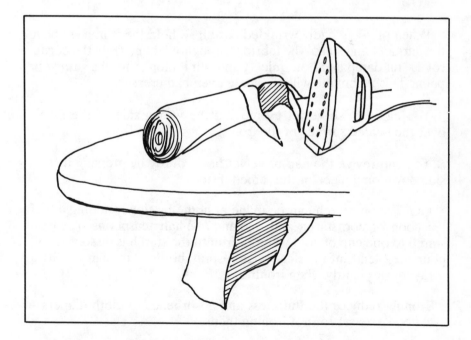

If you don't have a sleeve board, insert a rolled-up towel in sleeves so they can be pressed without leaving creases. Or make your own sleeve board from a heavy cardboard tube covered with a soft fabric.

So that shirt sleeves or tablecloths won't drag on the floor while you're ironing, slide a card table under the narrow end of your ironing board.

A thick magazine wrapped in heavy-duty aluminum foil makes an ideal iron rest.

Unwanted creases in a permanent-press fabric can sometimes be banished by pressing with a cloth moistened with a solution of two parts water and one part white vinegar.

Because acrylic knits stretch out of shape if moved when wet and warm, press each section dry and let it cool completely before moving it on the ironing board.

Hold pleats in place with paper clips when ironing. Be careful that the clips don't snag the fabric—particularly if the fabric has a loose weave.

When pressing badly wrinkled corduroy, hold the iron just above the garment and steam the fabric thoroughly. Then, while the corduroy is still damp and hot, quickly smooth it along the ribs with your palm. This technique will eliminate even bad creases.

You can refresh velvet by moving the wrong side of the fabric over the heated surface of the iron.

You can revive the nap of velvet or corduroy by pressing it right side down on a piece of the same fabric.

Quick spray starch can be made at home by slowly adding a half teaspoon of cornstarch and one-and-one-half teaspoons of wheat starch to one cup of cold water. Stir until the starch is dissolved and pour the blend into a clean, pump-spray bottle. You can use it to spray fabrics lightly when ironing.

Ironing reduces the fluffiness and absorbency of cloth diapers— two good excuses for not ironing them.

You can restore a shiny look to chintz by ironing the fabric right-side-down on waxed paper. This also adds body to the fabric.

To keep from giving your wash-and-wear garments a sheen when you do touch-up ironing, turn the clothing inside out and iron the wrong side.

To remove wrinkles from a tie, insert a piece of cardboard cut to fit the inside of the tie. Cover the tie with cheesecloth, and press lightly with a steam iron.

So that you won't flatten embroidery or eyelets when ironing, iron them face down on a thick towel. A towel is a good cushion for napped fabrics, too.

To avoid clogging the inside of a steam iron with mineral deposits from tap water, use distilled water. Better yet, use water collected from defrosting the freezer or from the air conditioner condenser—it works just as well.

If your iron is sticky from pressing starched clothes, clean it by running it across a piece of aluminum foil, fine sandpaper, or paper sprinkled with salt. If your iron is plastic-coated, though, avoid salt or other abrasives.

Remove cleaning-product residues from the soleplate vent areas of an electric iron with a cotton swab or a pipe cleaner.

TREATING SPOTS AND STAINS

Rubbing, folding, wringing, or squeezing a stained item can cause the stain to penetrate more deeply. Rough handling can also damage delicate fabrics. So always handle stained items gently.

You can remove some stubborn stains by gently applying liquid detergent to the stained area and then rinsing with cool water. If you sponge the area with rubbing alcohol after rinsing, the alcohol will help remove detergent residue and speed drying.

Rubbing alcohol cannot be used undiluted with all fabrics. One part alcohol should be diluted with two parts water for use on acetate, acrylic, modacrylic, rayon, triacetate, or vinyl.

Heat can make a stain impossible to remove. Avoid using hot water on stains; don't dry stained articles with heat; and never iron stained fabrics.

To lessen the likelihood of leaving a ring around a cleaned area, work from the center out when treating a stain.

Cornmeal, cornstarch, and fuller's earth are among the absorbent materials that can be used to soak up a stain. Use cornmeal or cornstarch on lighter colors; fuller's earth on darker colors.

When purchasing hydrogen peroxide for use in spot and stain removal, be careful not to purchase the stronger solution sold for bleaching hair. Buy the 3 percent hydrogen peroxide sold in drugstores as a mild antiseptic. It is a good bleach and is safe on most surfaces and all fibers. (Check dyed fabrics for color-fastness.)

If you're tempted to use nail polish remover on a stain, don't. Nail polish remover contains acetone, but it also contains other ingredients that could make stains worse. Use only pure acetone, and pretest dyed fabrics before treatment. Don't use acetone at all on fabrics that contain acetate.

When purchasing alcohol for stain-removal tasks, avoid products with added color or fragrance. Use common isopropyl alcohol (70 percent) which is adequate for most stain-removal jobs that call for alcohol.

Remove as much of a stain-producing agent as possible before treating the area with a stain-removal product. That way you'll avoid the possibility of enlarging the stain.

Pretest any stain-removing agent in an inconspicuous spot, such as the seam allowance or hem of a garment. Always run a sample test, since even water may damage some surfaces.

If you have to use more than one stain-removal agent in the cleaning process, thoroughly rinse each one away before applying the next.

When using or storing stain-removal products, be sure they're kept well out of reach of children.

As a safety measure, never transfer a stain-removal product to a new container. Keep it in the original container, which is correctly labeled and carries full instructions about the product's use.

Use only white vinegar for stain removal. Cider or wine vinegars contain color that can leave another stain. Dilute white vinegar for use on cotton or linen.

If white vinegar used as a stain remover changes the color of a dyed fabric, rinse the affected area with water and add a few drops of ammonia. Rinse thoroughly after this treatment.

When a stain-removal task calls for mild detergent, choose a white liquid dishwashing detergent. The dyes in nonwhite detergents may worsen the stain.

Detergent products used in automatic dishwashers or for heavy household tasks may contain alkalies that could set stains; they should not be used for stain-removal tasks.

Use laundry soap or pure white soap for removing stains. Avoid bath soaps that contain added moisturizers, fragrances, dyes, or deodorant.

If you don't have coconut oil to make a dry spotter (used for removal of many spots and stains), use mineral oil instead. It works almost as well. (A dry spotter can be made by combining one part coconut or mineral oil with eight parts liquid dry-cleaning solvent.)

You can make a soapless spot cleaner by mixing two cups of isopropyl rubbing alcohol (70 percent) and three quarters cup of white vinegar. To use, blot the soiled area until dry, apply the cleaner with a cloth or sponge, let it stand for several minutes, then blot the area dry again. Repeat if necessary. Blot the area with plain water after using the cleaner.

To make a wet spotter for nongreasy stains, combine in a small bowl one cup of water, two tablespoons of glycerin, and two tablespoons of liquid dishwashing detergent, stirring until the mixture is thoroughly blended. When using, blot the soiled area dry, apply the spotter and let it stand for several minutes, and then blot the soiled area dry again.

Stain Removal Techniques

A folded diaper makes a good absorbent pad on which to sponge a stained item. Be sure to lay the stained item on the diaper with the stained surface down, not up. This will allow the diaper to absorb the staining agent more readily.

When sponging a stain, work from the center of the stain outward toward the edge to minimize rings; sponge in an irregular pattern around the outside of the stain.

In order not to redeposit the staining substance on the fabric, change the absorbent or sponging pad as soon as the stain begins to transfer onto it.

When sponging a ring-prone fabric, barely touch the stain with the sponging pad so the stain absorbs the cleaner slowly. Then use a dry pad to blot up as much excess moisture as possible.

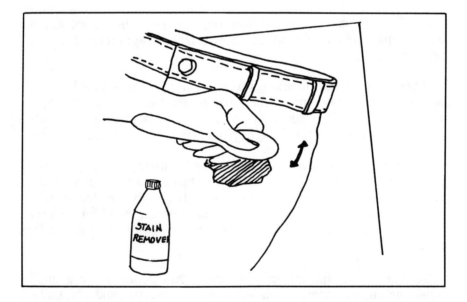

An effective way to remove many stains is by scraping with a teaspoon. The stain should be placed directly on the work surface, stain remover applied, and the edge of the spoon bowl moved back and forth in short strokes over the stain. Use firm but not hard pressure.

Although scraping with a teaspoon works well in removing stains from many fabrics, it is too harsh for use on delicate items; the treatment may harm the fabric more than the stain did.

Some stains can be removed from sturdy fabrics by tamping with a small dry brush with a handle (a toothbrush works well). The brush should be brought down squarely on the fabric from a height of several inches—rather like using a hammer. The action should be light enough not to bend the bristles.

An eyedropper or plant mister works well when flushing a stain from a nonwashable fabric. It allows you to apply a small quantity of water without wetting a large area. A plastic trigger bottle that can be adjusted to spray or fine stream also works successfully.

If you use water to flush a stain on a washable article, dip the stained area up and down in a bowl of warm water and change the water at least twice during the process.

If you want to use ice cubes to freeze a staining agent such as candle wax or chewing gum on a nonwashable item, place the ice in a plastic bag. You will get the desired freezing action without wetting the item. An item of suitable size can be put in a plastic bag in the freezer until the staining material solidifies; then it can be scraped off.

Removing Tough Stains

Try using salad oil to remove grease spots on cotton garments. Rub the oil into the grease, then wash the garment in hot, sudsy water.

Remove grease from fabrics by applying cornstarch or by dampening the area with salt dissolved in ammonia.

Perspiration stains will come out of clothing that is first soaked in salt water and then washed. Another way to remove perspiration stains is to apply a baking-soda paste and let it sit for a while before laundering.

To remove deodorant stains from fabrics, apply rubbing alcohol to the affected areas. Test for colorfastness before doing so.

To remove a bloodstain from a washable fabric, wash immediately with cold water (hot water sets stains); or cover still wet stains with a coating of dry starch. When the fabric dries, brush away the stains along with the starch.

A paste of meat tenderizer and cold water will lift stains from fabric.

If a fabric will not be harmed by the chemical, soak bloodstains with a solution of one tablespoon of ammonia to a pint of water.

Remove lipstick marks from a garment by rubbing with a slice of white bread.

Another way to remove lipstick smears is to dab the area with petroleum jelly and then apply a dry-cleaning solution.

Lipstick stains should also respond to this treatment: Pat salad oil on the smear, leave for five minutes, and then launder the fabric.

Makeup marks disappear from dark clothing if rubbed with bread.

Hardened stains sometimes can be loosened up by placing a pad dampened with stain remover on top of the stain and allowing it to penetrate for an hour or more. Also place a pad under the stain, and keep the top pad damp by adding more stain remover as needed.

Clothing that is badly mildewed should be soaked overnight in buttermilk, then laundered. If no buttermilk is available, dry-clean the clothing. Applying vinegar and exposing the clothing to sunshine also helps.

Mildew spots disappear from white fabrics if rubbed with a mixture of lemon juice and salt. Place the fabric in the sun to dry before washing.

There are several ways to remove chocolate or cocoa stains from fabrics. You can soak the stains thoroughly with club soda before washing, rub talcum powder into the stains to absorb them, apply milk to the stains because milk keeps them from setting, or rub shortening into the stains before laundering.

To remove grass stains from fabrics, rub lard into them. Denatured alcohol or a diluted solution of ammonia can also be used before laundering.

Another formula for removing grass stains: Combine a half cup of isopropyl rubbing alcohol (70 percent) and a half cup of water with one teaspoon of household ammonia and stir. To use, saturate the stained fabric with this mixture, let it stand for several minutes, rub to remove the stain, and launder as usual. (Use only on washable fabrics, and test fabrics for colorfastness before applying.)

Put scorched cotton in cold water immediately and let it soak for 24 hours. Often the scorched area will vanish without further treatment.

If you've scorched white fabric with an iron, sponge the stain gently with a cotton pad soaked in peroxide.

Treat scorch marks by rubbing them with an onion slice, soaking them in cold water, and laundering. Another way to treat fabric scorch marks is to dab them with an ammonia-dampened cloth, soak them in cold water, and launder. Or, try removing scorch marks by kneading them with a slice of dampened, stale white bread.

Treat an ink-stained fabric by soaking it overnight in sour milk or buttermilk. Speed the action of the milk by first rubbing salt into the stains.

Ink spots also respond to applications of lemon juice, hair spray, or denatured alcohol.

Water marks on clothing? Rub them with the rounded back of a silver spoon.

Remove ballpoint pen stains from clothing by sponging them with milk.

Another way to remove ballpoint pen stains or stamp pad stains (except red) is to sponge the affected area with water, or dampen the stain with a light mist of hair spray. Then apply a few drops of white vinegar, blotting every five minutes with a clean absorbent pad.

Erase pencil marks around shirt pockets before washing because they're more difficult to remove when wet.

Rub out mud spots in fabrics with a slice of raw potato.

You can remove shoe polish from clothing by applying rubbing alcohol. If traces of polish remain, add a tablespoon of borax powder to the water when laundering.

Try to rub soot from clothing with an art gum eraser. You also can sprinkle salt on a soot spot, let it settle, and then brush away both salt and soot with a stiff brush.

To eliminate a tar spot on fabric, apply shortening, let the tar soften for ten minutes, scrape it away, and launder the garment.

Nonoily spots on leather can be removed by buffing with an art gum eraser. Sponge with damp cheesecloth and saddle soap to remove surface dirt.

CHOOSING AND CARING FOR CLOTHES

Shopping for Clothes

Before heading off on a shopping trip, make sure you're wearing the kind of clothes and accessories you'd wear with the item for which you're shopping. For example, if you're looking for a jacket, wear a shirt and tie. This takes the guesswork out of how the item will look once you get it home.

Keep an updated index card in your purse or wallet with the sizes and measurements of all your family members. Then you'll be prepared to take advantage of an unexpected bargain without having to guess if it's going to fit.

If you're trying to match a color perfectly—for instance, you want a blouse exactly the same color as a skirt you've got—be sure to take the item with you. Your eye may not be as color-aware as you think.

Before shopping for a specific item or color of clothing, phone ahead to see if the store has what you're looking for. You may save yourself the time and trouble of going from store to store.

Staple fabric scraps snipped from skirt and pants hems or seams to a card, and carry it with you for help in coordinating shirts, sweaters, and accessories.

To see how a hose color will look on your legs pull the stocking over your forearm, not the back of your hand. Your hand is likely to be more tanned and will therefore alter the color of the hose. Also keep in mind that hosiery will look different in natural light than in the fluorescent light of the store.

When shopping for clothes, keep your eyes open for up-to-the-minute accessories—belts, scarves, earrings—that could give a fashion-conscious look to last year's basic dress or outfit. You may be able to put together a whole new look without buying a whole new outfit.

Factory outlets and fashion discount stores offer considerable savings on good-quality clothing. Some clothes offered at reduced prices as "seconds" have no visible flaws or have only minor flaws—a missing button or unraveled seam, for instance—that can be fixed easily without detracting from the overall appearance of the garment.

Buying clothes out of season allows you to save 50 percent or even more on in-season prices. Store-wide clearance sales are usually held after Easter, Independence Day, and Christmas, and offer values on off-season garments.

When budgeting for clothes, plan to spend the most money on items you'll wear frequently. An expensive winter coat is a more sensible buy, for example, than a costly evening dress that you'll wear only occasionally.

Buy hosiery, underwear, and handkerchiefs in multiple packs to save both money and shopping time.

Don't buy a garment with ornate or unusual buttons unless an extra button comes with the purchase. Otherwise you'll have to replace all the buttons if one of the originals gets lost.

Before purchasing a garment, check the cleaning directions. Some "dry clean only" garments may cost you more in cleaning bills than you're willing to pay.

Check the newspaper want ads and the yellow pages under "resale shops" to find stores that sell good used clothing. You may be able to pick up an as-new designer original for a fraction of the original cost.

If possible, look at yourself in a three-way mirror when trying on a new outfit. See how the garment fits in front, on the side, and in the back. Also check to see how it looks when you move about and when you sit down.

Before buying, test a stretch fabric garment by pulling it gently crosswise and lengthwise. If the material doesn't snap back into shape quickly you'll have trouble with bagging after wear.

When buying permanent-press garments, remember that you may not be able to lengthen the hemline without leaving an unsightly crease.

Never purchase a size smaller than you usually wear in the hope that you can alter the garment to fit. You can sometimes make a larger size smaller, but the reverse does not apply. Also, clothes that are too tight can actually make you feel tired.

Keep receipts for clothing; some faults may not show up until you put the garment on at home.

Fad fashions can be fun, but they aren't a good investment. Remember that you'll get only a few months wear out of a fad fashion, and budget accordingly.

Dressing to Suit Your Figure

When choosing clothes, keep in mind that dark colors tend to slim your figure and bright colors to enlarge it.

A vertically striped suit and a vest with waist points give the illusion of slimness and added height.

If you're overweight, wearing undersized clothes will accentuate the fact. Wear looser clothing to give the illusion of a slimmer figure.

If your legs are short, you'll look best in trousers that are straight, narrow, and uncuffed.

To de-emphasize a short, stocky figure, avoid horizontal stripes, large prints, plaids, and clingy fabrics.

Extra-tall women find that longer jackets and tops and cuffed pants help minimize height. A three-quarter-length coat will also minimize height.

If you're broad-shouldered, avoid oversized collars.

Your belt color can help to lengthen or shorten your torso. Match your belt to your shirt or sweater if you're short-waisted; match it to your skirt or slacks if you're long-waisted.

To lengthen a short torso, wear belts loosely so they fall below your natural waistline. Avoid wearing skirts or pants with wide waistbands.

To make your neck look longer, wear an open-collared shirt with a neck chain falling just below the collarbone.

Open-collared shirts and sweaters with oval, square, or V necks will help to elongate a short neck.

Coats and suits with broad shoulder lines can help draw attention away from a too-plump stomach.

Select shoes with heels in proportion to your height. Heels that are too high will make a person with short legs look awkward, not taller.

Shoes with wide straps that cut across the instep of your foot often make your legs look heavy.

Matching the tone of your stocking color to your shoe color helps create an unbroken line from your skirt hem to your feet, making you look taller and slimmer.

Heavy legs are flattered by sheer stockings or stockings with a thin vertical rib.

Dark stockings can help make your legs look more slender.

Slingback shoes make your legs look longer.

Nude stockings with an all-black outfit can make your legs look too stark against all that black. A darker tone may be better.

Dressing to Suit the Occasion

Dress conservatively for a job interview. Your prospective employer is concerned with your qualifications—not your familiarity with the latest fashion trends.

If you feel that your appearance is satisfactory but your voice doesn't do you justice, improve your voice quality by reading poetry aloud or talking and singing into a tape recorder.

Decide tonight what you're going to wear to work tomorrow. You'll feel better organized first thing in the morning and won't be surprised by missing buttons, stains, or ripped hemlines.

Keep an all-purpose outfit, complete with belt and other accessories, up front in your closet. It's a lifesaver on rushed mornings.

Always try on or at least check over a garment before you pack it for a trip. The morning of an important business meeting isn't the time to find that something needs cleaning or mending.

A man who keeps a sport coat and tie in the office closet, even if his normal attire is casual, will always be prepared for an unexpected luncheon or dinner invitation. Many good restaurants require male patrons to wear a jacket and tie.

A fresh flower at the neckline is a nice, light touch with a silk or chiffon party dress. Heavy, chunky jewelry doesn't enhance the delicacy of fine fabrics.

Double-Duty Dressing

A suitably styled leotard can do excellent double duty as a swimsuit.

A long skirt with a shirred waistline can be worn high as a strapless dress. Similarly, a poncho or strapless sundress pushed down to the waist makes a long skirt.

A bandanna can also become a scarf, headband, or halter.

A shawl or sarong can be improvised from any large piece of fabric.

Long narrow scarves can double as belts on pants or a skirt.

Buy gold or silver bedroom slippers to wear with your holiday evening dress. They look delicate and cost less than shoes, and if you choose well no one will know the difference.

Minimize vacation packing problems by choosing double-duty clothing. Look for nightdresses and pajamas that double as informal lounging or party wear; a bathrobe that you can also wear to the beach; and underwear pretty (and practical) enough to go in the swimming pool.

Caring for Your Clothes

When you buy a new garment, dab the center of each button with clear nail polish to seal the threads. The buttons will stay on longer.

Coating the edges of pockets with clear nail polish helps resist wear. The polish lasts through many washings. When it wears off, apply another coat.

Pegboard attached to the inside of the closet door provides easy storage for bags and belts. In the children's rooms, it's handy for all those items that inevitably end up on the floor of the closet or under the bed.

Hang your clothes on wooden or plastic hangers, being sure to close zippers and buttons. Make sure that shoulders, sleeves, and creases are straight and that collars are lying flat in place. The next time you search for that item in the closet you won't be disappointed to find a wrinkled, misshapen garment.

Hang up a suit or dress immediately after wearing. The wrinkles fall out more easily while the fabric still retains heat from your body.

Get into the habit of buttoning at least the top button of your coat or jacket when you hang it up. It will keep its shape better.

For longer wear and a better fit, cashmere and wool clothing should be shaken briskly after each wearing, and then hung to air before being put away in the closet.

To prevent a horizontal trouser crease midway up the trouser leg, put newspaper or tissue over a hanger rod, then fold the trousers over that. (Don't use newspaper for pale-colored pants—the newsprint may mark the fabric.)

Slip rubber bands on the ends of wire hangers to keep clothes from falling off.

Wind cellophane tape around wire hangers to prevent them from leaving rust stains on clothing.

Double the strength of wire hangers by taping two together with adhesive or cellophane. Then the hangers will withstand the weight of heavy garments.

When storing a hanging garment in a plastic bag from the cleaners, use a twist tie to seal any openings against dust.

Moths love grease spots as much as they love wool. Dry clean or launder woolen articles before storing.

Mothproofing products should be placed as high as possible in the closet because the fumes filter downward. Otherwise, your garments get only partial protection.

To store sweaters, fold them in a bureau drawer. Hangers can distort the shoulder shape of a sweater and stretch the garment unnecessarily.

Recycle those cardboard stiffeners that the laundry uses in your shirts. They're excellent for supporting the collars of shirts and turtleneck sweaters while they're hanging in the closet, and they keep the clothes from getting squished together.

Tired of having to press your scarves each time you wear them? Keep them wrinkle-free by pinning them with plastic clothespins to a coat-hanger in your closet.

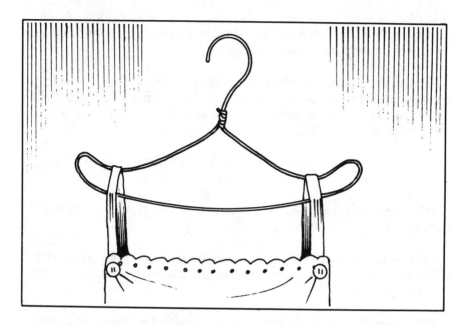

To prevent sleeveless garments from slipping off wire hangers, bend up both ends of the hanger.

To reduce wrinkles, lay a panel of tissue paper over the back of a garment before folding it.

Hanging heavily embroidered or sequined garments will distort their shape; store them flat.

Wrap adhesive or cellophane tape around your finger with the sticky side out to remove lint from a small area quickly.

Slip a clean blade in your safety razor and run it over a shirt collar to remove fuzz balls. You'll be able to scrape away the balls without snagging the shirt fabric.

To remove knots and fuzz balls from a sweater, gently rub them with sandpaper.

For a do-it-yourself lint remover, roll up a magazine and wrap wide adhesive tape around it, sticky side out. Pass it over lint, threads, and hairs.

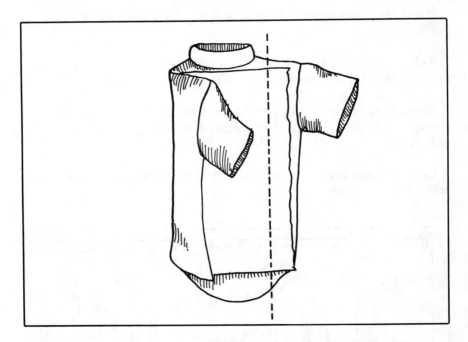

When folding clothes to be packed in a suitcase or stored for the season, lay the garment out flat and place a piece of tissue paper over it. For skirts, fold the garment twice vertically. For dresses, position the sleeves over the tissue paper, then fold the dress in thirds horizontally. Fold a coat or a sweater just as you would a dress but fold it over only once.

Line your bureau drawers with tissue paper to prevent clothing from catching and snagging on rough edges.

Loose dust and dirt won't harden and cut heavy fabric if you clean it with the small brush attachment on your vacuum cleaner, which will suck dirt out of tweeds and heavy woolens and revive the texture. Be sure the brush is clean before you start.

When brushing clothes to remove dust and lint you'll get better results if you brush with the nap rather than against it.

To remove the shine from wool, sponge the garment with a solution of one teaspoon ammonia to a quart of water. Press on the wrong side.

If a dress clings too much, wear a lightly starched cotton slip under it.

Rub zipper teeth occasionally with wax to keep the zipper working smoothly. Or rub the zipper with the stub of a candle.

To prevent mildew from forming in a leather-lined purse during storage, fill the purse with crumpled newspaper and leave it unfastened.

Keep an angora sweater from shedding by storing it in the refrigerator between wearings.

You can de-wrinkle clothing in a hurry by running hot water into the bathtub and hanging the garment on the shower rod. The steam will remove the wrinkles.

A business conference went on so long that your best suit smells like a tobacco factory? When you get home, run some hot water into the bathtub and add vinegar, then hang your suit on the shower rod and close the bathroom door. The vinegar in the rising steam will remove the smell of the smoke.

Take your jeans out of the dryer while they're still damp, smooth them carefully into shape and let them finish drying naturally. For a really trim fit, put them on and let them finish drying on you.

If you've let down the hems on an old pair of jeans, disguise the old hemlines by coloring them in with a permanent ink marker.

You can brighten up old jeans by washing them with a brand new pair. Some of the dye from the new pair will inevitably run out and into the faded jeans.

When the weather turns rainy or snowy, spray the hem of your coat with a stain repellant to protect it from mud and splashes.

Before trying a chemical stain or spot remover, test the remover on a hem, seam, or other hidden part of the garment. If the liquid discolors or stains the cloth, you won't have ruined the entire garment, and you'll know that you should have a professional dry cleaner take over.

Club soda, either straight from the bottle or flat, is a great emergency cleaner. Apply it with a damp cloth.

If you use a cleaning fluid on an item of clothing, don't use water on it as well.

When taking soiled garments to the dry cleaner, be sure no spots or stains are overlooked. Pin a note to each spot, explaining what the substance is, to call it to the dry cleaner's attention. Always have belts and accessories cleaned along with the main garment to be sure the whole outfit remains the same color.

Leather-look fabrics such as vinyl or polyurethane are easily cleaned with soap and water applied with a damp cloth.

Shoes, Boots, and Hosiery

To get a good fit, shop for new shoes when you've been on your feet for a while. Shoes that feel fine first thing in the morning may be painfully tight after you've been walking around and your feet have swollen.

Feet swell in the heat, so consider buying summer shoes a half-size larger for extra comfort.

When buying shoes you'll be wearing a lot, consider choosing a pair made of leather or woven fabric. Since these materials breathe, the shoes will be more comfortable to wear than those made of synthetics.

Sandpaper the soles of new shoes to keep them from slipping. Or rub the soles of the shoes against a cement step or sidewalk.

Insert shoe trees immediately after removing shoes, when the shoes are still warm and pliable.

Never store leather shoes in plastic bags. The plastic keeps the leather from breathing.

Shake baking soda into shoes to help banish perspiration odors.

Place strips of adhesive tape around the inside of boot tops to keep them from leaving dark rings on your stockings during rainy weather.

Make sure your shoe wardrobe includes a pair of shoes in a neutral color that goes well with a wide range of clothing colors.

Change shoes daily to double their life. Airing them out between wearings prevents perspiration from rotting the leather.

As a general fashion rule, shoe color should be the same color as, or darker than, your outfit.

To waterproof leather shoes or boots, apply silicone-based waterproofer and rub it on well with your hands.

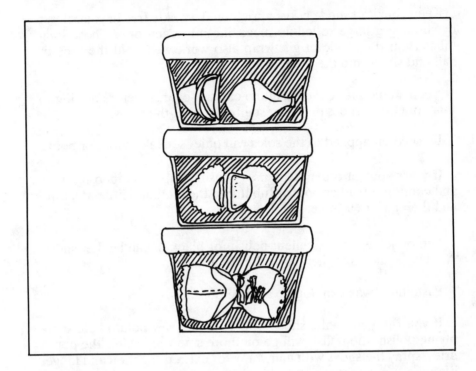

Rummaging through shoe boxes to find a certain pair of shoes is time-consuming and inconvenient. If you cut one end off each box, then stack the boxes on a shelf beside or on top of each other, you'll be able to select a pair at a glance.

A quick way to dry shoes is to hang them by their heels on a chair rung. Since they're off the floor, air can circulate on all sides.

Rain-soaked shoes sometimes stiffen up when they dry. Avoid stiffness by rubbing saddle soap into them before they dry completely.

Weather-proof and cream-polish new leather shoes and handbags before the first use to give them protection and shine. Keep them well polished to prolong their life span and to make it easier to remove surface dirt.

Remove water stains on leather shoes by rubbing with a cloth dipped in a vinegar and water solution.

Keep your soft suede boots upright and wrinkle free in your closet by slipping a large rolled-up magazine into each one. Those long tubes from the inside of gift wrap also work well; fold the tube in half and slip it into the boot.

Keep an old pair of shoes in the car and change before driving so that your good shoes don't get scuffed behind the heels.

Linseed oil applied to the soles will quiet squeaky shoes or boots.

If you're out of other cleaners, try using baby shampoo to clean and condition leather boots. Rub it into the leather a little at a time and then buff to a shine.

Lemon juice is an excellent polish for black or tan leather shoes. Apply the juice and then buff with a soft cloth.

Paste floor wax can double as shoe polish.

If you rub your white shoes with a slice of raw potato before applying polish, the polish will go on more smoothly. After the polish dries, spray the shoes with hair spray for extra protection and longer life.

If white shoes have dark heels, apply a coat of colorless nail polish to the heels. This prevents white polish from rubbing off on the heels later on. You can just wipe off any leaks with a damp cloth.

Scuff marks on white or pastel shoes can be removed by rubbing the spot with nail polish remover.

To remove surface dirt from suede and napped leather shoes, brush them with a bristle brush.

Remove rain spots from suede shoes, bags, and hats by rubbing the spots gently with an emery board.

A little petroleum jelly rubbed into patent leather shoes gives them a glistening shine. It also keeps them from cracking in winter.

You can rub dirt marks off suede shoes with an art gum eraser; then buff with fine sandpaper.

To keep patent leather shoes from cracking, treat them periodically with a leather conditioner or preservative. Don't wear them in very cold weather because cold causes patent leather to crack.

To clean stained suede shoes, first brush them, then hold them over the steam from a kettle or an iron just long enough to raise the nap but not to wet the shoes. Brush the nap with a soft brush.

Give black suede a face-lift with a sponge slightly moistened with cool, black coffee. Rub in the coffee gently.

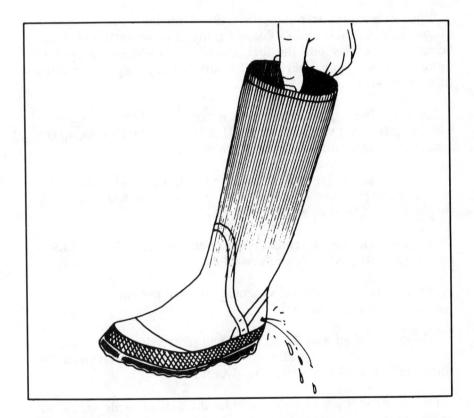

To find a pinhole leak in a rubber boot, fill it with water. Mark the leak and patch it.

If leather or vinyl shoes get wet, stuff them with paper to hold their shape and let them air dry. To preserve the finish on vinyl shoes, redampen with warm water and apply glycerin with a soft cloth.

Use cardboard tubing from gift wrap or paper towels to keep boots upright and in shape during nonwinter months. Or stuff the boots with newspaper so that they maintain the correct shape.

Weatherproof your boots against rain and snow by applying a silicone spray, especially at the seams.

A good cleaning with saddle soap will help remove road salt and other chemicals from leather boots. Check your boots daily for signs of salt stains; salt can eat away the leather if not removed promptly.

When wearing boots, put on two pairs of thin cotton socks instead of one pair of thick socks. The air trapped between the two thin layers will both insulate the feet and allow moisture to evaporate more quickly, keeping feet dry. Moisture doesn't evaporate readily from thick socks.

Lift off a fresh grease spot from a nonwashable fabric shoe by sprinkling the spot with cornstarch. Let the cornstarch soak up the grease for several minutes, then brush it away.

Lighter fluid can be used to remove tar and asphalt marks from synthetic shoes. Work in a well-ventilated area, and be extremely careful to keep fluid away from flames.

To clean shoe brushes, soak them in warm, sudsy water to which a few drops of turpentine have been added.

When metal tips come off shoelaces, harden the ends of the laces with a little nail polish.

Glycerin applied with a soft cloth will soften shoes that have become hard while drying after an outing in the rain. Dampen the shoes slightly before applying the glycerin.

Fine sandpaper works well to restore the nap on suede shoes, but use it gently.

Wear a pair of cotton or rubber gloves while putting on or removing your hose to reduce the chance of snagging the stockings with your fingernails.

Use an art gum eraser or emery board to clean suede shoes inexpensively.

Misplaced your shoehorn? Try using the handle of a tablespoon instead.

Neutral stockings worn with brightly colored evening shoes or slippers allow attention to be focused on the shoe color.

Your panty hose will last longer if given the following treatment before the first wearing. Immerse the hose in water, wring out, put in a plastic bag, and place the bag in the freezer. Once frozen, remove the hose from the freezer and hang up to dry. Sounds silly, but it works.

If you don't have any colorless nail polish to dab on a stocking to stop a run, try using hair spray instead.

If you have mismatched stockings left over from various pairs, you can dye them all the same color by boiling them in water along with two tea bags. Let them sit in the water until it cools, and then rinse and dry your newly matched hose.

Caring for Furs

Furs and down garments need breathing space, so give them plenty of room between other garments in your closet.

After you wear a fur, just shake it gently, rather than combing or brushing the garment.

To prevent your fur from losing its shape, always store it on a heavy wooden or plastic hanger designed to support the weight of a heavy garment.

Never store your fur coat in a plastic, cloth, or paper bag. Furs should be stored with no covering; they need good air circulation to prevent the hairs from drying and breaking.

If snow or rain dampens your fur, hang it to dry in a cool place where there's plenty of air circulation, perhaps on a shower curtain rod.

Avoid sitting for long periods in a fur coat. Excessive friction causes the fur to wear down.

Don't carry a shoulder bag when you're wearing a fur coat. The constant friction of the strap against the fur will wear down the hair.

Keeping your fur coat at home year-round in a cedar closet will damage the fur. Fur needs to be stored at cold temperatures and with proper ventilation if it is to keep its natural sheen and luster. At the first sign of spring weather, put your fur coat into cold storage where it will be guaranteed a constant, even temperature and correct humidity and air circulation. Your coat will last much longer.

Dust and grime on fur cannot be safely removed through dry cleaning or regular laundry methods. These cleaning techniques will strip the fur of its natural oils, causing drying and shedding of the hairs. Always have your fur professionally cleaned by a furrier.

Jewelry Care

Use fishing line to restring a broken necklace. It's easy to handle and extremely sturdy.

Bracelets and necklaces will stay tangle-free if they're stored on cup hooks attached to the inside of your closet door.

Hang long strings of beads on a man's tie rack in your closet. They're easy to get at and they won't tangle.

To keep necklaces and fine chains from tangling together in your jewelry box, cut a plastic drinking straw in half and slip one end of the chain through the straw; fasten the clasp closed. Slip each chain through a separate straw.

Because post earrings are easy to lose when traveling, hold them together on an index card.

For an instant jewelry chest, line a small drawer with foam rubber; the foam will keep things from slipping around.

If you lose a post-type pierced earring, you can put its double to new use as a tie or scarf pin or as a pushpin for a bulletin board.

To untangle a knot in a chain necklace, lay the chain on a piece of waxed paper and put a tiny drop of salad oil on the knot. Working with two straight pins, carefully loosen the knot.

Storing jewelry in plastic bags will reduce tarnish by protecting it from dust, lint, and moisture. Don't store pearls this way, however, because they need to breathe.

Protect pearls from dust, cosmetics, and perfume, all of which can dull them.

Separate jewelry in a jewel box so that the harder stones won't scratch the softer stones and metals.

Wear your silver jewelry frequently; it won't tarnish as quickly and your skin oils will eventually give the silver a protective satiny finish.

To restore luster to a dried-out emerald or jade, dip a toothpick in olive oil and gently rub it over the stone's surface. (Use this method only if the piece won't be resold, since the stone may darken.)

To clean around the settings of precious stones, use a cotton swab dipped in alcohol.

A piece of chalk in your jewelry box will prevent costume jewelry from tarnishing.

More Good Grooming Tips

When you're getting dressed, slip your skirt or dress over your head instead of stepping into it. You'll avoid broken zippers and ripped hems.

Go through your closets annually and discard any garment you haven't worn in the past 12 months. Make a mental note of any color or styling mistakes, and avoid repeating these on your next shopping trip.

Keep a "grocery list" of clothing needs inside your closet door. Then watch for sales and specials on the items you need.

To keep belts and handbags neatly in place, hang them on large shower curtain hooks on your clothes rod.

If you're short on closet space, you can put your hats, scarves, belts, and bags on display. Put up two lattice strips on the wall and add hooks.

Glue a piece of foam rubber to the underside of a shoulder bag strap or the straps on a schoolbag; the bags won't slip when you carry them.

Up to one-third of your body heat can escape through your head, so always wear a hat or scarf in cold, windy weather.

Natural fibers such as wool and cotton are warmer in cold weather than synthetics. Because natural fabrics breathe, they allow body perspiration to evaporate so that you don't feel damp and chilled.

White cotton is an ideal fabric for summer wear. White reflects the sun's rays and keeps you cool. Cotton also lets your skin breathe.

If you perspire heavily, include as many natural fiber garments as possible in your wardrobe, including cottons for summer. Remember that cotton blends will not wrinkle as easily as pure cotton fabrics.

CHILDREN'S CLOTHES

If you offer your child a choice of outfits he or she may be happier and more cooperative about getting dressed. Giving the child a choice of clothes is also a valuable introduction to decision-making.

You can buy a child's clothing without bringing the child along if you trace paper patterns of clothing that already fits.

Children will be more likely to hang up their clothes themselves if they can reach the hooks easily.

Iron-on patches on the insides of the knees of new jeans will help the jeans last longer.

When dressing a toddler, zippers are easier to deal with than buttons. Front fasteners help, too.

Offer a raisin or piece of dry cereal to a child who is resisting getting dressed. The child will close his or her hand around it and make it easier for you to get the hand through a sleeve.

It is easier to put shoes on a wiggly toddler who is "trapped" in a high chair.

Shoelaces will stay tied if you dampen them before tying.

Knots tied in the ends of your child's shoelaces will prevent the laces being pulled out altogether.

If your child is outgrowing his or her winter jacket and you need to make it last the season, add knitted cuffs to the sleeves. (You can buy knitted cuffs at department store notion counters.) As a bonus, the cuffs keep out cold air.

Most youngsters have a tough time telling right from left, especially when putting on shoes. You can help by putting a distinctive mark (such as a square of red tape) on the right shoe.

If your child seems to have trouble grasping the concept of matching the heel of his foot to the heel of his sock, take the easy way out—buy tube socks.

If you cut two tiny parellel slits in the tongue of a child's shoe and pull the laces through the slots to tie as usual, the tongue won't slip down out of place.

If you dip the ends of frayed shoelaces in clear fingernail polish, they'll be easier to poke through eyelets.

If your toddler has figured out how to take off mitten clips, attach his mittens to a long string that goes across his back and down both coat sleeves.

Her dad's shirt, with the collar and sleeves removed, makes a shortie nightgown for a daughter. Adult size T-shirts also make great nightshirts for kids.

If you use elastic thread to sew buttons on the cuffs of your child's shirts, the child won't have to button and unbutton the cuffs continually. The elastic provides just enough stretch to allow the child to slip his or her hand through the cuff even when it's buttoned.

An inexpensive inner tube repair kit from the hardware store can also be used to repair rubber boots.

Spray children's raincoats with silicone furniture polish to keep them looking new.

Put a plastic bag around your child's foot before slipping on galoshes. This makes fitting easier and keeps feet warmer, too.

Marking pens don't show up on dark-colored boots, so try writing the child's name with bleach on a cotton swab.

If your youngsters' boots are wet inside, you can dry them quickly and thoroughly with a portable hair dryer.

Mitten clasps can help hold overall straps so they don't slide off a toddler's shoulder. Or sew Velcro tabs on straps where they cross.

If a crease remains after you've lengthened a child's dress, disguise it with a row of lace, braid, or ribbon. Try to use the same trim elsewhere on the garment as well, to give a well-put-together look.

Extend the wear of your small daughter's pretty smock dresses that are too short by having her wear them as tops over jeans.

Masking tape can be used to mend torn tabs on disposable diapers.

You'll always have diaper pins handy away from home if you pin a few to your key chain.

A bar of soap makes a good pincushion for diaper pins and also lubricates them so that they slip through cloth diapers more easily.

If your baby's plastic pants are becoming dry and brittle, rub a little baby oil into them—or put the oil into the rinse water.

Personal Care

MAKING YOUR OWN
SKIN CARE AIDS

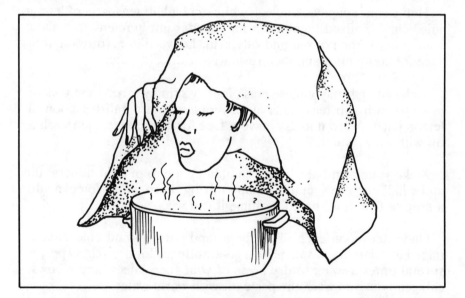

A few tablespoons of your favorite herbs boiled for several minutes in water make an easy, once-weekly facial sauna to unclog pores.

Just remove the pot from the heat and use a bath towel as a tent while you let the steam rise to your face for three to five minutes. If you then rinse your face with very cold water to close the pores, your skin will feel super-clean and smooth.

Three tablespoons of finely ground oatmeal mixed to a smooth paste with three tablespoons of witch hazel give you a super-economical homemade toning/cleansing mask for normal to oily skin. The paste should be applied to your face and allowed to dry for 20 to 30 minutes, then rinsed off with warm water.

A washed, unpeeled cucumber, sliced into your blender and pureed with a tablespoon of yogurt until smooth, makes a drying facial mask for oily skin. The mask should be applied to your face and allowed to dry for 20 minutes, then washed off with warm water. Finish with a cool water rinse.

Here's a homemade wash that will benefit any type of skin: Peel and core a large slice of pineapple and whip it to a pulp in the blender; drain off the juice and apply it to your face for 15 minutes. Then wash off.

Half a small papaya, one egg white, and a half teaspoon of lemon juice can be mixed together in the blender until creamy to make a toning mask for normal and oily skin. Leave the mixture on your face for 20 minutes and then rinse well with cold water.

Make an egg/mayonnaise mask for dry skin by mixing the yolk of one egg with two teaspoons of mayonnaise and a half teaspoon of lemon juice. Allow it to dry on your face for 20 minutes, then wash it off with warm water.

Make your own baby oil by combining a cup of light mineral oil and a half cup of vegetable oil and mixing thoroughly. You can add a drop or two of oil-based perfume if you wish.

One tablespoon each of finely ground oatmeal and cold cream, mixed to a smooth paste, make a good softener for dry skin. Apply it several times a week to dry areas of your feet, knees, and elbows; rub gently as you wash the paste off with warm water.

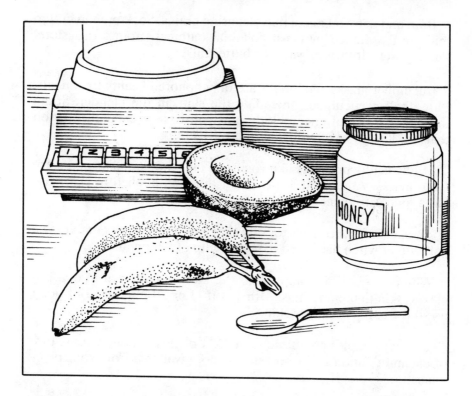

Banana and avocado combine to make a fruit mask for dry skin. The ingredients are a whole banana sliced with half the peel left on, half an avocado, and one teaspoon of honey. The mixture should be pureed until smooth, then allowed to dry on the face for 20 minutes. After washing it off with warm water, finish with a cool water rinse.

Remove rough skin with a mixture of a quarter cup of table salt, a quarter cup of Epsom salts, and a quarter cup of vegetable oil. Stir constantly as you mix the ingredients, then massage the paste into rough skin for several minutes. Remove by bathing or showering as usual.

Massage your face with a combination of sesame and olive oils. Leave the mixture on your face for a few minutes then scrape it away using a Popsicle stick or tongue depressor. You'll be peeling away dull dead skin cells in the process, leaving your skin glowing.

Bran and oatmeal make fine cleansing grains. Soak bran in buttermilk until softened or mash colloidal oatmeal (from a drugstore) into a paste with warm water or buttermilk.

Cucumber masks and lotions are time-honored beauty treatments. Puree half a cucumber, including the skin, in the blender. Strain through a piece of cheesecloth, and you have a cucumber lotion that will last for several days in the refrigerator.

Mildly acidic products like yogurt or buttermilk make good clarifying masks. Any acidic fruit, sliced thin and applied to skin, also has a mild astringent effect.

An excellent astringent for oily skin can be made by combining a half cup of witch hazel and a quarter cup of lemon juice.

Whipped egg white, applied to the face and allowed to dry, is a classic skin-tightening mask. Rinse off after 20 minutes. But don't use this treatment on dry skin.

To treat pimples and discourage skin blemishes, apply a mixture of calamine lotion and 1 percent phenol (available from your pharmacist).

Natural vegetable oils make excellent cleansing creams. Use them to remove makeup, then apply an astringent to be sure all the excess oil is removed.

If you run out of your favorite brand of moisturizer, apply a thin film of cold-pressed soy oil or almond oil. Your skin will be just as grateful.

Here's a great winter skin treatment. Soak a cloth in natural cider vinegar and lay it against your skin for 15 minutes. Remove the cloth and gently rub the skin with avocado oil, then rinse with warm water and apply a moisturizing lotion.

Add several handfuls of Epsom salts to your bathwater to help revive tired muscles.

Instead of buying bath oil, add two to three tablespoons of vegetable oil to your bath. For foaming oil, add a teaspoon of plain shampoo. (Never use special herbal, dandruff, coloring, or other treatment shampoos for this purpose.)

Toss two or three teaspoons of baking soda into the tub as a skin softener.

Before drawing your bath, mix equal parts of peanut, camphor, and castor oils for a soothing and fragrant skin massage.

To get rid of flaky skin or the remnants of last summer's tan, add a cup of natural cider vinegar or the juice of three fresh lemons to your bathwater. Slough away the dead skin cells with a dry sponge or brush.

Cornstarch sprayed with your favorite scent makes an excellent dusting powder.

Adding instant powdered milk to your bathwater does wonders for dry skin in cold weather. It not only softens the water but also makes your skin feel silky smooth without leaving a sticky film.

ALL-WEATHER
SKIN CARE

If you usually wear makeup, try to go without makeup completely one day a week to give your skin a chance to breathe.

A good night's rest does wonders for your complexion. If you're a poor sleeper, try this nightcap before bedtime: Mix one teaspoon of instant powdered milk into a cup of hot skim milk, add a teaspoon of honey or molasses, and sip it slowly.

If your face tends to be puffy when you wake up, keep skin freshener, astringent, and cotton pads for your eyelids in the fridge. These cooled skin aids offer a wonderful pickup to the skin in summer, too.

To lessen the drying effects of indoor heat on your skin in winter, place a humidifier or a basin of water in your bedroom at night.

Dry air at home or at work isn't healthy for your skin. House-plants, placed on trays containing pebbles and water, can act as natural humidifiers and add moisture to the air.

Try to schedule your bath for the evening so that you won't have to expose your skin immediately to outdoor air. Skin takes at least eight hours to replenish its natural oils after bathing.

It's best to apply perfume to your skin instead of to your clothes. Chemicals in the perfume may weaken a fabric or change its color.

For a smoother, softer finish when removing leg hair, rub moisturizing lotion on your legs before applying shaving foam.

When you buy fragrant soaps, unwrap them and tuck the bars into your linen closet or your lingerie drawers until you need them. They'll scent your linens or clothes, and the soaps will dry out and therefore last longer in use.

To protect your skin against cold, dry winter air, wear makeup that is oil- rather than water-based. This helps to moisturize and protect your skin.

If you love skiing and other snow sports, wear a moisturized sun-screen whenever you're outdoors. The sun's rays can still burn you even if the air feels cool, and sun reflected off the whiteness of snow can be particularly powerful.

When sunbathing, start with no more than 15 minutes' exposure. Increase the time to an hour gradually over a few weeks' time. Never stay out in strong sun for longer than an hour.

Use a water-based foundation to help moisturize your skin in summer, but use waterproof makeup for lips, eyes, and lashes to prevent running and smearing in the heat.

Whenever your body is tanning, it uses up more of the B-complex vitamins than usual. If you are deficient in these vitamins, you'll feel tired and drained. Supplement your diet with more foods that are rich in B vitamins.

To soothe sunburned skin, keep an aloe plant on your dresser or table. Break off a leaf as needed and squeeze the aloe gel onto reddened skin to soften and heal it.

Your skin can suffer most damage from the sun between the hours of 11:00 A.M. and 2:00 P.M. Always be sure to wear a sunscreen if you're outdoors during those times—and especially while swimming. The sun's rays penetrate water easily.

The color of your eyes can usually tell you how much sun protection you need—the lighter your eyes, the more easily you are likely to burn.

No matter what your skin type, use a high-protection lotion the first time you are in the sun. Use a total sunscreen on your face and the backs of your hands since these will be constantly exposed.

HAIR CARE

To promote healthy hair growth, follow this routine daily: Bend over and brush your scalp and hair from back to front until the scalp tingles. Then massage the scalp with your fingertips. This treatment stimulates the scalp and distributes your hair's natural oils.

Dull, lifeless hair can be a sign of poor diet. Keep your protein intake high, but cut down on your intake of calories, cholesterol, and fat. Your hair will reflect the improvement in your diet.

After shampooing, rinse your hair with cool water to seal in the moisture in the hair shafts.

Enrich plain, inexpensive shampoo by adding an egg or a pinch of unflavored gelatin. Do this with only as much shampoo as you can use at once, because this mixture won't keep.

Here's a treatment to help keep your hair bouncy and oil-free longer after shampooing: Chop a handful of watercress in the blender with a cup of water, boil the mixture for ten minutes, strain out the water, and let it cool. Apply the mixture to your hair and leave it for 20 minutes, then rinse it out.

Before shampooing, bend over and massage your head and scalp gently until it tingles. This helps the blood circulate to your hair roots.

Towel-dry your hair thoroughly before using your blow dryer. You'll save time and avoid damaging your hair with too much heat.

Add a packet of unflavored gelatin to a quart of water for an economical protein hair rinse.

To reduce static electricity, massage warm, polyunsaturated oil into your hair. Then wrap your head in a hot, damp towel for as long as possible before shampooing.

To cut down on static electricity, dampen your hairbrush before brushing dry hair.

Never use a brush on wet hair, because wet hair is elastic and subject to easy breakage. After shampooing, comb your hair gently.

Mayonnaise is a fine hair conditioning treatment. Spread a spoonful on your hair, then wrap your head in a warm towel. Wait an hour before shampooing thoroughly.

Baby powder makes a good dry shampoo. Rub it into the hair, then brush it out thoroughly.

To make your own dandruff remover, mix a half cup of white vinegar and a half cup of water in a bottle and shake vigorously to blend the ingredients. Dab the solution directly on your scalp with absorbent pads before each shampoo.

To make your own lemon rinse, blend a half cup of strained lemon juice and one cup of distilled water in a bottle. Comb the liquid through your hair after each shampoo.

Make your own egg conditioner this way: Separate the yolk from an egg and beat it until thick. Beat in one teaspoon of vegetable oil, and add a half cup of water. Work this mixture into your hair after your shampoo, leave it on for one to two minutes, and rinse thoroughly.

If you suffer from a flaky scalp, try the following treatment every two weeks: Section your hair and rub the scalp with a cotton pad saturated with plain rubbing alcohol. Let the alcohol dry, then brush your hair and rinse thoroughly with warm water, but don't shampoo.

Flat beer makes an excellent setting lotion for hair and gives curls extra body.

Before going out for the evening, set your hair before you take your bath or shower. The steam will help set your curls.

To perk up permed hair between shampoos, lightly mist your hair with fresh water and push the curls into place with your fingers.

Your hair will keep its style better if you sleep on a satin pillowcase.

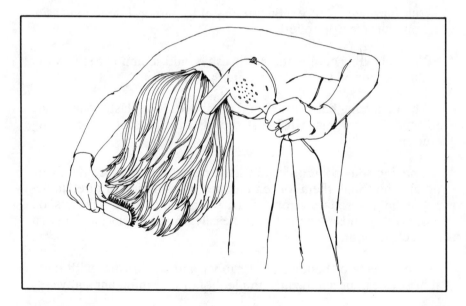

To get a fuller look to your hairstyle, bend over so your hair falls forward and blow the underneath layers dry before you dry the rest of the hair.

To make long hair look shorter, set the hair tightly on small rollers and comb the set into a pageboy style.

For a chic holiday hairstyle, wear your hair loose and held off the face with a thin gold or silver ribbon.

Use divided cutlery trays for storing bobby pins, curlers, combs, and other hair care items.

Your hairstyle can alter the shape of your face. Height at the crown of the head can lengthen a round face. Bangs can shorten a long face or add softness to an angular face.

During humid summer weather, use combs to hold your hair up and away from your face. You'll look and feel a lot cooler.

When temperatures drop below freezing, hair gets brittle and splits easily. Protect your hair by wearing a hat in cold weather.

Your hair needs more moisture in cold weather. Use the mist setting on your electric rollers.

When cleaning combs and hairbrushes, add shampoo to the water to remove hair oil trapped in the teeth or bristles.

When cleaning hairbrushes and combs (except plastic ones), one tablespoon ammonia will boost the effectiveness of the cleaning solution.

A baking soda solution cleans hairbrushes and combs effectively and cheaply. Soak them for ten minutes in a solution of three tablespoons baking soda and one quart warm water. The baking soda loosens oily deposits so they can be easily brushed away and leaves a fresh, clean odor.

Combs made of bone or hard rubber and hairbrushes with natural bristles can be sanitized with alcohol or a disinfectant spray.

HAND CARE

In winter, cream your hands with lanolin before you go to bed. Once a week, moisturize your hands as usual and wear white cotton gloves while you sleep.

Apply hand cream before putting on rubber gloves to do dishes or other chores.

Push back your cuticles with a towel every time you wash your hands.

If you're in the habit of biting your nails or chewing your cuticles, carry a tube of cuticle cream with you. Whenever you get the urge to start chewing, put the cream on your nails instead. You'll break yourself of a bad habit and promote healthy nail growth at the same time.

Any activity that requires fingers to be nimble—needlepoint, embroidery, typing, playing the piano—is good for the circulation and helps your fingernails to grow.

The acids in lemon and vegetable juices are harsh on your fingernails. When preparing these foods, rinse your hands often under cool running water.

Emergency treatment for dry, chapped hands: Once a week, soak your hands in a bath of warm baby oil mixed with sesame oil.

To soften cuticles, soak hands in a solution of one cup warm water and a teaspoon of dishwashing liquid.

A light color nail polish gives your hands the illusion of being longer and more graceful.

To quick-dry your nail polish, plunge your hands into a bowl of ice water while the polish is still wet, or place your hands into the freezer compartment of the refrigerator for a few seconds.

To prevent nail polish bottle tops from sticking, rub the inside of the cap and the neck of the bottle with a thin layer of petroleum jelly.

Cut metal nail files are hard on your nails. Use a diamond-dust file or an emery board instead, and file your nails in one direction only.

When cleaning around the house, wear cotton gloves to protect your manicure. Remove the gloves now and again and rinse your hands under warm water to remove any perspiration.

If you have a dial telephone, protect your manicure by using the blunt end of a pen or pencil to dial the number.

When nails chip excessively, it may be due to the use of polish remover. Leave your nails unpainted for a few days and see if their condition improves.

Don't throw out nail polish that has become hardened or gummy. Place the bottle into a pan of boiling water for a few seconds, and the polish will flow smoothly again.

Keep nail polish in the refrigerator to keep it from thickening.

Instead of buying nail polish remover, buy two ounces of acetone from the pharmacy.

CHOOSING AND USING COSMETICS

When shopping for foundation makeup, test the color by applying a drop to your face or neck, rather than to the back of your hand. If possible, check the color in natural light by a door or window rather than under fluorescent lights in the store.

To apply foundation like a professional, use a damp sea sponge. It blends the color evenly and gives the most natural looking coverage.

To emphasize facial contours, select a foundation that's a shade lighter than your tan during summer months.

Once you've applied your makeup, use a large makeup brush to dust translucent powder lightly over your whole face. You can further set your makeup with a light spray of mineral or ordinary water. A plant mister works fine for this purpose.

Your makeup foundation will last longer and give better coverage if you mix it with an equal amount of skin freshener.

Before reapplying makeup, or to remove excess oil or shine, pat your face gently with a tissue or a damp paper towel.

Before applying evening makeup, soak cotton balls in chamomile tea and place them over your closed eyes for ten minutes. Then lie down with your feet elevated. You'll feel really relaxed and refreshed afterward, and your face will show it.

If the powder in your compact has developed a hard surface, rub it gently with a piece of fine sandpaper to make it powdery again.

Use plain talcum powder (or any vegetable starch to which you aren't allergic) to take the shine off nose or forehead.

A rose-colored blusher brushed onto the sides of your throat will give your skin a healthy glow.

Make blusher yourself by blending a dab of lipstick with a little cream foundation.

To hide bags under your eyes, cover the area with a foundation darker than the shade you use for the rest of your face.

To shorten a long nose, blend dark foundation under the tip of your nose.

If you work under fluorescent light, avoid purple or blue eye shadows and blue-red lip colors. In candlelight, counteract the yellow glow from the candles by wearing rose, mauve, and grape tones.

If winter weather makes your skin look sallow, avoid makeup with gold or brown tints. Use colors that will highlight and brighten your face.

If you are wearing sequins or shiny materials, avoid wearing frosted cosmetics that will make your face look too shiny. Use matte powders, shadows, and creams, which will absorb the light reflected from your outfit.

During the hot, muggy days of summer, use only powder blusher and eye shadows; creams tend to stick and smudge. Also, powders help absorb excess oil and moisture. Dry skin, however, needs extra moisturizer to counteract the drying effect of hot sun.

To help camouflage a double chin, apply blusher under the chin, then blend it upward to the bone and across toward the edges of the jaw.

If your features are small, highlight them with a light foundation. Use a darker foundation to minimize large features.

To straighten a crooked nose, place a line of light-colored foundation down the center of your nose, blending well at the tip.

To slim down a broad nose, put dark foundation on either side of your nose and blend well.

Apply blusher from the top of your brow to your hairline to make a high forehead appear narrower.

Choker necklaces and beads have a shortening effect on long faces.

Long strands of neck jewelry lengthen a round face.

For the thickest-looking lashes, apply mascara and let it set for a few minutes. After curling the lashes, add a little more mascara to the tips to give the illusion of length.

Applying fresh mascara over the old will make your lashes brittle. Always remove your eye makeup before bedtime. Sleep with a little petroleum jelly on your lashes—it both conditions and darkens them.

When your mascara begins to dry out, don't throw it away. Run hot water over the tube for a minute and the mascara will soften again.

A tackle box is great for organizing and storing your cosmetics.

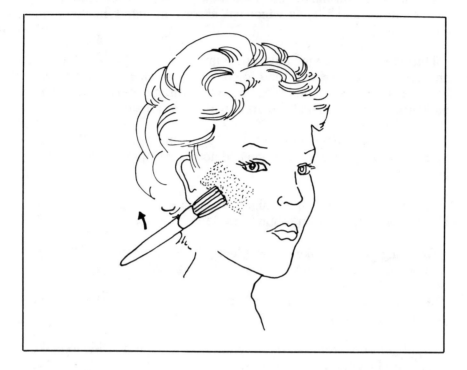

To help widen a long face, apply your blusher in a rectangular area at the cheekbone, centered under the eye, brushing up and out.

To make your eyebrows look darker, use an old toothbrush to brush eyebrows up toward your temples. Your eyes will look wider and brighter, too, even if you don't use eye makeup.

Using two shades of eyebrow pencil can help make your brow color look more natural.

Eyeliner pencil will flow more smoothly and be easier to apply if you gently heat the tip of the pencil for ten seconds over the flame of a match.

To make the whites of your eyes appear whiter, line your lower lashes with a deep blue color stick.

To bring out deep-set eyes, apply a light, frosted shadow on both your lids and brow bone, using a darker shade in the eyelid crease.

Small eyes can be made to look larger by applying eye shadow under your lower lashes, starting at the center of the eye and blending to the outer corner. Sweep the color along the brow bone out to the side of the eye.

If your eyes are too closely set, pluck your eyebrows so that they start farther apart.

If your hair is dark, lighten your eyebrows by brushing them lightly with your makeup foundation—this will actually make your eyes look bigger.

You can achieve a deep-set look for prominent eyes by applying lots of dark color in the crease of the eyelid. Pale or frosted eye shadow will have the opposite effect.

Don't match the color of your eye shadow to the exact shade of your eyes. The colors will cancel each other out, making your eyes look drab instead of exciting.

Sunlight bleaches and splits delicate eyelash hairs. Lubricate your lashes with a thin coat of waterproof mascara whenever you're outdoors.

Your lips have few natural oil glands and chap easily. Protect them with a thin coating of colorless lip balm whenever you aren't wearing lip gloss or lip color.

To make full lips appear slimmer, draw a lip line inside your natural lip line. Fill in with darker shade of lip color.

To brighten your makeup during the day outline your lips with a soft brown pencil and smudge slightly with your fingertips until the line is barely visible.

For a long-lasting lipstick, apply a generous coat. Then let it set for about two minutes. Blot with a tissue, puff on some powder, then apply another generous coat of lipstick. Wait again and blot.

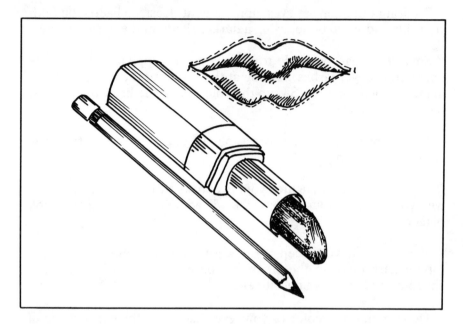

To make thin lips appear fuller, draw a lip line outside your natural lip line. Fill in with a lighter shade of lipstick.

If your upper and lower lips are uneven, apply makeup foundation over your lips; then fashion a new lip line with a pencil a shade darker than your lip color.

Mend a broken lipstick by holding the two ends over a gas burner, a match, or a lighter flame until the two pieces melt enough to adhere when pressed together. Let the lipstick cool and set before using.

Fluorescent lighting gives a garish cast to blues and reds, so choose warm, tawny lip colors for office light.

PERFUMES AND COLOGNES

Spray the inner hem of your skirt and inside of your gloves with your perfume. Spray sparingly, and don't put perfume on very pale or delicate fabrics—it may discolor them.

For fragrance that lasts all day, saturate a cotton pad with your favorite perfume and tuck it into your bra. Your body heat will help intensify the scent.

For a longer-lasting scent, apply perfume directly to pulse points such as the throat, the wrists, the insides of the elbows, and the backs of the knees.

Dab petroleum jelly on your pulse points before applying your perfume. The scent will last longer.

The scent of perfumes, colognes, or body oils will last longer if you apply them while you're still warm and damp from a shower or bath.

Keep a mister of cologne in the refrigerator during the summer. The fragrance makes a cool, tingly refresher after a shower or bath.

Apply perfumes and colognes before putting on your jewelry. The alcohol and oils in your favorite scent can cause a cloudy film on both real gold and costume jewelry.

Don't stick to one fragrance all year long. Temperatures affect the intensity of fragrance. Heavy scents and oils are perfect for winter, but hot weather calls for lighter fragrances in smaller quantities.

MORE PERSONAL CARE HINTS

To relieve facial tension, hold a cork between your teeth and lie down for ten minutes. Biting down gently on the cork will help you unclench tight facial muscles.

Limit your use of eye drops during the summer because overuse can prove harmful. Rinse chlorine and salt water from irritated eyes with pure mineral water instead.

If you've dropped a contact lens on the carpet, vacuum the area with the vacuum tube covered with a nylon stocking. The lens will cling to the stocking without being sucked through the tube.

If you can see your eyes clearly through the lenses of your sunglasses, the glasses are not dark enough to give adequate protection.

An easy trick to increase circulation to the gums, especially when your toothbrush isn't handy, is to chew a handful of pumpkin, sunflower, or melon seeds. They're nutritious, too.

Baking soda can be used as a tooth powder to help whiten and brighten your teeth. Make it taste good by adding powdered cinnamon or oil of cinnamon.

Go barefoot around the house as often as possible. Your feet contain 26 separate bones, all of which need freedom of movement and exercise—which they don't get while you're wearing heavy or highheeled shoes.

After standing on your feet all day or after a lengthy walk, soak away foot fatigue in a footbath of Epsom salts and warm water.

Sleeping with several pillows tucked under your lower legs can help prevent varicose veins.

To prevent ingrown toenails, cut the nails straight across, leaving no jagged edges.

Hopping on one foot 20 to 30 times while wearing exercise sandals helps to increase leg muscle tone and strengthen the feet.

If your eyes are puffy, cover them with cotton pads soaked in milk and relax for ten minutes.

Another treatment for puffy eyes: Dip two tea bags in boiling water for two minutes, then let the water cool slightly. Meanwhile, heat a teaspoon of olive oil until it's warm (not hot). Using an absorbent pad, carefully dab the oil around your eyes and on your eyelids. Lie down and cover each eye for ten minutes with a stillwarm tea bag. Remove the tea bags and gently wipe the oil from your skin with tissue.

Refresh tired eyes by laying cotton pads moistened with witch hazel over your closed eyelids for a few minutes.

To exercise and strengthen your eye muscles after an extended period of close reading or work, hold a pencil about ten inches from your face and look first at the tip of the pencil, then into the distance. Repeat ten times.

To moisturize the skin around your eyes while you sleep, apply odorless castor oil at bedtime.

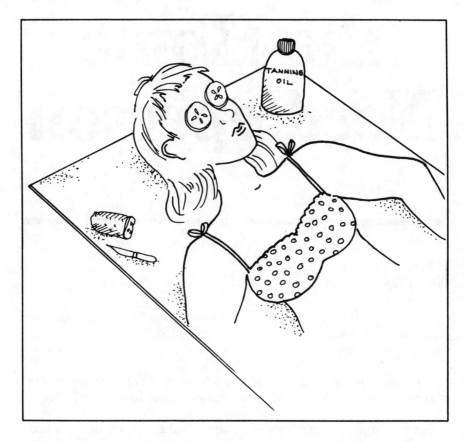

Place thin, freshly cut slices of cucumber over closed eyelids to help reduce swelling caused by overexposure to the sun.

Hints for the Home Needleperson

TIME AND TROUBLE SAVERS

It's easy to thread a needle if you spray your fingertips with hair spray and then stiffen the tip of the thread by rolling it back and forth in your fingers.

Attach your tape measure to the sewing table so that you won't have to rummage through all your equipment to find it.

Keep a small magnet in your sewing basket. When needles and pins drop on the carpet while you're sewing, retrieve them quickly with the magnet.

Sewing needles can get rusty and dull. Rub off any rust with an abrasive soap pad or steel wool. A dull needle or pin can be livened up by rubbing it over your hair, which contains natural oils.

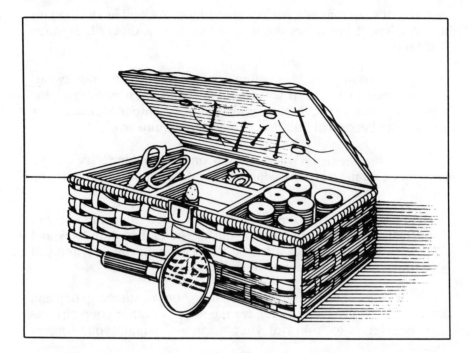

To help you thread needles, keep a magnifying glass in your sewing basket.

You can rejuvenate a blunted machine needle, at least temporarily, by rubbing it at an angle across the fine side of an emery board.

Make a habit of leaving a length of thread in a needle before storing it in a pincushion (or whatever you use as a pincushion). You'll be able to see it more easily, and the needle will be less likely to slip all the way into the pincushion.

To keep your scissors from damaging other items in your sewing basket, cover the points with the rubber protectors sold for knitting needles.

Try making this hang-up sewing center: Insert wood screws or nails across and down a breadboard with a handle, then hang all your spools of thread on it. If you want to hang scissors and other sewing utensils, add a row of cup hooks along the bottom.

A bar of soap makes a perfect pincushion. As well as storing pins and needles, it lubricates the tips so that they slide easily through stiff fabrics.

Sequins and tiny beads are often used together to decorate sweaters and other garments. If you get them mixed up, here's a trick for separating them: Drop both sequins and beads into a colander over a bowl; the beads will fall through and the sequins won't.

Do you get backache when you sew on the machine? Try using a secretary's chair, which is adjustable and designed to support the back.

Here's a quick way to mend a garment when appearance is not important. Put a piece of paper under the hole, then darn back and forth with an appropriate stitch on the sewing machine. When you wash the garment the paper will wash away.

If you've got sewer's cramp from a long bout of stitching, flap and shake your hands gently to relieve the ache. Another good circulation booster is to hold out your arms and wiggle your fingers vigorously.

To make a handy pincushion, glue a small sponge to the corner of your sewing machine.

File your clothes patterns by storing them upright in a shoe box.

Before pressing, sew as many seams and darts as possible at one time. You'll minimize the number of trips to the ironing board and find the project going much faster than if you stitched and pressed each seam individually.

The spongy filter tip from a cigarette makes a convenient small pincushion. Slip it into the center of a spool of thread, and then stick it full of pins or needles.

Plastic egg cartons make convenient storage containers for spools of thread.

Store tiny buttons in empty pill bottles.

For extra-strong stitching when sewing on buttons, double the thread before threading the needle. You'll have four strands of thread for each stitch.

To keep a four-hole button in place longer, sew through only two holes at a time. If one set of threads breaks loose, the other will hold the button securely.

Use dental floss to sew buttons on children's clothes. It's much stronger than thread.

Having trouble removing a button? Slide a comb under it, then slice through the lifted thread with a razor blade.

When you're mending the finger of a glove, a glass marble makes a good darning egg.

It's easier to repair seams on lingerie fabrics or nylon if you slide a sheet of paper under the seam. Stitch through both the fabric and the paper, and then carefully rip away the paper.

Thread looks darker on the spool than it will on fabric. Choose a thread a shade darker than the material you'll be using it on.

After ripping out a seam, pick up all the loose threads with a pencil eraser.

You can sharpen a sewing machine needle by stitching carefully through a piece of sandpaper.

Use a small paintbrush to clean dust and loose threads from your sewing machine.

If the foot control of your portable sewing machine creeps on the floor when you sew, glue a piece of foam rubber to the bottom surface and the foot control will stay in place.

After you've oiled your sewing machine, stitch through a blotter to soak up any excess lubricant that might remain in the machine and leak onto your fabric.

HINTS FOR THE
HOME DRESSMAKER

In order to sew for yourself, you must know your body measurements accurately. Ask a friend to help you, and take measurements over your usual undergarments (not over dresses, blouses, or slacks) using a nonstretch tape measure.

Sewing projects will proceed more quickly if you complete each phase before starting another. For example, if you cut out all garment, interfacing, and lining pieces at one time, you'll have all the pieces you need to construct the garment.

When you embark on a large-scale dressmaking project, fill a number of bobbins before you start. Then you won't find that just when you've gotten into the swing of it you have to stop to rewind the bobbin—which means you might as well go make a cup of coffee and check the mail, too, and you may not get back to your dressmaking at all that day.

Before sewing in a zipper, shrink it: Set the zipper in very hot water for a couple of minutes, then let it dry. Repeat the whole process once more before sewing in the zipper.

You can smooth wrinkled pattern pieces by pressing them with a warm, dry iron. Don't use steam; it will distort the pattern size.

A fork makes a great tracing wheel for marking out darts on a pattern with dressmaker's carbon.

Clear nail polish applied to the underside of the line where you have to cut open a machine-made buttonhole will prevent odd threads from unraveling and will keep the buttonhole firm.

If you're sewing a woman's blouse, sweater, or dress that will button down the front, make the buttonholes horizontal instead of vertical. The buttons will always stay firmly shut.

You can lengthen a very short skirt by adding a lace border or a wide band of ribbon, or by inserting a band of lace or contrasting fabric a few inches above the level of the hem.

A clean cardboard milk carton with the top cut off (gallon size) makes a great storage file for dress patterns.

Change a used full-length slip into a half-slip by cutting off the bodice and inserting a narrow elastic band at the waist.

If you're given a slip that's way too long, turn it into a camisole and half-slip: Cut a little below the waist, then hem the top part, and elasticize the waist of the skirt.

Repair worn and frayed elbows of jackets and sweaters by sewing on leather patches.

Cover a hole in a blouse or dress with a pretty piece of embroidery or an attractive applique.

Use elastic thread to sew buttons to the waistband of a skirt or pants; the garment will expand to fit even if the wearer gains a little weight.

When throwing out clothing you no longer wear, first stock up on notions by saving any usable zippers, buttons, or decorative trim. (Don't do this, however, with items you are donating to a charitable organization or a resale shop.)

Transform a pair of regular pants into maternity pants by removing the zipper and replacing it with a panel of stretch fabric.

Transform too-short slacks into knickers. Cut them below the knee and either insert elastic into a hem on each leg or make a buttoned band for each leg from the cut-off fabric.

Cutting heavy fabrics, such as quilts or coatings, will be more accurate if you pin through only one layer of fabric. If you pin all the way through, the fabric will pucker.

Cut through fake fur and other deep-pile fabric with a razor blade. Work from the wrong side, and cut through only the backing, since you want the furry side, or pile, to remain intact.

You can use a glue stick instead of pins and/or basting when making lapped seams. Apply the glue to the underside of the overlapping section. Press in place, allow to dry a minute or two, and topstitch.

You can hold nonfusible interfacing in place temporarily with adhesive from a glue stick. This eliminates the need to baste interfacing to the garment piece, and makes sewing faster.

When sewing an emblem on a uniform, first position and hold it in place with several dabs of white glue. After the glue sets, stitch the emblem by hand or machine. The glue will wash out with the first laundering.

Stitch darts from the widest portion toward the narrowest.

You can make a facing lie flat by stitching it to the seam allowance—not the fabric that will show—just inside the seam. Or, simply tack it at the seams. If you tack it all around the edge, the stitching will show on the right side of the fabric.

To prevent heavy materials from dragging on the floor while you're sewing, support them on an ironing board placed next to the sewing machine table.

Tissue paper can be useful when machine sewing delicate or hard-to-handle fabrics. Lay the tissue under nylon fabric to keep it from slipping. When sewing lace, place tissue between the fabric and the machine to keep the lace from snagging.

Some fabrics tend to pucker slightly when sewn. This can usually be prevented if the fabric layers are held taut as they go under the presser foot. Hold the fabric in front of and behind the presser foot, keeping it taut without stretching it or pulling it through the machine.

When a design calls for gathering the fabric, test-gather a scrap of your fabric to see if you're getting the desired look. If the gathering is too tight, use a longer stitch.

When sewing cuffs, you'll have more room for seam allowance when they're turned inside the cuff if you take one or more diagonal stitches across the points of square corners. The heavier the fabric, the longer the diagonal needs to be.

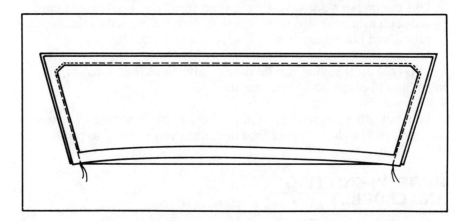

Shortening the stitch length when stitching around collar curves reinforces the seam and makes the curves smoother. On collar corners, shorten the stitch length and sew one or more diagonal stitches to reinforce the corners and make room for the seam allowances when the collar is turned.

When making an elastic waistband, fasten the ends of the elastic with a safety pin for the first few wearings and washings to make sure that the fit of the waistband is comfortable. Elastic sometimes shrinks or relaxes after the first washings. When you are confident that the fit is right, remove the safety pin, stitch the ends of the elastic, and neaten the waistband.

When sewing snaps in place, stitch in the top half and rub a little chalk over its tip. Press it against the other side of the garment to mark the exact spot where you should sew in the bottom half of the fastener.

If very small snaps slip out of your fingers, tape them in place on the fabric and sew through the tape. Lift off the tape when you're done.

Before you hem a skirt, a dress, or pants, let the garment hang for a day on a hanger. The fabric will settle, and you'll get a more accurate hem. This is especially important for fabrics with a lot of "give," like knits; if they're not pre-hung you may find that parts of the hemline drop after a few wearings.

You can make your own hem gauge from any lightweight cardboard such as a postcard or index card. Notch the card at the depth required and pin up the hem.

Clip-type clothespins can be more convenient than pins for holding a hem in place while you sew it.

You can often steam out small puckers at the top edge of a hem. So, don't redo a slightly puckered hem until you've tried to press out the pucker.

HINTS ON KNITTING
AND CROCHET

When buying yarn, check the label on each ball or skein to be sure it's all from the same dye lot; otherwise you could end up with yarn of slightly different shades. Keep a note of the dye lot in case you run short unexpectedly.

There's an easy test that will tell you whether an unlabeled skein of yarn is wool or synthetic. Put a small piece of the yarn in a large ashtray, and set a match to it. If the yarn burns to ashes, it's wool. Synthetics will harden into a dark lump when burned.

You can recycle still usable yarn from knitted items you no longer wear. After unraveling the yarn, wind it loosely around a cake rack, dip the rack into water, and then let the whole thing dry out. All the kinks will be "ironed out" of the yarn, and you can then rewind it.

To keep metallic yarns from unraveling, dip the ends in clear fingernail polish.

Attach a paper clip to the page of your knitting book, and move the clip up or down the page to keep your place when following detailed instructions.

When teaching a beginner how to knit, use a red needle to mark the purl row and a white needle for the plain row.

It's easy to pick up the wrong directions for size when working with a knitting pattern. Before you begin, use a black felt-tip marker to circle the directions that apply to your size. If you decide to make the same pattern in a different size later on, use a different colored marker to circle the new directions.

Before buying yarn, consider the advantages and disadvantages of both wool and synthetics. Although wool will keep you warm even when wet, it needs special handling when laundering. Most synthetic yarns can be machine washed, but some synthetics may gradually stretch out of shape. Wool may be irritating or allergenic to some people; synthetics are less likely to cause an allergic reaction.

Make markers for your knitting from the little plastic price tags used to fasten bread wrappers. Or, if you're working with fine yarns, tie a piece of yarn of a contrasting color into a circle for use as a marker.

If you carry your knitting around with you, you can make a carrier from a well-washed plastic bleach bottle. Cut off about two inches from the top of the handle and spout, and drop in the ball of yarn. Draw up the end of the skein through the spout as you work.

You can test your knitting pattern for gauge size by doing a test run. Using the needles and yarn required by the pattern, knit a sample piece about four inches square. When you measure this, you'll have a good idea of any adjustments that may be necessary.

Here are two of the best ways to wind a hank of yarn into a manageable ball. Have a friend hold the hank taut between two hands while you wind the ball. If no help is available, a ladder-backed chair works just as well. Always wind the ball loosely to keep from stretching the yarn out of shape.

The plastic hairpins that come with brush hair rollers are better than straight pins for pinning seams on a knitted garment. The plastic pins are longer and stay firmly in place.

To make sure knitted sleeves are identical, knit them on the needle at the same time.

Looking for a good place to store skeins of yarn? Tuck them into the slots of a wine rack.

For a smoother look, try splicing instead of knotting the ends of your knitting. Unravel about an inch of each yarn end, then loosely weave the strands together.

It's easier to camouflage the place where you've knotted two lengths of yarn if you do it at the edge rather than in the middle of an item. At the edge, you can cover the knot with a seam or edging.

A knitting needle can do double duty as a ruler. Starting from the top down, mark off every inch with nail polish or with a waterproof marking pen.

Here's a foolproof way to keep your yarn clean while you knit or crochet. Put the ball of yarn into a plastic bag, and thread the end of the skein through a hole in the bottom of the bag. Draw out the yarn a little at a time as you work.

If you break a knitting needle, recycle it as a stake to prop up a houseplant.

You can make a double-pointed knitting needle from a broken plastic one. Sharpen the broken end of the needle with a pencil sharpener.

Knitted cuffs have a tendency to lose shape. To help them keep their shape interweave elastic thread through the cuffs or knit sewing silk of the same color into the first couple of rows.

Knitted cuffs and other ribbed edges will keep their shape better if you use needles a size or two smaller than those used for the rest of the garment.

Ribbed edges should never be ironed with steam. This causes the ribbing to flatten out and lose its flexibility.

You can prevent the strap of a knitted or crocheted shoulder bag from curling up or stretching out of shape. When making the strap, use two separate knitted or crocheted pieces, and bind them together with fusible webbing.

When your hands feel stiff from too much knitting, powder them with talc. The yarn will glide easily again.

Many people are sensitive to wool clothing. To make a wool sweater less scratchy, rinse it in cool water to which you've added a very small amount of glycerin. Or line the sleeves of a wool sweater by tacking in the legs from an old pair of nylon hose.

If you want to make a sweater for an expected baby, make buttonholes down both sides of the front opening of the garment. It'll be easy enough to sew buttons on the correct side, thus closing the extra openings, when you find out if the baby is a boy or a girl.

Use a length of leftover yarn instead of ribbon when you gift-wrap a knitted or crocheted gift. The recipient can use this remnant for future mending. Slip the washing instructions from the yarn label into the package, too.

Treat your crochet hooks to a paraffin rub from time to time to keep them in good working condition.

Use plastic toothbrush tubes for storing your crochet hooks.

HINTS ON EMBROIDERY

To keep embroidery floss from tangling, wind it onto knitting bobbins.

Styrofoam meat trays make good sewing cards for children. Punch out a design with a paper puncher, and let the children sew in the design with colorful yarn. To make a safe substitute for a needle, wrap cellophane tape around the tip of the yarn.

To separate embroidery floss, cut the length of thread you'll need, then moisten it with a damp sponge. The moist strands will separate easily and dry quickly for use.

Use a larger needle than usual when embroidering with metallic floss. Because the eye of the needle is larger, the thread won't catch and fray so easily.

Instead of using buttons or beads, which a small child can pull off and perhaps swallow, embroider the eyes, mouth, and nose on stuffed animals.

HINTS ON NEEDLEPOINT

Some domestic and many imported yarns are not colorfast. When in doubt, dampen a few threads and rub them against a scrap of white cloth. If the colors run, it means you can't wash or otherwise wet the needlework in which the thread is used.

Ordinary tea can be used to dye white cotton or linen needlepoint canvas. The stronger the tea, the darker the color you'll get. Use one to three teabags to a cup of hot water (depending on how deep a color you want). Brush the tea on your canvas, then block it and let it dry.

Crewel work can collect a lot of dust and grime. Use a fabric waterproofing spray to keep it dustfree.

When doing needlepoint, cover the rough edges of your canvas with masking tape. This prevents the yarn from catching and fraying.

Never fold a needlepoint canvas when you're not working on it. To keep the canvas sturdy, roll it up instead.

You'll be able to draw designs on needlepoint canvas more easily if you pull rather than push the pencil.

You can waterproof paints you've used on your needlepoint design by spraying the canvas with acrylic spray.

When blocking needlepoint worked with noncolorfast yarn, douse it liberally with salt before wetting it down with cold water. Then just let it dry.

You can check for any stitches you may have missed by holding a finished needlepoint canvas up to the light.

Another way to block needlepoint worked with noncolorfast yarn is to combine two tablespoons of white vinegar with a cup of cold water, and use this mixture to moisten both sides of the finished canvas thoroughly. Be careful not to saturate the needlepoint, however. This technique will also keep the underlying inks of the design from bleeding.

HINTS FOR QUILTERS

If you prefer not to mark up your quilt face with a pencil, "draw" in the straight lines with strips of masking tape.

For interesting markings that won't show up on the finished quilt, dip cookie cutters into cocoa or cinnamon, and stamp the spice design on the quilt top. No marks—and it smells good too.

Cardboard templates become worn quickly. Edge templates with tape so that repeated use won't appreciably change the size of the pattern.

You can keep track of your patchwork squares by storing the pieces in large-size coffee cans. Note the number of pieces on the lid.

You can make a sturdy master pattern for patchwork pieces from an iron-on mending patch. It won't slip or fray, and it will hold its shape for a long time.

Iron some fusible bond onto the backs of lightweight quilting appliques. They'll stay flat and keep their shape. You can get the same effect by treating them with spray starch and then ironing.

After sorting your patchwork pieces, slip a doubled thread through a pile of patches, leaving the knotted end of the thread at the bottom of the stack. With the top end left unknotted, you can peel off each square as it's needed.

Part 3:

Hints About Food

Kitchen Planning and Organization

SAVING SPACE IN THE KITCHEN

If your kitchen is too small to accommodate a table and chairs permanently, install a pull-out extension table or workspace that slides back into a "drawer." Or, make a flip-up counter and eating area that folds back down when not in use.

To make the most of available space when storing tapered glassware, position every other glass upside down.

A wall-hung canvas "apron" with lots of pockets makes a decorative and space-saving holder for all sorts of kitchen gadgets and utensils.

If you hang your sharp knives inside or on the side of a high cabinet, you'll save drawer space and keep these utensils out of the children's reach.

To economize on drawer space, arrange wooden spoons and other utensils bouquet-style in a handsome pitcher, canister, or wooden bucket near the range or on the counter.

If you lack drawer space for kitchen linens and towels, store them in attractive baskets on the counter.

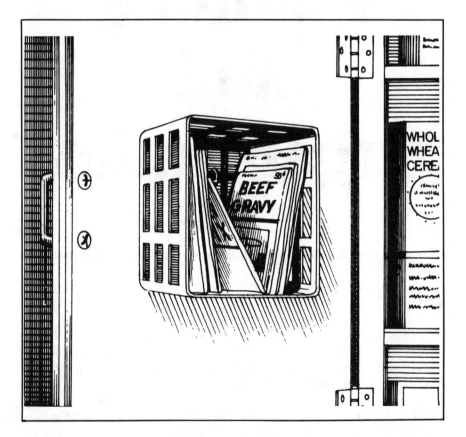

Staple plastic berry baskets to the pantry wall or the inside of a cabinet door to hold small packages of sauce mixes, seasonings, and cold drink mixes.

If you don't have cabinet space for your pots and pans, put a small wooden ladder—painted to match your kitchen—in a corner and place the pots and pans on the steps.

Hanging mugs on cup hooks underneath your cabinets saves shelf space.

To save space in the kitchen, hang pots, pans, and other items from the ceiling. Use hooks meant for hanging swag lamps and screw them directly into the joists.

KITCHEN EQUIPMENT AND SUPPLIES

If your dishpan leaks, don't throw it away. Use it as an under-the-sink storage bin for waxes, brushes, and soaps. It will slide in and out like a drawer.

If you keep your brooms, mops, and buckets hanging on hooks inside the broom closet they won't fall every time you open the door.

You can cut counter clutter with stackable plastic canisters or a four-in-one turntable canister.

Purchase food storage containers that do several jobs. Freezer-to-oven casserole dishes are more useful than freezer containers that store casseroles adequately but can't be used in the oven.

Plastic or wire baskets that hang under your shelves make excellent space savers for extra storage. Use them for unrefrigerated vegetables or cooking utensils.

Use the plastic lids that come with some tins as separators when you freeze hamburger patties.

Floor tiles make perfect linings for pantry shelves. They last longer than self-adhesive paper and are easier to fit in place.

If your kitchen and dining room area are combined and you dislike looking at the pots and pans while you eat, install a ceiling-hung venetian blind to separate the two areas.

Since pots, pans, and casseroles can be heavy, store them at lower levels to avoid having to reach up for them.

Toss a few extra plastic clothespins into your kitchen drawer. Use them to seal packages of partially used foods such as pretzels, chips, noodles, or rice.

Save screw-top glass containers for storing dry goods in the pantry.

A small glass salt shaker makes an excellent container for lemon juice, because you can sprinkle exactly the amount you need without risk of pouring too much and ruining the flavor of a dish.

The shaker bottles and containers that some spices come in can be filled with flour for no-mess flouring of cutlets and other foods. If you add seasonings to the flour you've got an instant seasoned coating mix.

Recycle those tall, cylindrical potato chip containers for picnic food. They'll hold cutlery, rolled up paper napkins, apples, or the baby's food jars (put folded paper towels between the jars for cushioning).

Well-scrubbed empty bleach bottles are great household helpers, too. Cut them to shape as flour or sugar scoops or as sun shades for the seedlings in your garden. The bottoms make good stands for indoor plant pots, too.

Make a knife holder out of your empty thread spools. Insert screws in the spool holes and attach them to a cabinet door. Place the spools in a row, one butted right next to the other. The blades will fit in the gaps between the spools while the handles rest on the spools.

If you store your sharp knives in drawers, keep the knives in a holder to prevent the blades from getting dull. They are safer stored this way, too.

If you've nowhere to hang a memo board for your notes, paint part of your kitchen door with three coats of blackboard paint.

A phone center with a writing surface can be installed between two wall studs in your kitchen. Cut the wall between the two studs and build the center to fit the space.

A large pair of tweezers can help you get olives and pickles out of narrow jars; tweezers are also useful for placing garnishes on food without touching the food with your hands, or for removing bones from fish fillets.

Keep an aloe plant growing in your kitchen. The gel squeezed from a leaf can soothe insect bites, prickly heat, or sunburn.

Washing your ice cube trays occasionally in hot soapy water will keep the cubes from sticking.

A rubber-coated plate rack makes a great cookbook holder.

Plastic or wire baskets on casters provide excellent, easy-to-maneuver storage for unrefrigerated vegetables or loose cooking utensils.

Make your own kitchen sink splashback by cutting a piece of clear plexiglass to size. Drill two small holes in it and nail it up on the wall.

To keep recipes clipped from newspapers and magazines so they'll be readily available, fold them into an envelope fastened to an inside cover of a cookbook.

If you find a recipe that's an improvement over one featured in your cookbook, tape a copy of it right over the recipe in the book. The next time you need it, you'll be able to locate it easily by referring to the book's own index.

If you store your dishes in open dish racks instead of in cabinets, position the racks over the sink. That way you can wash the dishes, put them in place, and they'll drip-dry into the sink.

Napkins, paper towels, or cloth protectors placed between pieces of fine china when stacking will help prevent scratching.

Most plastic food containers can be recycled for storing or refrigerating food.

Mesh bags, wire baskets, and even old nylon stockings make good storage containers for potatoes and onions because they allow the necessary air circulation.

Even when soap bars wear down, they're still useful. Slit a sponge to make a pocket to hold the slivers, wet and squeeze the sponge for foamy suds. Or fill a sock with soap slivers and use it the same way.

Thin, leftover soap bars can be tossed into a blender with water and transformed into creamy, liquid soap. Pour this substance into empty squeeze bottles, and keep one at each sink.

A bar of soap will stay high and dry in a soap dish if it rests on a small sponge.

You can mend a crack in a china cup with milk. Just immerse the cup in a pan of milk, simmer for three-quarters of an hour, and then wash and dry the cup. The protein in the milk is what works the miracle.

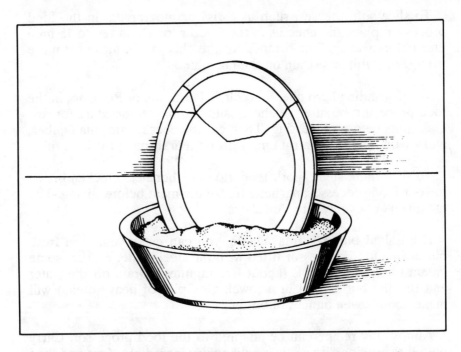

To mend a broken plate, fill a pan with sand. Embed the largest broken portion of the plate in the sand, with the broken edge straight up. The glued pieces will be held in place by gravity. If necessary, use clothespins to clamp the pieces together.

Modeling clay can be shaped to support pieces of broken cups, glasses, or other objects while they are being glued back together.

KITCHEN TIME AND TROUBLE SAVERS

To chop parsley successfully in the food processor, make sure the leaves are very dry by first whirling them in a salad spinner or patting them dry with a heavy towel.

Citrus zest used in a dessert recipe can be chopped in a food processor with a steel blade if some of the sugar from the recipe is placed in the work bowl with the zest.

To slice soft cheeses, such as Swiss or mozzarella, in the food processor, place the cheeses in the freezer for about ten to 15 minutes before slicing. The firmness of the cheese will make for more even slices with less strain on the machine.

When grinding hard cheese, such as Parmesan or Romano, in the food processor, be sure the cheese sits at room temperature for several hours before processing. Then cut the cheese into small cubes, and—with the machine running—drop them through the feed tube.

To slice flank steak, pork tenderloin, or boneless chicken breast in your food processor, partially freeze the meat before slicing. The meat will cut evenly into thin slices.

If unsalted butter is unavailable, you can make your own fresh butter in a food processor fitted with the steel blade. Process some cream until butter forms (about five minutes). Drain off the water and dry the butter well in a towel. One pint of heavy cream will make about seven ounces of butter.

Almost any recipe can be adapted to the food processor. Carry out all the recipe directions involving dry ingredients first and then just wipe the bowl clean with a paper towel. Process the wet ingredients last.

Select cooking pans that are durable and made from a good heat conductor, such as copper, cast aluminum, heavy rolled steel, or cast iron. Specially treated aluminum pots and porcelain-lined cast iron pans won't react to acid or cream foods.

Top-quality carbon steel or combination carbon and stainless steel knives are essential to good cooking. Knife edges should be sharpened on a steel or ceramic sharpener before each use. Knives should be reground professionally every four to six months.

When cooking with a wok on an electric stove, position the ring so that the narrow opening is on the bottom. This will bring the wok closer to the high heat needed for successful stir frying.

The best type of pastry bag is plastic lined. The canvas makes the bag easy to grip, and the plastic lining makes it easy to clean.

You'll ingest more iron if you cook in cast iron pots because foods absorb iron from the pots. For example, stew simmered for several hours in an iron pot contains at least 25 times as much iron as stew simmered in an aluminum pot.

Create extra counter space when cooking for a crowd or baking for a holiday by placing trays or cookie sheets across pulled out drawers.

If you put marbles or a jar lid in the bottom of a double boiler, their rattling will alert you if the water boils away.

To make a tray of fresh ice cubes quickly, leave three or four cubes in the tray when you refill it. The already frozen cubes help cool the fresh water and speed the freezing process.

To prevent ice cube trays from sticking to the freezer shelf, line the shelf with waxed paper.

To be sure that cake tins are completely dry before you store them, place them in a warm oven for a few minutes.

If one drinking glass is tightly nested inside another, don't try to force them apart. You may crack both. Rather, fill the top glass with cold water and immerse the lower one in hot water. The top glass will contract slightly and the bottom one will expand, so they'll come apart easily.

If you keep plastic wrap in your refrigerator, it won't cling to itself when handled.

If the rubber gloves you're wearing won't come off because you've forgotten to sprinkle powder on your hands, hold your gloved hands under the cold tap water. The gloves will slip right off.

To start a fresh bottle of ketchup flowing, push a drinking straw to the bottom of the bottle. When you remove the straw, the ketchup will pour easily.

An electric beater won't sound so loud if you put a damp dish-cloth under the bowl to muffle the noise.

A gravy boat makes a good server for spaghetti sauce.

If salt pours out of your salt shaker too liberally, plug up some of the holes with clear nail polish.

Put a few grains of rice in your salt shaker to keep the salt from caking.

If you put a dab of butter under the spout of a pitcher the contents won't run down the side after you pour.

New drinking glasses sometimes crack when you pour hot liquids into them. They won't if you "season" them this way: Put them in a large pot filled with cold water, bring the water slowly to a boil, and then turn off the heat and let the water cool.

When you buy an electric coffee maker, look for one with water markings on the *inside*. They're easier to read than markings on the outside.

Pot holders protect against cold as well as heat, so wear your kitchen mitts to protect your hands when rearranging frozen foods in the freezer.

Selling your offerings at a bake sale? They'll move faster if you include the recipe. People like to know the ingredients—and how to duplicate your goodies.

You can improvise a sink or tub stopper from the plastic cover of a coffee can. Lay the cover across the drain and suction will hold it firmly in place.

Is the key or tab on a can missing or damaged? Just turn the can over and open it with an ordinary can opener.

You can do more with toothpaste than brush your teeth or remove spots. It also works as an adhesive, perhaps for hanging lightweight pictures and posters on your kitchen walls. When you eventually remove the pictures or posters, just wipe away the toothpaste with damp cloth. There will be no nail holes to repair.

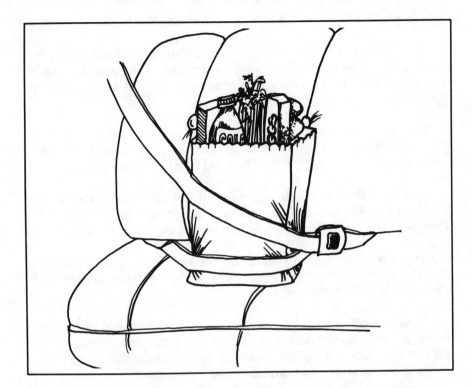

When driving home from the store, strap seat belts that aren't being used around bags containing items that could be spilled or broken.

You can sharpen garbage disposer blades by running ice cubes through them.

Because instructions on bottle labels are frequently in tiny, almost unreadable print, it's a good idea to keep a magnifying glass handy.

KITCHEN CLEANUP

If you're using an inexpensive dishwashing detergent but find that it leaves spots on the dishes, simply put a few tablespoons of vinegar in the rinse water.

Out of liquid dishwashing detergent? Substitute any mild shampoo.

It's usually possible to remove burned-on foods from a pan by coating the burned-on food generously with baking soda barely moistened with water. Leave the paste on overnight and then wash the pan as usual.

Another way of removing burned-on foods from a pan is to fill the pan with water, drop in one or two fabric softener sheets, and let the water stand for an hour or so. The food crust will lift right off.

To rid a teakettle of lime deposits, fill it with a mix of half water and half vinegar and boil the mixture. Let it stand overnight, and then pour the cooled-off liquid—and the lime—down the drain.

Keep a jar of hot, soapy water on the sink when you're cooking and slip silverware into it as you finish using it. Rinse quickly, and the utensils will be clean again.

If you take off your rings, watch, or bracelet while washing dishes, fasten a large cup hook near the kitchen sink and hang these valuables on it. Position the hook so that there's no chance of a small ring slipping out of your hands and down an open drain.

Use a crumpled sheet of newspaper to soak up excess grease from a pan before cleaning the pan in the regular manner.

Loosen leftover egg and cheese residue on dinnerware by soaking in cool water.

A soiled white porcelain sink will gleam like new if you line it with paper towels, spray them until soaked with household bleach, and wait an hour before rinsing.

You can deodorize your kitchen by putting a spoonful of ground coffee in a container and heating it in the oven, or by boiling water containing a little ammonia.

Banish sink odors by washing the sink with a strong salt solution or with laundry bleach.

For stains on acrylic kitchen utensils, wipe at once with a damp cloth. If the stains persist, use an all-purpose cleaner or moistened bicarbonate of soda. Always act as quickly as possible and never use harsh abrasives.

Soft cheeses can be cleaned from a grater by rubbing a raw potato over its teeth and openings. (A lemon rind or a toothbrush also does a first-rate cleanup job.)

You never clean the top of the refrigerator because you're only five-foot-two and you can't *see* the top of the refrigerator? Cover it with a towel. Then when it does occur to you to investigate, just whip off the towel and replace it.

A rubber window squeegee is ideal for scraping crumbs from tables.

Scorched pans (other than aluminum) can be cleaned by bringing one teaspoon baking soda and one cup water to a boil in the pan. Allow to cool, then wash. For aluminum pans, substitute vinegar for the baking soda.

When washing delicate objects in the sink, guard against breakage by padding the sink bottom with a towel; wrap another towel, held in place with a rubber band, around the faucet.

To protect your wok from rust when not in use, coat it lightly with cooking oil before storing it.

To retard tarnish on polished brass, rub it with a cloth moistened with olive oil. When it eventually tarnishes, clean it by rubbing with a lemon wedge dipped in salt. Rinse with water and dry with a soft cloth.

You can remove all traces of fish, onion, or other odors from your hands if you wet them and sprinkle on baking soda. Work the paste over your hands and then rinse away both soda and odor.

If odors linger in pots and pans or other cooking utensils, try washing the utensils with a baking soda and water solution, or boil vinegar in them.

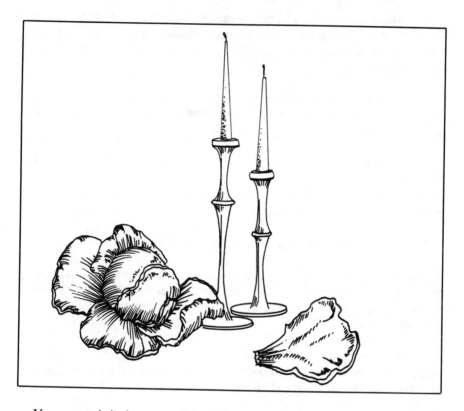

You can minimize scratching when you polish pewter if you rub it with cabbage leaves or very fine steel wool. Then rinse with water and dry with a soft cloth.

You can get rid of rust marks in a stainless steel sink by rubbing them with lighter fluid. Afterward, thoroughly wash the sink and your hands.

Hard lime deposits around faucets can be softened for easy removal by covering with vinegar-soaked paper towels for about an hour before cleaning.

The fastest and cheapest way to remove stains from nonstick-coated cookware is to mix two tablespoons baking soda with one cup water and a half cup liquid bleach. If you boil the solution in the pan for several minutes the stains will disappear. After washing the pan, wipe the inner surface with cooking oil to reseason it.

One way to clean porcelain surfaces is to rub them with cream of tartar sprinkled on a damp cloth. You can remove rust spots from metal surfaces the same way.

A paste made of baking soda and water is very effective in removing stubborn soil and stains from plastic and rubber utensils, and it deodorizes them at the same time. Apply the paste with a synthetic scouring pad and watch the stains disappear.

A good way to remove odor from plastic containers without spending a cent is to crumple a piece of newspaper into the container, secure the lid tightly, and leave overnight. It takes the odor away very effectively.

Metal-trimmed china should not be soaked for long periods. Soaking will damage the trim.

Be sure the water is not too hot when you rinse glazed dinnerware. Boiling water will cause the glaze to craze, or develop minute cracks.

Pasta dishes can make for heavy-duty cleanup chores. Ease the task by spraying nonstick cooking spray on the inside of the pot you're cooking the noodles in; the water won't boil over. Spray the cheese grater to keep the cheese from sticking. And spray the pizza pan and the inside of the lasagna dish; the food will come out easily and cleanup will be a snap.

If the children spill rice on the floor, try to resist the temptation to clean it up immediately. It will be much easier to sweep up when it has dried.

Aluminum Cookware

Try removing dark stains from an aluminum pan by filling the pan with water containing one tablespoon of cream of tartar per quart of water and boiling the mixture. White vinegar added to water and boiled works equally well.

To remove discolorations from an aluminum pot, cook tomatoes or applesauce in it; the acid in the food will brighten up the metal.

Aluminum cookware should be washed by hand. If washed in the dishwasher, the strong detergent used can discolor polished or satin finishes and remove the color from an anodized finish.

Food should not be stored in aluminum cookware. The food may discolor or pit the metal.

The least expensive way to clean aluminum cookware is with baking soda. After rinsing the pot, don't dry it; just sprinkle one table-spoon baking soda on the wet surface to make a paste, then use a synthetic scouring pad to spread the paste and clean off any stains. Rinse and polish to give a bright finish.

Cast Iron Cookware

You can remove charred food spots from the interior of a cast iron utensil by sprinkling salt on the spots, adding enough vinegar to cover, and boiling the mixture.

Moisture causes cast iron to deteriorate, so after washing and towel drying a cast iron skillet, put it in a warm oven to complete the drying process. It's also a good idea to place paper towels between cast iron pans when you stack them so that moisture can't get trapped between them.

The easiest way to clean the outside of a cast iron skillet is with oven cleaner. Spray it on, let it stand for an hour, and wipe it off with a solution of water and vinegar.

You can maintain the seasoning of cast iron cookware by scouring the pots and pans occasionally, wiping them with oil, and placing them in a warm oven for two hours. Then wipe off the excess oil.

Remove the lids before storing cast iron pots and pans. If they are stored with the lids in place, rust can form.

Washing in the dishwasher will remove the seasoning from cast iron cookware and may cause rust. Wash these utensils by hand.

Season cast iron cookware the easy way with nonstick cooking spray.

Clay Cookware

Before you use a clay cooking utensil for the first time, soak both the top and the bottom in water for about half an hour, then scrub well with a stiff brush to remove any clay dust.

To remove stubborn soil or pungent odors from clay cookware, fill it with water to which you have added one to four tablespoons of baking soda and leave it overnight.

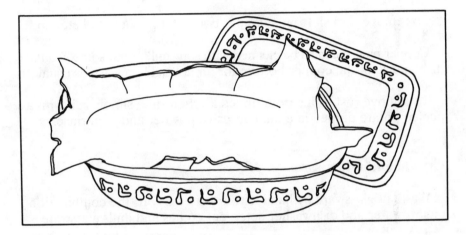

If you line a clay cooker with baking parchment paper you will prevent the porous clay from absorbing food stains and strong flavors.

Clay cookware won't develop mold if you always make sure it is thoroughly dry before storing it, and always store it without the lid in place.

If mold spots do appear on your clay cooker, you can remove them with a paste of equal parts baking soda and water, which should be brushed on and allowed to stand for 30 minutes, preferably in strong sunlight. After brushing away the paste be sure to rinse and dry the cooker thoroughly before storing.

Copper Cookware

If your copper cookware comes with a protective lacquer coating that must be removed before the cookware is used, place the utensil in a solution of one cup baking soda and two gallons boiling water. Let it stand until the water cools, peel off the lacquer, wash, rinse, and dry.

Vinegar is the featured ingredient in two inexpensive copper cleaners. The first consists of a paste made of one tablespoon each salt, white vinegar, and flour. This can be used to clean a discolored skillet. Because the vinegar is acid, the skillet must then be washed with hot soapy water and rinsed. You can get equally good results with a paste of two tablespoons vinegar and one tablespoon salt.

To remove tarnish from a copper pot, rub the pot with ketchup.

Copper pans can also be cleaned with sour milk. Pour some in a flat dish and soak the copper bottom for an hour. Then wash as usual.

To remove rust stains from tinned kitchenware, simply rub with a peeled potato dipped in a mild abrasive powder and then rinse.

Crystal and Glassware

Wash all glassware by hand if your water is soft; the combination of soft water and dishwasher detergent etches and dulls glassware.

A stained glass decanter can be cleaned by filling it with water to which you have added a cup of ammonia or vinegar. Allow the mixture to stand overnight.

For persistent stains on the interior of a glass decanter, add two packs of powdered denture cleaner, dissolved in water, to the water/ ammonia mixture given in the previous hint.

"Dry dusting" crystal or displayed glassware may scratch the surface. Instead, wipe these items with a soft cloth dipped in an ammonia solution.

You can remove stains from crystal by rubbing with a cut lemon or washing in a vinegar solution.

Milk glass will yellow if washed in the dishwasher. Wash these items by hand.

Stubborn food spots on glassware will dissolve if rubbed with baking soda.

Greasy glassware will come sparkling clean if washed in an ammonia solution.

If there are stubborn lime and water spots on your glassware, try polishing the spots away with a soft chamois cloth.

Here's an easy way to remove the cloudiness from your fine crystal: Fill the glasses with ordinary water and drop a denture tablet in each. Wait until the tablets dissolve and then rinse the glasses; the film will be gone.

To prevent cracking, slip delicate stemware into the wash water edgewise—not bottom first. For real sparkle add a little vinegar to the warm rinse water.

To dry delicate stemware, stand it upside down on a soft towel, or polish it gently with a soft, lint-free cloth.

Use a soft brush to remove dirt from crevices in glassware.

A good way to clean a glass decanter is to cut a potato into small pieces, drop the pieces into the decanter, add warm water, and shake until the decanter's inside surfaces are spotless. Throw out the potato pieces, and then rinse the decanter with clean water.

A vase with a narrow neck appears to be hard to clean, but you can freshen it by dampening the inside with water, sprinkling in some toilet bowl cleaner, and waiting ten minutes before rinsing thoroughly. Or fill the vase with hot water, add rice and two teaspoons of vinegar, and shake vigorously.

If your glass coffee percolator looks dull, make it sparkle again by boiling vinegar in it.

Silver and Flatware

Retard silver tarnishing by placing a piece of alum in the silverware drawer.

When silver does tarnish, apply silver polish with a sponge instead of a cloth. The sponge squeezes into crevices a cloth can't reach.

Silverware should be washed by hand rather than in the dishwasher, then buffed dry to bring up the shine and prevent waterspots. The same method should be used for brass and pewter.

Using sterling silver flatware regularly slows the tarnishing process and gives the pieces a beautiful patina.

If you do wash sterling silver in the dishwasher, separate it from stainless steel. Contact between the two produces an electrolytic action that pits the stainless steel.

Because contact with rubber darkens silver, wear cloth instead of rubber gloves when cleaning it. Also, never fasten pieces of silverware together with rubber bands.

Even the slightest dampness causes silver to tarnish, so after you've washed or polished sterling silver it's a good idea to let it air dry for a few hours before putting it away.

You can keep stainless steel shiny by rubbing it with a lemon peel or a cloth dampened with rubbing alcohol, and then washing it as usual.

When black spots appear on carbon steel knives, you can remove them with an old wine bottle cork. Sprinkle cleanser on the side of the blade, wet the cork, and scrub the blade with the flat end of the cork. Clean the other side the same way.

If you want carving knives to remain sharp, wash them in cool water.

Cutting Boards and Countertops

Wooden cutting boards should be cleaned and oiled periodically to restore their smooth finish and protect them from moisture.

To deodorize a wooden cutting board, mix a half cup baking soda with one quart warm water and rub it on the surface. Use a synthetic scouring pad to clean away the gummy residue on the edges. Rinse and dry well.

You can restore the natural finish to a wooden cutting board by applying two coats of boiled linseed oil (salad oil will do in a pinch) 24 hours apart. Rub the oil in with a fine steel-wool pad, and clean off the excess between applications.

Rubbing salt into a wooden cutting board will both eliminate odors and lift stains.

To remove countertop stains, simply sprinkle with baking soda, rub with a damp cloth or sponge, and rinse with clear water.

To brighten a dulled plastic laminate countertop surface, apply an appliance wax or a light furniture wax.

Coffee or tea stains can be removed by rubbing them with a damp cloth dipped in baking soda.

To prevent staining, coat rubber drainboard trays with a thin film of furniture polish. Remove any stains with a mixture of bleach and water before applying the polish.

If your laminated plastic countertop is marred by hard-to-remove stains, don't rub it with steel wool or abrasive cleaners; instead, try a solution of milk, bleach, and water. Let it sit for a minute and immediately rinse with water.

Has the dye used to mark food products left a stubborn stain on your laminated kitchen counter? The solution is simple. Sprinkle baking soda on the stain, rub it in with a damp cloth or sponge, and rinse with clear water.

APPLIANCES:
USE AND CARE

You'll make defrosting the refrigerator easier if you rub the inside of the freezer section with shortening. As an alternative, spray it with a commercial coating that prevents food from sticking to pans. Either way, ice will slide right off when you defrost.

Do you defrost your refrigerator by letting water drip into a tray beneath the freezer compartment? You can avoid spilling the water on the way to the sink if you leave the tray in position, let its contents refreeze, and then drop the frozen chunk in the sink to melt.

A frost-free refrigerator should be cleaned thoroughly every four to six months; a manual-defrost refrigerator should be cleaned when frost is half an inch thick.

You can speed up the task of defrosting a manual-defrost refrigerator by placing shallow pans of hot water on the shelves.

Refrigerator and freezer odors can sometimes be eliminated by rubbing interior surfaces with a few drops of vanilla extract diluted in a cup of water. Some homemakers keep a cotton ball soaked with the extract inside the refrigerator all the time.

Here are other ways to keep the refrigerator free of odors: Leave an open box of baking soda, a dish of charcoal briquettes, or a lemon half in the unit. If odors still linger, clean all interior surfaces with club soda or a baking soda and water solution.

While defrosting the freezer, wrap perishables in newspaper to keep them cold. Make sure frozen food packages are wiped dry of condensation before returning them to the freezer.

As well as using baking soda in the refrigerator to cut down on odors, you can put a second box in the freezer. It will absorb stale odors and keep ice cubes (and ice cream) fresh longer.

Ice trays should not be washed in a detergent solution. This can remove the special nonstick coating that some ice trays have.

Occasionally remove the burners from a gas stove and wash them thoroughly. Clean the holes with a fine wire cleaner or a pipe cleaner, then quickly dry the just-washed burners in a warm oven. (Don't try to clean a gas burner's holes with a toothpick; it may break off and clog a hole.)

A cheap, effective way to clean a soiled oven is with ordinary household ammonia. Pour one cup of ammonia in a glass or ceramic bowl, place it in the oven, and allow it to sit in the closed oven overnight. Next morning, pour the ammonia into a pail of warm water and use this solution to sponge out loosened soil. The fumes are strong at first, but they soon dissipate.

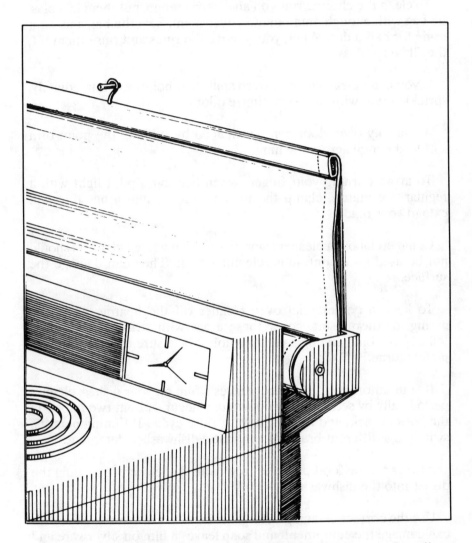

Protect your wall behind your stove from grease splatters. Install a washable vinyl shade. Position it upside down so that the roller is hidden by the stove. When cooking, pull the shade up and fasten it to a hook several feet above the stove. When finished, roll the shade down out of sight.

After you've cleaned an oven, bake a few orange peels in it at 350°F to dispel cleaning odors.

To clean the chrome rings on an electric range, put them in a plastic bag with enough ammonia to cover them. Seal the bag and set it aside for half a day. When you remove the rings and rinse them off, they'll be spotless.

If you can't clean stove or oven spills and boil-overs immediately, sprinkle them with salt to minimize odor.

A squeaky oven door can be silenced by rubbing the point of a soft lead pencil across the hinges.

To avoid burning your fingers when lighting a pilot light with a regular-size match, clamp the match with kitchen tongs that will extend your reach.

Commercial oven cleaners, abrasives, or powdered cleaners should not be used on a continuous-cleaning oven. They can damage the surface.

To keep a commercial oven cleaner off the heating elements, wiring, or thermostat, cover these areas with strips of aluminum foil before commencing a cleaning job. Make sure the oven is completely turned off.

If your automatic dishwasher leaves a film on your dishes, clean it periodically by setting a bowl of white vinegar—about two cups—in the bottom rack, and running a wash-rinse cycle. If filming persists, switch to a different brand of automatic dishwasher detergent.

Always scrape food particles from your dishes before loading the dishes into the dishwasher.

Use the correct cleaning detergents in your dishwasher. Soapsuds can damage the equipment, and soap leaves a film on silverware and glasses.

Leave the dishwasher door open occasionally to air out any odors retained in the liner.

You can remove hard water and mineral deposits from the interior porcelain tank of your dishwasher by placing a glass bowl containing three quarters cup of bleach on the lower rack. Load the dishwasher with glass and china only, and run it through the wash and rinse cycle. Then put one cup vinegar in the bowl and run the machine through a complete cycle.

If the interior of the dishwasher retains stubborn odors, sprinkle three tablespoons baking soda in the bottom of the machine and allow it to sit overnight. The odors will be washed away with the baking soda during the next wash cycle.

Sprinkle a handful of baking soda over the dirty dishes in the dishwasher. It will take the place of detergent in the first wash cycle, and will also help to deodorize the dishes.

Let the blender scrub itself clean. Fill it less than halfway with hot water, add a few drops of dishwashing liquid, and run for ten seconds. Rinse and dry.

There are several ways to keep chrome surfaces glistening. You can rub them with dry baking soda sprinkled on a dry cloth, a cloth dampened with hot water and ammonia, or a cloth dampened with rubbing alcohol.

To clean chrome knobs or decorations on an appliance, apply nail polish remover. (First make sure that the unit is unplugged, because polish remover is flammable.) Rinse the knobs or decorations with water.

Use a toothbrush dipped in warm soapsuds to clean the tiny crevices between appliance push buttons or raised-letter nameplates.

To flush food particles from a meat grinder, run a raw potato or a slice of stale bread through it before washing it.

The polished-metal surface of your toaster/oven broiler or toaster will come clean with baking soda or flour rubbed on with a dry cloth. Use baking soda only on a moistened cloth for stubborn stains.

To remove coffee or tea stains from the interior of a thermos bottle, partially fill the container with crushed eggshells, add hot water, and shake well.

To remove general stains from the interior of a thermos bottle, fill the container with warm water and one tablespoon bicarbonate of soda, let stand for three hours, then wash.

Sweeten a coffee maker's plastic basket by occasionally rubbing it with a paste of baking soda and water.

Built-up oil deposits in your electric coffee maker can give the coffee a bitter taste. With the stem and basket in place, fill the percolator to the limit with cold water and add six tablespoons of baking soda. Plug the coffee maker in and run it through the complete cycle. Wait for 15 minutes, unplug, and empty out the solution. Then wash in a mild detergent, rinse, and dry.

Coffee and teapots can be freshened easily by washing with a solution of baking soda and water. Baking soda on a damp sponge will clean away stubborn stains.

Tear up a citrus fruit peel and put it into your food waste disposer to eliminate stale odors. You'll enjoy the fresh scent of citrus instead. Your kitchen standby, baking soda, also works well to deodorize the disposer; sprinkle baking soda over several ice cubes and grind them in the disposer.

TIPS ON KITCHEN TECHNIQUES

Range-Top and Oven Cooking

Tired of boil-overs that take a lot of time to clean up? You can prevent them by inserting a toothpick horizontally between pot and lid so that steam can escape harmlessly.

You can prevent steam from scalding your wrists and hands when you drain boiling water from a pot of vegetables if you first turn on the cold water tap.

Using the wrong size cooking utensils on your range top is inefficient and wastes energy. If a pan is larger than the electric element, it may overheat. It it's too small, fuel is wasted. On a gas range, a pan smaller than the burner allows heat to extend beyond the side of the pan; this wastes energy and may damage the pan.

For even cooking in a conventional oven, allow two inches between pans and two inches between pans and the oven wall. This allows adequate room for circulation of the hot air.

If your oven doesn't have an indicator light, allow ten minutes for preheating before putting in breads or cookies. Preheat at the setting required in the recipes.

Shiny aluminum pans reflect heat and give a golden color to breads and cookies. For pies, use dark pans to absorb heat and keep the crust from getting soggy.

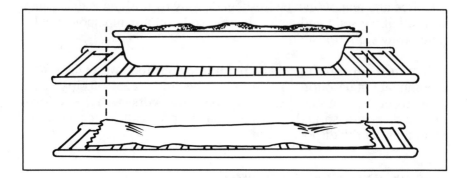

If you want to use aluminum foil in the oven to catch spills, place it on the rack below the one used for baking. If it is directly under the utensil it will reduce air circulation. Use foil only on the part of the lower rack that is directly under the utensil; do not cover the entire rack.

Warped or bent pans cause uneven baking results and unevenly shaped baked goods. Find another use for warped pans (put them under your houseplants, for example), and buy new ones for baking.

Racks left in the oven during the self-clean cycle may become discolored and hard to slide in and out of the oven. Remove the racks before the cycle starts and wash them by hand. Or, if you want to leave them in the oven, use a soap-filled steel-wool pad to polish the edges of the racks and guides, and rub a little oil (use salad oil) on them to make them slide more easily.

Frying and Broiling

Dripping fat can smoke and catch fire while you're broiling meat. Guard against this by placing dry bread in the broiler pan to soak up the fat.

If grease on your broiler catches fire, sprinkle salt or baking soda on the flames. (Partially burned meat may still be edible after you've rinsed off the soda.) Don't try to use flour as a fire extinguisher—it's explosive.

If you're going to sauté or fry a food, dry it thoroughly before placing it in hot oil. Cold, wet food may splatter dangerously.

A temperature test for sautéing in butter: It's time to add the food just after the foam on the butter subsides.

Sprinkling a little salt in the frying pan before you start cooking prevents hot fat from splattering.

To be able to use vegetable oil several times, heat it slowly to frying temperature so that it doesn't decompose. Use a thermometer to avoid overheating.

Don't use the same vegetable oil for frying more than a few times. Old oil soaks into fried foods.

Before you save hot oil, test it by dropping a piece of white bread into the pan. If dark spots appear on the bread, the oil isn't worth saving.

You can use a baster to remove grease from the frying pan when you're cooking hamburger or other fatty foods.

Is your frying pan splattering? Punch a lot of holes in an aluminum-foil pie plate and place it upside down over the pan. The punctured pie plate confines grease but lets steam escape.

For an extra-light, delicate crust on fried foods, mix your batter with club soda and add three quarters of a teaspoon of baking soda.

Broiling with gas is different from broiling with electricity. When you broil with gas, you should keep the oven door closed because gas flames absorb moisture and consume smoke. When you broil with electricity, keep the door slightly open so the oven can expel moisture.

Think twice before lining a broiling pan with foil. Foil promotes frying rather than broiling because it prevents fat from draining away.

Instead of clarifying butter for sautéing foods, add a small amount of vegetable oil to unsalted butter. The vegetable oil will allow the butter to reach a higher temperature without burning.

You can give your skillet a nonstick finish by sprinkling the pan with salt and then warming it for five minutes. Remove, wipe out the salt, and use as usual.

Cooking in the Microwave Oven

For microwave cooking, cut meats and vegetables in uniform sizes to make sure that they cook evenly.

Baked foods rise higher in a microwave oven. To avoid spillage, fill cake and bread pans only half full with batter.

To ensure that food cooks fully and evenly in the microwave oven, stir food pieces and turn dishes periodically while they're cooking.

Remove large bones from meat before microwaving it, because the dense bone may keep the area around it from cooking. The deboned meat will cook more evenly if you use a middle temperature range.

When microwaving a food that needs thorough cooking to destroy possibly harmful organisms, be particularly careful to observe the recommended standing time. Let the food stand outside the oven for the full time recommended to complete cooking; cover with foil to keep hot.

Here's a way to find out if a certain (nonmetal) cooking utensil can be used in your microwave oven:

Place the utensil in the oven and put a cup of cool water on it or next to it. Microwave on High for one minute. If the utensil is hot after one minute, it is not safe for microwave oven use. If it's warm, use it only for short-term heating. If it's cold, but the water is hot, you can use the utensil safely in the microwave oven.

Rehydrate dried fruits by covering them with water in a bowl and microwaving for four to five minutes. Use high power.

To get more juice from a lemon, pop it in the microwave on high power for 30 seconds. The same process works for other citrus fruits.

Paper towels around sandwiches, rolls, or other baked goods will absorb moisture that would otherwise make the food soggy.

Potato chips that have lost their crunch can be placed on paper towels in the microwave oven and heated briefly. The towels will absorb moisture and restore the chips to crispness.

Although correctly used utensils will not heat up in a microwave oven, they may get hot from the food itself. So don't throw out your pot holders. Be careful, too, of escaping steam when you lift the cover of a dish.

Paper plates, cups, and napkins can be used in the microwave oven. But don't use foil-lined paper products, paper towels than include nylon or synthetic fibers, or newspaper—some newspaper inks may absorb microwaves and cause the paper to catch fire.

When using plastic roasting or cooking bags in the microwave oven, discard the wire twist tie and use a plastic fastener or a piece of string instead.

Thick-skinned foods such as potatoes, squash, and tomatoes trap steam during microwave cooking. Pierce the skins before cooking to allow steam to escape. The same applies to eggs in the shell.

You can use your microwave to make shelling nuts a cinch. Put two cups of nuts into a one-quart casserole with a cup of water, and microwave for four to five minutes on High. Then, when you crack the nuts, the meats will come out in one piece.

If your brown sugar has turned into an intractable lump, just place a piece of dampened paper towel in the box, close the box tightly, and put the whole thing in the microwave for 20 to 30 seconds on High. The sugar will soften up nicely.

Your microwave oven can ease the chore of peeling such foods as tomatoes or peaches. Heat for 30 seconds on High, then allow to stand for two minutes. The peel will slip off easily.

Microwave ice cream? Ridiculous, wouldn't you say? In fact, ice cream that has hardened too much in the freezer can be returned to usable consistency if you microwave it on Warm for 10 to 15 seconds.

Several food items (such as potatoes) will cook more evenly in a microwave oven if they are arranged in a circle around the center with two inches between them to allow the microwave energy to circulate adequately. Similarly, chicken pieces will cook more evenly if arranged in the dish with the thicker or bigger portions toward the outside edges of the dish.

The metal clamps used to hold the legs of poultry in place need not be removed before cooking the bird in a microwave oven, so long as the metal does not touch the walls of the oven.

With foods that require browning—breads, cookies, and some meats, for example—a conventional oven produces better results than a microwave oven unless the microwave oven has a broiling element.

Storing and Preserving Food

SAFE FOOD STORAGE AND HANDLING

When you unload your groceries into the freezer, be sure to place the new items behind previously purchased items of the same type. Then you'll automatically reach for the older items at the front of the freezer first.

Defrosting food under cold instead of hot water helps keep the food cold so that bacteria are less likely to grow in the thawed portions before the center areas are completely defrosted. Secure the frozen package in a watertight plastic bag, and change the cold water frequently.

Be conservative about following the "sell by" and "use by" dates on purchased products; they do not tell you how much the food has been handled or how well it has been refrigerated before you buy it.

Wash kitchen linens frequently. Bacteria can lodge in tea towels and washcloths that are reused a lot without laundering. Throw out dish sponges when they get dirty.

Adding mayonnaise to food may make the food slightly more resistant to food poisoning organisms—which is contrary to what you may have learned about mayonnaise being particularly susceptible to harboring hostile organisms. The fact is that most commercially prepared mayonnaises and salad dressings contain some kind of acid (lemon juice, for instance) which slows down the growth of bacteria.

Mayonnaise keeps best at 50°F, so after opening it should be kept in the warmest part of the refrigerator—in the door shelf or away from the freezing compartment. Use up the jar within two months for best flavor.

Mayonnaise separates during freezing, and when you defrost it you get just the separated components. So don't try to freeze salads made with mayonnaise—egg, tuna, or chicken salad, for example.

If you have storage cabinets above your kitchen range, use them only for nonfood items. Even foods such as dry cake mixes, which can be kept safely at room temperature, will not keep well if exposed to heat rising from the range.

Not all boxed or canned foods can be kept at room temperature. Unopened canned cheeses (Brie or Camembert, for example) should be stored in the refrigerator. Check the labels for instructions.

Some grated Parmesan cheese products can be kept out of the refrigerator after opening, but others cannot. Check the label each time you purchase a different brand, and if you've failed to refrigerate a product so labeled, throw it out.

Unshelled nuts will keep at room temperature for up to six months, but other nuts have a high fat content and should be stored in airtight containers in the refrigerator or freezer to keep them from becoming rancid. Throw out any that have mold.

Tofu can be kept in the refrigerator for about a week, but it will stay fresh longer if the water in the container is changed every other day. Once opened, transfer tofu to an airtight plastic container.

Canned foods store well, but they don't keep forever. Cans can rust over time, and if the rust gets deep enough it can cause tiny holes that allow the entry of food spoilage organisms. Check cans regularly.

Canned foods that are high in acid (tomatoes, for instance) should only be stored for 12 to 18 months, compared to low-acid foods that can be satisfactorily stored for two to five years. (High-acid foods react with the metal container, and this reaction eventually causes changes in taste, texture, and nutritional value.)

Canned foods that have been accidentally frozen can present health problems. If the cans are swollen and you're sure that the cause of the swelling is freezing and nothing else, you can use the contents: Cook them thoroughly and eat or refreeze right away. If the seams of the can have rusted or split, the food must be discarded.

What do you do with a product you suspect to be a potential source of food poisoning? Seal it in a strong plastic bag, mark the bag to indicate that the contents are dangerous, and place it on a high shelf in the refrigerator (where children can't reach it). Place a paper plate under the package to avoid leakage. Then report it to health officials.

When preparing a stuffed chicken or turkey, check the stuffing as well as the bird for doneness. Place the thermometer in the stuffing and leave for five minutes before taking a reading. For complete cooking, the stuffing should register 165°F and the bird 185°F.

Stuffed poultry that has been commercially frozen should not be defrosted before cooking. Follow the package directions carefully.

Always stuff a chicken or turkey loosely—don't cram dressing into the cavity. If the bird is stuffed loosely the oven heat will penetrate more easily to cook the stuffing all the way through.

Don't worry about the separation of the fat from the meat and the oil from the marinade that occurs when you freeze marinated meat. The components will combine satisfactorily when reheated.

Although the acid in a marinade will help slow the growth of dangerous bacteria, it won't prevent it altogether, so it's not safe to allow food to marinate on the countertop. If the marinating process takes longer than an hour, refrigerate the container.

Foods should not be marinated in any container—like metal—that can be affected by the acid in the marinade. Use only glass or plastic containers for marinating.

Keep potatoes in a dry, dark place. Light affects the vitamin C content.

Sweet potatoes, regular potatoes, and hard-shelled squash should not be refrigerated because cold temperatures cause the starch to convert to sugar, affecting the taste. Keep these vegetables at room temperature.

Egg dishes are susceptible to bacteria growth and should be handled carefully. Serve egg-rich hot dishes immediately after cooking and refrigerate leftovers quickly. If the dish is to be served cold, put it in the refrigerator immediately after preparation and keep it there until you're ready to serve it.

Hard-cooked eggs can be refrigerated for up to a week. Maximum keeping time for fresh eggs in the refrigerator is about five weeks; then they begin to lose quality.

Cracked or soiled eggs may contain disease-causing organisms. Use these eggs only in dishes where they will be fully cooked. Choose only clean, intact eggs for soft-boiled or scrambled eggs or any recipe—such as a salad dressing—where they are eaten raw.

Although cooking destroys most of the bacteria that can lead to food poisoning, it does not destroy the staph *(staphylococcus aureus)* organism. For this reason, two hours is the longest that prepared foods—especially starchy foods, cheese, and meat dishes such as cooked meats and meat salads—should be allowed to sit at room temperature.

Partial cooking may speed up your food preparation program, but it's inadvisable because partial cooking may encourage bacteria growth before cooking is complete. So don't interrupt cooking of meat and poultry; cook it completely at one time.

As a rule of thumb, cook frozen foods one and one-half times as long as thawed foods.

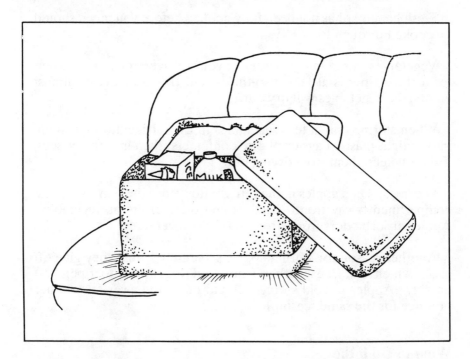

If you live a long way from the store, be especially careful of how you handle food between purchase and home storage, particularly in hot weather. Pick up perishables last in your trek around the supermarket, and if you live more than 30 miles from the store keep an ice chest in your car and transfer perishables to it for the journey home.

Don't handle meat and poultry more than necessary, because frequent handling can introduce bacteria into these products. Unless the store wrap is damaged, leave it in place when you store the food. If the wrap is damaged, replace it before storage.

Even canned hams should be refrigerated. Check the label for storage information. Packaged ham slices or whole hams should be stored in the coldest part of the refrigerator. Use ham slices within three or four days; whole hams within a week.

Ham does not freeze well; it loses flavor and texture when frozen. If you must freeze ham, try to use it within a month or so.

Fresh ham that has not been fully cooked before you buy it should be cooked through to 170°F.

Vegetables stored in the crisper of your refrigerator will keep better if the crisper is at least two-thirds full. If it is empty or almost empty, the vegetables will dry out.

When storing only a few vegetables in the refrigerator, put them into airtight plastic bags or plastic containers, then into the crisper. This will keep them from drying out.

When you keep apples in the refrigerator, store them in a separate compartment away from tomatoes and other fruits or vegetables. Apples absorb odors from strong-flavored vegetables.

Another reason for storing apples separately is that they give off gases which can cause other fruits and vegetables to ripen too quickly. (Apples in cold storage should be stored away from other produce for the same reason.)

What to Do if the Freezer Fails

If your freezer goes out but you expect the stoppage to be temporary, avoid opening the freezer to check on the contents. Every time you open it you're letting out cold air and reducing the effectiveness of the appliance.

If you expect your freezer to be out of action for more than a day or two, call around to find a school, church, or store with a freezer in which you can store your frozen goods temporarily.

It's also possible to rent space in a commercial freezer or cold storage plant if your freezer goes on the fritz and you expect it to take a while to fix.

Dry ice will keep your food frozen in a freezer that's temporarily out of commission, but dry ice must be handled carefully. Never touch dry ice with your bare hands—it freezes everything, including skin; handle it only with tongs or with your hands protected by heavy gloves. Also, work in a well-ventilated area because as dry ice evaporates, it uses oxygen very quickly.

If you use dry ice to preserve the contents of a nonfunctioning freezer, avoid letting it touch the packages themselves. Place the ice on empty shelves, or cover the frozen goods with a layer of cardboard and place the dry ice on top of that.

How much dry ice do you need to keep your frozen foods in good condition? If you have a ten-cubic-foot freezer that is full, reckon on 25 pounds of dry ice to keep the contents below freezing for three to four days. If the freezer is only half full, the same amount of ice will only keep the produce frozen for two to three days.

After a thaw, check if meat or poultry still contains ice crystals. If it does, you can refreeze it safely. Otherwise it should be cooked. Of course, you can refreeze the food after cooking.

COLD STORAGE FOR VEGETABLES AND FRUITS

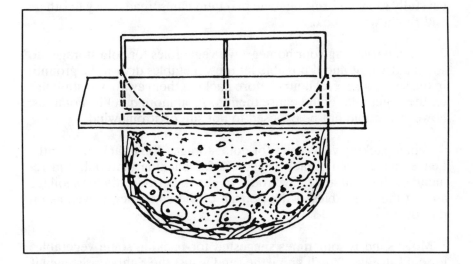

You can make an excellent cold-storage area for vegetables in a window well (provided it doesn't collect and hold water). Line a dry window well with straw or hay, put in the vegetables, and cover with a board and more straw.

If you have a cold-storage area for fruits and vegetables indoors, keep a humidity gauge there—without adequate humidity the produce will dry up and shrivel. You don't need fancy equipment for maintaining the right humidity; you can just put pans of water or a tub of dampened sand on the floor, or cover the floor with damp straw, sand, or sawdust.

The outside stairs to your basement can make a good vegetable storage area. Set a plank on each step for insulation. Check the temperature on each step and put boxes or barrels of vegetables on the steps where the temperature is right. (If you live in a cold climate, you may need to cover the outside door to keep the produce from freezing.)

A garage or storage shed can be a useful storage area for vegetables, but only if it is free of oil and gasoline odors, which can be absorbed by some fruits and vegetables.

Pick only perfect vegetables for cold storage, and handle them carefully to avoid bruising. One bad item can spread decay to others and ruin a whole box.

When harvesting your homegrown vegetables for cold storage, do so on a dry day, and if possible let the vegetables dry on the ground, in the sun, for several hours before packing them away. Moisture left on the vegetables could cause them to spoil more quickly. Potatoes, however, should not be exposed to hot sun or strong wind.

When packing vegetables for cold storage, don't pack too tightly. Leave space around each vegetable for packing material, and remember that you must have room to check periodically for spoilage among the vegetables at the bottom of the container as well as on the top.

Moist sand is sometimes suggested for packing some vegetables for cold storage. You'll know the sand is just the right consistency if it feels cold and falls apart in your hand when squeezed, leaving just a few particles sticking to your skin.

When your vegetables mature, you may want to harvest seeds for sprouting. If so, leave the seeds on the plant until they're dry and fully mature, then store the dried seeds in airtight plastic bags in a metal container, or in airtight glass jars. If you wrap newspaper around the containers it will keep light from reaching the seeds. You can keep seeds this way in a cool, dry place for up to 12 months.

If you want to store your tomatoes, plant late so that the vines will still be vigorous when you pick the tomatoes for storage. Harvest green tomatoes just before the time when you expect the first killing frost in your area.

When selecting apples for cold storage, choose late-season varieties. The following varieties keep well: Winesap, Northern Spy, Jonathan, McIntosh, Cortland, and Golden and Red Delicious.

Select dessert pears for cold storage. Anjou keep best, followed by Bosc or Commice.

For storage, harvest mature pears that are still hard. Pears that have begun to ripen will decay quickly.

Underripe bunches of grapes can be cold-stored for one to two months between layers of clean straw and hay. Catawba grapes keep best. Second in line are Tokay and Concord.

FREEZING FOODS
AT HOME

Freeze slightly under-mature vegetables rather than those that are past their prime. Under-mature vegetables retain flavor and shape when frozen. (Different rules apply to fruit.)

For peak flavor, rush vegetables from the garden to the freezer within two hours. If you can't freeze them within that time, cool the vegetables quickly in ice water, drain well, and keep refrigerated until ready to prepare for freezing.

Since cooling is an important part of preparing vegetables for freezing, keep a good supply of ice in reserve for your home freezing needs by filling heavy-duty plastic bags with ice cubes, or by freezing water in empty milk cartons.

Blanching—precooking vegetables slightly before freezing—is necessary to arrest the chemical changes that are caused by enzyme activity. For a homemade blancher, use a six- to eight-quart pot with a cover, and a colander, sieve, deep-frying basket, or cheesecloth bag to lift the vegetables from the boiling water.

If you buy a commercial blancher, it need not gather dust when you're not using it to prepare vegetables for freezing. The blancher can double as a spaghetti cooker, or steamer, or a deep-fat fryer.

When blanching large quantities of vegetables for freezing, you'll get best results if you start with only the amount that can be blanched and cooled in a 15-minute period. (Put the rest in the refrigerator.) Package, label, and freeze each blanched group before starting on the next. Don't forget that blanching means the vegetables have already been cooked slightly. This shortens the cooking time required for frozen vegetables.

To help estimate how much ice you'll need to have on hand for cooling vegetables after blanching, reckon on one pound of ice for every pound of vegetables.

If you pack foods in containers with narrow mouths, the food expands upward in the container even more and you must allow more head space: Three-quarters inch for pint containers; one-and-one-half inches for quarts.

Use your hands to press as much air as possible out of a filled freezer bag before sealing it.

It's sometimes hard to get the air out of an odd-shaped bag of produce to be frozen. Make it easier by lowering the filled bag into a sink full of water and letting the water press the air out. Then twist the top of the bag, fold the twisted section over, and fasten it with a rubber band, pipe cleaner, or twist tie.

For fastest freezing, foods newly prepared for freezing should be placed in a single layer in the coldest part of your freezer. Leave the freezer closed for 24 hours, then move the packages—which should be frozen solid—to another area of the freezer to free up the coldest area for the next batch.

Remember that your freezer can only freeze a limited amount of food at a time. A good estimate is two to three pounds of food for each cubic foot of freezer space.

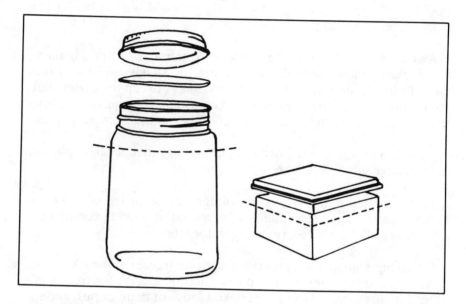

Foods that are packed in liquid expand as they freeze, and room— or head space—must be allowed for this expansion to keep lids from popping off or freezer bags from bursting. Allow a quarter inch of head space for pints, a half inch for quarts.

If you freeze a lot of garden produce, plan your freezer's annual or semi-annual defrosting for when the weather is cold, preferably before you start planning your garden. Then you can take an inventory and determine what to plant in spring. For instance, if you have lots of green beans left in March, that's a clue that supply is exceeding demand. Put up fewer beans next year and fill the freezer space with something else.

Don't use a hair dryer or other heating appliance to speed up the freezer's defrosting process; the heat could melt or warp some of the materials on the inside of the freezer.

If your freezer develops an odor, put a piece or two of charcoal on an paper towel and leave in the freezer for a few days.

A plastic windshield wiper is a good tool for scraping loosened ice from the inside of your freezer.

Use your home-frozen fruits and vegetables within a year. Although they keep longer than many foods, they should not be stored for longer than 12 months.

Avoid ice crystals forming in the foods you freeze by freezing them fast at zero temperatures. If foods freeze too slowly, moisture from the cells in the food fibers forms ice crystals between the fibers, and the product loses liquid and may darken. Quick freezing at very low temperatures locks the cells in the food fiber in their proper places.

Liquid foods are safest frozen in plastic bags that are then placed in protective cardboard boxes.

Plastic-coated milk cartons or cottage cheese or ice cream containers are not airtight enough to be reused as freezer containers. Use them only for short-term refrigerator storage.

Grouping similar foods together in your freezer will make your inventory more organized. Keep one shelf or section for fruits, another for vegetables, a third for cooked foods or main dishes, and so on. Hang a chart or clipboard on the freezer door handle or nearby, then note what goes in or out, how much, and when.

As you use your frozen foods, it's a good idea to keep a running check on your methods and packaging. If you notice that a particular bag, container, or sealing method isn't doing the job, jot down a mental note about it and try a different procedure next time.

If you want the blueberries you freeze to retain their shape and color, don't wash them. Simply freeze them in their containers, and wash them just before use.

To prevent foods such as berries from sticking together when frozen, flashfreeze them first. Here's how: Separate them on a cookie sheet, freeze, remove, and—while still frozen—pack them together in airtight containers before replacing them in the freezer.

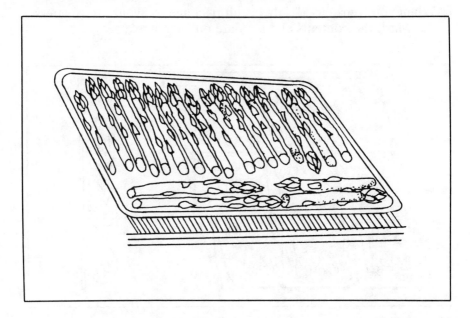

Delicate vegetables like asparagus should be briefly tray-frozen before they're packaged. First blanch the vegetables and drain them well, then spread them in a single layer on a cookie sheet and freeze them until just solid. Then transfer them to containers and store them in the freezer.

The best plums for freezing are large sugar plums. Save Damson plums for making jellies and sauces.

Fruits with pits, like plums and cherries, must be pitted before freezing. The stone imparts an off flavor to the fruit during long-term freezer storage.

You can freeze whole lemons or limes. Just wash and dry the fruit, twist a freezer bag tightly around it, seal, and freeze.

The best way to freeze strawberries is in low-sugar pectin syrup. You will need about two cups of syrup to coat about three pounds of berries. To make the syrup, combine one cup water and one box powdered fruit pectin and boil until pectin is dissolved (one minute). Stir in one-half cup sugar until dissolved. Remove from heat and add cold water to make two cups. Chill before use.

When you freeze food, label each package to avoid future guess-work. Mark the contents and the date on each package.

Freeze small amounts of herbs in individual plastic packets; seal each packet well, label it, and staple the packets to a piece of cardboard.

For ready made *bouquets garnis*, tie together several sprigs of different herbs (for instance, parsley, bay leaf, and thyme), and freeze in individual plastic bags stapled to a piece of cardboard.

Cooking Frozen Foods

Most frozen vegetables should be cooked without thawing, but one major exception is corn on the cob. It should be thawed completely before cooking; otherwise you'll have to cook it too long and it will get tough.

Instant beef stock can come from the freezer. When you cook a beef roast, save and refrigerate the pan juices. After the fat has hardened, remove and discard it. Pour the remaining juice into an ice cube tray; when the juice is frozen, wrap the cubes individually in foil and store in the freezer for later use.

If you have leftover tomatoes, freeze them for later use in stews and soups. Freezing makes them soft, but this won't affect their taste.

Uncooked soufflés can be successfully frozen. Pour the batter into the soufflé dish, then cover the dish tightly with plastic wrap before placing it on a level spot in the freezer. If using a freezer-to-oven dish, the soufflé can be baked directly from the freezer. If using a china or porcelain soufflé dish, remove it from the freezer 30 minutes before baking. In both cases, bake the soufflé for twice as long as the recipe indicates.

Thaw frozen foods by placing the container under cold running water for a few minutes. Then place the container in a pan of lukewarm water until the food slips out easily.

CANNING FOODS AT HOME

Hints on Safe Food Canning

Never try to shortcut correct canning methods by using substitutions or gimmicks such as preserving powders, aspirin, dishwasher canning, oven canning, "steam" canning in a shallow pan over boiling water, or microwave oven canning. Taking any shortcuts is asking for trouble—spoiled food, illness, or poisoning.

Note that the old-fashioned method of open-kettle processing is no longer considered safe because it has you cook food in an open kettle, pack it into jars, and seal it without any processing. Because of the lack of processing, the chances of spoilage are great. Stick to recommended, up-to-date canning methods.

You can reuse canning jars and the screw bands used to fasten them year after year, provided they are in perfect condition (throw out or use for other storage needs any jar that has even a nick in it). Lids, however, cannot be reused. Make quite sure you don't use an old lid by accident by opening a sealed jar with a pointed opener, piercing the lid so that it cannot be saved or reused.

Peanut butter, mayonnaise, instant coffee, or other food jars are not suitable for home canning. They are not tempered to withstand heat processing, and their top rims may not be right for the lids. Don't risk losing food or cutting yourself on a cracked jar by using substitutes for proper canning jars.

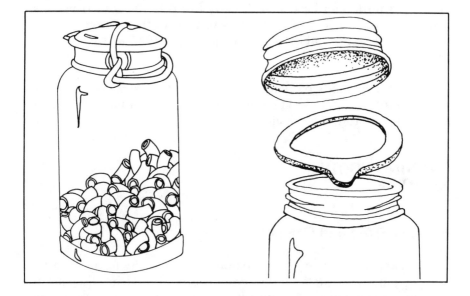

Don't risk anyone's health by using outdated canning equipment. Although they haven't been manufactured for years, there are still some old-fashioned, even antique, jars around. They may be decorative, but they are not safe for canning. Do not use the type of jar that is sealed with a glass lid and wire bails, nor the type of jar that has a zinc lid lined with porcelain that screws on over a rubber ring.

If you use one of your big pots or saucepans as a preserving kettle, remember that iron, copper, brass, aluminum, galvanized zinc, or tin should not be used—they may discolor food or cause bad flavors.

Canning Equipment and Techniques

When selecting fruit and vegetables for home canning, try to buy them in approximately the same size so they'll cook more evenly before canning.

To make sure that canned foods keep a fresh flavor, choose only those foods that are firm, ripe, and fresh, with no bruises that will spoil over time.

Always wash foods thoroughly before canning; discard any rotting sections.

It's easier to fill the jars if you use a wide-neck funnel placed on top of the jar, then spoon the contents into the funnel.

Don't open a processed jar to add more liquid. You'll have to reprocess the jar to prevent the contents from spoiling.

To prevent canned foods from darkening, rinse the foods in a quart of cold water mixed with one and one half teaspoons of salt. Discoloration can also be prevented by adding 50 mg of vitamin C to each quart jar.

You can process two layers of jars in your canner if you place a small wire rack between them, so that water and steam can circulate evenly in the space between the two layers.

An easy way to check whether a jar is sealed is to tap the lid with a metal spoon. If you hear a ringing sound, the jar is sealed.

If the seal of a canned jar won't move down when pressed, the jar is properly sealed and ready for storage.

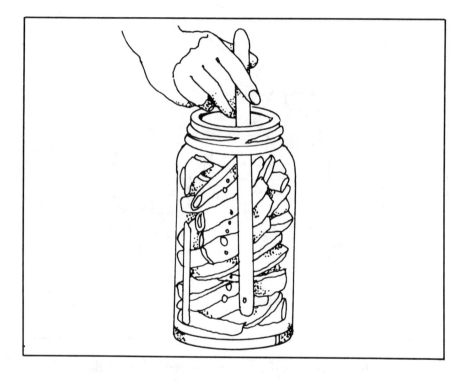

A non-metal spatula or tool with a slim handle is best for releasing air bubbles from filled jars before sealing. You can buy a special bubble-freer, but a rubber spatula, wooden spoon, or plastic knife will do fine. Avoid metal knives or spatulas—they might nick the glass.

A cheesecloth liner can turn a colander into a strainer.

Avoid sudden changes in temperature when working with hot jars of hot food. Putting a hot jar on a cool counter or in a cold draft could cause the glass to break.

When you are canning, the underside of the lid of the jar may discolor from chemicals in the food or water, but you needn't worry about this. It is common and presents no danger.

If you find a scum or milky powder on the outside of canning jars after processing or cooling, wipe it off with a cloth and don't worry about it—it's due merely to the minerals in the water. Next time, however, add a tablespoon or two of vinegar or a teaspoon of cream of tartar to the water in the canner to help prevent staining the inside of the canner.

Remove screw bands before storing jars of canned goods, because if they are left on they may rust in place. To remove a stuck screw band, wring out a cloth in hot water and wrap it around the band for a minute or two to help loosen it.

It's a good additional safety precaution to heat home-canned foods before using them. Heat home-canned acid food to boiling and boil for ten minutes; boil low-acid foods for 20 minutes.

If someone in your family is on a special diet, you may omit sugar and/or salt from many recipes for home-canned goods, because these ingredients are only added for flavor. The exceptions are sauces, pickles, relishes, and preserves, in which the salt or sugar serves a necessary purpose and should not be omitted.

Before canning fresh fish, soak it in a solution of brine (eight ounces of salt to one gallon of water) for between ten and sixty minutes depending on the size of the fish.

For pickling, be sure your vinegar has at least 5 percent acidity; otherwise your pickles may soften and spoil.

If you're putting up pickles or sauerkraut and don't have a crock in which to ferment the ingredients, you can substitute a perfectly clean (preferably new) plastic bucket—which is a lot cheaper than a crock pot.

Preserve cucumbers within 24 hours of harvesting, before they have a chance to get soft or hollow.

Large, mature carrots don't can well. Use young, tender carrots for best results.

A sugar-salt mixture really brings out the flavor of canned peas. Mix one part salt with two parts sugar and add two teaspoons of this mixture to each pint jar before sealing.

Soybeans start to lose flavor almost as soon as they are picked. Rush them from the field to the jar.

Boiling Water Bath Canning

If you own a very large pot, you can probably turn it into a boiling water bath canner by finding a rack that will fit down in the pot, covering the bottom. A rack or a cushion (make one from a folded towel) is necessary to keep the jars from touching the hot bottom of the pot and possibly breaking before processing is complete. The pot must be big enough to allow at least four inches of space above the jars as they sit on the rack or towel—measure *before* you start canning.

How do you judge if a pot is big enough for canning? For pint jars you need a pot at least ten to twelve inches deep; for quart jars you need a pot at least eleven to thirteen inches deep.

Low-acid tomatoes should not be canned in a boiling water bath canner. Tomatoes are traditionally considered acid fruits, but some new varieties are low-acid. Consult your Cooperative Extension Service if you are unsure about how to process your tomatoes. (Low-acid foods support botulism bacteria, which are not destroyed until the temperature of the food reaches 240°F. Since water boils at only 212°F, any food that will support the botulism bacteria must be processed in a steam-pressure canner, where the pressure creates temperatures above boiling.)

The acid content of tomatoes becomes lower as they get overripe, therefore overripe tomatoes should not be canned. You can tell tomatoes are overripe when the skin is dark (and sometimes wrinkled) and they are soft to the touch.

Homemade Pickles

To avoid discovering after the fact that your homemade whole pickles are hollow, check the cucumbers before processing by putting them in water; hollow cucumbers will usually float. Use the hollow ones for relishes.

To keep your homemade pickles from tasting musty, use only fresh whole or ground spices.

If you pickle using whole spices tied in a cheesecloth bag, be sure to remove the spice bag before filling the jars. If the spices are left in the jars they may cause the pickles to darken.

Iodized table salt causes pickles to darken, and noniodized salt contains additives that can make the pickling liquid cloudy. For these reasons, it's best to use only pure granulated pickling salt in your recipes for homemade pickles.

If the water in your area is hard, it may cause your pickles to darken. If soft water is not available, boil tap water and let it cool; then remove any scum before using it in your pickle recipes.

Select slightly underripe cucumbers for pickling; they keep their shape and texture better than riper specimens.

For a subtle fruit flavor when making fruit-based pickle recipes, try substituting apple cider or apple cider flavored distilled vinegar for the distilled white vinegar in the recipe.

If you want to make a double batch of pickles, make up the recipe twice rather than trying to double the ingredients. Doubling or tripling a pickle recipe may alter the ratio of vinegar to the other ingredients, and this will affect flavor and texture and may even cause spoilage.

Signs of Spoilage

When you open a jar of canned food that has been stored for some time, watch for spurting liquid. If any liquid does spurt out, the contents have spoiled.

If canned food smells strange or looks cloudy after opening, discard it immediately without tasting it.

If the lid on a canning jar is bulging, the contents may be spoiled.

To avoid spoilage and explosions, home canned foods should be stored out of direct light and away from direct heat sources.

Disposing of Spoiled Food

Spoiled home-canned products may be contaminated with botulism toxins which are not necessarily destroyed by sewage treatment plants, so spoiled food cannot safely be flushed down the toilet. Instead, bury it deeply enough that it cannot be dug up by animals and none of it can seep up to the surface.

Another way of making spoiled food safe for disposal is to boil it for ten minutes. This will produce a horrible smell, but it will destroy the toxins. After boiling, you can safely dispose of the food.

Spoiled food can also be chemically inactivated: Put the food in a glass container and mix in one-half to one cup chlorine bleach or several tablespoons of strong lye. Let it stand overnight somewhere where you are quite certain it is out of reach of children and animals. After treatment the spoiled food can be flushed down the toilet or wrapped in newspaper and put in the garbage.

Protect yourself. Always wear rubber or plastic gloves when handling spoiled food, and dispose of the gloves afterward.

You don't have to throw out jars that have held spoiled food. If you boil the jars and screw bands for 15 minutes in a strong detergent solution you can reuse them safely. You cannot reuse the lids anyway, so dispose of them along with the spoiled food.

Jams and Jellies

Maintaining the correct temperature is very important in making jams and jellies. Clip a candy thermometer to the side of the pot to help you check the temperature.

Even half a minute of overcooking can scorch jellies. Keep a timer and/or a clock with a second hand beside you when preparing jellies.

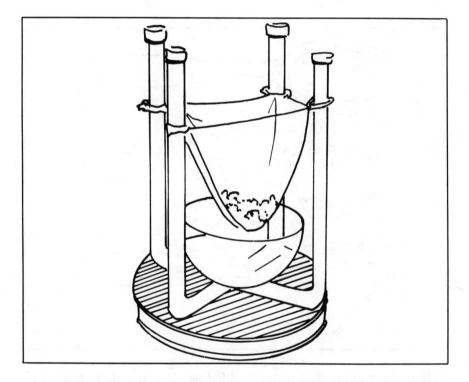

A homemade jelly bag can be a simple length of cheesecloth or muslin hung from an upended stool or chair, with a bowl underneath to catch the juice from the fruit. Or you can knot the corners of the cheesecloth together loosely and hang your homemade jelly bag from a cupboard door handle, a faucet in the sink, or a broomstick across two chairs.

Liquid and powdered pectin are added at different stages in the recipe and cannot be used interchangeably in jelly-making, so resist the temptation to substitute one for the other—even if not doing so means a trip to the store. Always use the type of pectin called for in the recipe.

Don't forget to check the expiration date on powdered or liquid pectin boxes. Because pectin does not hold its strength from one year to the next, it must be discarded after the freshness date has expired.

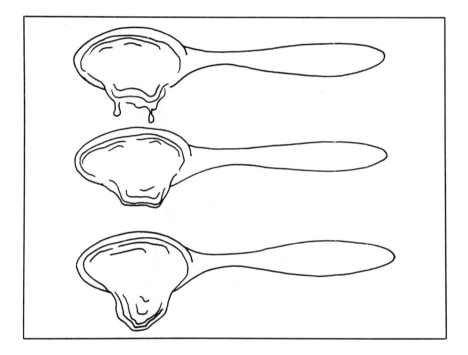

If you're making jelly without added pectin and want to test it for jell, do it like this: Dip a cool metal spoon into the boiling juice, fill it, and lift the spoon above the kettle. Tilt the spoon slowly (allow the jelly to drip back into the kettle) so the jelly runs off the side. When the jelly is cooked enough it will flow together and come off the spoon in a sheet or flake.

Another way to test jell is to wait until the jelly has boiled for several minutes, then spoon a tablespoon or so of juice onto a cool saucer or plate. Put the plate in a freezer section of your refrigerator for about five minutes. If the mixture jells, the jelly is done.

Nobody's perfect, and sometimes your best efforts result in soft jelly. If you don't want to recook it, use the soft jelly as a delicious topping for ice cream, cheesecake, pound cake, puddings, or custards.

Soft jelly also makes an excellent glaze for ham.

How do you check that your jelly jars are sealed correctly? After jars have cooled, the center of the lid or flat should be slightly concave, pulled down by the partial vacuum formed inside the jar during processing. The popping sound you hear when the jars vent and the lids are snapped down tells you that the jar is properly sealed.

Does it hurt you to throw away a full jar of jam or jelly because there's a little mold on the top? Throw it out anyway. It's unsafe to scrape off the layer of mold and serve the rest of the contents because there's nothing to tell you which molds are harmful and which aren't. So treat them all as potentially harmful.

Even if you're diet-conscious, never reduce the amount of sugar in proportion to fruit in a jam or jelly recipe. To do so may result in a soft, syrupy product or—because sugar is a preservative—in mold growth.

To test whether fruit juice contains enough pectin to jell, mix two tablespoons of cooked fruit juice with two teaspoons of sugar and one tablespoon Epsom salts and let stand for 20 minutes. If the juice contains enough pectin the mixture should form into a semisolid.

Place several marbles in the kettle when you're making jelly, preserves, apple butter, or other foods requiring continuous stirring. The marbles will roll constantly across the kettle bottom and prevent sticking.

When you're mixing homemade jelly, use a potato masher for stirring. The handle is long enough to keep your hand cool and the shape prevents the masher from slipping into the pot.

DRYING FOODS AT HOME

Drying fruit does not improve the quality, so begin with fully ripened fruit. Fruit that is ready to eat is ready to dry.

When drying fruits such as ripe plums and grapes, blanch them by dipping them in boiling water for 30 seconds to help break the skins and allow the centers to dry out.

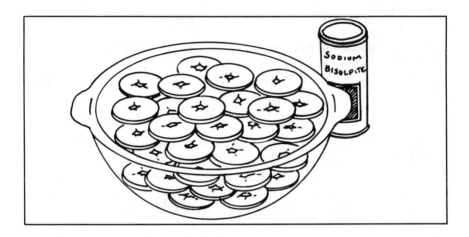

When buying sodium bisulfite to prepare a sulfur solution to pretreat light-colored fruits before drying, select only pure, food-grade sodium bisulfite from a drugstore or health food store. Neither garden-dusting sulfur nor practical-grade sulfur should be used; neither is pure enough for eating.

Instead of using a commercial antioxidant to prevent foods from darkening, you can use inexpensive ascorbic acid crystals purchased at the drugstore. Two-and-one-half teaspoons of ascorbic acid mixed in one cup water will coat about five quarts of fruit.

An easy-to-make oven drying tray can be constructed from narrow wooden slats and nylon netting or cheesecloth. Measure your oven rack and build the tray two inches smaller than the oven rack in all directions; the extra space is needed to allow air to circulate around the food.

An even simpler way to use your oven rack for drying is to cover it with nylon netting. You can also make a cheesecloth cover using two thicknesses of cheesecloth.

If you want to use more trays than your oven has racks, place blocks at the corners of the oven racks and stack the trays at least one-and-one-half inches apart. (Remember that a big load takes longer to dry than a smaller one.)

Since the temperature varies inside your oven, you will need to shift your drying trays every half hour, rotating them from front to back and moving them from top to bottom. To avoid getting thoroughly confused, number the trays; it will help you keep track of the rotation order.

Don't use the top position of the oven rack in an electric oven for drying. The food on the top tray will dry too quickly.

Use a hot pad, or other item, to prop your oven door slightly open while food is drying so that moist air can escape. Prop the oven door open about one inch for an electric oven, four to six inches for a gas oven.

You can help to keep air circulating while food is drying by placing an electric fan set on "low" in front of the oven door. Don't use a fan for a gas oven with a pilot light, though; it could blow out the pilot.

If you're drying food in a convection oven, keep in mind that drying times in a convection oven are usually shorter than in a conventional oven. Check food for doneness at the lower range of times given in the recipe.

Baking sheets or cookie trays should not be used as drying trays. These metal trays do not allow free airflow around the produce, and the top of the food will dry out while the underside remains wet.

If you're handy with tools and want to make your own dehydrator, use cheesecloth, nylon netting, or muslin to cover galvanized screening. Avoid aluminum, which discolors and corrodes easily, and copper, which destroys vitamin C. Also avoid fiberglass mesh; the fibers can get into the food and become dangerous.

Chili peppers can be air-dried without the use of either your oven or an electric dryer. Thread them on a sturdy string and hang them up to dry in a warm area for about two weeks (cover the whole thing with cheesecloth if dust is a problem). When they're ready for use, just break them from the stem as needed.

Wash your hands carefully after handling dried chilies; the oils may cause burning.

Schedule your home drying for a day when your work is not likely to be interrupted, because you should never suspend the drying process once it's begun. If you cool partly dried food and then start it up later there's a chance that bacteria, molds, and yeasts will find a home in it.

Choose a bright, sunny day for your home drying; that way you'll keep the dried foods from picking up moisture from the surrounding air after they leave the oven or dryer.

Dry strong-smelling vegetables such as onions, cabbage, and carrots separately from other vegetables or fruits which might absorb the odors.

Dried fruits are best when prepared with other fruits; stick to batches of berries or batches of cut fruits, but don't mix the two.

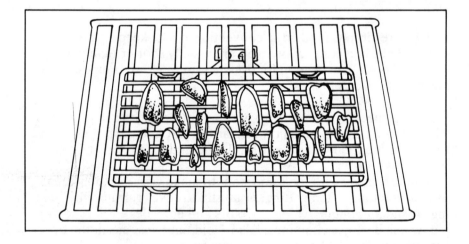

A rule of thumb is that properly dried vegetables are brittle to the touch. Exceptions to this rule are mushrooms, sweet peppers, and squash, which will feel pliable and leathery when dried. Some experts recommend the hammer test: If sufficiently dry, the vegetable pieces will shatter when struck with a hammer.

Coffee cans make good storage containers for dried foods, but first wrap the food in a plastic bag to keep the metal of the can from affecting the flavor of the food.

Small plastic bags are useful for packaging dried foods, and you can save space by packing several into a large jar or a coffee can. That way you can use small portions as needed, without exposing the whole container to possible contamination each time it's opened.

Many dried fruits and vegetables will keep up to twelve months if properly stored, but use your dried carrots, onions, and cabbage within six months because they spoil more quickly.

Rehydrating Dried Foods

When rehydrating fruit, enhance the flavor by soaking it in fruit juice instead of water.

Sugar should be added to fruits, if desired, *after* it has been rehydrated. If added earlier, the sugar will toughen the fruit.

You'll know your produce is fully rehydrated when it has regained nearly the same size as when fresh.

Remember that rehydrated vegetables require less cooking time than fresh vegetables. Simply simmer them to the required degree of firmness.

Drying Herbs

Harvest herbs to be stored when the flowers of the plant are just beginning to open; this is the moment when the flavor is at its peak.

For best flavor, cut herbs for storage on a dry, sunny morning— after the dew has dried but before the sun gets too hot.

If you're growing herbs for their seeds, harvest the seeds as soon as the heads turn brown, but before they ripen completely and begin to fall off. Harvest the seeds on a warm, dry day.

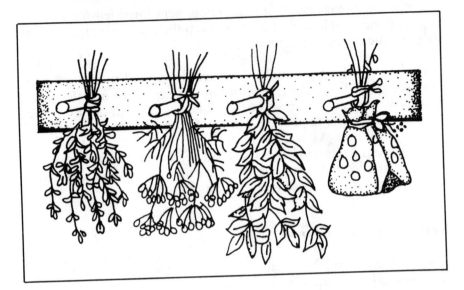

Hang bunches of herbs in a warm, dry place to dry; tie a paper bag over the bunch of seed herbs to catch the ripening seeds.

Dry seeds in their pods, husks, or coverings. You can then remove these coverings by winnowing—rubbing a few seeds at a time between your palms to loosen the pods or husks, which will then fall away.

When cutting herbs for drying, cut off the tender, fresh top two-thirds of the plant; trim off brown leaves and lower leaves.

You can dry herbs in the microwave oven by placing three or four stalks between several thicknesses of paper towels on a drying rack and drying at medium power for two or three minutes, or until the leaves crumble easily. If the herbs still aren't dry, return the leaves to the oven at the same heat for an additional 30 seconds.

Coffee cans lined with a plastic bag or tinted glass containers are best for storing dried herbs because they keep out the light, which can affect flavor.

If you use cheesecloth on which to dry herbs, use a double thickness to prevent the seeds or crumpled pieces from falling through the mesh—the pieces will shrink even smaller as they dry.

To verify the freshness of herbs you've been storing for some time, rub a little between your palms. If the herb is still potent, a strong aroma will be released. If there's little or no fragrance released, the flavor has faded and you'll need to put up a fresh supply.

A cup of plain herbal tea (no cream or sugar) makes a no-calorie, no-caffeine, low-cost beverage.

A low-calorie substitute for sour cream: Mix cottage cheese in the blender until smooth and flavor it with herbs.

Cooking With Dried Herbs

Add sprigs of herbs to vinegar to provide wonderful flavor. (Pretty bottles of your own herb vinegars make fine gifts, too.) Tarragon in white wine vinegar; basil and garlic in red wine vinegar; and mint or savory in white or cider vinegar are just a few examples. In fact, you can use any herb you like, or any combination you prefer.

When using dried herbs, first crush or chop the leaves to release the flavor and aroma.

When substituting dried herbs for fresh in a recipe, use one quarter the amount specified. One teaspoon dried herbs is the equivalent of four teaspoons of fresh herbs.

When preparing soups or stews that must cook for several hours, add herbs during the last half hour of cooking time. The flavor and aroma of herbs can be lost if they cook too long. In foods that cook quickly, add the herbs immediately.

You'll get best results if you add herbs to the liquid portion of your recipe before mixing in the rest of the ingredients. Moistening the herbs first with a little water, oil, or other suitable liquid and allowing them to stand for ten minutes will bring out the flavor even more.

Fresh herbs have long been favorites for use in infusions, or teas, but these teas can be expensive to buy. Make your own by steeping about one teaspoon of a dried herb (or a combination of herbs) in one teacup (six ounces) of boiling water. Add boiling water to herbs in a teapot, or use a tea ball. Steep for five to ten minutes, and sweeten if desired with honey or sugar. Mint, rosemary, marjoram, and thyme are favorites for making herb tea.

Purchasing and Preparing Food

MEAT AND MAIN DISHES

Roasts, Burgers, and Beef

The meat that appears cheapest according to price per pound may not be the best buy. Look at the price per serving instead—a more expensive cut that has no bones or fats may be more economical in the long run.

When wrapping chops, chicken parts, or hamburgers for your freezer, place sheets of waxed paper between the pieces of meat. That way the meat will separate easily and defrost faster.

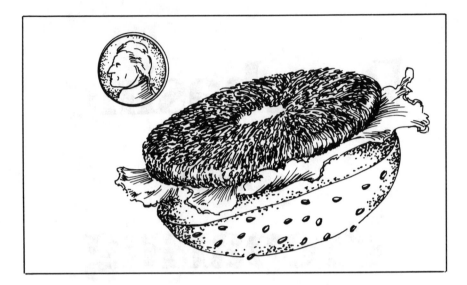

When you're making hamburger patties to freeze, make a nickel-size hole in the center of each patty. You won't have to thaw the hamburger before cooking, and the hole will close during cooking.

Dropping a few tomatoes in the pan will help tenderize a pot roast. Acid from the tomatoes helps break down the roast's stringy fibers.

When a recipe specifies thinly sliced meat, it will help to put the meat in the freezer for a short time before cutting it. Meat slices more easily if it's slightly frozen.

A mixture of olive oil and vinegar will tenderize meat. Rub the mixture on the meat and let it stand several hours before cooking.

Another way to tenderize meat is to rub baking soda into it, let it stand for several hours, and then wash and cook it.

Meats can be marinated in a plastic bag: Put the meat in the bag along with the marinade, seal the bag, and turn it a few times during the day.

If you've forgotten to thaw meat but want to cook it anyway, cook it half as long again as you would if it were thawed.

Meat will shrink less during roasting if it's cooked longer at a lower temperature.

Since a roast will thaw more quickly if all sides are exposed to air, elevate it on a cake cooling rack—or use the burner grill from your range. Put newspaper or a plate under the rack to catch the water and other drippings.

A shallow pan is better than a deep one for cooking a roast because it allows heat to circulate around the meat.

If you need to defrost frozen ground beef quickly, try sprinkling it with the amount of salt recommended for cooking (salt is a great thawing agent), or heat it in your dishwasher turned to its drying cycle.

You can slice a roast more easily if you let it stand for about 15 minutes after taking it from the oven.

To eliminate most of the smoke and grease when broiling fatty meats, pour a cup of water into the bottom portion of the broiler pan before putting it in the oven.

For pan drippings that have fine flavor, support poultry or meat on a grid of celery sticks and carrots rather than a metal roasting rack. Roast as usual.

To make relatively grease-free hamburgers in an electric frying pan, prop up one of the legs of the pan and then fry on the pan's elevated side. The grease will drain down to the lower side of the pan. Be careful, especially if there are children around, that the pan cannot tip over or the contents spill out.

Want perfectly rounded, flat meat patties? Press down on a piece of meat with a can and trim off the excess.

For particularly juicy burgers, put a tablespoon of cottage cheese in the center of each before frying or broiling.

If you plan to freeze meat stews like *coq au vin* or *boeuf bourguignonne,* undercook them slightly. When they're thawed and reheated, the stews won't have the muddy flavor and mushy texture of overcooked meat.

When sautéing meats, be careful not to overcrowd the pan. If there are too many pieces in the pan, the meat will steam instead of brown.

For best results when sautéing meats or vegetables, make sure they're completely dry before cooking.

A meat loaf can be stretched with raw oatmeal, grated carrots, crushed cornflakes, or instant potato flakes.

If you want to keep your hands clean when mixing meat loaf, place the ingredients in a plastic bag and knead them through the bag. Still using the bag, shape the mixture into the form of a loaf, and gently ease it out of the bag and into a loaf pan.

Meat loaf won't stick to the bottom of the pan if you bake it on top of a few raw bacon slices. The bacon adds flavor, too.

You can cut the cooking time for meat loaf by cooking the mixture in muffin tins or in a flat, shallow pan.

So that meatballs won't fall apart when you cook them, chill them first.

An ice cream scoop is useful in shaping perfectly round meatballs. For smaller meatballs, use a melon scoop.

Do you like your steaks rare on the inside but well done on the outside? If so, grill them straight from the freezer without thawing.

When cooking red meats, it's time to turn the meat over to brown the other side when juices bubble to the surface of the meat.

An unopened tin can can be used to pound flour into meat for Swiss steak—but *wash* the can first.

For particularly tender liver, soak it in milk and refrigerate it for two hours. Then dry the liver, sprinkle on bread crumbs, and sauté.

Another tenderizer for liver: Soak it in tomato juice for three hours before frying or broiling.

If you partially freeze liver before slicing it, the skin will peel off easily.

To make breaded pork chops that are almost greaseless, bake them on a wire rack in a baking pan. Any grease will drip into the pan.

Bacon and Ham

It is more economical to buy slab bacon and slice it as you need it. Slab bacon with the rind on is cheaper than sliced bacon, and it keeps better.

Bacon slices won't stick together if you roll the package into a tube held with a rubber band before refrigerating.

Bacon will curl less during frying if it has first been soaked in cold water.

Bacon curls make wonderful hors d'oeuvres. Fry strips short of crispness, then remove them from the skillet and twist them round the tines of a fork. Pierce the curls with wooden toothpicks and broil them under a low flame until they're crisp.

If you want bacon strips to maintain their shape with minimum shrinkage, start frying them on a cold skillet and periodically prick them with a fork during cooking.

When you have leftover pieces of cooked bacon, crumble and freeze them for future use as baked potato toppings or salad garnish.

If salt pork is unavailable for a recipe, substitute bacon that's been blanched in boiling water for ten minutes to remove the smoked flavor.

You won't have to clean a greasy frying pan every time you want bacon if you fry a large quantity and freeze it. Place the slices on cookie sheets so that they won't stick together, and when they're frozen, repackage them in plastic bags and store. Reheat foil-wrapped slices in the oven for just a few minutes.

Before opening a canned ham, run hot tap water over the container for several minutes. The gelatin will melt and the ham will slide right out.

Frying thin slices of ham for breakfast may be more economical than frying bacon.

It's best not to freeze cured, smoked, or canned ham, because freezing causes flavor and texture changes. Refrigerate this type of ham instead.

Save time and effort when broiling sausages by putting the links on a skewer so you can turn them all with one movement.

Chicken and Turkey

If you chill a chicken for an hour after flouring it for frying, the coating will adhere better during cooking.

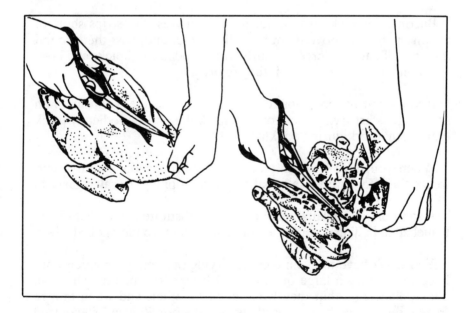

You needn't slam away at a chicken with a knife in order to debone it. Kitchen shears make the job easier.

For guaranteed tenderness, marinate chicken breasts in buttermilk, cream, or ordinary milk for three hours in the refrigerator before baking.

Unpleasant poultry odors can usually be eliminated by washing the bird with lemon juice and rubbing it with salt.

Boneless chicken or turkey breasts—which are much cheaper—can be substituted for veal scallopini or cutlets.

Does your broiled chicken dry out during cooking? Brush it with lemon juice to keep it moist and add a touch of extra flavor.

When frying, broiling, or grilling chicken, always use tongs to turn the pieces. If you use a fork you're likely to pierce the skin, and natural juices will escape.

If you want a fresh chicken to stay fresh longer, loosely wrap it with waxed paper (not plastic wrap) and refrigerate. Cook it within three days.

For pure white breast meat, defrost a chicken by letting it stand for a time in heavily salted cold water. The salt draws out all traces of blood. Rinse well with clean water before cooking.

A chicken will baste itself if you cover the bird with strips of bacon during roasting. Remove the bacon before the end of cooking to brown the bird further.

Chicken livers won't splatter during cooking if you first perforate them with a fork. Puncture several holes in each.

It's best to baste a chicken only during the final 30 minutes of cooking. Sauce won't penetrate during the early cooking stages and may cause the chicken to brown too quickly.

Don't risk having your hands and wrists splattered with hot fat when adding steaming water to a browning chicken. Use ice cubes and place the lid on the pan before they melt.

If you don't care for dressing with roast poultry you still can make the bird flavorsome and juicy by pouring a cup of water mixed with a quarter cup of pineapple juice into the body cavity.

If you want a turkey to be extra juicy, use a basting needle to inject the raw bird with a quarter pound of melted margarine in six to eight places around the breast and thighs. Then roast according to your usual recipe.

For the most accurate thermometer reading of a roasting turkey, immerse the thermometer in warm water before sliding it into the turkey. When you insert it, keep it away from fat and bones, both of which render inaccurate readings.

To hold in stuffing, truss a turkey with unwaxed dental floss—it's extra strong and doesn't burn. Or, instead of trussing, use two heels of dampened bread to block the cavity and keep the dressing in place. Position the crusts so that they face out and then overlap each other. One or two raw potatoes could also be used to seal the cavity.

Fish and Seafood

It's easy to make your own fish scaler. Nail three bottle caps, serrated edges up, side by side at the end of a piece of wood. To make scaling easier, rub the entire fish with vinegar to loosen the scales.

To tell whether a fish is fresh or stale check the eyes. If they're slightly protruding, bright, and clear, the fish is fresh. If they're pink, sunken, or cloudy, the fish is stale. If the gills are gray, the fish is stale; they should be red or pink.

One way to freeze fish is to put the fillets in clean milk cartons filled with water. When the ice that surrounded the fish thaws in the defrosting process, use the liquid to water your houseplants—it's ideal fertilizer.

When poaching a whole fish, wrap it in a length of cheesecloth for easy removal from the poaching liquid.

Give frozen fish a fresh flavor by thawing it in milk. The milk eliminates the frozen taste.

You can make any fish taste tender and sweet by soaking it in a quarter cup of lemon juice and water, or vinegar, or wine before cooking.

To remove most of the salty taste from saltwater fish, soak it in vinegar and rinse under cold water before cooking.

If you like halibut as white as popcorn, add a little milk and lemon juice to the seasoned liquid in which you cook it.

After handling fish, you can rid your hands of the odor by rubbing them with salt or vinegar.

If you're having a hard time prying clams or oysters from their shells, soak them for a few minutes in club soda to loosen both muscles and shell hinges. Or wash them in cold water, place in a plastic bag, and freeze for 30 minutes. Or plunge the plastic bag into boiling water for several minutes. Either freezing or boiling makes it easy to open the shells with a beer-can opener or knife.

When a recipe calls for fish to be cooked *en papillote* (in a parchment paper casing), aluminum foil can be substituted for the parchment paper.

If you can't get a fishy odor out of a pan used for frying fish, sprinkle the pan with salt, pour hot water in it, let it stand for a while, and then wash as usual.

Fish won't stick to the pan during baking if you lay it on a bed of parsley, celery, and chopped onions. This vegetable bed also adds flavor.

If you chill canned shrimp before adding them to hot mixtures they'll hold their shape better.

If you don't like the tinny taste of canned shrimp, soak for 15 minutes in a mixture of one teaspoon sherry and two tablespoons vinegar.

If you've put too much mayonnaise in the tuna salad and you have no more tuna to add, substitute bread crumbs.

If you enjoy fish but don't appreciate a fishy odor in the kitchen, brush the fish with lemon juice before cooking, or add a little lemon juice to cold oil or butter before frying the fish.

FRUITS AND VEGETABLES

Selecting Fruit

Though their appearance might not be perfect, standard grades of fruits are as high in nutrition as the more expensive "fancy" grades. Unless appearance is important, you can buy the cheaper grades and save money with no loss in food value.

Whenever possible, avoid buying prepackaged fruits and vegetables. The packaging may disguise rotten spots.

When shopping for berries, examine the container bottoms. If they are wet or stained much of the fruit is probably moldy or mushy, so select only those containers that have dry bottoms. If you discover one or two bruised and spoiled berries when you get home, discard them; molds quickly spread from berry to berry.

There's an old-fashioned "thumping test" for gauging a watermelon's ripeness. Whack your index finger against it. If you can hear a high plink, the melon isn't ripe. If you hear a low plunk, it is.

How can you tell when a melon is ripe? Hold it to your ear and shake it. It's ripe if you can hear the juice and seeds sloshing around.

When selecting oranges, don't be misled by the intensity of their color—most oranges are dyed to make them look more appetizing. Instead, look for brown spots—surprisingly enough, they indicate top quality. And remember that the sweetest oranges have the biggest navel holes.

If oranges seem spongy, light in weight, or puffy, they won't be juicy.

To select the juiciest grapefruits, look for those with the thinnest skins. The "yellowness" of grapefruit skin doesn't indicate anything.

To get the juiciest, most flavorful lemons, pick those with smooth skins and small points at each end.

You can judge if an avocado is ripe by sticking a toothpick in the stem end. If it slides in and out with ease, the avocado is ready to eat.

Fresh papayas will be soft when you squeeze them gently.

A sure sign that an apple is ripe is a light green color at the bottom of the fruit.

Shake a coconut before you buy it to make sure that it is full of "milk." To release the milk, pierce the three "eyes" on the shell and drain the liquid. Coconut milk can be refrigerated for 24 hours or frozen for future use.

When choosing a coconut from the display, check that the three soft "eyes" on the shell are intact, dry, and free of mold.

Ripening Fruit

You can make your own fruit-ripening "bowl" from a perforated plastic bag. The perforations permit air movement, yet the bag will retain the fruit gases that hasten ripening.

To speed up the ripening of pears, tomatoes, or peaches, put them in a brown paper bag with a ripe apple. Punch some holes in the bag, and put it in a cool place out of direct sunlight. Or, put the fruit in a box and cover it with a newspaper to seal in the natural gases that promote ripening.

To speed up the ripening of avocados, place them in a brown paper bag and store the bag in a warm place. Once ripe, you can retard spoilage by keeping them in the refrigerator.

To hasten the ripening of green bananas, place them so that they touch overripe ones, or wrap them in a damp cloth and put them in a bag.

If a fresh pineapple isn't quite ripe, but you're eager to eat it, you can make it taste ripe this way: Prepare it as usual and then put the pieces in a pot, cover them with water, add sugar, and boil for a few minutes. Then drain off the water, let the fruit cool, and chill it in the refrigerator.

Refrigerate apples to slow down the ripening process. If you don't have room in the refrigerator, keep your apples stored in a cool place, with a wet towel placed over the top of the container to keep the apples moist but not wet. Don't let apples freeze—they will spoil.

The kiwifruit you buy in the store has probably been harvested when mature but still hard. To ripen the fruit at home, place it in a plastic bag with an apple, and leave it at room temperature. For slower ripening, just refrigerate it for several weeks.

When storing ripe kiwifruit in the refrigerator, place it in the fruit bin away from other fruits so that the flavors don't get mixed.

Handling Fruit After Purchase

Store apples in clear plastic rather than in a paper bag. You'll be able to spot any that are spoiling and remove them before they contaminate other fruit.

Artichokes will maintain their freshly picked texture for almost a week if they're wrapped (unwashed) in a damp towel and stored in a plastic bag in the refrigerator.

Lettuce will rust more slowly if there is no excess moisture in its container. To keep your lettuce bag or refrigerator vegetable compartment relatively dry, put in a few dry paper towels or dry sponges to absorb excess water.

Because carrot tops can rob the vegetable of moisture during storage, slice off the tops before refrigerating the carrots.

To maintain the moisture content that keeps asparagus fresh, cut a small slice off the bottom of each stalk, then stand all stalks upright in a container with an inch of water at the bottom and store in the refrigerator. Celery can be stored the same way—cut a slice from the bottom of the head of celery and store like asparagus.

If a head of lettuce won't drop down into a plastic storage bag because it sticks to the sides, try putting it in the bag this way: Turn the bag inside out, put your hand in the bag, grab the lettuce head through the bag, and pull the bag right-side-out over the lettuce.

Because mushrooms can become slimy if refrigerated in a sealed plastic bag, it's better to refrigerate them in a brown paper bag. Brown paper confines the humidity that keeps mushrooms fresh and permits them to breathe.

Preparing and Using Fruit

To keep an unused avocado half from turning dark, press the pit back into place before refrigerating the uneaten half.

For a perfect avocado half, cut the fruit in half lengthwise, pull the halves apart, and plunge a very sharp chef's knife into the pit. The pit will pull away cleanly with the knife. Remove the avocado halves from the shell with a spoon, or very gently with your fingers.

As soon as you bring lemons home from the store, put them in the refrigerator in a tightly sealed container of water. Doing so encourages them to yield more juice. (You can get the same result by immersing a lemon in hot water for about 15 minutes before squeezing it.)

If you need only a drop or two of fresh lemon juice, you needn't cut into the whole lemon. Just puncture it and squeeze out the desired amount. If you then store the lemon in the refrigerator, its freshness and flavor will be unaffected.

Save the liquids from canned fruits; add a little cornstarch to the juice to make an instant sauce for cake or pudding.

Juices saved from canned fruits can be combined with flavored or unflavored gelatin for a dessert or salad. If you don't want to use the juice at once, freeze it.

Enhance the good fresh taste of cantaloupe or honeydew melon by sprinkling with a few drops of lemon juice.

When working with fruits that stain your hands, cut down on the mess by spraying your hands with nonstick cooking spray before handling the fruit. If you spray the pot, too, fruits and berries won't stick.

To keep berries in tip-top condition don't wash them until you're ready to eat them.

Strawberries will stay firm for several days if they are stored in a colander in the refrigerator. The colander allows cold air to circulate through and around them, keeping them fresh.

Hull strawberries after you've washed them; if you do it beforehand they'll soak up water and turn mushy.

If you store ripe bananas in your refrigerator they won't go soft so quickly. The cold darkens their skins, but it doesn't affect the fruit.

To keep dried fruit fresh for a longer period, keep it in the freezer.

Since carbon steel knives react with fruit and cause discoloration, cut your fruit with stainless steel knives.

To maintain the crispness of apple slices and to prevent them from browning, immerse them in salted water for ten minutes before use.

When dicing several apples to make a large apple salad, mix them with dressing or mayonnaise as you chop. If you wait until you've cut all the apples, the first ones cut may discolor; coating them with mayonnaise will prevent this.

You can restore flavor to dried-out apples by slicing them into sections and sprinkling the sections with apple cider.

So that apples won't shrink when you bake them, remove a horizontal belt of peel from around the middle of each one. So that they won't wrinkle during baking, cut random slits in each one before placing them in the oven.

If you want to freeze homemade cider, use clean waxed cardboard containers or plastic jugs with screw tops; be sure to leave two inches of head room for expansion of the liquid when frozen.

Apples for cider-making should be fully ripe. Immature apples contain too little sugar and too much acid and starch to make satisfactory cider.

To tell if an unpicked apple is ripe, twist it clockwise on the stem. A ripe apple should come away from the tree easily.

If you have an apple tree in your garden, you can test apples for ripeness by cutting one open and looking at the seeds. A mature apple will have dark brown seeds. In an immature apple the seeds are pale tan or white in color.

Windfall apples—fruit that has been knocked from the tree before it's fully mature—will not give well-flavored cider. Use these immature fruits for jellies instead.

Apple cider can be kept in the freezer for a year. Let it thaw in the refrigerator for 24 hours before use.

Frozen grapes make cooling warm weather snacks. They look attractive, too.

A quick way to remove seeds from grapes is to slice the grapes slightly off-center. This exposes the seeds and makes them easy to flick away.

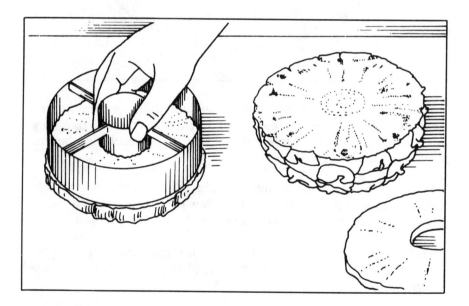

The center ring of a doughnut cutter is ideal for removing the core from slices of fresh pineapple. Just press the ring on each pineapple slice.

If a recipe calls for gelatin and pineapple, use either canned fruit or fresh pineapple that has been boiled for five minutes. There is an enzyme in fresh pineapple that will prevent gelatin from setting.

Taking a watermelon on a picnic? If you wrap it in dry newspaper or burlap as soon as you remove it from the refrigerator, it will stay refreshingly cool till you're ready to eat it.

To peel a difficult-to-skin fruit, hold it on a fork over a gas flame until the skin cracks, and then slide off the skin.

Another trick for peeling thick-skinned fruit: Put the fruit in a bowl, pour boiling water over it, wait 60 seconds, then remove the fruit and peel the skin with a paring knife.

To prevent freshly cut fruit from browning, place it in a bowl of cool water in which you've dissolved two powdered vitamin-C tablets; or keep the fruit submerged in water to which you've added juice from a half a lemon.

Cooking cranberries requires less sugar if you add a quarter teaspoon of baking soda to the pot.

When cooking cranberries, add a teaspoon of butter to each pound of berries to prevent overboiling and "foaming."

Cranberries are done cooking when they look as though they're *ready* to burst. If you cook them until they actually pop, they'll taste bitter.

Remove the shell from a coconut like a pro. Heat the coconut in the oven for 15 minutes at 350°F. Then tap it all over with a hammer, remove the cracked shell, and peel away the brown skin.

Serve mangoes as a source of vitamins A and C. For a change, cook the peeled, chopped fruit with water, sugar, and orange juice to make a hot or cold sauce for ice cream or fruit salad.

Kiwifruit contain an enzyme which prevents gelatin from setting, so don't include them in a gelatin salad mold. You can, however, use the slices as a pretty garnish on top of the mold.

Did you know you can use kiwifruit as a meat tenderizer? It's the enzymes in the fruit that do the trick.

Ice cream and dairy products are good with kiwifruit, but another enzyme in the fruit causes composition changes when combined with milk. If you use the two together, serve the dish immediately after combining the kiwifruit and the dairy product.

You can eat the seeds as well as the flesh of papayas. Grind the seeds and add them to a salad dressing for an unusual flavor.

Selecting Vegetables

Sometimes produce that's a day or two old offers a better buy than higher priced fresh produce. If older produce merely has a few blemishes that you can cut away, and it's drastically reduced in price, go ahead and buy it.

Canned mushrooms cost more than fresh ones, so you'll save if you buy fresh ones—especially if they're on sale—and freeze them for future use.

Fresh vegetables in season can be considerably cheaper than the same foods frozen or canned.

Store root vegetables such as potatoes and carrots in a cool, moist place to slow down loss of their vitamin content.

Let unripe tomatoes ripen at room temperature but away from direct sunlight. Store ripe tomatoes at cool temperatures or in the refrigerator to slow down loss of their vitamin C.

Seal leafy vegetables in plastic bags before storing them in the vegetable crisper. They'll retain their moisture and stay fresh longer.

Preparing and Using Vegetables

If you want to freshen blemished or wilted produce, snip off all brown edges, sprinkle the vegetables with cold water, wrap them in toweling, and place them in your refrigerator for an hour or more.

When slicing raw vegetables it sometimes helps to cut a small slice off one side to form a steady base.

If you're simmering vegetables and you need to add more water, use *hot* water, not cold. Adding cold water may toughen the vegetable fibers.

Economize on time and fuel by steaming two vegetables simultaneously in the same pot. If you want to serve them separately, loosely wrap each in aluminum foil during cooking.

To make frozen vegetables taste as much as possible like fresh ones, pour boiling water on them before cooking. This flushes away all traces of frozen water.

Cooking artichokes in iron or aluminum pots will turn the pots gray; use stainless steel or glass pots instead.

To keep artichokes from discoloring as you clean them, squeeze a lemon half into a bowl of cold water. As you clean each artichoke, rub it with the other half of the lemon, and then drop it into the acidulated water. Remember to cook the artichokes in a nonaluminum pan.

Fresh asparagus can be cooked to perfection in a coffee percolator. Position the asparagus upright and add an inch or two of water. The stalks will be cooked tender, while the tips will stay crisp.

To firm uncooked asparagus stalks that have gone limp, position them upright in a deep pot. Add ice water, and cover the pot with a plastic bag. Put the pot in the refrigerator for an hour, and when you're ready to cook the asparagus, the stalks will be firm.

You will avoid damaging the delicate tips of canned asparagus if you open the can from the bottom rather than the top.

To prevent beets from fading during cooking, leave an inch or two of stem attached and add a few tablespoons of vinegar to the water.

If you've purchased asparagus with thick, tough stalks, peel the lower parts of the stalks with a potato peeler until you reach the soft interior. Cook as usual and the stalks will taste as tender as the flowers.

The pervasive smell of broccoli or cabbage while it's cooking can be reduced by dropping a slice of stale bread into the cooking water. Placing a cup of vinegar (which absorbs odors) on the range, or dropping a lemon wedge into the pot will also lessen the offensive odor.

You'll speed the cooking time for brussels sprouts by marking an "X" with a knife on the bottom of each before putting it in the pot.

If you've purchased fresh broccoli, cabbage, or cauliflower, and find live insects in the vegetable, drive them out by soaking the food for 30 minutes in cold water to which you've added a few tablespoons of salt or vinegar.

Peel the thick skin off broccoli stalks (the part you're often tempted to throw out), then slice the stalks very thinly and add the slices to a tossed salad. They're crisp and delicious. Do the same with the center core of a lettuce head (but you don't need to peel it first).

Cabbage that has been frozen before cooking will not have the characteristic overpowering odor. (Wash the cabbage and dry it with a paper towel before putting it in a plastic bag and freezing it.) After defrosting, there will be no odor when the vegetable is boiled.

You can prevent red cabbage from turning purple during cooking by adding a tablespoon of vinegar to the cooking water.

The unappealing scent of cooking cauliflower will be reduced if you drop unshelled walnuts into the cooking water.

Add a dash of milk during cooking to keep cauliflower white.

Carrots can be skinned in seconds if they're first dropped into boiling hot water for five minutes and then plunged into cold water. The skins will slip right off.

Out of lettuce for bacon, lettuce, and tomato sandwiches? Use celery-stalk leaves instead.

If you like to grill corn with the husks on, try it this way: First soak the cobs—husks and all—in water for 60 minutes. Then, fasten the ends with wire twist ties so that the husks won't slip off and place the corn on the grill. Turn it every ten minutes for 40 minutes, remove it from the grill, peel off the husks, and serve.

For extra succulent corn on the cob, strip green leaves from the cobs and use the most tender ones to line the bottom of the pot before adding water and cooking.

If your preference is corn off the cob, shave off kernels easily with a shoehorn.

A damp paper towel rubbed over corn on the cob easily removes the corn silk.

A dampened toothbrush is effective in brushing the last stubborn strands of corn silk from corncobs.

One way to cover hot corn evenly with butter is to melt the butter and spread it on with a pastry brush.

To cut fresh mushrooms into uniform sections, try using an egg slicer.

When cleaning mushrooms, try just to brush them clean with your fingers, or rinse them off quickly. Soaking them will make them soggy.

To maintain the whiteness and firmness of mushrooms while sautéing them, add a teaspoon of lemon juice for every quarter pound of melted butter.

Your eyes will be less likely to water when you're slicing or chopping onions if you refrigerate the onions before cutting and slice off the root ends last. It also helps to breathe through your nose only and to run the exhaust fan.

You know about using lemon juice to preserve the color of fruits you're preparing for a fruit salad. But did you know you can also use it on light-colored vegetables such as cauliflower or mushrooms?

You can peel fresh white onions quickly if you first immerse them in boiling water for a minute or two.

If you make an "X" at the root end of an onion with a sharp knife, the onion won't pop apart during cooking.

If you soak onion rings in cold water for an hour they'll be milder and more suitable for use in salads.

After you cut raw onions, get the onion scent off your hands by washing them with baking soda or salt.

If you're out of onions, packaged onion soup mix can be substituted in many recipes.

Why waste time laboriously shelling peas? Just drop the pods in boiling water. The pods will split open and release the peas, and the pods will float to the surface, where you can skim them off.

Peppers and tomatoes will keep their shape during baking if they are supported in greased muffin tins.

Peppers will stay bright green during baking if you coat them with salad oil or olive oil before stuffing and cooking them.

Exposure to air turns peeled potatoes dark, so if you want to peel potatoes ahead of time, cover them with water and refrigerate.

To firm raw potatoes that have gone soft, immerse them in ice water for 30 minutes.

To cook a baked potato in half the usual time, boil it for five minutes before putting it in a hot oven to get the "baked" flavor.

If you need to bake potatoes quickly, use baking nails. Insert a nail lengthwise in each potato; it will heat rapidly and then radiate heat to the inside of the potato, decreasing baking time by as much as 15 minutes.

You can bake potatoes in less time by slicing them in half lengthwise and cooking them on a lightly greased baking sheet, cut side down.

Do the skins crack when you bake potatoes? Keep them smooth by rubbing fat or butter all over the potatoes before putting them in the oven.

To make delicious, fat-free "French fries," cut the potatoes into half-inch thick pieces and soak them in a large bowl of cold water for at least two hours. Place the "fries" on a baking sheet with at least one inch of space between the pieces. Preheat your oven to 400°F and bake the "fries" about 35 or 40 minutes, until they're nicely puffed and browned.

If you bake potatoes on *top* of a gas range you don't have to heat the whole oven. Wrap several medium-size potatoes, side by side, in aluminum foil, and place them on a burner set at the lowest possible heat. In 15 minutes, flip the package over. The potatoes should be ready to eat in 30 minutes.

Sprinkle a little flour on potatoes before frying them and they'll be extra crisp and crunchy.

Hash browns that are stuck to the bottom of a pan will lift right out if you nestle the pan in a larger one containing an inch or so of cold water. It will then be easy to loosen the potatoes with a spatula.

Some people say the very best French fries are made by frying them twice. Here's how: Let potato strips stand in cold water for an hour and wipe them off before an initial, short-duration frying. Drain off the grease, and fry them for the second time until they're golden brown.

You can use unpeeled potatoes when making hash browns. Just run them through the grater, skin and all, and you won't lose the nutrients that are just under the potato skin.

To keep potato pancakes from discoloring, add sour cream to the grated potatoes. Or grate the potatoes into a bowl of ice water; and drain before use.

For extra nutrition, add powdered milk to mashed potatoes and beat well to mix.

Hungry for a new kind of nutritious snack? Cut potato skins into strips, season them to taste, and bake them in a hot oven until crisp.

The strong odor of sauerkraut can be eliminated by adding a few celery stalks to the juice.

You can also eliminate the smell of sauerkraut by adding red wine to it before cooking.

To test string beans for freshness, snap one in half. If it breaks easily, it's just right.

The quickest way to peel sweet potatoes is to boil them until just tender and then drop them into cold water. The skins will slip right off.

Looking for the ripest tomatoes in a batch? Put all your tomatoes in a large container filled with water. The ripe tomatoes will sink to the bottom, and the unripe ones will float.

You can peel several tomatoes simultaneously by putting them in a net onion or orange bag and submerging them in a pot of boiling water for one minute. The skins will drop right off.

For firm tomato slices, cut parallel to the stem axis.

To heighten the flavor when cooking tomatoes, add a pinch of sugar to the cooking water.

To lock color and flavor into cooked spinach, begin by washing the spinach well in cold water and removing the stems and spines. Lift the spinach leaves from the water and place them in a heavy nonaluminum pan (enameled cast iron is excellent). The spinach should fit in tightly. Cover and steam over medium heat, tossing occasionally until the spinach is *just* wilted.

When you want to use cooked spinach in stuffings or molded vegetable dishes, cook it as in the preceding hint, then drain well. Place the spinach in a cotton or linen towel. Holding it over a bowl or the sink, squeeze the spinach until all excess moisture has been removed.

You can save energy by roasting a lot of red peppers at one time, using the just-lit coals of a barbecue. Char the peppers on all sides, then place them in a heavy plastic bag and seal for ten minutes. Then use a small, sharp knife or your fingers to lift off the skin, stem, and seeds of each pepper. Slice and store the peppers in a jar in the refrigerator. They'll keep for several weeks and can be used in hot vegetable dishes, in salads, or as an antipasto.

To remove the bitter juices from eggplant before cooking, cut it into slices or cubes as directed in the recipe. Sprinkle the eggplant liberally with coarse or kosher salt, and set the pieces on several layers of paper towels for 30 minutes. Rinse the slices or cubes quickly under cold running water and pat them dry before continuing with the recipe.

To soften and peel whole cabbage leaves for stuffed cabbage effortlessly, core the cabbage head and freeze it for several days. Put the head into a large bowl of hot water, and the leaves will peel right off.

The inner layers of leeks are often very dirty. To clean them thoroughly, cut two perpendicular slits, starting about three inches from the root end and running all the way through the stem end. Wash the vegetables thoroughly under cold running water to remove all dirt.

Let your vegetable and fruit peelings do double duty: Add them to a compost pile in the garden, and use the compost to feed your vegetable garden.

EGGS, CHEESE, AND OTHER DAIRY PRODUCTS

Eggs and Egg Dishes

Medium or large eggs should be used in recipes calling for eggs; using small or extra-large eggs may create a slight imbalance in the ingredients.

You can freeze egg whites for up to a year, but after you defrost them remember that two tablespoons of egg white that's been frozen equal one tablespoon of fresh egg white.

For the greatest volume, whip egg whites at room temperature in a grease-free bowl that's been rinsed first with warm water, then with lemon juice or vinegar, and dried with paper towels.

Before adding eggs to a yeast mixture, bring them to room temperature. Cold eggs slow down the action of the yeast.

You don't need an eggbeater to beat eggs. Simply break the eggs into a jar, screw the lid on tightly, and shake the jar vigorously.

You can store egg yolks for up to three days by covering them with water in a covered container in the refrigerator.

You can tell whether an egg is fresh or not by putting it in a pan of cool salted water. If the egg sinks to the bottom, it's fresh. If it rises to the surface, it's not.

Store eggs with the large end up to maintain quality.

Poached eggs can be refrigerated in cold water for several days. To reheat, place the eggs in a strainer, lower into boiling water for about one minute, and serve right away.

Raw eggs won't slip from your fingers if you moisten your fingertips before picking up the eggs.

Egg yolks won't curdle when poured into a hot mixture if you first add some of the mixture to the yolks to raise their temperature.

Give stability and body to beaten egg whites by adding a quarter teaspoon of cream of tartar for every two whites.

For maximum volume, let egg whites warm to room temperature before beating and add just under one tablespoon of water for each egg white.

Remember that egg whites won't beat properly if any trace of yolk remains. Flecks of yolk can be removed with the moistened tip of a cotton swab.

If an egg cracks when you boil it, add a little vinegar to the water. The vinegar will prevent the white from streaming out of the shell.

If you want to keep yolks perfectly centered in hard-boiled eggs (perhaps for deviled eggs) stir the water constantly while cooking.

Hard-boiled eggs will be easier to shell if you submerge them in cold water for a minute or so after cooking. Then, when you crack the egg's shell, gently roll the egg between the palms of your hands. The shell should slip right off.

Rings for frying eggs or homemade English muffins can be made by cutting the bottom and top from clean tuna fish or pet food cans.

To prevent an egg from cracking when placed in boiling water, pierce it with a sharp needle.

The shell of a hard-boiled egg will slide right off if you crack it against the side of your sink several times and then peel it under cold running water.

When slicing hard-boiled eggs, the yolk will not crumble if you first dip your knife or egg slicer in cold water.

You'll be able to tell the raw eggs from the hard-boiled ones stored in your refrigerator if you hard-boil eggs in water to which you've added food coloring. Or mark hard-boiled eggs with a pencil or crayon before you put them away.

If you haven't marked them, the quickest way to distinguish hard-boiled eggs from uncooked ones is to spin them. A hard-boiled egg will spin; a raw one won't.

If you need a boiled egg and the last egg in the carton cracks, don't despair. Just boil the egg in a "shell" fashioned from aluminum foil.

If you want an omelet to be extra tender, add a little water to the beaten egg mixture instead of milk or cream. Water slows down yolk coagulation; milk or cream accelerates it.

If you rub salt on your omelet pan with paper toweling both before and after cooking, you'll make your own nonstick finish.

When you're preparing to make several omelets, you can still beat all the eggs together if you remember this handy measuring rule: Two large eggs equal one third cup beaten eggs.

For extra fluffy omelets add a little cornstarch before beating the eggs.

A few drops of vinegar in the cooking water will keep a poached egg from running.

If you make poached eggs and can't serve them right away, don't discard them. Simply place them in cool water. Later, when you're ready to serve, you can reheat them slowly in hot salted water; the flavor will be unimpaired.

For added flavor, poach eggs in white wine, beer, milk, cream, meat or vegetable stock, tea, or vegetable juice instead of water.

To store boiled and poached eggs dishes made a day in advance, cover the eggs with a sauce or aspic, and then refrigerate. Bake or broil the eggs the next day to serve them hot.

The secret of superb scrambled eggs is to cook the eggs slowly, starting with a cool—not heated—buttered pan. When their texture is almost perfect, mix in one tablespoon of evaporated milk or cream per portion. (If you're serving a large group, extend the mixture by stirring in a white sauce.)

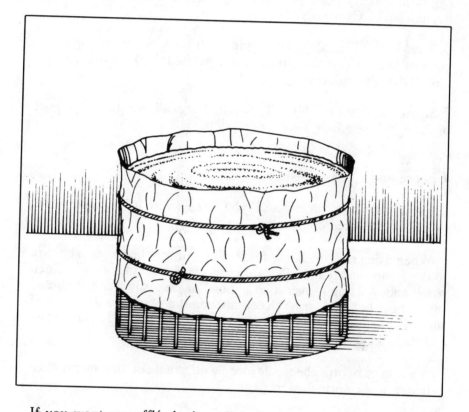

If you want a soufflé that's so light it practically floats, make a collar with aluminum foil, waxed paper, or brown paper. After buttering it thoroughly, wrap it to a height of five inches around a soufflé mold, fasten it with twine, and pour the soufflé mixture into this container. Remove the collar before serving.

Before pouring a soufflé mixture into the dish, spray the dish and the waxed paper collar with nonstick cooking spray. The soufflé won't flop when you serve it and you'll have less baked-on residue to clean.

If you want to stretch scrambled eggs, just add water and a little baking powder. The taste won't be affected and the eggs will be fluffier.

If you want to beat up a lot of eggs in a hurry—for a scrambled egg brunch party, perhaps—break the eggs into a jar, screw on the lid, and shake vigorously.

Peeled hard-boiled eggs will stay fresh for a couple of days in a glass jar filled with cold water and refrigerated. Make sure the water covers the eggs completely.

So you don't get the filling for deviled eggs all over the white part of the eggs, use a baby's spoon or a demitasse spoon.

Cheese and Cheese Dishes

Mold won't form on cheese if you store it with a few sugar cubes in a tightly covered container.

When using ricotta cheese for stuffings or for cheesecake, be sure to dry it thoroughly first. Place the ricotta in a clean cotton or linen towel and, holding it over a large bowl or sink, squeeze the cheese into a tight ball and wring. Keep moving the ricotta to dry parts of the towel and wring until all excess moisture is gone. To remove all ricotta from the towel, use a spatula or pastry scraper.

A scoop of ricotta cheese flavored with vanilla or almond makes a delicious low-calorie dessert or snack.

If cheese does get moldy, cut or scrape the mold off and then dab the exposed surfaces with vinegar, which retards mold growth.

Cheese will have added freshness and flavor if it's wrapped in a cloth soaked in wine and vinegar and then stored in the refrigerator.

Store cottage cheese upside down in the refrigerator to keep it fresh longer.

If you don't have a cheese slicer, you can cut cheese easily with extra-strength thread held taut.

When cheese gets too hard, you can soften it by soaking it in buttermilk. To prevent cheese from drying out and hardening, apply butter to the cut end, or wrap tightly in aluminum foil.

It's easier to grate Cheddar or any soft cheese if you chill it in the freezer for a few minutes before grating.

You can make thinner, neater slices of processed cheese if you dip your knife in hot water before cutting.

If you like to use cheese strips in salads and as garnish, try cutting strips with a potato peeler.

Frozen cream cheese that appears grainy after defrosting can be whipped smooth again.

Grate together odds and ends of hard cheese left after fixing the family's box lunches, and keep the mixture in a jar. You've got an instant cheese topping for pizza, spaghetti, or other dishes.

A good way of cleaning the grater after grating cheese is to rub a slice of bread over it. As a bonus, you've made cheese-flavored bread crumbs for topping a casserole.

Other Dairy Products

Dairy products that have almost reached expiration date sometimes offer good values with little compromise in quality. Ask your store manager about such "unadvertised specials."

If you're going to store unsalted butter in your freezer for a long time, wrap it carefully and seal it airtight. Salted butter that you're freezing for a short time can be stored in its original container.

Always use unsalted (often labeled sweet) butter for cooking. It's generally fresher than salted butter because salt is a preservative that can mask flavors.

Always store butter in the butter keeper or on the bottom shelf of the refrigerator; otherwise it will absorb flavors from other foods.

Ice cream that's been opened and put back in the freezer may develop a waxlike film on its exposed surface. A film won't form if you press a piece of waxed paper against the exposed surface before resealing the carton.

Melted ice cream shouldn't be refrozen, but you can refrigerate it and use it on breakfast cereal.

It's safe to store milk in the freezer, but be sure to defrost it in the refrigerator, not at room temperature.

Skim-milk yogurt makes an excellent low-calorie substitute for sour cream in many recipes. Take care when adding it to hot foods, however. Too much heat or over-vigorous stirring can cause yogurt to become stringy or to separate. Always add it at the last minute and stir gently.

If you live alone or have a family of nonmilk-drinkers, a carton of milk may sit in your refrigerator and go sour before it's used. Instead, keep nonfat dry milk in the cupboard and reliquify it for use in place of whole or skim milk.

Half-and-half or undiluted evaporated milk can be substituted in a recipe that calls for light cream. In a pinch, just use whole milk.

Short on butter? Stretch it by adding evaporated milk. Two cups of evaporated milk added to one pound of butter makes almost two pounds. Add the milk a little at a time to butter which has been brought to room temperature and beaten until creamy. Chill. (Don't use this mixture in cakes such as pound cake.)

Homemade *crème fraîche* has a more natural taste and texture than the store-bought kind and can be prepared much more economically. Mix one teaspoon of buttermilk and one pint of heavy cream in a glass jar. Put the covered jar in a warm spot (75-85°F) for about 24 hours, until the cream is the consistency of pudding. This cream can be refrigerated for several weeks.

Add a little chopped fresh fruit to plain yogurt for a fresh-tasting snack that's a good alternative to flavored yogurt. Or add a teaspoon of your favorite preserves.

If you are out of buttermilk, a good substitute is regular whole milk to which you have added some lemon juice. Use a tablespoon of lemon juice to a cup of milk, and let the mixture stand until it thickens—it will only take a few minutes.

Soy milk can be used in most recipes that call for cow's milk. The tastes are similar enough in cooked dishes.

SOUPS, SAUCES, GRAVIES, AND STUFFINGS

Soups and Stocks

If you want rich, brown beef stock, add beef bones that have been browned in the broiler (about six inches from the heating unit).

Your homemade soup will be free of fat if you make it ahead of time and then store it in the refrigerator until the fat solidifies and rises to the top of the container, where it's easy to remove.

If fatty soups and stews aren't your dish, render them fat-free by stirring either lettuce leaves or ice cubes into the pot (don't allow the cubes to melt). Fat will cling to either, and you can then discard the fat along with the lettuce or ice cubes.

Worried about scorching and boil-overs when cooking soup in a large stock pot? You needn't be. Position two or three bricks around the burner so that the pot is elevated above the heating coils or the gas flames. Then simmer the contents as long as necessary over low heat.

If you want a soup to have more body, add bones to the pot. Marrow bones and veal bones are especially good, they contribute gelatin, which is a thickening agent.

To maximize flavor when making soup, start heating bones and meat in cold, salted water, instead of dropping them into boiling water.

Freeze water from boiling or steaming vegetables and use it in soup stock. You'll have the added benefit of nutrients from the vegetables.

If the stew or soup you're preparing seems too salty, add sugar or a few slices of raw potato. (Discard the potato slices before serving.)

Soup too thin? Add mashed potatoes or instant rice, stirring until you get the desired consistency.

When saving meat juices for stock, leave the fat in place on the surface. When it solidifies, it will seal the stock and its flavor.

If you want to clear a broth, add a few eggshells to the stock, and simmer it for ten minutes. The eggshells will attract the "sediment."

When cutting chickens into pieces, save the carcasses, necks, and gizzards. Freeze them, along with roast turkey and chicken carcasses; when you have enough, use the carcasses to make delicious chicken stock.

It's easy to make a concentrated stock that will add a chef's touch to your soups. Reduce brown beef or chicken stock to a heavy, syrup-like consistency, being careful not to burn the stock. Store it in the refrigerator or freezer and just break or cut off small pieces as needed to flavor soups or sauces.

To save money, trim beef and veal roasts yourself. Store the bones in a heavy bag in the freezer, and use them to make beef stock.

When making stock, never allow the liquid to boil. Boiling will make the stock cloudy.

There's no need to thaw frozen stock before using. Just pop a frozen block of stock into a covered saucepan and heat it gently until boiling.

If freezer space is tight and you want to store homemade stocks, simply cook down the stock until it's reduced by half, then freeze it. To use, you can restore the stock to its original volume by adding water.

To avoid having all your plastic containers filled with frozen stock, line each container with a heavy-duty freezer bag and fill it with stock. Cover and freeze. Slide the bag with the frozen stock from the plastic container. Seal the bag with tape or a twist tie, and return it to the freezer.

For tastier clam chowder, add the minced clams at the last moment and cook just long enough to heat. As a bonus, the clams won't become mushy.

To keep milk from curdling when you prepare tomato soup, add the soup stock to the milk, instead of the milk to the stock.

Pureed leftover vegetables lend additional flavoring to soup stocks. If soup isn't on the menu, freeze the puree in ice cube trays and use the vegetable "cubes" later as needed.

To skim fat from stock, add a tablespoon of cold water while the stock is simmering, and discard the film that rises to the surface.

Sauces

Your brown sauce won't thicken if you add acids, such as citrus juice or vinegar, before the sauce has been reduced.

If your brown sauce is too thick, you can thin it with more meat stock or a tablespoon or two of light cream.

Don't cover meat sauces while keeping them warm. Moisture will build up and will dilute your sauce.

Substitute beef, veal, or pork fat for butter when making a brown sauce for gravies.

To give your sauce an extra-shiny appearance, whip in two tablespoons of cold butter just before serving.

If a sauce begins to separate, add a little cold water. If the sauce begins to cool too quickly, alternate cold and hot water.

You can freeze leftover hollandaise sauce in boilable plastic bags. Thaw as needed by running warm water over the bag.

If you make béarnaise sauce several hours ahead of time, keep it in a tightly closed, preheated vacuum bottle.

If an egg-based sauce curdles, it's probably because it's been boiled. Keep the temperature moderate when making egg sauces.

A *beurre manié* makes a useful sauce thickener. For every tablespoon of softened butter, mix in one tablespoon of all-purpose flour. The *beurre manié* can be formed into small balls and stored well covered in the refrigerator for several weeks. To thicken a sauce, just break off part of a ball and whisk it into the sauce just before serving. Continue adding pieces of *beurre manié* until the sauce is the desired consistency.

Gravies

If gravy's too salty, add several *pinches* of brown sugar. It'll remove the salty taste without sweetening.

Does your gravy taste burned? It won't if you stir in a teaspoon of peanut butter.

There are two quick ways to darken gravy. The first is to mix a tablespoon of water with a tablespoon of sugar, heating the blend in a pan until the sugar browns and the water evaporates. Pour the gravy into this pan. The second method is to add coffee to the gravy; it will add color without affecting the flavor.

One way of making rich brown gravy for your roast is to put flour in a pie pan and let it brown in the oven along with the roast. When the meat is done, mix the toasty brown flour with a little cold water and heat it with the meat juice.

If you want greaseless gravy, let the pan drippings sit for a few minutes. The grease will rise to the top where it can be skimmed off, leaving stock for grease-free gravy.

Stuffings

You'll be able to remove the dressing from a turkey easily if it's held in a cheesecloth bag that you've pushed into the cavity. When you're ready to serve, pull out the bag and turn the dressing into a bowl.

Here's how to prepare fresh chestnuts for a stuffing: With a small, sharp knife, slit the flat side of each chestnut; put the nuts in a saucepan; cover them with cold water; and bring to a boil. Cook for several minutes, then remove the pan from the heat. Working quickly with only a few nuts at a time, peel the outer and inner shells. Cook the peeled nuts covered with water or stock in a saucepan. Simmer until tender (about 30 minutes).

Leftover turkey dressing can be baked in muffin tins and served with butter as an interesting alternative to dinner rolls.

If you don't have a bowl large enough to hold the turkey dressing you're mixing, try using a large plastic bag.

Here's a quick way to stuff a small turkey: Sprinkle several bread slices with herbs and chopped onion, fold them in half, and push them into the cavity.

SALADS AND SALAD DRESSINGS

You can make soggy lettuce crisp and firm again by submerging it in a bowl of cold water and lemon juice in the refrigerator. After an hour, remove the lettuce from the refrigerator and dip it briefly in hot water, then in ice water to which you've added a dash of apple cider vinegar. Pat the lettuce dry with a paper towel.

Another way to make lettuce (or celery) crisp is to place it in a pan of cold water to which you've added slices of raw potato.

If you want to remove the core from a head of lettuce without causing the brown spots that form when you cut out the core with a knife, just smack the core end against the countertop. The core can be twisted right out and the leaves will stay unblemished.

If you put washed salad greens in the freezer about ten minutes before preparing the salad they will be even crunchier.

You can prepare a salad up to six hours ahead of time if you place the vinaigrette dressing in the bottom of the bowl and carefully place well-dried salad greens on top. Cover and refrigerate, but don't toss until just before serving.

To make scalloped edges on the cucumber rounds you use in salads, simply run fork tines over a peeled cucumber, then slice as usual.

For a more elegant presentation, remove the seeds from cucumbers before serving them in a salad or as a vegetable side dish. Cut the peeled or unpeeled cucumber in half lengthwise; remove the seeds with a melon baller or a small spoon.

For extra-crisp cucumber slices, soak them in salted ice water for 30 minutes. Just before serving, drain and rinse well under cold running water. Pat dry and toss with dressing.

Be sure that lettuce leaves are well dried before tossing or the salad dressing won't cling.

When dressing a salad with vinegar and oil, remember to pour the vinegar first. If you pour the oil first, the vinegar won't stick to the greens.

Don't pour vinaigrette dressing over salad greens until the moment before serving. Only shredded cabbage or tomatoes can stand a vinaigrette bath for up to an hour before serving without losing firmness.

Don't toss sliced tomatoes into your salad. Their water content will dilute the salad dressing. Add them on top at the last minute, or use whole cherry tomatoes.

A soggy salad never garners compliments for the chef. You can keep your salads crisp if you invert a saucer in the bottom of the bowl to allow any liquid to drain and collect under the saucer, away from the greens.

A sticky wooden bowl will look and feel smoother if it's washed and dried and then vigorously rubbed, inside and out, with waxed paper.

For instantly cold, well-blended oil and vinegar salad dressing, pour the dressing into a screw-top jar, add an ice cube, and shake. Remove the ice cube before pouring the dressing. Here's another twist: Place your greens in a plastic bag, add the dressing, and shake the entire mixture. The greens will be evenly coated on all sides.

If you wanted crumbled Roquefort or blue cheese for your salads, freeze it; then it will crumble easily when scraped with a paring knife. (This does not work well with other cheeses.)

For extra-creamy salad dressings, place dressing ingredients in a slow-running blender and slowly add the oil.

If salt is used as a salad seasoning, it's best to add it at the last minute. If you add the salt ahead of time the lettuce will wilt.

A crushed garlic clove rubbed on the inside of a salad bowl will heighten the taste of the salad ingredients.

To keep fruit salad, potato salad, or shrimp as cold as possible for serving, place it in a bowl and put that bowl in a larger one filled to the rim with crushed ice. If you want to make the ice even colder, add coarse kitchen salt to it.

For easy unmolding of gelatin salads or aspics, lightly grease the mold with vegetable oil (or sweet almond oil for desserts) before pouring in the gelatin mixture. Chill until solid.

For a gourmet-style potato salad, cut your potato slices extra thin with a wire cheese cutter.

When you make a gelatin salad with cream cheese, does the hot gelatin turn it lumpy? It won't if you mix the cheese with dry gelatin before adding liquid.

Salvage leftover mixed salad greens by blending them with a can of tomato juice and spices for a quick cup of gazpacho.

HERBS AND SEASONINGS

To separate the cloves of a head of garlic, lay the head on a flat surface, then hit it sharply with the palm of your hand.

To remove garlic peel easily, lay the clove on a cutting board and smack it sharply with the flat side of a chef's knife or cleaver.

Freshly made chili powder has more kick than the store-bought kind. Buy dried chilies in a Spanish or Mexican grocery store. Remove the seeds and stems, then grind the chili pods in a blender or in a food processor with a steel blade.

If you want hot chilies to keep their kick, store them loosely sealed in a brown paper bag in your refrigerator.

When working with hot chilies, it's a good idea to wear rubber gloves. Be careful not to touch your face and eyes; the oil from the chilies can irritate your skin.

For maximum flavor, buy whole spices and crush or grind them with a mortar and pestle or an electric spice grinder just before using.

To save money and enjoy fresher flavor, make gourmet mustards and vinegars at home. For mustards: Add freshly ground or cracked spices or chopped fresh herb leaves to Dijon mustard. Flavor to taste. Store in the refrigerator. For herb vinegars: Heat one quart of white wine vinegar with one cup of minced fresh herbs (or a quarter cup dried herbs) in a nonaluminum saucepan. Steep at room temperature overnight, then strain through a fine sieve lined with cheesecloth. Store in airtight glass bottles.

If cilantro (fresh coriander leaves, sometimes called Chinese parsley) is unavailable, substitute by adding one teaspoon of finely chopped or grated lemon or lime zest to every two tablespoons of chopped parsley leaves.

Instead of using expensive cheesecloth to hold a *bouquet garni,* substitute a large, reusable, stainless steel tea ball.

A piece of dried or fresh lemon or orange peel makes a tasty, unusual addition to a *bouquet garni* for meat or chicken stews.

The best salt is sea salt or coarse kosher salt. Iodized salt can add an unpleasant harsh taste to foods.

In selecting bay leaves, look for leaves that are imported— preferably Turkish. Many cooks consider they have better flavor than the California bay leaf, which tends to be stronger and oilier.

For uniform texture in chopped chives, cut the chives at the root end of the plant and bunch them together tightly with one hand. Hold the bunch on a cutting board and chop finely with a sharp knife.

Any dish that's prepared to be served cold should be slightly overseasoned, because chilling subdues flavors.

If you're preparing a slow-cooking dish, it's preferable to use whole spices rather than minced spices. Whole spices impart their flavor gradually, matching the pace of the cooking process.

If fresh herbs are unavailable, dried herbs can be given a fresher flavor if you chop them with an equal amount of fresh parsley leaves.

You can boost the flavor oils in fresh or dried herbs by kneading the herbs between your fingertips to release the oil bouquet.

If a recipe specifies dried herbs and you have only fresh, triple the amount called for.

If you add a half teaspoon of whole peppers to the ground pepper in your pepper shaker, the pepper will pour better and taste snappier, too.

Using minced parsley (dried or fresh) with other herbs enhances their tastes.

The skins will slip right off garlic cloves after they are soaked in warm water.

Herb butters are convenient garnishes for broiled meats, poached fish, or steamed vegetables. For every half pound of softened butter, mix in the juice of half a lemon or lime, two tablespoons of fresh, chopped herbs, and salt and pepper to taste. Put the butter on a length of waxed paper and roll it all into a tube. The tube can be frozen or refrigerated.

It's easy to make garlic salt: Sprinkle table salt on a board and cut garlic on it. After the salt absorbs all the garlic juice, store it for future use. Similarly, onion salt can be made by squeezing onion juice over table salt.

Seasoned salt is much cheaper to make than to buy. Blend iodized table salt with garlic powder, pepper, paprika, dry mustard, thyme, sesame seeds, and anything else you like. Put the seasoned salt in a shaker and let it stand for a few days to blend the flavors. Use it on salads, vegetables, soups, and casseroles.

You can maintain the freshness and flavor of herbs by soaking them in olive oil and refrigerating them.

You can chop parsley or chives with a grater if you keep both seasonings in your freezer. When you want a small amount of either, remove it from the freezer, grate as much as you need, and put the remainder back "on ice."

Parsley will be easier to chop if you rinse it and refrigerate in a sealed plastic bag or other container until crisp.

Because fresh basil leaves discolor easily, always use a stainless steel or carbon and stainless steel knife to cut them. Lay the leaves one on top of the other and roll them into a tight tube. Slice thinly with a sharp knife, then unravel the leaves. This is called a *chiffonade* cut.

Since chili powder, paprika, and red pepper deteriorate under humid and hot conditions, store them in dark containers in your refrigerator during the summer.

Since rosemary can be hard and tough, even after cooking, grind it in a pepper mill before use.

Italian or flat leaf parsley has much more flavor than curly parsley, which is best used as a garnish or in recipes requiring little or no cooking. Add the stems to a *bouquet garni* for flavoring long-cooking dishes, such as soups or stews.

You can make your own celery powder—which makes a good flavoring for stews, soups, and salad dressings—by drying celery leaves and then forcing them through a sieve.

Peeled fresh ginger root will stay fresh for months if stored in white wine or dry sherry, tightly covered, and refrigerated.

A vegetable peeler works well in removing citrus zest. Take care not to remove the bitter white underskin along with the colored zest.

After grating ginger root or citrus zest on the fine side of a vegetable grater, you can use a pastry brush to remove the little bits that stick to the grater.

CEREALS, RICE, AND PASTA

Cooked too much rice? Freeze it, and when ready to use put it in a sieve and run hot water through it. You have your own instant rice—and at a lower cost than the store-bought kind.

If you like rice that's snowy white, add some lemon juice to the cooking water.

If the rice you're cooking has burned slightly, you can remove the burned flavor by adding a heel from a loaf of fresh white bread and covering the pot for a few minutes.

When cooking potatoes or rice, add a pinch of rosemary to the water instead of salt; it adds a special flavor.

When cooking dry beans, a little baking soda will keep them from getting mushy.

Whole-grain cereals stay fresh longer if they're refrigerated; this is true whether the container is open or unopened.

You can make chocolate flavored oatmeal—without buying the more expensive packaged kind—by adding cocoa mix to regular oatmeal as you cook it. Mix in enough cocoa to please your taste.

If your hot cereal has lumps in it, next time make sure the water is boiling before adding the cereal a little at a time.

A large strainer or a French fry basket can make it easy to drain pasta. Sit either device inside the cooking pot before you add the pasta; after cooking you can simply lift the pasta from the pot.

When buying pasta, make sure it's made from semolina rather than ordinary flour. Pasta made from semolina holds its shape better and doesn't become mushy.

Instead of discarding leftover spaghetti noodles, cut them into small pieces and store in your freezer. The next time you make spaghetti sauce, add the noodles to the mixture.

When boiling water for spaghetti or macaroni, add a teaspoon or so of cooking oil. Then the pasta won't stick together (or to the pot), and you needn't stir it constantly.

For perfect *al dente* pasta every time, use the old Italian method of testing for doneness. Remove a strand of pasta from the boiling water and throw it against the wall or refrigerator. If it sticks, the pasta is cooked *al dente* and should be drained and served right away.

Homemade egg pastas can be rolled, cut, and partially dried (until still pliable but not sticky), then laid on cloth or heavy paper dusted with semolina flour or cornmeal. Cover the pasta with another towel and store in the refrigerator for up to 24 hours. When cooked, the pasta will have the same flavor as freshly made.

There are several ways to prevent the pot boiling over when cooking pasta. You can lay a large metal spatula across the top of the pot; or rub shortening around the rim before cooking; or add several teaspoons of cooking oil or a dab of butter to the cooking water.

To preserve the freshness of the unused portion of pasta in a box you've opened, store the remaining pasta in a tightly covered glass container.

For superior pasta, let salted water come to a boil, stir the pasta into the water, cover the pot, and turn off the heat. After the pasta sits for 15 minutes it will be ready to eat.

To prevent cooked spaghetti strands from becoming sticky, run fresh, *hot* water into the spaghetti pot before draining.

If you've made a pot of spaghetti but can't serve it at once, leave it in water, but make it cool enough to stop the cooking process. To reheat the spaghetti, put it in a strainer and shake it thoroughly as you run it under hot tap water.

If you're going to use pasta in a dish that requires further cooking, reduce the pasta cooking time by one-third.

It is possible to remove ravioli from a can without damaging the "pillows." Open the can; place it in a pan, open-end down; puncture the other end of the can with a can opener, and lift the can straight off the ravioli. Every pillow will be intact.

Hang homemade pasta over a clothes hanger to dry.

You can cut a thin-crust pizza more easily with kitchen scissors than with a knife.

BREAD, COOKIES, CAKES, AND DESSERTS

Breads and Rolls

To make yeast bread more moist, use water in which you've boiled potatoes. As a bonus, the bread will be slightly larger; it will stay fresh longer, too.

If you find it hard to knead rye, whole wheat, or pumpernickel dough, rub a little oil on your hands. The oil makes the dough more pliable.

So dough won't form a crust while rising in a bowl, first grease the bowl and press the dough into it. Then, turn over the dough, greased side up, and cover it lightly with a dish towel.

A nonstick cookie sheet is ideal for kneading and shaping bread dough; you won't have to cope with the powdery mess left by a pastry board or cloth.

To check whether bread dough has risen sufficiently, press two fingertips into the dough; if a dent remains, the dough is ready for the oven.

To make bread extra crusty, brush the dough with an egg white beaten with a tablespoon of water.

Dough rises best in a warm spot. Try putting the dough bowl on a heating pad set at medium, or on a table in front of a sunny window. Another good place is inside a gas oven where the warmth of the pilot light encourages dough to rise. Or, let your television set do double duty if you're making bread while watching your favorite TV show. Let the dough rise on top of the set, where heat from the picture tube will warm it.

Allow a few extra minutes of baking time to brown bread crust that has been baked in a shiny metal pan.

If your bread crust gets too hard while you're baking the loaves, next time place a small pan of water in the oven. Also, when the bread has just been taken from the oven, spread soft butter on the warm crust.

Home-baked bread can be cut neatly into equal slices if you cool the bread on a wire rack and then use the slight impressions left by the wires as your guide.

For round-shaped homemade bread, bake your dough in two-pound coffee tins—or try a frying pan with a non-metal or detachable handle.

If you allow bread to cool in the baking pan, the bottom and sides will get soggy. Cool bread on a rack instead.

Put a celery stalk into the bag with a loaf of bread; moisture from the celery will help keep the bread fresh longer.

If you want your rolls to have a crystalline glaze, brush them with a mixture of a quarter cup of milk and one tablespoon of sugar before sliding them into the oven. Or brush the dough with a mixture of one tablespoon of milk and a beaten egg.

To keep dinner rolls piping hot in a straw serving basket, place them on a napkin-covered hot ceramic tile on a trivet. You can heat the tile in the oven at the same time you're heating the rolls.

If you've made and buttered slices of toast and your youngsters are slow in showing up for breakfast, keep the slices warm by wrapping them in aluminum foil.

Leftover rolls that have become wrinkly can be made smooth again by placing them for a few minutes in a 350°F oven.

If you sift flour directly into your canister you won't have to sift it again when you use it for baking.

Flour freezes well, so stock up when it's on sale at the supermarket.

If you need to thaw a loaf of frozen unsliced bread in a hurry, put it in a brown paper bag in a 325°F oven for about five minutes.

Rolls will stay hot longer in a serving basket if you spread aluminum foil under the napkin they're wrapped in.

If leftover rolls have hardened, make them soft again by sprinkling them lightly with water, covering them with foil, and heating them in the oven for a few minutes.

A baking stone (available in specialty cookware shops) or unglazed red tiles (available at tile supply stores) simulate the old-fashioned brick ovens used by bakers. When bread or pizzas are baked directly on a preheated stone or tiles, the texture is light with a superb, crisp crust.

For a crisp crust on French or Italian bread, spray the loaves with a fine mist of cold water at five-minute intervals during the first 15 minutes of baking.

Allow chilled dough to stand at room temperature until it's pliable enough to roll out easily.

When making a cold cuts and pickles sandwich, layer the pickle slices between the cold cuts, *not* next to the bread. This keeps the bread from getting soggy.

If you make sandwiches with frozen bread, use peanut butter, cream cheese, and other spreads that can be smoothed more evenly and won't be likely to tear the bread.

When making croutons for salads or stuffing you'll find that frozen bread is easier to cut, especially with an electric knife.

To make Melba toast, remove the crust from a loaf of French bread. Slice the bread thin, and bake the slices until crisp and light brown in a 200°F oven. Remove and cool. Store in an airtight container.

Save stale French and Italian bread for making your own bread crumbs. Trim off the crusts and lay the bread on a platter covered with a cloth. Let the bread sit at room temperature for two or three days or lay the bread pieces on a baking sheet and leave overnight in a gas oven with a pilot light. Cut the hardened bread into chunks, and process in a food processor (with the steel blade) or in a blender. For very fine bread crumbs, pass them through a medium sieve. Store in an airtight container in a cool spot.

Leftover hot dog and hamburger buns can be deliciously recycled. Spread them with butter, garlic powder, and Parmesan cheese, toast them in an oven, and crumble them over salads.

Does the breading sometimes refuse to stick to cutlets? Here's how the pros do it: First dust the cutlet with flour, then brush off the excess. Next, brush the cutlet with an *anglaise* (beaten egg, oil, water, salt, and pepper). Dip it into fine bread crumbs, pressing the crumbs so they'll adhere, then shake off the excess. For best results, breaded cutlets should be refrigerated one or two hours before cooking.

Instead of buying prepared bread crumbs, make your own by crumbling leftover bread ends, crackers, or cereal crumbs (the sugarless variety) in the food processor.

Want to pack additional flavor into bread crumbs? Mix them in your blender with broken crackers and cookies.

Pastry and Pies

For best results, roll out pastry dough on either a marble or a formica countertop. The cold surface keeps the shortening in the dough from softening.

If you can't roll out your pastry dough on a marble or formica surface, chill your working area by rubbing it with a plastic bag filled with ice cubes. Wipe away any excess moisture before rolling the pastry.

If you want a tender and flaky pie crust, don't over-flour your pastry crust as you roll it out.

To prevent pie crust from over-browning, place a shield of aluminum foil over the edge of your pastry crust when it's baking; remove this shield for the last 15 minutes of baking time.

Use dried beans or rice as inexpensive pie weights when you're baking an empty pie crust; the beans or rice can be cooled and reused many times. You can also keep the pie crust from bubbling by pricking it all over with a fork.

Whenever possible, use the size of baking pan specified in the recipe. If a slightly smaller or larger pan must be substituted, adjust the baking time accordingly.

Lemon juice, vinegar, sour cream, or milk can be substituted for water in pie crust recipes. Any of these will provide a tender and flavorful crust.

Opt for lard rather than butter when making pie dough. Butter may give a little more flavor, but lard makes a flakier crust.

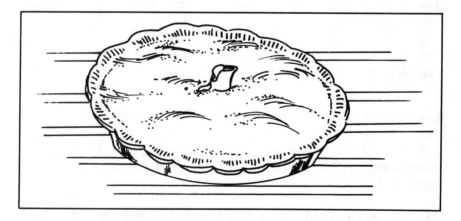

So juice can bubble out of a pie harmlessly and in one place, insert a piece of tube-type macaroni in the center of the pie before baking.

When you must cool a pie in a hurry, set the pie pan on top of a larger pan lined with ice cubes.

A powder puff kept in the flour canister is perfect for dusting flour on pastry boards and rolling pins.

To prevent pastry dough from clinging to your rolling pin, chill the pin in the freezer before flouring.

When you roll dough on waxed paper, dampen the counter before spreading the paper; then the waxed paper will cling smoothly to the counter.

To thaw unbaked puff pastry, wrap the frozen dough in a nonterry cloth towel and let it defrost for 24 hours in the refrigerator.

When brushing puff pastry tarts with an egg wash, don't let the wash drip down the sides of the pastry. If it does, the egg wash will glue the puff pastry layers together and they won't rise properly.

Pate à choux puffs that have been stored in a tin for several days benefit from being crisped in a 350°F oven, then cooled before filling.

Pate à choux puffs freeze well and don't need to be defrosted before serving. Just heat them in a 400°F oven for a few minutes, then cool before filling.

For a tempting brown glaze on your pie, brush the top with milk before sliding the pie in the oven.

Here's a real time- and money-saver. When fresh fruits are in season and on sale, prepare enough pie filling for several pies. Line pie pans with aluminum foil or waxed paper, fill with the fruit, cover, and stack in freezer. The next time you want a pie, just slide one of your pie-shaped fillings into a crust and pop it in the oven.

Frozen pies sometimes have a "dry" taste. You can eliminate this dryness by brushing them with melted butter before baking.

To keep a fruit pie from getting soggy, dust the crust with flour before adding the filling, or sprinkle ground nuts over the bottom crust.

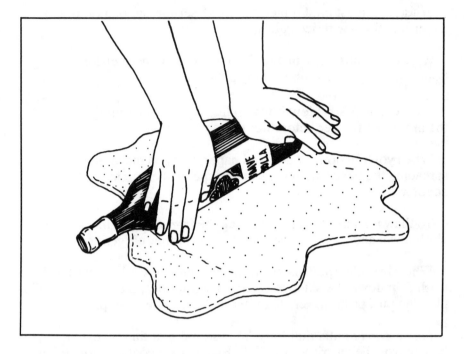

No rolling pin handy? Use a full wine bottle.

To make an upper pie crust extra flaky, brush its surface with a little cold water before baking.

If the fruit filling in a pie is too juicy, add a spoonful of tapioca to absorb extra juice.

To thicken juice of a fruit pie so that it won't be too runny, add a beaten egg white to the sugar you use when preparing the pie, or add a dash of flour to the fruit itself during preparation.

Before baking a frozen pie, it's sometimes difficult to make slits in the top crust, since the crust is too hard. Warm the pie in the oven for a few minutes and then make the slits.

When making a pumpkin pie, put a layer of marshmallows on the crust before adding the filling. As the pie bakes, the marshmallows will rise and form a perfect topping.

The inverted flat top of a two-quart, ovenproof casserole dish can double as an eight-inch pie plate.

You can avoid oven spills when baking a pie by putting it in a plain paper bag or an oven browning bag that you've cut several slits in. Bake the "bagged" pie ten minutes longer than called for in the recipe.

Baked custard will slip out of the cups easily if you have coated the cups with nonstick cooking spray. You can also use the spray on your ice cream scoop, and to ease other sticky jobs like candy-making—spray the pan, the thermometer, and the tray you cool the candy on.

Cookies

If you want your rolled cookies to be thinner and crisper, put dollops of dough on a baking sheet, and then press on each with the bottom of a water glass that has been floured or moistened and dipped in sugar.

Here's one sure method of getting rolled cookies of equal thickness so some won't burn before others are fully baked. Cut a yardstick in half, and place each half flat on the right and left sides of a pastry cloth close enough to each other so your rolling pin spans them. Roll your dough between the sticks until it can't be flattened further. (The dough will be precisely the thickness of the yardstick— or any other pieces of wood you use.)

An easy way to cut refrigerated cookie dough is with a wire cheese cutter.

Beaten egg yolk thinned with water makes a shiny cookie coating. When it dries, it also forms a good surface for icing designs.

You can give cookies a crisp coating by sprinkling a sugar and flour mixture on a pastry board and rolling the dough on it.

When cookies get hard and stale, crumble them to use as toppings for pies and coffee cakes.

Need another cookie sheet? Flip a baking pan over and bake your cookies on the underside of the pan.

Cookies are more difficult to remove from a baking sheet after they've cooled completely. If you're having trouble lifting them, try using a greased spatula, or reheat the cookie sheet for a moment by running it over a stove burner or briefly returning it to a warm oven.

If you want your homemade cookies to retain moisture as long as possible, use honey rather than sugar when mixing the batter.

Cakes and Frostings

To make all-purpose flour as much like cake flour as possible, use seven-eighths cup for every cup of cake flour listed in the recipe, and sift it twice to make it as light as possible.

You won't have dry pockets of powder on the bottom of a bowl after stirring a cake mix if you put the liquid in the bowl before adding the mix.

If you like your cakes more moist than crumbly, mix two to four tablespoons of salad oil into the batter.

Fruits, nuts, and raisins often sink to the bottom of cake batter. To keep them evenly dispersed, try heating them or rolling them in melted butter before adding them to the batter.

When you're making an upside-down cake, spray the bottom of the pan with nonstick cooking spray. It will keep the sugar and fruit from sticking to the pan and ruining the decorative effect when the cake is turned right side up.

You don't need to grease and flour a cake pan if you use nonstick cooking spray instead. The baked goods will slide out easily. (But don't use this spray when you're making an angel food cake—the spray won't allow the batter to rise up the sides of the pan.)

If you're out of chocolate for baking, you can substitute three tablespoons of cocoa plus one tablespoon butter or margarine for one ounce of chocolate.

For a richer flavor, substitute devil's food cake mix for cocoa in frostings.

Worried about cholesterol? Substitute two stiffly beaten egg whites for every whole egg that a cake recipe calls for.

If you want a chocolate cake that's extra moist and fluffy, add a spoonful of vinegar to the baking soda.

Before you put a cake on a plate, sprinkle sugar on the plate to absorb moisture. Otherwise, the bottom of the cake may get gooey and stick to the plate.

Any cake you bake or buy will stay fresh longer if you place half an apple with it in its container. Moisture released gradually by the apple will keep the cake moist.

If the top of a cake is browning too quickly, place a pan of warm water on a rack above the cake. The browning will slow down.

When testing to see if a cake is done, you can use a stick of un-cooked spaghetti if you're out of toothpicks.

Has your fruitcake dried out? It can be freshened if you turn it over, poke some holes in its bottom surface, and place a dab of frozen orange juice in each hole. As the frozen juice melts, it will spread evenly throughout the cake and make it moist. When the cake is thoroughly—but lightly—saturated, flip it over again. It will taste fresh as new.

One surefire way to prevent a cake from sticking to the bottom of a pan is to position a waxed paper cutout on the bottom of the pan before pouring in the batter.

If you want to make a quick fancy cake topping, position an open-design paper doily on top of the cake. Dust on powdered sugar, which will sift through the doily and create an instant work of art. Lift off the doily and serve the cake.

Cake icings won't crystallize if you add a dash of salt to the sugar.

If the tiers of a multilayer cake slip as you frost it, try taming them by inserting strands of dry spaghetti. Carefully pull out the spaghetti when you're finished.

You can fashion your own cake decorating tube by rolling an ordinary piece of paper into a cone, open just slightly at the tip. Fill the cone with the icing, fold over the large end, and squeeze, holding the large end closed.

If you need to cut a cake when it's hot, use unwaxed dental floss. It won't damage the cake as much as a knife would.

You'll be able to slice cleanly through cake icing if you first dip the knife blade in boiling water.

A spill-proof way to pour cupcake batter into muffin tins is to pour it first into a clean half-gallon milk carton. The carton's spout lets you pour with precision.

You can slice an angel food cake neatly and without crumbs if you freeze it and then thaw it before cutting.

So that frozen cheesecake won't lose its butter-smooth texture, thaw it slowly in your refrigerator, not at room temperature.

Stale angel food cake can be transformed into wonderful cookies. Cut the cake into half-inch-thick slices, shape them with a cookie cutter if desired, then toast, frost, and eat.

If you want to cut a cake into decorative party shapes, freeze it first. You'll find it much less messy to handle the frozen cake, and you'll be able to make intricate shapes more easily.

Grated citrus fruit rinds make wonderful flavorings for cakes. Store them in a covered jar in the refrigerator until needed.

A quick way to cool a cake layer is to place the cake pan on an upside-down colander.

Sometimes a baked cake is reluctant to come out of its pan because it has cooled too much and the grease used to coat the pan has hardened again. Loosen it—and the cake—by returning the cake to a warm oven just long enough for the pan to become warm to the touch.

Dust the layers of your cake lightly with powdered sugar before spreading on the cake filling to keep the filling from soaking into the cake.

To decorate white frosting on a cake, top it with gumdrops shaved paper thin. They'll curl up like tiny flowers.

For an unusual, delectable frosting, add several drops of chocolate syrup to a prepared whipped topping.

If you like fudge frosting but find that it hardens too quickly as you apply it, mix in a teaspoon of cornstarch and keep the bowl in a pan of hot water. Spreading it on the cake will be as easy as buttering a slice of toast.

To frost a very crumbly cake, apply a thin layer of icing and let it harden completely. When this coat is set, spread a second layer of icing—it will go on easily, with no crumbs.

If you wrap a cake in waxed paper that's been sprinkled with powdered sugar, the frosting won't cling to the paper.

Pancakes and Breakfast Treats

A toothbrush or pastry brush is helpful in spreading oil evenly on the surface of a waffle iron. A toothbrush can aid in cleanup, too: Use it to brush batter from the crevices.

When pancakes stick to a griddle it means they don't contain enough shortening. Mix a little more oil or melted butter into the next batch.

If your family can't eat all the waffles or pancakes you make, you can store the extras flat in plastic bags in your freezer. They can be reheated in your toaster.

To reheat pancakes without overcooking them, wrap them in a dish towel and put them in a 250°F oven for a few minutes.

You can speed up the chore of cutting up pancakes for small children by using a pizza cutter—even a stack is easy to cut this way.

If you've given up pancakes for breakfast because you want to avoid the sugar content of the syrup, sweeten the batter with artificial sweetener. Then you won't need to add syrup anyway.

Keep small slices of bread from disappearing into your toaster by sticking a toothpick through the bread so that the toothpick lies across the toaster.

The trick to freezing crepes—whether flat or rolled—is to stack them (sandwiched between sheets of waxed paper), cool them, and then wrap them tightly before storing them in the freezer.

Make waffles and pancakes extra light by replacing the liquid you usually use with club soda. Don't store any of the club soda batter, because continuing effervescence will alter its texture. Use it all, or discard it.

If the kids forgot to tell you they finished the pancake syrup, make a quick substitute by boiling together equal parts of water, brown sugar, and white sugar.

Crepes will be lighter if, instead of cream or milk, you use a liquid composed of one part water to three parts skim milk.

For extra delicate and tender crepes, use just enough batter to cover the pan bottom with a paper-thin layer.

When making muffins, you can prevent burning by filling one of the pan's cups with water rather than batter.

If you separate English muffin halves before freezing them you'll be able to toast them straight from the freezer.

To prevent doughnuts from burning, add potato slices to the grease.

For instant bakery treats, deep-fry refrigerator biscuit dough. You can pull the biscuits into a long-john shape, twist them like French twists, or cut holes for doughnuts. Roll the hot biscuits in sugar or frost them; for bismarks, slit them and push-in a spoonful of jelly.

Have your leftover doughnuts become stale? For a different breakfast treat, just slice them in half, dip them in French-toast batter, and brown them in butter.

Scoop the seeds out of half a cantaloupe and fill the center with dry cereal and milk for an easy breakfast in an edible "dish."

Your kids won't eat hot cereal? Tempt them by stirring in a few chocolate morsels. A dollop of ice cream on top of the cereal should soften up a reluctant young eater, too.

Meringue

Egg whites that have been refrigerated produce a fuller, more fluffy meringue than fresh egg whites.

To stabilize meringue, add a teaspoon of lemon juice to every three egg whites.

Meringue shells won't darken while baking if you grease your baking sheets with a solid vegetable shortening.

To make meringue that's extra high, add a little baking powder to the room-temperature egg whites you beat or whip for the recipe.

Meringues were never easier. Separate the eggs while they're still cold, then let the whites warm up to room temperature before beating them.

To avoid shrinkage and watery edges in the meringue topping on a pie, spread the meringue all the way to the edge of the pie crust.

Meringue pie topping won't split or crack if you cook the pie slowly. Instead of removing the pie from the oven when the meringue turns brown, just shut off the oven, open the oven door slightly, and leave the pie for several minutes.

There are several ways to prevent meringue from sticking to the knife when you cut a pie. You can dip your knife in boiling water or butter it before slicing the pie, or you can sprinkle a bit of sugar over the top of the meringue before you brown it.

To make vanilla sugar for flavoring meringues and icings, cut open two vanilla beans and place them in a quart container. Fill the container with confectioners' sugar and allow the sugar to ripen for a week before using. Keep refilling the container with sugar until the beans are spent (two or three months).

Whipped Cream

Before whipping cream, chill the beater, the bowl, and the cream.

To prevent cream whipped ahead of time from separating, add a quarter teaspoon of unflavored gelatin to each cup of cream during whipping.

If you whip half a pint of cream at a time, rather than a full pint, it'll be much fluffier.

Adding a few drops of lemon juice to cream will speed the whipping process.

If you want whipped cream with good body—and in no time— whip it in a double boiler over salt and ice cubes.

For best results when adding sweetener to cream, add it after the cream has been whipped.

You can maintain whipped cream's shape—and prevent it from getting watery—if you use powdered instead of granulated sugar.

Don't be dismayed if ice crystals remain in heavy cream after you defrost it. The cream whips better in that condition.

If you have leftover whipped cream, flash-freeze scoops of it on a cookie sheet and store it in your freezer in plastic bags. You'll have instant cream when you need it.

When buying whipping cream, don't choose the ultrapasteurized brands. They whip up poorly and have an unnatural, chalky taste.

If a large spatula is unavailable for folding in beaten egg whites or whipped cream, use the palm of your hand to fold ingredients together gently.

Chocolate

Chocolate melts more quickly if it is first broken or chopped into small pieces with a chef's knife or in a food processor fitted with a steel blade.

If chocolate contracts into a hard lump while melting, stir in one to two tablespoons of solid vegetable shortening (not butter or oil), and beat vigorously.

When you want a pronounced chocolate flavor in your baked goods, use dark or bitter chocolate in the recipe.

Once sweet chocolate, milk chocolate, or white chocolate are melted, they must be used immediately. Unsweetened and semisweet chocolate will be usable for up to 15 minutes after melting.

If melted chocolate used for dipping becomes too thick to coat evenly, add a tablespoon or two of warm water or brewed coffee to thin it to the proper dipping consistency.

For best results, chocolate should be melted in a double boiler over hot, *not* boiling, water. Working the chocolate back and forth with a spatula helps the chocolate to melt evenly.

Semisweet chocolate with its higher sugar content is best for dipping and icings because it hardens to a beautiful, glossy sheen.

To make thin chocolate curls for dessert decorations, shave room-temperature chocolate with a vegetable peeler. Refrigerate the chocolate curls after shaving.

If unsweetened baking chocolate is unavailable for a recipe, substitute three tablespoons of cocoa powder plus one tablespoon of vegetable shortening or unsalted butter for each ounce of chocolate called for in the recipe.

Puddings and Parfaits

You can remove lumps from curdled egg custard by putting the custard in a jar and shaking the jar vigorously.

For feather-light steamed pudding, replace half the flour called for with bread crumbs.

You can prevent "skin" from forming on pudding by resting plastic wrap on its surface before it cools.

Make your own parfaits by spooning different kinds of jelly between ice cream layers. Or, spoon different kinds of sherbet between ice cream layers.

Half the fun of a parfait is seeing what you're eating, so make your concoction in a crystal water glass.

Frozen orange, tangerine, or lemon shells make lovely serving dishes for ices, sherbets, and ice creams. Keep them well wrapped in the freezer. After using them, rinse out the shells and refreeze them for another day.

BEVERAGES

Coffee and Hot Chocolate

Keep freshly ground coffee stored in a glass jar in the refrigerator to prevent it from going rancid.

Ground coffee or coffee beans will stay fresh indefinitely if frozen.

It's annoying when ground coffee spills into the stem opening when you're filling the basket of a percolator pot. You can keep the ground coffee out by holding a fingertip over the stem opening when filling the basket.

Remove coffee grounds immediately after brewing so your coffee won't taste bitter.

If you run out of filters for your drip pot or percolator, simply cut a paper towel to size.

There are several ways to save on coffee. One is to grind beans until they're powdery and use less coffee than usual. Or use one half the ground coffee you normally use, but circulate the water through the grounds twice. Or reuse old coffee grounds. Spread them on a flat pan and put them in the oven for 30 minutes at 350°F. Cool them and mix with half your usual portion of fresh ground coffee.

If your coffee is too bitter because you heated it too long, just toss in a pinch of salt to banish the bitter taste.

You can make café mocha without a special mix by adding an envelope of instant cocoa mix to a cup of black coffee.

If the coffee you've just brewed tastes weak, add a little instant coffee.

Out of cream? Lighten your coffee or tea with beaten egg white.

If your coffee tends to look muddy, next time start with cold water and drop in a few unwashed egg shells after brewing.

If cream curdles in your hot coffee, add a pinch of baking soda to the cream before fixing your next cup.

Trying to cut out sugar in your coffee? Try adding a drop of vanilla, which is a natural sweetener, instead.

Keep your coffee hot longer by pouring it into a preheated cup or mug. Just fill the cup with very hot water while the coffee is brewing. By the time the coffee is ready, the cup will be hot.

Does your hot chocolate sometimes have an acid taste? Reduce the acidity by adding a pinch of salt before mixing with boiling water.

To give hot chocolate a butter-smooth texture, add to each potful a pinch of salt and a teaspoon of cornstarch dissolved in water.

Tea

To keep the flavor fresh, store tea bags or loose tea in an airtight tin can.

For tea with intensified flavor and fragrance, store dried orange blossoms or dried orange rind in the canister.

Tea won't get cloudy if you add a pinch of baking soda to the pot.

You'll get a tastier cup of tea if you brew it in a clean china or earthenware pot, using fresh cold water that's been brought quickly to a boil.

The paper tag on your tea bag won't fall into your cup if you tuck it through the cup's handle. Another trick—moisten the string and stick it to the rim of the cup.

To get the last remaining spoonful of honey from the jar, pour in some hot tea, close the lid, and shake gently. Not only is your jar clean, but your tea is sweetened and ready to drink.

If you don't have fresh lemon for your pitcher of iced tea you can get the same taste by adding a little lemon gelatin.

Freeze leftover tea, and add the cubes to your next glass of iced tea.

To keep iced tea from clouding over, keep the tea at room temperature. When it's time to serve, just pour it over ice cubes.

When making instant iced tea, the crystals will dissolve better if you add a little very hot water before adding cold water.

Juices and Soft Drinks

When squeezing your own orange juice, press the orange and roll it gently on the table or countertop. You'll get more juice.

The quickest way to thaw frozen orange juice concentrate is to mix it with water in a blender.

A quick way to dissolve frozen orange juice concentrate is to stir it with a potato masher or whisk.

It's easy to make tomato juice into something special, fast. Pour a large can of tomato juice into a large glass jar, and add a chopped-up celery stalk and a chopped green onion. Let the mixture stand for several minutes before serving.

To make fruit soda pop at home, partially fill a glass with a frozen juice concentrate, dissolved in water according to the instructions, and top off the glass with club soda.

If diet cola doesn't have enough "kick" or seems too artificially sweet, squeeze a lemon wedge into it. It'll taste just right.

You can cut the foam when pouring a carbonated drink over ice cubes if you first rinse the cubes with water.

Alcoholic Beverages

It's best to keep bottled beer away from light, particularly sunlight, if you're not storing it in your refrigerator; light alters the taste—and not for the better.

Vodka will be more flavorful if kept in the refrigerator or freezer rather than in the liquor cabinet.

To extend the life of wine remaining in a jug, transfer what's left to a regular wine bottle, leaving a minimum of air space between the cork and the wine. This will help maintain the flavor of the wine.

Want to serve drinks with a flair? Freeze cherries, mint leaves, cocktail onions, and green olives in ice cubes. They're a conversation topic when added to martinis, manhattans, or other drinks.

Long, slender slices of peeled cucumber make perfect swizzle sticks for Bloody Marys.

When you chill a champagne bottle in an ice bucket, cover the bottle with ice just up to its neck. If the ice is any higher, you may have a tough time removing the cork.

For best champagne flavor, avoid overchilling it in the refrigerator. Champagne lovers know the secret is to chill the wine briefly in an ice bucket.

Plastic corks sometimes seem impossible to remove from champagne bottles, but if you pour warm water on the bottle's neck the heat will make the bottle's neck expand and the cork will pop or slide out easily.

Wine that has turned sour need not be thrown out—you can use it as a vinegar substitute.

A good way to save leftover dinner wine for cooking is to pour a thin film of vegetable or olive oil over its surface. The film will preserve its flavor by sealing out air.

BARBECUES AND PICNICS

Barbecues and Open-Air Cooking

Before the barbecue season starts, fill brown paper bags with enough briquettes for a cookout and fold over the tops of the bags. When you're ready to light the fire, place a bag in the grill and touch a match to it. Your hands will stay clean; and heat from the burning paper will light the briquettes quickly. An alternative is to pack briquettes in empty egg cartons with the covers closed. You'll still have a quick fire and clean hands.

An empty plastic squeeze bottle makes a handy bellows for barbecue coals.

If you spray your barbecue grill with nonstick cooking spray you'll be able to turn chicken pieces without tearing. Hamburger patties will stay whole, too. The spray also means that cleanup will be much easier—you may only need to wipe off the grill with a damp towel.

When you barbecue juicy meat, fat dripping on the hot coals can cause flames to flare up. Put out the flames by dropping lettuce leaves on the coals, or by squirting water on the coals with a spray bottle or turkey baster.

A proven way to spice up the flavor of food on the barbecue is to sprinkle the coals with fresh herbs that have been soaked in water.

You can cook an entire meal—not just meat, baked potatoes, and ears of corn—on an outdoor grill. Put vegetables and appetizers in covered kettles, and place these on the grill. You'll save on household energy and keep the kitchen cool.

If you're barbecuing hamburgers for a large group of people, you can save on grill time by partially cooking the burgers indoors. Line the bottom of a baking pan with foil and lay down a layer of patties; set a piece of foil over this layer, and add another tier of patties.

Repeat this procedure till you have four tiers. Place this oversized layer cake in a 350°F oven for about 15 minutes; then finish grilling the patties outside.

To tenderize pork chops or chicken pieces before barbecuing, boil them in a saucepan for 15 minutes, drain them, and then marinate them in barbecue sauce for half an hour. Then position them on the grill and barbecue as usual.

How long does it take to cook a whole turkey on the barbecue grill? Allow 15 to 18 minutes a pound for an unstuffed turkey, 18 to 24 minutes for a stuffed one.

Chicken for your barbecue will stay moist and tender if you pre-cook it for 30 minutes in the oven, then put it on the grill and baste frequently with barbecue sauce during the last five to ten minutes of grilling time. As an alternative to oven cooking, put the chicken in the microwave oven for 15 minutes, then grill.

If you're cooking a variety of vegetables on skewers on the grill, make sure they all finish cooking at the same time by blanching or par-boiling long-cooking vegetables (potato or carrot chunks, for instance) ahead of time.

Here are some interesting desserts to offer as a change from ice cream or watermelon chunks at a barbecue: Grill apple or peach halves, cut side down, and top with plain yogurt (a little sherry or honey spooned on each half is a good touch for extra flavor). Or sprinkle orange segments with sugar (and cinnamon, if liked), wrap in foil, and grill.

Chunks of fresh vegetables, threaded on a skewer and grilled, make a tasty accompaniment to barbecued meats, or a satisfying alternative to meat for vegetarians. But have you tried the same trick with fruits? If not, skewer chunks of peach, pineapple, banana, and other fruits and barbecue over medium heat. Baste with a mixture of melted butter, sugar, and cinnamon, and be sure to turn the skewers often.

Add zip to the skewered vegetables you barbecue by brushing them with salad dressing—Italian is good—instead of butter.

You can cook potatoes, carrots, or winter squash directly on the coals of your barbecue or campfire if you first wrap the vegetables thoroughly in foil. They'll take 30 to 45 minutes to cook.

Use spare space on your barbecue grill to heat bread or rolls. Either brush the bread or rolls with butter and heat face down on the grill for a minute or two; or wrap in foil and heat for ten to twenty minutes.

Here's a way to cook potatoes on the barbecue grill if you're tired of plain baked potatoes. Cut unpeeled potatoes into half-inch slices, brush with equal parts of melted butter and barbecue sauce, and wrap in foil, making sure the package is tightly sealed. Place the package on the grill and cook for 30 minutes; flip the package and cook for 30 minutes more.

There are several ways to make cleaning the grill less of a chore. A grill will steam-clean itself if wrapped in wet newspapers or sprayed with window cleaner while it's still hot. Or, you can wipe it with crumpled aluminum foil while it's still warm. To coat it protectively before cooking, use vegetable oil and wipe it off as soon as the grill is cool enough to touch.

A beer-can opener makes a great scraper for cleaning barbecue grills; file a notch in the end of the opener opposite the sharp point.

Cooking with pots and pans over an open fire can leave black scorch marks on the bottoms of metal utensils. Permanent scorching can be prevented by coating the bottoms of pots and pans with bar soap or shaving cream, or painting on liquid detergent with a pastry brush before using the pan on an open flame. When the metalware cools, you'll be able to remove black marks with little effort.

A disposable pie pan can help protect against burns when you're roasting marshmallows or hot dogs on sticks over an open fire. Make a hole in the center of a pan, slide the stick through the hole, and let the pan serve as a heat shield.

Picnics

If you use thumbtacks to secure paper plates to a picnic table, you won't have to worry about them blowing away in the wind.

When you pack a picnic, keep the salt and pepper from spilling out of shakers by wrapping waxed paper or plastic wrap around the necks of the containers before screwing the tops on.

When organizing your picnic basket, be sure to include a cutting board, a knife, plastic bags and ties, and a damp washcloth for cleanup.

A plastic window shade makes a wonderful tablecloth for a picnic. When the picnic's over, just wipe off the shade, roll it up, and store it.

If you need a cutting board for a picnic, use a smooth piece of the scrap wood meant for the campfire, or make a board by covering a thick magazine with heavy-duty aluminum foil.

Keep dessert foods covered when you picnic outdoors. Insects are attracted to sugary foods.

Protect soft picnic foods and fruits from being crushed by packing them in old egg cartons.

If your picnic cooler leaks, try plugging the leaks inside and out with melted paraffin wax.

Dust talcum powder on the edge of your ice cooler to keep it from sticking in hot weather.

When you're outdoors, consider storing ice in a sugar bag, which is thicker than a plastic bag and offers better insulation.

If you accidentally pierce a hole in the plastic liner of a cooler when breaking ice, dab the hole with fingernail polish until it's filled in. Don't use household glues; some of them can damage the liner.

Keep a wading pool near your backyard swimming pool so that people can wash sand, grass, and dirt from their feet before entering the pool. The water in the swimming pool will stay clean longer.

Save watermelon rinds from meals or picnics. Keep them in a plastic bag in the refrigerator until you have enough to pickle.

MORE GOOD ADVICE ABOUT FOOD

If you have a large family of independent eaters, it's hard to keep track of what's in the food cupboard. Keep a memo pad in a conspicuous place and train (or try to train) everyone to write down replacement items each time they empty a package or jar. That way the person to finish off the peanut butter is responsible for making sure that item appears on your shopping list, and the person who uses the last lunch bag in the packet notes that you need another pack.

To keep brown sugar from drying out, store it in a jar with a piece of apple.

If brown sugar gets hard, grate it or run it through the blender to make it powdery.

When you buy peanut butter that isn't homogenized, store it upside down to prevent the oil from rising to the top. Stir before use.

If humid weather is making your crackers soggy, store them in the freezer.

Whole unblanched nuts, purchased in bulk, are generally cheaper than packaged nuts. They can be stored in the freezer and used as needed.

Opened tomato paste should be refrigerated. Cover it with a little vegetable oil, which can be poured off when you want to use the paste again.

To avoid spoilage after a can of tomato paste has been opened and partially used, freeze the remainder in tablespoon-size portions. The frozen paste can be dropped into a sauce when needed.

When a jar of jam, mustard, or mayonnaise is almost empty, store the container on its side. This makes it easier to scrape out the last of the contents.

To keep your cooking oil fresh, store it tightly sealed in a dark glass or plastic container in a cool place.

Olive oil marked "virgin" or "extra-virgin" has the truest olive flavor because it comes from the first cold pressing of the olives. Pure olive oil comes from a second pressing and doesn't have as intense an olive flavor.

For Oriental dishes, use only sesame oil pressed from roasted sesame seeds (available in Oriental grocery stores). The cold pressed sesame oil found in health food stores doesn't have the same distinctive flavor.

The best way to keep leftover cold cuts fresh, without freezing them, is to roll them up and put them in a covered glass container in your refrigerator.

To keep a leftover onion slice fresh as long as possible, rub the open side with butter.

Leftover mashed potatoes make patties that can be coated with flour and fried.

If you run ice cold water over popcorn kernels before tossing them into the popper, there'll be fewer kernels left after popping.

To minimize the number of popcorn kernels that won't pop when heated, keep unpopped popcorn in your freezer.

There's no need to buy a special jar for making bean sprouts. Just use a canning jar with a screw-on ring top. Place the beans in the jar, and cover the jar top with a double thickness of cheesecloth. Screw on the ring top over the cheesecloth. Rinse with warm water and drain twice a day until the beans sprout.

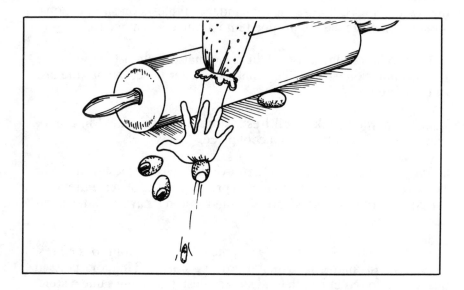

One way to remove pits from olives is to place the olives on a paper towel, roll them gently with a rolling pin, and then press them with the heel of your hand. The pits will pop right out.

When the last olive or pickle in a jar is gone, don't throw out the juice. Use it to season deviled eggs.

Leftover mincemeat can be stirred into rice pudding or vanilla yogurt for a spicy, unusual treat.

Because honey weighs more than other sweeteners, adjust the quantity when substituting honey in a recipe. As a rule of thumb, remember that a 12-ounce jar of honey is equal to one standard eight-ounce measuring cup.

If you want to use honey instead of a dry sweetener in a recipe, allow two-thirds to three-quarters cup of honey (according to taste) for one cup of dry sweetener.

Out of honey for a recipe? Substitute molasses.

Honey that has become granulated can be restored to smooth texture by placing the jar in boiling water. This works for syrup or jelly as well.

To store honey for long periods, freeze it in ice cube trays. Transfer the cubes to freezer bags, seal, and store.

When a recipe calls for nuts and you don't have any, you can use coarse bran instead.

You can transform regular granulated sugar into superfine sugar in your blender.

Ordinary wine works as well as the more expensive cooking wine for marinating or preparing gourmet recipes. You'll also avoid the added salt in cooking wine.

A potato peeler makes a perfect peach peeler, or cheese or chocolate grater.

If you mix the ingredients for instant gelatin or pudding in a large pitcher, it will be easy to pour the gelatin into individual molds without spilling it.

When measuring syrup or other sticky liquids, first wet the measuring cup, or oil it with cooking oil and then rinse it in hot water so it will release all of the gooey fluids after they're measured. And pour into the center of the measuring cup, *not* down the sides.

It's much less expensive (and healthier) to buy unsweetened cereals and add your own sugar than it is to buy presweetened varieties.

Different foods require varied uses of salt during cooking. For instance, it's best to cook most vegetables in salted water and to salt soups and stews quite early in the cooking process. But salt should be sprinkled on meat just before it is removed from the oven or range top.

An envelope with the corner clipped off makes a quick funnel for flour, salt, or sugar.

Grating two or more foods for the same dish? If you grate the softest one first, the harder or firmer foods that follow will clean out the grater's openings.

You don't always need mixing bowls to mix foods. To save time and cut down on dishwashing, pour all your ingredients into a sturdy plastic bag, close it, and shake to mix the food.

To prevent unnecessary spills, store your sugar in a plastic container with a handle and a snap-on lid.

If you want to serve a recipe to a larger number of people than the recipe is designed for, you may get better results by making up the original recipe several times rather than by doubling or tripling the ingredients.

To prevent splattering on a cookbook or recipe card while you're mixing ingredients or cooking, cover the paper with a glass plate or pie pan.

To protect a recipe card from cooking splatters, spray it with hair spray. After the spray dries, you can wipe any smudges off the card with a damp cloth.

Here's another way to keep a recipe card from getting lost amid the clutter of utensils and ingredients: Cut a slit in the top of a cork that you have glued to the lid of your recipe box. The cork holds the recipe card while you work.

Do you find it easy to mislay a recipe card while you're cooking? Next time, keep your card handy by slipping it between the tines of a fork and standing the fork in a glass.

Sausage casings can be stuffed using a large pastry bag and a plain tube. Fill the bag with the sausage, then pull the end of the casing around the pastry tube, and hold it tightly with one hand while squeezing the pastry bag with the other.

Keep a bowl from slipping on a countertop while mixing ingredients by placing it on a damp folded towel.

If oven racks refuse to slide easily, coat the gliders with a film of petroleum jelly.

To get a good grasp on jar lids and bottle tops, open them by covering the lid with a piece of sandpaper.

You'll conserve range energy as well as elbow grease when heating small amounts of leftover food if you wrap each type of food in a separate aluminum foil package, place the packages side-by-side in a frying pan containing an inch of water, and heat over a single burner. This way there's only one pan to clean.

For unusual finger sandwiches, add powdered or liquid vegetable coloring to cream cheese fillings.

You can freeze olives, pickles, and similar condiments in containers (but not glass jars) of their own liquid.

Try this hors d'oeuvre buffet to keep snacks from getting soggy: Put out a plate of empty pastry puffs with an assortment of meat and cheese fillings, and let guests fill their own.

For a delicious pastry-puff glaze, brush puffs right from the oven with mayonnaise, then sprinkle with Parmesan cheese and a dash of paprika.

To blanch almonds, place them in boiling water for one minute. Then peel off the skins, using either your fingernails or a small, sharp knife.

To toast almonds, place the blanched almonds on a baking sheet in a 200°F oven for five minutes, or until dry and lightly toasted.

Cracking nuts can be fun for the family, but the shells tend to mix with the meat. You can separate the meat by dropping both shells and meat into a bowl of water. The meat will sink and the shells will float to the surface, where you can skim them off.

Marshmallows stay soft and fresh when you store them in the freezer. They are also easier to cut.

When preparing a recipe that calls for marshmallows, remember that one large marshmallow equals ten small ones.

It's best to reheat most foods in a thick, covered pot. A heavy pot with a tight lid keeps food from drying out.

It's easy to reheat leftover baked potatoes: Run hot water over them, and then bake them for 20 minutes in a 350°F oven.

If shredded coconut dries out, sprinkle it with milk and let it stand for 30 minutes. It will taste moist and fresh again.

Pan-fried slices of leftover meat loaf can be used as a filling for regular or open-faced sandwiches.

When you fix dinner, prepare extra foods and freeze single-person portions in divided containers. This way you have on hand "TV dinners" that are much more cost-effective than the purchased variety.

You can do more with nonstick cooking spray than use it on your frying pan and cake pans: Spray the inside of a measuring cup before pouring syrup or honey to avoid having half the sticky stuff stick to the cup. Coat cookie cutters and cookie guns so the dough won't stick. Try spraying it on your egg whisk, too.

Nonstick cooking spray on your kitchen shears makes easy work of slicing candied fruits, dates, and citrus rinds.

Bottles of oil, molasses, and other sticky substances always seem to leak onto your kitchen shelves, no matter how careful you are. Solve the problem by cutting off the ankle parts of mismatched socks and slipping one of these bands over the bottle. It will catch the sticky drips, and you can launder the band easily when necessary.

Another way to keep sticky drips off kitchen shelves and countertops: Cut down empty salt containers and similar round containers and sit the sticky bottles in them. No more mess.

If your youngsters get more jelly on the table than on the sandwich, transfer the jelly to one of those squeeze containers used for mustard or ketchup. The kids can squeeze the jelly on the bread without any problem.

Use a muffin tray to carry drinks from one room to another or into the garden for a summer picnic. The glasses will stand firm in the muffin cups instead of sliding around as they would on a tray.

Try using a pastry blender for mixing dips and similar foods that are too thick to go in the food blender. It works like a charm.

When your children outgrow their cute lunch boxes with Superman or whoever on them, use the boxes as files for letters, recipes, newspaper clippings, or other odds and ends.

Tofu, a mild-flavored cheese-like product made from soybeans, is popular with vegetarians and makes a good protein replacement for other cooks, too. Whisk it into thin gravies and sauces to add body. Use a wire whisk.

If you want dry, crumbly tofu for stir-frying, wrap it in a clean towel and wring the water out.

To firm a cake of tofu, wrap it with paper towels and weight with a one-pound can placed on top of a saucer. Drain for about 15 minutes.

Another way of making tofu more dry is to parboil it.

If tofu looks pink around the edges, it is about to go bad. You can still use it if you first parboil it; place the tofu in water, bring to a boil, and simmer for about three minutes. Then use.

Tofu can be frozen, but it may turn a light yellow or brown color. Also, freezing changes the texture; when thawed, the tofu will be soft and spongy. Drain tofu before freezing.

If you make your own tofu, feed the leftover bean mash to your pets for added nutrition. Mix it in with their regular food. (You can use this mash in cooking, but most of the nutritional value will have been transferred to the tofu.)

Diet and Nutrition

EATING FOR FITNESS

Take a positive approach to making healthy changes in your diet and life-style. Instead of mourning what you're giving up, concentrate on all the benefits you're getting from your improved diet.

You can improve your chances for a long and healthy life by cutting down on the fat, salt, caffeine, and sugar in your diet. The average American eats four times more fat, 40 times more salt and caffeine, and 100 times more sugar than the body normally needs.

Eating a nutritious breakfast every morning and avoiding snacks between meals are two of the easiest ways to improve your eating habits.

Vitamin and mineral supplements aren't necessary for most people. A well-balanced diet should provide you with all the vitamins and minerals required for good health.

Smoking destroys your body's supply of vitamin C. Drink a glass of orange juice in the morning instead of lighting up a cigarette.

Eating between meals upsets the proper functioning of your metabolism. If you must snack, try raisins, nuts, apples, or crunchy vegetables instead of sugary foods.

Drink plenty of water daily. Water cleanses your system and promotes healthy-looking skin.

Sugar plays a role in the development of tooth decay, obesity, diabetes, and cardiovascular disease. If you do nothing else to improve your diet, at least cut down on your intake of sugar.

Add natural sugar to your diet by replacing baked goods and fattening desserts with fresh fruits.

When you need a pick-me-up, try drinking a glass of fruit juice or fresh, cold water instead of a sweetened soft drink.

Sugar is sugar, no matter what form it takes. Don't be misled by "sugarless" products that contain corn syrup, honey, molasses, maltose, glucose, dextrose, and invert sugar. These are just other names for sugar. If you must avoid sugar for medical reasons, read labels carefully and be aware of the many names that sugar goes under.

Under normal circumstances your body needs no more than a teaspoon of salt a day. Too much salt in the diet can lead to high blood pressure, obesity, and heart and circulatory problems. You can cut down on salt painlessly by leaving it out of your cooking, by removing the salt shaker from the table, and by using salt substitutes if you really miss the taste.

Substitute herbs, spices, and pepper in place of salt when seasoning foods.

Use lemon and lime juices to flavor vegetables in place of salt.

Reduce the salt content of instant broth by using twice as much water as the package directions indicate.

Be aware that many commercial canned foods contain high levels of salt. Canned soups are often especially high in salt. Read labels carefully.

A high-fat diet can be dangerous to your health. When cooking, consider using polyunsaturated fats such as corn, soybean, and sunflower oil instead of saturated fats such as lard, butter, chicken fat, coconut oil, or hydrogenated vegetable oils.

Low-fat skim milk contains considerably less fat than whole milk. The same is true of skim milk cheeses, low-fat cottage cheese, and yogurt.

When buying meats, look for the leanest cuts. Trim off any visible fat before cooking, and whenever possible choose broiling over any other preparation method; broiling can reduce the fat content of meat by up to one-half.

Although broiling is the best cooking method for meat if you're trying to avoid fat, you can also substantially reduce the fat and calorie content of meat by boiling or pot-roasting it and skimming off the fat.

You can improve your whole family's diet by beginning to replace some meat dishes with fish and poultry. You'll be eating less fat and fewer calories.

Legumes, especially peas and beans, are an excellent source of protein and should be included in your weekly menus.

Experiment with meatless meals to cut down on your fat intake. Meatless spaghetti sauce, chili, and vegetable soup can taste just as delicious as the meaty versions.

Eat plenty of whole-grain bread, pasta, potatoes, and rice and other grains; they are good energy foods and sources of protein.

Avoid eating too many preserved meats such as ham, hot dogs, and corned beef. Processed meats contain chemical additives.

Don't toss away the darker outer leaves of your lettuce head. They're higher in nutrients than the leaves found closer to the core.

Scrub vegetables with a vegetable brush to remove any surface dirt before cooking. Don't remove the skins, because you'll also be throwing out most of the vitamins and minerals.

Cook your vegetables briefly by steaming them. Overcooked vegetables lose their vitamin C and mineral content.

Be sure your child's diet contains lots of milk and milk products, as well as enriched breads and green, leafy vegetables. These foods are high in calcium, which is essential in building strong bones and healthy teeth.

If you are allergic to wheat, use any of the following substitutes for one cup of wheat flour: One-and-one-quarter cups rye flour; three quarters cup rice flour; one-and-one-third cups oat flour; one cup corn flour; three-quarters cup coarse oatmeal; one cup fine cornmeal; or five-eighths cup potato starch flour.

Accustom your children's taste buds to nonsugared foods by preparing their breakfasts with sugar-free cereals. Sweeten with raw honey, sliced bananas, chopped apples, or raisins.

In place of candy, potato chips, and pretzels, give your youngsters healthy snacks like sunflower seeds, raw almonds or cashews, roasted soy nuts, or fresh or dried fruits.

Fry your foods in a nonstick pan that requires no additional oil for frying.

Cut out as much sugar as possible from your diet in the summer. Mosquitoes are attracted to people who eat a lot of sugar.

If you're often out in the sun, stay away from caffeine drinks such as coffee, tea, or cola. Caffeine makes your skin more sensitive.

Eat smaller but more frequent meals in summer. Your body will have to work less to digest the foods, and you'll feel cooler.

Use more salt in your foods during the summer months, especially if you perspire a lot. Heavy perspiration depletes the salt content of your body.

If you're susceptible to colds, fortify your diet with extra vitamin C by drinking lots of fruit juice or rose-hip tea.

To keep your bones from getting brittle as you get older, be sure that your diet is rich in calcium from milk products, and vitamins A, C, and D that are present in citrus and vegetable juices.

A tablespoon of brewer's yeast added to a glass of fruit or vegetable juice or milk acts as a natural laxative.

Substitute honey for sugar as a sweetener. It serves as a natural laxative.

To calm an upset stomach, drink a glass of buttermilk or skim milk mixed with a tablespoon of cider vinegar.

When you're pregnant, follow these tips:

- To control weight gain during pregnancy, cut down on sweets but not on whole-grain bread and potatoes that you need for energy.
- To reduce feelings of nausea during pregnancy, try eating only cold foods.
- If you can't tolerate any other foods in the morning, at least eat bread or dry toast with milk.
- To ensure that your diet contains a good supply of vitamins A and D, eat liver or an oily fish such as herring, sardines, or mackerel once a week.
- To prevent constipation, eat fiber-rich foods such as whole-grain breads and lots of fresh fruits and vegetables.
- To control nausea, take small sips of cola or bites of bland food, such as custard, gelatin, or mashed potatoes, throughout the day.
- Nibbling on nuts, cheese, or other high-protein foods every two or three hours can help relieve feelings of nausea in early pregnancy. Substitute frequent nutritious snacks for three heavy meals a day.
- Eating a cracker with a glass of milk before bedtime helps reduce heartburn and ensures a sound sleep.

It's estimated that during pregnancy a woman needs about 300 extra calories a day. These should be obtained from nutritious foods, not from high-calorie snacks that are low in food value.

HEALTHY LUNCHTIME IDEAS

Freeze a carton of yogurt overnight and take it to work with you. The yogurt will be thawed but still cold by lunchtime the next day; it's a delicious, low-calorie lunch.

You can fix lunches for the entire week on Sunday night. Hard-boil a dozen eggs and fry two chickens. Then wrap each piece of chicken securely in plastic wrap and divide these prepared foods into lunch bags, with a different piece of fruit and cheese for each day of the week. Store the bags in the refrigerator and take one out each morning on your way to work.

You can make and freeze sandwiches up to two weeks ahead of time, provided you use no jelly, mayonnaise, eggs, lettuce, or tomato in the filling. Butter the bread, add the sandwich filling, and wrap the sandwiches tightly in plastic wrap before storing in the freezer. A sandwich removed from the freezer in the morning will be ready to eat by lunchtime.

If your work place offers nowhere to keep your lunch refrigerated during hot weather, freeze sandwiches containing mayonnaise or salad dressing the night before, even though mayonnaise separates when it's frozen. The sandwiches will thaw by lunchtime without spoiling from the heat.

Plan well-balanced box lunches. Include a protein-rich food, a crisp fruit or vegetable, a beverage or soup, and a treat.

Make extra servings of chili and stews to use in your lunch box. Pour them hot into vacuum containers for eating the next day, or freeze in serving-size portions for later in the week.

Good fillings for pita bread are grated cheese, cottage cheese mixed with tomatoes, onions, and cucumbers, a spread made from chick-peas, or paté. Add plain yogurt and shredded lettuce just before eating.

Freeze cartons of prepared shrimp or crab cocktail. They'll thaw out but still be cold by the time you're ready to eat lunch.

To prevent soggy sandwiches, moisture-proof your sandwich bread by spreading on a thin layer of margarine or butter before adding the filling.

For more food value—and to give you more energy—make lunchtime sandwiches from whole-grain breads and buns instead of white bread.

You can cut down on calories at lunch (or at any other time) by eating hamburgers and sandwiches open-faced, with only one slice of bread or bun.

A 40-ounce plastic freezer container provides the perfect lunch box for carrying salad fixings to the office. Add a low-calorie dressing of lemon juice and herbs just before eating your salad. If the salad is dressed ahead of time it will go limp.

You can avoid that mid-afternoon slump that usually follows close on the heels of a heavy lunch by sticking to salads or light foods at lunchtime.

Try to use part of your lunch hour to visit a museum, do some shopping, or take a lunchtime exercise class—the break will refresh you more than a long, sedentary lunch.

Fill plastic sandwich bags with an assortment of fresh vegetable sticks for a light vegetarian lunch, or for snacks to nibble if you're trying to avoid sugar-laden between-meal snacks.

A packet of powdered skim milk provides a quick, vitamin-packed, liquid lunch food. It's also a great source of protein, calcium, and vitamin B[2].

For an eat-on-the-run lunch, mix one fresh egg yolk into a glass of orange juice. Add a teaspoon of honey to sweeten.

Even if you're in a hurry, don't gulp down your lunch. You'll only get indigestion later. Eat slowly, chewing your food well.

Instead of taking a coffee and doughnut break, take an exercise break. Treat yourself to a handful of raw seeds or nuts afterward.

Several ice cubes sealed with a twist tie in a plastic bag is an easy ice bag for keeping your lunch cold.

HINTS FOR WEIGHT WATCHERS

Gaining or losing weight is basically a matter of addition or subtraction. Each pound on your body is worth 3500 calories. In order to lose one pound, you must cut back by 3500 calories. In order to gain one pound you must increase your food intake by 3500 calories.

Despite extravagant claims by certain advertisers and certain health clubs, vibrating machines, body massages, saunas, and steam baths won't really reduce your weight. You'll lose a lot of body fluid because of perspiration, but the fluid will return as soon as you drink water.

Don't expect to lose weight through exercise alone. Sensible dieting will help you lose weight, and exercise will help you maintain a firm, healthy body.

If you're in the habit of eating while you're busy doing something else, such as watching TV or reading, make an effort to stop doing so. Making just a single change in your snacking habits can help you shed unwanted pounds.

Instead of spending extra money on diet foods or low-calorie items, eat what you normally do but eat less of it.

A glass of water can fill you up enough to distract you from hunger pangs and help you resist between-meal snacks.

If you're having trouble losing weight, avoid having in the house 'instant' foods that can be eaten without extensive preparation. The thought of having to spend time preparing foods may deter you from eating them.

Cutting down on alcohol can significantly reduce the amount of calories you take in. For some people it's possible to lose weight simply by eliminating alcohol from the diet altogether.

If you're on a diet, it may help to turn after meal cleanup over to somebody else. That way you won't be tempted to munch on leftovers as you're putting them away.

Keep a record of everything you eat, and it'll be easier to reinforce your goals for weight loss. The record will also be a reminder of how often you are cheating on your diet.

If you eat your meals with someone whose company you enjoy, you'll probably talk more and eat less.

When you're tempted to have a second helping of some food, tell yourself you can have it in five minutes. During the five minutes, keep busy doing something else. You'll probably forget about wanting the extra food.

Use smaller plates for your diet-size meals. Smaller portions look more satisfying on a proportionately smaller plate, and you won't feel that you're on starvation rations. The same strategy applies to wine glasses and dessert dishes.

When you're on a diet, foods that take longer to eat can be more satisfying than easy-to-eat foods. For example, corn on the cob seems like more than the same amount of cut corn, and lobster in the shell will keep you busy longer than a boneless steak.

When making stews and other dishes containing grease or fats, prepare them ahead and then store them in the refrigerator. The fat will rise to the surface, where you can easily lift it off before reheating and serving the dish.

Substitute yogurt for whipped cream or artificial dessert toppings.

Dieters can snack, too, if their diet allows for it. There are many snacks that fall under 100 calories. Try five ounces of ginger ale over a peeled and sectioned orange. Or add a spritz of orange and lemon to tomato juice, then blend with ice cubes. Or prepare raw vegetables along with one third cup of plain yogurt splashed with herbs for dipping.

Substitute club soda or mineral water for an evening cocktail. Eat fresh vegetables from a relish tray instead of fattening hors d'oeuvres.

To cut down on calories, dress your vegetables with lemon juice and herbs instead of butter.

Dips made from packaged mixes pack a weighty wallop of calories, but it isn't the mix that makes them fattening—it's what they're mixed with. Most packaged mixes add only 50 calories, but the directions call for a base of sour cream (485 calories per cup) or cream cheese (850 calories in an eight-ounce package). You can cut calories dramatically by substituting plain, unsweetened yogurt—only 130 calories—for sour cream or the low calorie, low-fat "imitation" cream cheese—only 416 calories—for the real thing.

If you check the nutrition information printed on competing packaged products and choose the one with the lowest calorie count, you can save calories the same way a cost-conscious shopper saves money.

The lower the fat content in dairy products, the fewer calories they contain. For example, cottage cheese that's labeled 99 percent fat-free has only 160 to 180 calories a cup, while regular creamed cottage cheese has 240 to 260 calories.

The word "imitation" on low-calorie, low-sugar, or low-fat products doesn't necessarily mean that the product is made up of chemicals, only that the lower sugar or fat content keeps the product from conforming to standard recipes. Often the imitations are more nutritious than the real thing. For example, some low-sugar jams and preserves contain more fruit and less sugar, and some imitation low-fat cheeses have a higher protein content.

It's best to look for specific calorie information on "dietetic" foods. A "dietetic" product doesn't always contain fewer calories; for example, some "dietetic" candies for diabetics have just as many calories as regular candy.